Intangible Assets and Va

Intangible Assets and Value Creation

Juergen H. Daum

WILEY

Copyright © 2003 John Wiley & Sons Ltd, The Atrium, Southern Gate, Chichester,
West Sussex PO19 8SQ, England
Telephone (+44) 1243 779777

Email (for orders and customer service enquiries): cs-books@wiley.co.uk
Visit our Home Page on www.wileyeurope.com or www.wiley.com

Translation from the German language edition *Intangible Assets – oder die Kunst,
Mehrwert zu schaffen* by Juergen H. Daum. Copyright © 2001 Galileo Press GmbH, Bonn, Germany

Other Wiley Editorial Offices

John Wiley & Sons Inc., 111 River Street, Hoboken, NJ 07030, USA

Jossey-Bass, 989 Market Street, San Francisco, CA 94103-1741, USA

Wiley-VCH Verlag GmbH, Boschstr. 12, D-69469 Weinheim, Germany

John Wiley & Sons Australia Ltd, 33 Park Road, Milton, Queensland 4064, Australia

John Wiley & Sons (Asia) Pte Ltd, 2 Clementi Loop #0201, Jin Xing Distripark, Singapore 129809

John Wiley & Sons Canada Ltd, 22 Worcester Road, Etobicoke, Ontario, Canada M9W 1L1

Wiley also publishes its books in a variety of electronic formats. Some content that appears in print
may not be available in electronic books.

British Library Cataloguing in Publication Data

A catalogue record for this book is available from the British Library

ISBN 0-470-84512-0

Project management by Originator, Gt Yarmouth (typeset in $9\frac{1}{2}/13\frac{1}{2}$pt Stone Sans)
Printed and bound in Great Britain by Antony Rowe Ltd, Chippenham, Wiltshire
This book is printed on acid-free paper responsibly manufactured from sustainable forestry
in which at least two trees are planted for each one used for paper production.

Contents

Interviews

Foreword

Conceptual value added rather than physical value added, as recently described by Alan Greenspan,[1] makes up an increasingly larger part of the gross national product of developed countries. Intellectual capital, in contrast to tangible assets and financial capital, is becoming an ever more important basis for the creation of economic value and increasingly creates a competitive advantage for companies and economies.

In developed countries the economy and companies are therefore increasingly influenced by the economics of intangible assets, in particular, intellectual capital. This opens up new opportunities, as demonstrated by effects such as increasing returns and network effects for knowledge-based companies and their products, but also involves larger risks, for example, in the form of higher market and technology risks. The value of knowledge assets and intangibles is also largely dependent on the reputation and the "perception" of a company with its customers, business partners, employees, the stock market, and the public. But image and reputation can soon disappear into thin air, even with no fault of the company in question.

The increasing importance of this so-called knowledge economy, which is often associated with industries such as software, pharmaceuticals, the media, and financial services, will continue to change our image of the economy and value creation. Factories and assembly lines will no longer form the wealth of a company; instead it will be the creativity and capacity for learning of the employees, innovation, and the ability to maintain long-term customer and business partner relationships. And this applies to companies in all industries.

In spite of this, there is no exclusive "either–or" between the industrial economy and the knowledge economy. Many products will continue to be manufactured industrially. However, the share of intellectual capital and therefore intangible assets that flows into the development and design of

---

[1] US Federal Reserve Board's *Semiannual Monetary Policy Report* to the US Congress, February 27/March 7, 2002 (www.federalreserve.gov/boarddocs/hh/2002/march/testimony.htm).

these products and that forms the basis for modern competitive production and supply chain processes will increase. The same applies to the increasingly important service and customer relationship management processes for production companies that are often decisive factors for a company's financial results.

However, the basic rules of business still apply to new knowledge-based companies – even though in the dotcom era people sometimes think differently. Converting intellectual capital into results requires a certain degree of tangible and financial capital, and only profit-creating company activities ensure long-term success.

This is currently demonstrated by companies such as SAP AG, which is a typical example of the knowledge economy. The company has grown strongly over the last decades. Management focused on setting the right course in product development, sales and marketing, and on building human capital and partnerships in order to take advantage of the fast-growing market opportunities and convert them into corresponding market share and sales revenue. The additional value created through long-term customer relationships was demonstrated in the last fiscal year, as growth in the industry levelled out, but SAP was still able to increase its market share in comparison with competitors. Disciplined financial management was always necessary, guaranteeing solid financing of product and market development projects even in the growth phase. This is even more valid today, as the software industry develops into a mature industry. With lower growth rates, it is clear that, in addition to innovation, customer relationships and human capital, discipline in the areas of finance, cost management and resource utilization is a decisive success factor.

It is no longer a case of ''New Economy'' versus ''Old Economy'', since traditional industrial companies are turning into knowledge-based companies and the newcomers are getting used to tried and trusted reputable business practices, such as being and staying profitable. The recipe for success for companies in all branches today and in the future is therefore the combination of new and old success factors.

But to convert their knowledge capital into a measurable performance and results, companies also require appropriate instruments for control. A combination of ''old'' and ''new'' is also valid here – for example, efficient cost management in combination with effective innovation, market, sales and customer relationship management. Here we need to catch up, both regarding business science and theory as well as the practical aspects. This book covers exactly this subject and therefore represents a valuable contribution toward making the intangible assets that are so valuable to a company today more manageable by integrating them into a comprehensive enterprise management and control system.

Walldorf, September 2002
Dr Werner Brandt
Member of the executive board of SAP AG

Foreword to the German edition

Intangible assets have grown in importance for both investors and managers in recent years. Companies today create value to a large degree through business processes and activities that are based on knowledge assets, on productive relationships with customers and other business partners, on their public reputation and on the recognition of their brands and products in the global marketplace, and in particular on their innovative power and on new technologies.

The growing gap between the market value of a company and between what it reports in its financial statements demonstrates that the real value drivers are no longer captured through traditional management and accounting instruments such as the balance sheet and the income statement. Managers can no longer run a company successfully, and investors cannot make judgements about a possible investment, based on this information alone.

A more intensive discussion about the treatment of these immaterial value drivers in accounting, controlling and management systems of companies and in external corporate reports started a couple of years ago in the Anglo-Saxon countries under terms such as "intellectual capital", "intangible assets", or just "intangibles". This discussion has now also reached Germany, since German corporations whose stocks are listed on a US stock exchange are obliged by the new US GAAP rules to subject their reported goodwill to an impairment test; that is, a fair market valuation at least once a year. This has not only far-reaching consequences for accounting and financial reporting but also for the future design of corporate planning, controlling and management systems.

It is highly probable that these new accounting rules will lead financial analysts to pay more attention to reported goodwill and to ask companies to provide them with more information about their intangibles and the sustainability of the reported value – even if a company is not listed on a US stock exchange. A new general standard could emerge that will force companies not only to enhance their external reporting but also to adapt their internal management accounting and controlling systems in order to be able to manage internally what they have to report externally.

Corporations that are obliged to carry out this impairment test will experience this need as soon as they have to justify impaired goodwill. Repeated and sudden, unexpected adjustments to the value of goodwill may lead analysts to think that management lacks the necessary discipline or even the competence to manage corporate assets. In order to avoid such surprises and to inform the financial community proactively, as was the case with income statement and balance sheet figures in the past, not only the procedures related to external accounting need to be enhanced but also those related to management accounting and controlling. Sound planning systems based on modern technologies are therefore increasing in significance. The corporate planning system and resulting future return expectations form the basis for fair market valuation by an impairment test. Business plans are no longer only internal benchmarks and objectives for managers, they will also play a central role in the auditing process in the future.

Senior executives and their consultants, controllers and accountants, as well as auditors, financial analysts and institutional investors are therefore well advised to pay more attention to the "intangibles", which have become important economic factors both on the corporate and on the national level. Only through a better understanding of the economics of these intangible assets can sound internal and external investment decisions be made today to enable our companies to advance in the future. Traditional financial statement analysis concepts have to be expanded to enable a comprehensive enterprise analysis. We therefore need new instruments to support both internal management control and external reporting, as well as traditional monthly, quarterly and annual financial statements to provide managers and investors with the relevant additional information about these intangible value drivers that they need to make their decisions. This book will contribute toward achieving this goal.

Frankfurt/Main, Germany, February 2002
Karlheinz Hornung
Chief Financial Officer and member of the executive board of
MG Technologies AG

About the Author

Juergen H. Daum is a recognized expert and consultant for enterprise management concepts and systems. As senior business consultant at SAP AG he provides advice to enterprises and business managers worldwide in the area of finance, financial accounting, management accounting, controlling and business intelligence, management information systems and IT, and enterprise management. Until recently he led, as Director of Program Management, the strategic repositioning of SAP's finance, accounting, and analytical management applications, then called mySAP Financials, and has substantially contributed to the definition of its future development strategy. Earlier, as product manager of SEM, he was responsible for the definition of the concept for SAP Strategic Enterprise Management (SAP SEM), now part of the mySAP Financials solution, and was then leading its market roll-out. Before joining SAP, he was the CFO of an IT company in Germany.

Since his early career days, Juergen Daum has been engaged in operational tasks, strategy work and organizational development. He has always acted at the interface between the practical application of enterprise management concepts and the design of supporting IT and software solutions. In addition to his expert knowledge, he owns significant entrepreneurial and visionary capabilities, developed as a student in his own small company. For 10 years he worked in an international environment at SAP on the concept of the "enterprise management system", collaborating with global and local companies in Europe and North America – both at an executive level and with corporate specialists and with experts from finance, controlling, strategic planning, and IT.

Juergen H. Daum was born in 1960 and lives with his family near Heidelberg in Germany. He is a member of the German Controller Association (Controller Verein e.V.) and of an international management organization and publishes regularly on enterprise management and management systems.

Contact: jhd@juergendaum.com
           www.juergendaum.com

Introduction

Today's companies have become the least transparent organizations ever, and the status of their production and risk factors and the economic performance of their business systems are difficult to grasp. For managers, investors and economists this situation is alarming. We risk our companies being unable to exploit their full economic potential to create value-added and wealth. A large portion of their activities that create value-added for shareholders and stakeholders is no longer recorded in a systematic way and is therefore not transparent internally and externally.

The reason is the limitations of today's management, accounting and controlling instruments. They have not kept pace with the economic realities of the last few decades. They originate from another economic era and are oriented on the industrial value-creation systems of the past. They provide a too narrow view and exclude the most important production factors of our increasingly knowledge- and service-based enterprises and economies: intangible assets – nonfinancial, immaterial, "invisible" production factors – and their value-creation potential and inherent risks.

The USA was long proud to have the best, most accurate and most transparent accounting and financial reporting system. The gold standard of accounting, the generally accepted American/US-GAAP, accounting principles recently suffered a heavy setback. And this, despite the fact that US-GAAP is oriented, in contrast to traditional European accounting rules which have as their basis the caution principle and the minimum value principle, on the true and fair view principle, and that US-GAAP tries to make sure that companies report their actual performance as accurately as possible.

The largest insolvency in American economic history, the sudden breakdown of Enron, the previously profitable and successful power trading giant, created a real shock. Americans were suddenly questioning the quality of their accounting rules. Never before were investors so skeptical about the financial reports of American corporations. This mistrust even extended to blue chips like General Electric and IBM.

US president George W. Bush announced in January 2002 that the reporting rules for corporations would be carefully reviewed. The main criticism centered around the fact that the US-GAAP are based on many detailed rules, but that they lack broader principles to ensure that information that is really relevant for judging today's companies is disclosed.

What is specifically missing includes, for example, standards and rules that define how investments in intangibles should be treated in accounting and financial reporting. In his congressional testimony in the Enron case, Professor Baruch Lev from New York University identified the most critical limitation of current financial reporting as being too narrow and too much focused on just the financial aspects of transactions that had already been executed. Instead, companies should report on their intangible assets and, in a comprehensive way, on their risk exposure.[2]

The first step to increase the transparency of corporate intangible assets has already been taken. The new US-GAAP rules concerning goodwill (SFAS 141 and 142[3]), which have to be applied by companies in fiscal year 2002 for the first time, will let financial analysts and investors investigate in more detail the components of goodwill, which are intangible assets. However, these rules only apply to acquired intangible assets that emerge as an accounting item labeled "goodwill" in the accounting process of first consolidation of an acquired company and that have to be tested annually against its fair market value for possible impairment. Therefore, these new rules are not sufficient to provide the full picture of how a company is creating value-added with its intangible assets and how successful it is in this process.

The discussion about the inadequacy of traditional corporate reporting and whether companies should report in a comprehensive way about their new value drivers – intangible assets – started some years ago – especially in the Anglo-Saxon countries and in Scandinavia. For example, a task force of the US Securities and Exchange Commission (SEC) investigated how the traditional, financial reporting practice of companies could be improved. In its final report in May 2001 it recommended that the SEC should come up with a framework for voluntary "Supplementary Reporting", which should report on the status of intangibles and other operational performance drivers of a company's business system.[4]

---

[2] The testimony is available at: www.stern.nyu.edu~blev/
[3] For more detail about these rules, see the report on the website of the author at: www.juergendaum.com/news/11_10_2001.htm
[4] The report of the SEC taskforce is available at: www.fei.org/finrep/files/SEC-Taskforce-Final-6-6-2kl.pdf

Denmark has already taken a lead. It is the first country to oblige its companies to disclose (from 2002) an intellectual capital statement in addition to their traditional financial reports. The concept is based on the experiences of several Danish and Swedish companies that acted as pioneers for such a reporting practice. One is the Swedish financial service company Skandia, which was the first company to introduce this kind of reporting under the direction of Leif Edvinsson.

All these initiatives demonstrate that our current accounting practice is due for a major change and overhaul. Accounting and corporate reporting has to reflect the economic reality of today's companies in a better way so that they can serve as reliable instruments to support decisions made by investors. At the same time managers need better control and management tools to be able to manage internally what has been reported externally. Only in this way will investors and managers be able to get a better understanding of the company's performance and its future prospects.

At the beginning of the 20th century industrial mass production, as the engine to generate value, required more complex cost accounting, beyond the abilities of previous accounting practices, to enable management to control and optimize these new value-creation processes. In the same way, we must now expand accounting and control systems to a new level, to enable companies to optimize, manage and report on today's new value-creating activities and processes.

In the booming economy and capital markets of the 1990s crude measurement and valuation models could be tolerated. In today's slow-growth economy and stagnant capital markets, more attention to corporate resource allocation is required from managers. So, managers should develop the capability to assess the expected return on investment in R&D, employee training, information technology (IT), brand enhancement, etc. and compare these returns with those of physical investment in an effort to achieve optimal allocation of corporate resources.

To include information about nonfinancial success factors in management reports is a step in the right direction, but is not sufficient to enable management to manage the intangible assets of the company and to exploit their potential fully. Value creation on the basis of intangible assets is a quite complex process in most organizations. Conceiving the framework for a new management system therefore requires a deep understanding of the nature and characteristics of intangible assets.

The enterprise strategy that describes how a company wants to create value for its stakeholders with a unique combination of its assets becomes more important in the highly competitive environment of the knowledge-based economy. It is critical that strategy moves into the operational area, to get new strategies into action and to adapt quickly to changing market conditions.

This requires a management system that makes strategy work continuously rather than as a one-off process, and establishes ongoing strategic dialog within the enterprise. This is because one of the main characteristics of intangible assets is that their value is normally far more dependent on external factors, such as for example market perception, than is the case with the value of physical assets. And these external factors are not under the control of management. Unique competitive positions in the market based on intangible assets can only be retained or even expanded if the enterprise is always one step ahead in this kind of external development, and has already adapted its own strategy before a change occurs.

The control instruments of the company have to include a measurement system that provides a focused view of all success-critical areas of the company. This measure or KPI (Key Performance Indicators) system represents not only the foundation for performance monitoring, but also for planning and risk management, especially for the rolling forecasting process that serves as the main integration platform for the different management processes. The concept of the Tableau de Bord as the main measurement and reporting tool was developed by the author (see pp. 257–297) and reports on the total performance of a company as well as on the status and prospects of the most important value-creating processes, could serve as the framework for management information, performance measurement, control and risk-monitoring system. It could represent the basis for the new management system and for external reporting.

To design, introduce and work with a new management system is not only a challenge for consultants, controllers, strategic planners, corporate accountants and IT experts, but is also especially so for managers. In order to make full use of the new concepts and the new system, managers need to enhance their mental scope. Most managers are trained to limit risk and to solve day-to-day problems. This is no longer sufficient. Enterprise success in the new economy does not depend on eliminating risks, but on limiting them and especially on leveraging opportunities quickly by translating them into strategies and corresponding actions fast. Managers have to mistrust their "gut feeling" and have to base their decision instead on hard facts. They should get used to techniques like systems thinking and scenario planning. Because they tend, like every human being, to underestimate large risks and to overestimate small ones and to avoid a small loss at any price rather than make a major gain – as Patrick George said in his interview in this book.

The structure of the book

The intention of this book is to demonstrate and prove the necessity of adopting new concepts for the enterprise organization and for the enterprise management system in the 21st century. This is complemented by examples showing not only how leading companies have started to reorganize themselves internally but also their relationships with their stakeholders in order to enable them to leverage and harness the new success factors. However, the core objective of the book and its main topic is to show what tasks the new management systems has to solve, how the underlying accounting and measurement systems and management processes should be conceived, and how it is linked and integrated with an improved external reporting and communication system. For this, I have tried to gather and consolidate the latest expert discussion on these topics, the appropriate tools, instruments and methods, and to link them together to one integrated concept.

Part 1 of the book explains, by describing the new enterprise environment and the conditions of the new economy using many examples, why the traditional enterprise model and traditional management systems are no longer sufficient. It shows the limitations of traditional enterprise organization models, of traditional management systems and of traditional accounting and control systems. In addition, taking several examples from leading companies, the new success factors for enterprises in the new environment are presented.

Part 2 describes how companies react to the changing role they play in society and how they adapt their organization structures and processes and their culture in order to create value-added for their shareholders and stakeholders. Taking the case of ABB, we demonstrate how an enterprise developed from a traditional industrial company, based on a standard hierarchical structure, into a global enterprise that functions as a string of smaller entrepreneurial units. This part ends by giving an example of a company (Cisco) and describes its evolution from a global company into a networked e-business enterprise.

Part 3 presents concepts and examples for a new management system that should enable companies to master the challenges of the era of intangible assets. This includes a comprehensive description of a framework for a new accounting, measurement and management system, as well as for an improved external reporting system. The framework integrates concepts such as Kaplan and Norton's Balanced Scorecard, Lev's Value Chain Blueprint and other modern management, accounting and performance management concepts. This part ends with a description of the new challenges and tasks for the CFO and the CIO and of a model for the necessary information technology infrastructure.

What a knowledge and intangible asset-based economy on the macrolevel means and what the new economic success factors of nations are, constitute our discussion in Part 4, the Epilogue.

You can read every part of the book separately. If you are interested more in accounting, controlling and in performance management issues, you should focus on Part 3. If you want to learn more about what managers have done to lead their companies to success in the new environment and to create new structural capital, I recommend Part 2. A general overview about the book's topics and about challenges and opportunities related to intangible assets is provided in Part 1.

Why this book?

Managerial diseconomies that are caused by a company's incapacity to manage its intangible assets properly are the major factor that limits the use of intangible assets and inhibits economic growth that would be possible through them. To avoid bad managerial decision making systematically by adopting an improved management system can therefore have significant impact on enterprise performance. When companies act in a more forward-looking way, when they are able to estimate risks and opportunities better and when they make better use of their real value drivers, they will improve their performance and their returns.

This can bring the economy forward in a way that could exceed the productivity gains that were achieved in the 1990s in the USA by improvements in enterprise structures, in operative business processes and by the intensified use of information technology.

In Europe, especially, there exists a need to catch up when we consider the productivity of national economies. As I write this introduction, I have just received the latest figures for 2001. Despite its slowing economy, the USA still managed to maintain its high productivity rate from the late 1990s. The slightly decreased economic growth rate is due to a decreased employment rate. The productivity gap between the USA and the rest of the world is widening. Europe is in the hunt to catch up. European and Asian enterprises should take care not to miss the train again: that is, a complete overhaul of their management systems and the next wave of possible productivity improvements.

Heidelberg, February 2002

Juergen H. Daum

jhd@juergendaum.com

http://www.juergendaum.com

Part 1
New Corporate Values

1 Intangible Assets: The Foundation of a New Economy

Information and knowledge are the thermonuclear competitive weapons of our time. Knowledge is more valuable and more powerful than natural resources, big factories, or fat bankrolls. In industry after industry, success comes to the companies that have the best information or wield it most effectively – not necessarily the companies with the most muscle.

Thomas A. Stewart[1]

In the last two decades of the 20th century an almost unnoticed (by the public) revolution in the corporate world took place: the transition from industrial capitalism, where business was based on tangible physical assets, to a new economy, where the production of goods and services and value creation in general depends and relies on invisible intangible assets. In 1982, of every $100 invested in stocks of US manufacturers and mining companies on average $62.3 were still spent on tangible assets, such as land, plant, machinery, equipment and inventories. In 1992, 10 years later, only $37.9 out of every $100 invested into stocks was spent on tangible assets. More than half of the investment went into so-called intangible assets – corporate values which are not reported on a company's balance sheet.[2] Since then, the rate one had to pay for tangible assets with every dollar invested in stock has dropped further to only 16% in 1999 (see Figure 1.1). While these statistics relate to S&P 500 companies in the USA,[3] the same trend can be observed in other developed economies all over the world.

In knowledge-intensive industries, like the software business, the book-to-market value has often dropped below 10%. The book value of a company, also named "shareholders equity" by accountants, reflects the value of a company's reported assets less liabilities (= net assets) and represents the company's value reported to shareholders and to the financial community through financial statements.

---

[1] Thomas A. Stewart (1997) *Intellectual Capital*, New York: Doubleday Dell, p. xix. Interestingly, this book by Stewart and the books by Karl Erik Sveiby and Leif Edvinsson (collaborating with Michael S. Malone) were all published in the same year, 1997. All three titles are quoted throughout this chapter.

[2] Stewart, *Intellectual Capital*, p. 33.

[3] Buruch Lev (January, 2000) "Knowledge and shareholder value". In this article, Lev reports an average market-to-book ratio of the S&P 500 companies for 1999 of 6.25. See: www.stern.nyu.edu/~blev/knowledge&shareholdervalue.doc).

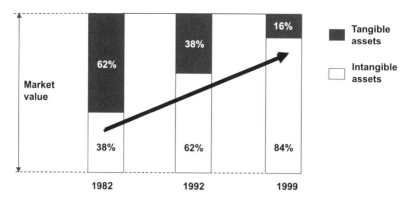

Figure 1.1   Development of the value of intangible assets as a percentage of total market value of S&P 500 companies between 1982 and 1999.

The portion of a company's reported net assets compared with its market value has in many cases become so small today that the relevance of a balance sheet, which reports on these assets, and the effort accountants and auditors put in to set it up properly, has become questionable.

Take, for example, Microsoft. At the end of its fiscal year 1999 on June 30, 1999, the net assets of Microsoft – those appearing on the balance sheet – accounted only for 6.2% of its market value of $460 billion (see Figure 1.2). One year later, after a sharp correction of technology stocks in April, 2000, this rate was still at 9.8%. But nobody believes that Microsoft's future cash flows,

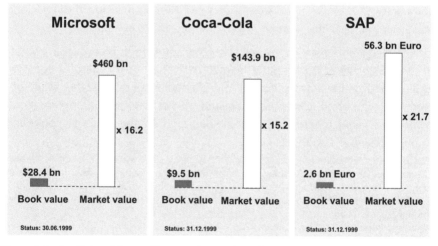

Figure 1.2   For "intangible asset" companies, market value can exceed book value by up to 20 times.

whose net present value was estimated at $460 billion by the financial market, are generated through office buildings and equipment – which are probably most of the physical assets you will find on Microsoft's balance sheet.

Microsoft's value originates from its software development knowledge and from its involvement in an environment and a culture that stimulates development of superior software products. It also originates from creative marketing and sales capabilities and platforms, consisting mainly of Microsoft's worldwide customer base, to which it can continuously sell new products, and of its dominant position within the huge ecosystem of the "Wintel" community. This community consists in thousands of software companies that provide solutions based on "Windows", in Intel, the company which has set the standard for the hardware side of the business, and in PC vendors like Compaq, Dell, IBM, HP, etc. |Most of Microsoft's capital is not traditional capital such as land and machinery. It's intellectual capital and intangible assets, such as human capital in the form of talented employees who come up with ideas for new products and patents, and structural capital in the form of procedures and organizational structures that facilitate productive collaboration between employees, and in the form of the relationships the company maintains with customers and business partners on which its marketing and sales capabilities are based. |

Likewise for SAP, the German market leader for enterprise resource planning (ERP) and e-business software solutions: only 4.6% of its market value as of December 31, 1999 appears as net assets or shareholders equity on its balance sheet, with its market value more than 21-fold higher (see Figure 1.2). Most of SAP's value consists in its ability to create superior business software solutions and in its capabilities to sell them successfully worldwide. Similar to Microsoft, SAP is based on a large existing customer base of more than 13,500 worldwide corporate customers in 120 countries and on the dominant role the company plays within a large ecosystem of consulting, software and hardware partners. These partners are all engaged in marketing, implementation and consultancy activities around SAP's ERP product R/3 and its e-business platform mySAP.com, and the revenues generated by this ecosystem related to SAP products are more than five times higher than the revenues of SAP itself. But Microsoft and SAP are not exceptional examples. Knowledge businesses create a large part of today's wealth and jobs. Businesses such as those producing software were the pioneers. Because software is nothing more than pure knowledge in codified form, software companies are 100% knowledge businesses. However, other businesses, like the pharmaceutical industry, where the bulk of company value is made up of its R&D pipeline, its capability and knowledge, its ability to create "blockbuster" compounds with huge revenue potential, are also examples of intangible corporation pioneers.

It is not by accident that the software and pharmaceutical industries were rated by institutional investors and financial analysts as the "top investment theme" in the last decade. Knowledge and intangible asset-based businesses can create much more wealth than traditional financial assets-based businesses, because economics works much better for them: for example, the economic law of diminishing returns, known from tangible assets-based businesses, is no longer valid, expenditures which are costs in traditional businesses turn into investments in knowledge businesses and create future revenue-generating assets, which are, by the way, no longer under the full control of the investing company. And, as we will see later, the phenomena of diminishing returns known from traditional businesses is converted into the phenomena of increasing returns. All this was unimaginable in the old industrial age.

Nevertheless, even traditional companies can create intangible assets and knowledge-based value. By concentrating on their core competencies, they will at the same time be able to create brand value, extend their customer base and grow revenue, reduce costs while keeping an attractive pricing level, communicate a better "story" to investors and gain a much more attractive investment profile. Take Coca-Cola, a company doing business in the more traditional industry, as an example: only 6.6% of Coca-Cola's market value was reported as book value on its balance sheet on December 31, 1999. Of each $100 invested in Coca-Cola stock more than $93 had to be paid for the intangible assets of the company – mainly for its brand and the related ability to get higher prices for its products and to generate more revenue than competitors are able to do, but also for Coca-Cola's global network of bottlers, which represents an exclusive global sales channel (see Figure 1.2).

Every company in the future will have to convert itself into an organization that is able to create in a systematic way intellectual capital and intangible assets by leveraging and exploiting knowledge work. And businesses have to learn how to increase return not only on tangible, physical assets but also on intangible assets.

This requires a new model for the business corporation and new management systems that are better adapted to these new intangible drivers of corporate value than the traditional financial-based management, accounting, control and reporting concepts. It requires an enterprise organization that is able to support the systematic transformation of individual knowledge and relations with business partners into intangible assets, which can serve as the basis to generate additional revenues. Management systems are needed that can make value that is created or destroyed visible and manageable – including the value that relates to intangible assets. Organizational concepts and forms are required that enable an enterprise to adapt to changes in its markets in a more forward-looking way and provide it with the ability to reconfigure not only its tangible value chain, but – much more important today – its intangible value chain as well by developing new strategies and implementing them at light speed.

For this, new managers are required who have a deep understanding of the nature of intellectual capital, intangibles and their economics. They will create through flexible organizational structures, through the appropriate internal and external business processes and knowledge-management procedures an environment that helps to make knowledge workers more productive and to transform their work results into sustained value for the corporation. Partnerships, economic webs and net communities will play an important role for a business organization to be successful – as we have already seen in the cases Coca-Cola, SAP and Microsoft. Management has to treat all three elements: human capital (the source of individual knowledge as the "base material" for value creation), the internal organization structure and business processes (which represents the corporate knowledge base) and relations with business partners, economic webs and the net communities (which represent the external marketing and sales base), as the real corporate assets that represent the foundation for economic value creation in today's new knowledge-based economy.

Businesses and managers who are focused on creating and exploiting intangible assets have to also make intensive use of IT and the Internet, because information and the flow of information form the basis of any intellectual asset-creation process. Digitizing its business and management systems, not only within the four walls of the company but across the ecosystem and business network of all partner companies as well, will become one of the top themes for corporations in the years to come, in order to increase productivity and especially productivity of knowledge work and economic networks.

Only in this way will management be able to create, accumulate, maintain and leverage intangible assets and intellectual capital in order to create value-added for both shareholders and stakeholders in the more challenging and demanding new economy with its higher stakes. But this requires a totally new approach to management. To understand necessity and urgency for such a transition, let us have a closer look at the underlying revolutionary change in our economies and at what happened in recent years.

The end of industrial capitalism and of traditional management

Knowledge-worker productivity is the biggest of the 21st century management challenges. In the developed countries it is their first survival requirement. In no other way can the developed countries hope to maintain themselves, let alone to maintain their leadership and their standard of living.

Peter F. Drucker[4]

Industrial capitalism, which emerged in the 19th century as a new economic structure, gave rise to the business corporation and its basic management techniques – such as financial accounting – and was based almost exclusively on financial capital. Financial capital – money – bought land, machinery and other equipment to produce goods. It also bought labor from workers, needed for the production process. Most work was not very sophisticated and required no specific skills a worker could not learn within a few days. He or she was therefore easily replaceable. Labor was cheap and abundantly available. The one who owned financial capital – the capitalist – owned everything: the tools to produce goods with and the result of the production process, the product itself.

The capitalist was the only one to gain the added-value of the production process, in the form of profits. Reinvested profits together with a so far unknown economic growth rate (the preindustrial economic growth rate used to be nearly 0%) generated even more wealth and enormous economic and also political power for capitalists.

While economic power was concentrated in the hands of a few capitalists, the workers' destiny was to live in poverty. No wonder that Karl Marx predicted the end of industrial capitalism. He estimated that the accumulation of capital in the hands of a few people would accelerate and cause even more poverty for the rest. He was convinced that this situation would provoke enough social instability that workers would take their destiny into their own hands and create a socialist society where all production tools and capital would be owned by the proletariat – the community of the workers.

---

[4] Peter F. Drucker, *Management Challenges for the 21st Century*, New York: HarperCollins, p. 157.

The essence of Karl Marx's theory, that the owner of the production factor ''labor'' – the worker – should also get his or her share of the added-value generated in the production process and should participate in capital accumulation, was revolutionary thinking at this time. It led to many armed conflicts and wars and determined the political landscape until the end of the 20th century. But socialism, as an outcome of the ideas of Karl Marx, was not able to keep its promises. And after the collapse of the former Soviet Union, Karl Marx would be surprised to see how his dream of a ''capitalist worker'' has materialized in, for example, Silicon Valley: in the form of the knowledge worker, who owns his working tools (his brain, etc.) and who participates in the economic success of his company through stock options. This became possible at the end of the 20th century because information and knowledge has gained more importance as a production factor than financial capital and has replaced it as the engine for wealth creation. New kinds of business, based on knowledge work, have been created in recent years. Companies that were more flexible, more adaptive and more fluid in their structures, producing ''smart'' products and services that featured mass customization, customer participation in product design and manufacture and the linking of suppliers, distributors and strategic partners into chains of common destiny. Companies emerged that have created and own more intellectual capital and value-creating potential than traditional businesses. It is these knowledge-intensive firms, found in many industries from software and semiconductors to steel mills, that have led the revolution, leaving other companies – and other nations – to catch up. These agile, virtual and intangible corporations feature at their philosophical centre an entirely different notion of what constitutes an asset. They value activities that create invisible intellectual capital like employee competence building, ''packaging'' of knowledge by identifying and describing best practice business processes, collaborating with partners instead of doing everything itself or activities to improve customer relations more than activities that help to preserve physical assets and increase short-term profitability.

These ''intangible'' activities may not impact the bottom line of a company for years, such as R&D investments in the pharmaceutical and software sectors. But, increasingly, created intangible assets are recognized and valued by investors. Some 10 or 20 years ago, nobody would have invested money in a company that was not able to generate any profit for years. With the Internet boom the significance of investments in the intellectual capital and intangible assets of corporations for their future value-creation potential was increasingly acknowledged by the financial community.

Unfortunately some of the dotcoms exaggerated massively in marketing their capabilities – which in some cases came close to fraud. But even when the Internet bubble burst and the hype at the Nasdaq in the USA, at the Neuer Markt in Germany and at other similar stock exchanges in other countries ended, one thing remained: that investors and managers recognize that enterprises, which should create sustaining value for investors and stakeholders, have to focus not just on short-term earnings but also on long-term business potential, that is on the creation of intangible assets. But at the same time they have to prove their economic health and strength through regular short-term performance. Promises for the future alone are not sufficient. But the pressure on management through the earnings game, through the focus of the financial community on short-term performance can be reduced for companies that invest massively in the future and in intangibles. The precondition is the existence of a management and reporting system that can inform management and the external financial community in a reliable way about the status of intangible assets.

The corporation and its shareholders no longer exclusively own corporate assets

The knowledge worker of today, unlike his or her industrial worker great-grandfather, owns the tools needed for production: knowledge, competencies and skills. These workers can walk out of the door of a company and take their knowledge with them. But knowledge workers also take with them the knowledge they brought in, and that they gained in the company as partici-pants in intellectual capital accumulation. This is the accumulation of human capital: knowledge gained and built up through work experiences and through collaboration with other knowledge workers, business partners and customers.

That companies no longer own this kind of capital, intellectual capital, alone might be reflected in the fact that more and more companies, especially in knowledge-intensive businesses, reward the accumulation of intellectual capital by their employees by letting them also participate in the accumulation of financial capital in the form of stock options the company grant to them. These companies want to bind their workers' talents to the enterprise and make them shareholders, legally co-owners of the company's assets made up of a large portion of intangible assets that they helped to create. Microsoft alone estimates to have created between 5,000 and 10,000 millionaires through its stock option programs. In Silicon Valley, the heart of the software industry, the number of millionaires grew by 44% in 1996, totaling

55,000 in San Jose; many of these new millionaires were programmers.[5] The flip side of the coin is that jobs which do not require special skills or special knowledge are losing value, salaries and wages are dropping and often these jobs disappear completely through automation.

This is leading to situations such as those in Germany in 2001: the country is still suffering from the highest unemployment rate for years and at the same time German software companies are struggling to find qualified people. Some 75,000 positions in the German software and IT industry cannot be filled due to the lack of qualified experts. And it is likely that this number will grow within the next few years up to 250,000. The German government reacted in the meantime by introducing its "green card" initiative, allowing highly-skilled people such as software programmers to enter the country for a limited time. Being able to hire enough talented people and retaining their skills and knowledge for the company represents a major challenge for management in any knowledge-intensive business today.

Similar is true for the creation of relationships with customers and business partners. Many enterprises have to reach certain market-related growth targets in order to be successful. For example, they have to reach a certain level of market share within a certain time frame in a new product segment in order to be able to generate the returns necessary to cover the upfront invest-ment and to reward shareholders and stakeholders. Because companies are no longer able to achieve this alone, they are dependent on the existence of large partner networks in sales and marketing. These partner networks therefore represent a valuable asset for these companies, because they are the founda-tion of their capability to grow fast enough and to dominate a market in the future and to generate superior earnings. But the network is not legally owned by the corporation. Partners can terminate the partnership at any point in time and walk away with a new partner – often a major competitor of the company. Each partner has some influence on this asset "partner network". Therefore it is economically owned by all partners. Likewise with customers: customer relations are the basis on which to do future business with these customers, they represent an option to sell new products to these customers, which is definitely easier than winning new customers. Existing customer relations are therefore of great value for a company. But as customer relations are often a product of the activities of the company, its partners and of the customers themselves, it is economically owned by all parties together, and, what is

---

[5] Detlev J. Hoch et al. (1999) *Secrets of Software Success*, Boston: Harvard Business School Press, p. 7.

even more important, these assets are not under the full control of management.

Intellectual capital is often not owned exclusively by a corporation and its shareholders. The stakeholders of a company – that means its shareholders, employees, customers and business partners – have a shared ownership in the intellectual capital and the intangible assets the company is using as the basis for its business or value-creation system. This is a real revolution and is changing one of the most important fundamentals of industrial capitalism: that economic control is based on *ownership* of financial capital and assets.

Henry Ford owned the means of production of his automobiles. He also owned the output – the car – until a customer bought it, at which point Ford had no further claim on it. The production and output of knowledge work, however, do not belong only to the company that employs the knowledge worker. Says Thomas Stewart, editor of the American magazine *Fortune*: "When I write an article in *Fortune*, the magazine owns the copyright for the words I use – but *Fortune* doesn't have exclusive ownership of the underlying knowledge. I still have it. *Fortune* has it. And if you read it, you have it too. In other words, when knowledge is the chief resource and result – the input and output, the raw material and finished product – ownership of that knowledge becomes fuzzy, shared: the worker is part-owner, the capitalist/shareholder is part-owner, and the customer is part-owner."[6] The rise of the knowledge worker, the increase in customer sophistication and global highly competitive markets as well as the need for partnerships in today's complex turbo-businesses on the one hand and the economic power of networks on the other, all this fundamentally alters the nature and work and the agenda of management.

It represents the end of management as we know it. There is no one right structure for an organization, there is no one right way to manage people, technologies. Especially because of the growing dominance of intangible assets, markets can change faster than in the past. Corporations not only have to adapt quickly to such changes; rather, they have to be able to anticipate such changes and have to act in a proactive way. If profits slip relegating the corporation to some lower point in their industry, companies will have to change to restore their place in the industry's value chain, where they can get a good share of overall generated value in the chain and to participate in its growth. In such a highly dynamic environment, organizations have to find new

---

[6] Stewart, *Intellectual Capital*, p. 103.

structures and management systems that allow them to create value systematically together with the co-owners of their assets.

The fact that a new economy corporation no longer owns some of its major assets or even full control over them represents a major challenge – not only from an accounting or legal point of view, but, probably much more importantly, from a management point of view as well. *If control of the business of a corporation is not based on ownership, as it used to be in so far known management systems, how do you manage this business?*

And knowledge workers do not perform in a command structure, with the result that the ''boss'' no longer knows how the job gets done. *How do you control your human capital in such an environment?*

In an economic web of partners, in a stakeholder network, nobody is ''the boss'' either. Alliances and partnerships are also not ''teams'' – every member works independently and with his or her own goals, objectives and tasks. *How do you lead and shape such an economic web for the sake of the company and all its partners?*

By treating these partner networks, customer relations, employee knowledge and skills, the company's processes, culture, organization, information and knowledge databases as assets, a manager takes the first step in the right direction. Every manager learns in business school that assets have to be managed actively, otherwise the company will not fulfil its purpose: to create value and to earn money. In a new economy we have to find a new approach to management, one which allows companies to implement new business systems successfully, to enhance them and be sustainably successful, even if the corporation does not have full control of its major assets.

This is no easy task and it requires a deep understanding of how knowledge- and relation-based assets are created, increased and used to create value, in order to be able to build the appropriate organization structure, culture and management systems. Says Peter Drucker: ''Making these new structures perform and work is a good deal more difficult than making the traditional command structure based on ownership and control work. But where they do work, they produce superior performance and superior results.''[7]

---

[7] Peter F. Drucker (1999) ''The real meaning of the merger boom'', *The Conference Board 1999 Annual Essay and Report*, New York: The Conference Board, p. 6.

In Part 2 and Part 3, I present examples, case studies and concepts for creating new structures and management systems. But, first, in order to provide a better basic understanding for the new enterprise model, I will describe in the remainder of this chapter and Chapter 2 the specific characteristics of intangible assets and related business success factors, also including the role IT is playing in this.

Information technology is replacing tangible assets

The role of IT has changed nearly everything we have become used to in business. Information and knowledge represent the foundation of intangible assets and of the new economics of the business enterprise of today. The power of information and knowledge is so big that it can replace financial and tangible assets.

Wal-Mart, the biggest retailing company in the world, has spent more than a billion dollars on information technology and was one of the first in industry to wire their retail stores with their logistic system. At the end of the day they knew exactly what customers bought and preferred and could process orders to suppliers immediately and come close to deliveries just-in-time when sold, reducing necessary stocks and working capital and avoiding the ''sold-out'' situation of specific products for customers (this is called ''efficient consumer response'' today and is perceived as a standard of best practice for the retail industry). Through new IT-based logistics and inventory management systems many businesses have started to follow Wal-Mart and replace inventory with information.

Inventories and stocks in a company mainly serve as buffers to bridge the time, for example, between the moment someone recognizes that raw material stock is out and the moment the supplier delivers new material. This time can be long, if you consider the complicated, traditional process of inventory management and purchasing, when someone has to fill out a form for a purchase requisition, someone has to process it in the purchase department, as does someone else on the supplier side. The longer it takes, the larger the stocks have to be to bridge that time.

But if a company links the supplier into its own electronic inventory management system, or even better into its production planning system, and allows the supplier to manage the company's inventories of raw materials or merchandise (so-called ''vendor-managed inventories''), the supplier is able to deliver raw material just-in-time, because the supplier now has the information, when the company exactly needs what quantities of material and where in its production process.

Japanese automotive companies in the 1980s taught the rest of the world how suppliers could deliver components and raw materials just-in-time as and when needed on the production belt, saving time, processing costs, working capital and storage space. Other automotive companies and other industries followed with similar improvements and many of them went even further. They not only replaced raw material inventories but also the inventories of semi-finished goods and of finished products with information, by linking different work processes in the internal production chain through integrated ERP software systems and by linking their company with its customers through electronic data interchange (EDI). Many companies have recently started to go some steps further through Internet-based Supply Chain Management (SCM) and Customer Relationship Management (CRM) software applications.

All of them have significantly reduced their working capital and at the same time improved responsiveness to customers and markets by streamlining the complete supply chain process. This is one of the reasons why investments in IT can yield a much greater return – experts estimate between five to ten times – than investments in traditional assets.

Since 1991 American companies have spent more money on equipment that gathers, processes, analyses and distributes information than on machines that stamp, cut, assemble, lift and otherwise manipulate the physical world.[8] But the focus of IT investments is still today to automate operations and process customer orders, purchase requisitions, payments and so on. But these IT and software systems generate simultaneously – while processing a customer order – a lot of additional information about the process and the business itself – such as information about customer ordering and buying patterns and customer preferences. Using this information, companies are now able with their analytical software applications to convert such information into knowledge, which can be used to optimize future marketing campaigns.

Sure, automation of formerly manually processed tasks enabled businesses to bring in more continuity and save time, cut costs and reduce inventories/ working capital and other current assets like receivables. But information converted to knowledge can replace not only working capital but also fixed assets.

---

[8] Stewart, *Intellectual Capital*, p. 21.

If an enterprise has the best knowledge in its industry about the preferences and needs of a specific group of potential customers, it is able to concentrate just on serving these customers, outsourcing the production plant to someone else. Because it is concentrating its forces, it will meet customer expectations and needs better than others and customers will readily pay a premium. It will have a much lighter, tangible balance sheet and simultaneously its profit margin will increase.

Information has become so valuable today that 90% of American companies, except those in steel, mining, transportation and real estate, pay more today for information than to attract financial capital.[9] Investment in information and knowledge represent an investment in the capability to create intangible assets. IT is helping corporations to replace tangible assets by intangible ones and to increase the portion of the total value of a corporation made up of intangible assets.

What exactly are intangible assets?

Assets are everything owned economically by a company that has money value. Assets come in four forms:

▶   *current assets*, meaning that they are likely to be consumed or sold within one year;

▶   *fixed assets*, which in the form of plant, equipment and property have a useful life of more than one year;

▶   *investments*, a company's holdings in stock and bonds; and

▶   *intangible assets*, which is everything that is not physical or investment, but is of value to the company. Typically they are long term, and just as typically they cannot be accurately valued until the company is sold, being then converted to and lumped under the title "goodwill", which is calculated as the difference between purchase price and book value. In more and more companies the role and amount of these intangibles increasingly gets greater to such a point that their value completely overwhelms the value of all the other assets combined, and it becomes obvious to everyone that these assets have to be identified and analyzed in more detail. Intangible assets can be described as a

---

[9] Paul A. Strassmann (January 30, 1996) "The value of computers, information and knowledge". See www.strassmann.comabgeruienwerdenkann).

company's intangible resources. They are therefore also called "intellectual capital".

Intellectual capital comprises human capital, structural capital, partner capital and customer capital, which is the result of the quality of the relations a company maintains with its customers (see Figure 1.3). In addition a company's culture and strategic capabilities count as intellectual capital or intangible assets. Intangible assets are the basis of an enterprise's innovation power, the raw material from which the bulk of its future economic and financial results are made.

Human capital

Human capital has developed into one of the most important intangible assets. In a knowledge-based economy everything starts with the people who have the necessary new ideas and the knowledge about customer needs. Human capital is therefore the source of innovation and renewal, because new, good ideas are created by people. This includes, for example, the engineer who invented a new technology that helped his company to construct a new innovative market-leading CD player, which is not only able to play CDs but to rewrite them as well. It is the product manager in a consumer products business who had the idea to sell a product in novel packaging, which enabled his company to attract many more consumers. It comprises the people who conceived new organizational processes within the company and processes that link the company to its suppliers in such a way that it is now able to deliver customers with ordered products and services timely as promised or just-in-time when needed. It also includes managers who came up with a new, powerful strategy that outsmarts the competition for years.

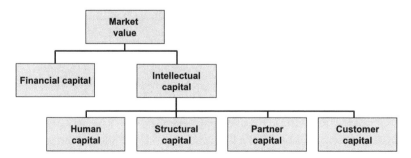

Figure 1.3 The value components of an enterprise.[10]

---

[10] Leif Edvinsson and Michael S. Malone (1997) *Intellectual Capital: Realizing Your Company's True Value by Finding Its Hidden Brainpower*, New York: HarperCollins.

The human capital of a company includes the individual capabilities of people who are working for this company, both employees and managers: their knowledge, skills, competencies and experiences. But not all these personal assets and not all employees and managers count as human capital. Only those individuals whose capabilities are of great value for the company, which can be used and incorporated in its operations and value-creating processes, are of strategic importance. People with skills and competencies, which are abundantly available on the labor market in equal form, do represent human resources but not human capital. They don't contribute to the firm's capability to make a difference in the market. Therefore, individual capabilities have to be assessed in the scope of a company's actual strategy and its value-creation system or business model to decide whether a specific person counts as human capital or just as a human resource.

Identified human capital can only be preserved if these employees and managers constantly upgrade their skills and add new ones. This is not only of vital interest for the company but also for the employees or managers themselves, as they are the owners of their human capital. The company just rents it and "owns" it only for the period when the employees are on its payroll. Both by matching the degree or gaps in actual skills with those required according to strategy and the actual business model, and their development over time, has to be monitored and managed in order to protect one of the most important ingredients of corporate assets today: that of human capital. Otherwise, the company risks continuing to draw on a body of aging and increasingly obsolete skills, ignoring at the same time new valuable competencies gained by individual employees, thus gradually losing its innovation capabilities and its competitive edge and destroying shareholder value. Many companies in knowledge-intensive businesses – professional services, software or high-tech have therefore started to identify and track skills available and skills required as well as the development and build-up of the required skills and competencies of their employees. Such skill databases are very valuable for enterprises not only from a strategic point of view, they are also used to optimize operative tasks. For example, skill databases can also be used to link different call centres at different locations to one single resource pool. The appropriate qualified person who is able to solve a specific customer problem can be found by using the skill database from all available employees across all call centres instead of from only the local one. Skill databases are also used in management development programs of multinationals to identify "high potentials". But what is often missing, especially in more traditional industries, are skill databases that cover all employees and therefore allow systematic enhancement of the total human capital of the enterprise.

So the core of intellectual capital is made up of human capital, of the talent pool consisting of the individuals working for the company. Human capital thus encompasses individual value in an economic sense. The Swedish company Skandia – a pioneer in intellectual capital management – divides human capital into three subcomponents: values, competence and relationship.[11]

It is the individual's *values* that determine whether an action is perceived as being meaningful or not. Values define the desirable and therefore the selection of modes, means and ends of actions. Values thus serve as a filter. Common values are the basis on which people are able to understand each other and work together toward a common objective in a partnership. The common core of values can be called an organization's culture which is a part of its structural capital (see the following section).

Competence has three dimensions: professional, social and commercial. According to Skandia, professional competence is defined as the human ability to act in a productive way within an organization and its business processes, which means utilizing the structural capital of that organization. Commercial competence is the ability to collaborate with customers and other external partners in value-creating constellations. Competence in general can be described as knowledge, will and skill.

The importance of transforming knowledge to action comes to light when looking at *relationship competencies*. This can be done either by individual actions or by sharing knowledge and networking with colleagues or partners. Interactive ability is often exemplified in knowledge sharing. Knowledge sharing is dependent on mutual trust and confidence, which in turn emanate from attitudes and values.

The topic of relationship competencies and knowledge sharing leads us to the next topic, because, even if human capital is the source of innovation and an essential basis for corporate value creation, it is not enough for creating and leveraging corporate intellectual capital.

Structural capital

The reason is that smart individuals do not necessarily make for smart enterprises. If people do not interact with each other, if knowledge does not flow

---

[11] Skandia Insurance Ltd (1998) *Human Capital in Transformation – Intellectual Capital Prototype Report*, Stockholm: Skandia, pp. 6–7.

between them, the group is not intelligent as a whole, there is no collective brilliance. And real leading-edge knowledge and innovation comes from interaction between knowledge workers, from the sharing of ideas and experiences.

To make this happen, a company needs the right organizational infrastructure, an innovative and stimulating culture and, the procedures and working schemes which support smooth and efficient knowledge and information flows within the entire organization and between internal and external experts. Also, an appropriate IT infrastructure is required to support this and one that helps knowledge workers to work in a productive way. Processes and techniques are required that help increase the effectiveness of knowledge-based value creation (for example, by supporting the development of products and services that create significant new value from a customer point of view) or that help develop very efficient manufacturing or sales methods.

All this represents structural capital, which can be subdivided into organizational, innovation and process capital. Structural capital is packed human capital: it permits individual human capital, individual knowledge, to be used again and again to create value.

Compiling human knowledge into structural capital helped Skandia to move quickly and take advantage of the worldwide trend toward deregulation of insurance and other financial services. It also helped Skandia to cut the time involved in opening an office in a new country from seven years to seven months. The company did it by identifying techniques and technology that could be transplanted anywhere. Skandia created what it calls a "prototype concept" – a collection of software applications, manuals and other structured know-how that can easily be customized to take account of local laws or support any line of financial products. Now, if a new team has to open a new subsidiary somewhere in the world, they are able to use, in most cases directly or with some minor modifications, the collected knowledge and past experiences from previous launches to open a prototype branch office quickly and therefore save time and money.[12]

One of the most important tasks of management is to implement structures, processes and procedures that help convert individual knowledge, human capital, as quickly as possible into the structural capital the company owns, because it is the job of management to build corporate assets. Structural capital belongs to the organization as a whole. It can be reproduced and shared.

---

[12] Stewart, *Intellectual Capital*, p. 77.

Structural capital and shareholder value is therefore created through the continuous recycling and creative utilization of shared knowledge and experience. This in turn requires the structuring and packaging of competencies and skills with the help of technology, process description, manuals, networks and the like to ensure that competence will remain with the company, when the employees go home.

Structural capital creates the conditions for the rapid sharing of knowledge and sustained, collective knowledge growth. Lead times between learning and knowledge shared have to be shortened systematically. Human capital will also become much more productive through structured, easily accessible and intelligent work processes. "Only the organization can provide the basic continuity that knowledge workers need in order to be effective. Only the organization can convert the specialized knowledge of the knowledge worker into performance," says Peter Drucker.[13] If every person were able to gain the full value of their services, there would be no corporations and only individuals. Structural capital provides added value and makes human capital much more productive. That is what motivates talented people to stay with their company, as long as it can provide them with the needed resources to work on interesting projects where they can leverage their knowledge and increase their human capital through collaboration with other experts and through work experience.

Structural capital is also an organization's capability to learn, innovate and adapt quickly to changes in technologies and in markets. In contrast to the opinion of many people, learning is mainly a social activity and not something that is done privately by, for example, reading a book. Real learning occurs if you talk about new ideas you may have, for example, found in a book. Through comments and other ideas discussed in a community, new concepts are created that can be used in an organization or in a personal work environment to improve work and productivity.

Communities of practice as the basis for professional learning

The term "communities of practice" is the modern name for the shop floor where new human capital, knowledge, is created. A community of practice is usually formed by a group of experts who work on similar topics or in the same discipline and who would like to communicate and exchange ideas and concepts at an expert level. These are, for example, development engineers, marketing, sales and human resource specialists or accountants and controllers

---

[13] Peter F. Drucker, (November, 1994) "The age of social transformation", *Atlantic Monthly*, p. 68.

within an enterprise. They all share within their group similar professional experiences and expert knowledge. But communities of practice can also be found outside the enterprise in the form of communities of physicians, lawyers, accountants or controllers (e.g., like the ICAEW in the UK or the Controller Verein e.V. in Germany). These are external communities that are not related to a specific company. Communities perform the main jobs of human capital formation: knowledge transfer and inovation. Therefore, company internal communities also represent structural capital. But learning communities that cross the boundaries of corporations are far more productive in terms of innovation and human capital creation. The bad news is that this type of community cannot be owned or controlled by a company.

The ground where communities grow is the internally networked organization. The greatest challenge for the new economy manager is to create an organization that can share knowledge. Networks connect people to people and people to data. They allow information that once flowed through a hierarchy – from the worker to manager, from manager to senior executive and then down another line finally to another worker – to flow between workers directly, enabling the corporation to react immediately to new customer requirements and needs. IT tools like email, teleconferencing and groupware changed the way organizations are run. This stimulus for the networked organization that is capable of delivering information and knowledge just-in-time to the place where it is actually needed, in addition enabled real organizational learning. In such an organization you see constant self-reorganization and self-redesign, without the need for a whole lot of co-ordination across the company. Such structural capital, an internal network, allows a company to act and react almost reflexively. A network organization might not look like one on its formal chart. Sometimes the network organiza-tion exists as an informal network in the form of different communities beside or behind the official organization.

In addition, an enterprise should not be entirely unhierarchical, because business organizations need to be pointed in the right direction and even pushed to take it. Take 3M: on the official organization chart, researchers are scattered in many different labs. There is a central R&D lab and there are labs attached to business units, and there are several centres dedicated to particular basic technologies. But there are a lot of networks that guarantee innovation and fast commercialization of research results across the entire organization.

A scientist who cannot get money for a project from a business unit his lab is linked with is encouraged to see if someone else will fund it. At the other end of the innovation pipeline new ideas are evaluated for commercial potential not only by people with hierarchical responsibility for them but also by a technical audit panel of scientists, manufacturing people and marketing specialists, none of whom work for the sponsoring business. Twice a year, in addition, 3M holds technology fairs, one run by scientists hawking inventions that need business sponsors, the other put on by business units promoting a marketing opportunity that needs an invention.[14]

Because a network organization, rather than the traditional corporation, is not based on a hierarchy, the question is: how to manage such an organization? In a network, supervision changes. There is less supervision of the content of the work and of single activities, more supervision of a person's overall performance and career. Basic management jobs, such as planning, budgeting and supervising must be done differently. To build, maintain and retain structural capital in the form of internal networks, corporations have to find new management methods and processes.

Customer capital and user communities

Customer capital is the value of a company's relationship with the people or organizations to which it sells. Customer capital would have been a truly alien notion to accountants just a few decades ago. But with today's mega-acquisitions, it is clear that customer capital counts. In recent acquisitions in the telecommunication industry, the acquisition price is often calculated by the number of customers the acquired company owns, multiplied by an average customer price which is the net present value of estimated future earnings per customer. Usually, the total acquisition price exceeded by far the book value of the acquired firm, while most of the excess price was paid for its customer base.

Another example: the Ford Motor Company estimates that every percentage point increase in customer loyalty – that means every percent more of existing customers who again buy a car from Ford – is worth $100 million a year in profits.[15] These are real big ticket numbers and the reason why the customer side has become so important in valuing a business. The quality of the customer relationship determines whether cash flows generated by this customer are sustainable in the future or can even grow. The company that has the better relationship with its customers has a better chance to keep them and to extend business with them beyond normal business and sell them new products or services. This increases a company's future cash flow generation

---

[14] Stewart, *Intellectual Capital*, pp. 189–190.
[15] Ibid., p. 144.

potential and therefore the overall value of the company. But many businesses still do not know their end-customers.

To know its customers and, more importantly, to know their preferences and needs is of inestimable value for corporations today. The industrial age with its mass production and standardized products is gone. While the consumer of the 1960s was accustomed to one-size-fits-all/single-transaction/zero-service relationships with his or her vendors, the consumer of today, having enjoyed a decade of growing control over the purchase process, expects to be able personally to define the products or service to match his or her needs. That is the reason why the company that is closest to the customer and really understands customer needs and expectations is able to provide the customer with the appropriate solution and product, building trust and very strong customer loyalty as a result.

By controlling the relationship with the end-customer, a company is able to dominate the complete supply chain of the customer and earn most of the value created in this supply chain. Its partners on the back end, upstream, have to be satisfied with smaller margins and profits. Power flows downstream from the manufacturers toward the companies who own the most knowledge about what happens at the customer end, where you find the folks who pay for all the upstream activities. So great is the power of this knowledge and information about customers that whoever controls it in many cases controls the complete business.

In 1990 IBM made between $10 billion and $11 billion in profits. No company has made that kind of money before or since (in 1997 the most profitable companies in the world, General Electric and Exxon, each made just a little more than $8 billion). In the next four years, IBM lost $23 billion – more money than any company in human history.[16] IBM did not notice that profits in the computer business were moving – due to a major technology change, the rise of the personal computer – from those assembling computers in the middle of the value-added chain to those at the beginning of the chain making components (Intel, Microsoft) and to those selling computers at the end of the chain (Dell, Compaq). Dell and Compaq had more information and knowledge about what the customer, the consumer, really expected from buying a personal computer and from the computer itself.

Merck,[17] with the best research labs in the prescription drug business, was

[16] Lester C. Thurow, "If God spoke to John Akers", *Across the Board* (January, 2000), p. 11.
[17] Stewart, *Intellectual Capital*, pp. 145–149.

America's most admired company in *Fortune*'s annual survey of corporate reputations for seven consecutive years. The company was admired and respected by its customers, mainly physicians and hospitals. Intellectual assets are what made Merck successful, but they were not – till recently – strictly customer capital. They were the human and structural intellectual capital employed in discovering, designing and patenting new drugs, and getting regulatory approval to sell them.

In the late 1980s a new type of company emerged: companies that set themselves up as "pharmaceutical benefit managers". They struck deals with HMOs (health maintenance organizations = companies dealing in health insurance) and employer-sponsored, managed care plans that allowed them to get information about prescriptions. They delivered pills directly to the patient, cutting out the traditional middlemen, drugstores and wholesalers.

One of these companies, Medco, obtained information about customers at the individual level – knowledge previously in the possession of doctors and druggists. Merck and the other drug companies knew their customers – doctors, hospitals, wholesalers and drugstores – but Medco knew the ultimate customer – the patient. Using this information, Medco did two things to provide value for their customers and shareholders: they bypassed retail distribution entirely for some customers, particularly people who had to take a drug regularly for a chronic condition, and they intervened directly with physicians, pressing them to prescribe generic lower cost versions of costly brand name drugs or suggesting less expensive alternative medication for a specific disease. In this way they were able to deliver drugs to their customers at a much lower price while still making a good profit margin.

Between 1987 and 1992 managed care companies and pharmaceutical benefit managers doubled their market share and more than doubled the discounts they received from manufacturers. Their knowledge of customers trumped the drug manufacturer's knowledge of chemistry. In 1993 Merck bought Medco. They were now buying access to the information flow about individual customers. In doing so, Merck acknowledged that the intangible assets that controlled the market had changed.

Nearly half of the $6.6 billion Merck paid for Medco had been spent on acquiring "customer relationships"; that is, customer capital. In less than a decade, the whole structure of the pharmaceutical industry in the USA changed, not because of new laboratory techniques or regulatory regimes but because a new class of customer – pharmaceutical benefit managers and managed care plans – came upon the scene. The drug makers had valuable relationships – customer capital – with their old customers. The newcomers destroyed it. Their power to negotiate prices and determine what drugs were prescribed vitiated the value of those old relationships. Customer capital, as it is not fully owned and exclusively controlled by the corporation, can be destroyed very quickly by changes in the ecosystem and the environment of a company – as it is with intellectual capital in general. For the drug industry, the collapse in the value of their customer capital was a grave crisis. They had to move fast and aggressively to rebuild it.

The greatest value always tends to belong to people who own knowledge – particularly about what happens at the customer end of a value chain. Therefore it is not the flow of material, but the flow of information that is important for controlling a business. In industrial capitalism the manufacturer controlled the complete supply chain. The buyer, the customer, was not so important. He or she was a one-time target who could be forgotten once the sale was made. But, today, the importance of customers has changed. Companies can no longer survive in business if they are not able to customize their products and services to individual customers. Customer in-formation became a strategic asset, it became customer capital. Whoever owns information about customers controls the entire business and its supply chain and is able to create new intellectual capital and to increase the value of his or her customer capital.

So, one important task for management in the new economy is to look for and track information in its own industry's value chain. It has constantly to monitor what information drives the business, who has it and to whom in the value chain it is worth most. With this knowledge a company is able to change the physical activities it performs to take advantage of the flow in intellectual activities.

This is what, for example, many retail companies did by entering into e-commerce. They tried to move into the field where a new type of customer relationship and customer capital had been created, pioneered by companies like Amazon. This new customer relationship was characterized by direct one-on-one communication, actually triggered by the customer via the Internet. Information about the buying behaviour of the customer, gathered as a by-product during the transaction, is used by the online bookseller to recommend new books about the same topic at a later visit or to inform other buyers, who are interested in a specific book, about similar books that buyers of the book in question have bought – increasing the likelihood of new sales and customer satisfaction at the same time. By creating online stores themselves, retailers tried to adapt to the new sales standards of its industry.

Besides customer capital which is tied to individual existing customers, there can be found two other more general forms of customer or market capital: brand capital and public reputation capital. Both are of the same type: they represent intellectual capital that is tied to the image or reputation of a company.

Brand capital is related to products. To customers and potential customers a brand symbolizes the reputation of a product. Customers and prospective customers expect a certain constant level of product quality. It is a form of condensed trust and stands for reliability or confidence in the value of the product or service. This allows the company that owns the brand to ask for a premium for its products over and above the price of other competitive products on the market.

Corporate image or reputation capital is tied to a company as a whole, independently of any specific product. The public expects from such a corporation that it meets certain standards, whether they are in the area of working conditions for its employees or in the area of environmental behaviour. Image or reputation capital allows a company to gain an advantage over competitors not only on product markets but also on labor and business partner markets. Accordingly, more and more companies are working not only to establish product brands in the market but also the company name as a kind of corporate brand, attracting stakeholders such as employees, business partners, investors and customers in the long term.

Business partner or economic web capital

The customer of today wants immediate, customized, flawless delivery. And some vendor out there has already found the right combination of personnel and technology to raise the service bar just that much higher to beat the competition. And once customers see it can be done, they demand it from everyone. The result is that companies are increasingly trapped in a race to guarantee the success of their customers – and that creates a whole new set of challenges. Incorporating the new technology and dealing with rising customer expectations have forced companies into the realization that they cannot fulfil any of their long-term strategies without completely revising their organizations and relying heavily on partners and alliances.

Another reason that partnerships have become more attractive for companies today is a change in the economics of partnerships as a result of IT. If a company outsources certain activities or buys them from the market, the costs for these activities are usually lower than it would be by accomplishing them itself. However, it has higher transaction and coordination costs: additional costs because of purchasing processes and a higher degree of co-ordination. In the industrial economy the advantage of lower costs for the activities themselves was offset by higher transaction and coordination costs in many cases. So, it did not make sense to outsource these activities from an economic point of view.

If you can buy by means of an electronic network and process transactions between companies nearly as easily as within a company using the Internet, e-business software applications and electronic marketplaces, the costs change. The old model of owning the complete value chain in an industry begins to lose its competitive advantage when coordination costs drop, when sellers and buyers find each other more easily. The result is that more companies decide to buy what they once produced in-house.

In such a partnership, every partner can concentrate forces so that the end result is a much better one, creating more value for all business partners and for end-customers than the old model. Very often, in highly dynamic markets and industries, a single company alone is no longer able to keep track of market developments. To surf on the leading edge of an emerging business or new market, time becomes critical and the business need partners who can add their resources and brain power to the company's. Such partnerships can be found as: "virtual corporations" or more loosely as organized economic webs.

Skandia's Assurance and Financial Services (AFS) division defines itself as a virtual corporation. Its focus is not on traditional life insurance, but on a combined product consisting of savings and insurance such as variable annuities, where a part of the payment is invested in mutual funds, the value of which forms the ultimate policy value. AFS puts its money and brain-power into developing insurance products, operating an internal and external network, and opening global markets. But AFS neither manages mutual funds nor deals directly with the public. That is done by partners. Downstream there are local sellers – banks, brokerages and financial advisers – who want to sell insurance and value AFS's product-development expertise. Upstream are well-known fund managers such as J.P. Morgan, and others, who value AFS as a stable source of long-term funds from an inexpensive distribution channel.[18]

It is a similar story with the German financial services company MLP. The company specializes in selling insurance and fund products designed to the individual needs of academics, such as doctors, engineers and lawyers, whose large salaries and other sources of income create a major income gap after retirement, especially if they simply relied on public pensions, which would cover but a small portion of their average salary. Like AFS the company partnered on the upstream side with professional insurance companies and fund managers in order to be able to develop and provide specialized financial products for its target group. However, unlike Skandia, MLP markets and sells its products directly.

Both AFS and MLP reported a record financial earnings growth rate in recent years. By focusing on their core competencies and by outsourcing other tasks of their value chain, they have been able to generate more value than their competitors, rewarding their shareholders with superior earnings.

Another example of virtual organizations are car manufacturers. They have partners on the supply side who have been outsourced a large amount of development and production work for car components. On the selling side, they have their car dealers as partners who concentrate on the car retail business. The partner network on the selling side and the network on the upstream side at AFS, MLP and car manufacturers clearly represent intellectual capital for these organizations. They are able to leverage it by making supplier and customer relations and transactions more efficient to better source and sell within their existing business and to save costs, increase cycle times and reliability of delivery dates for end-customers. But once such a network has been established, it could also be used to sell by-products, goods and services of the partners to other companies outside the network. This is often the main business case behind the recently created e-marketplaces like Covisint in the automotive industry.

A partner network based on the model of virtual corporations increases a company's future earning potential and can represent a market entry hurdle for competitors, dependent on how tightly it can control its partners. In virtual corporations the "shaper" company control its partners very tightly, as we know from the automotive industry.

---

[18] Stewart, *Intellectual Capital*, pp. 196–197.

In economic webs, the control of partners is much looser, but the opportunities for value creation exceed those of virtual corporations. Economic webs are the best way to cooperate in new businesses or industries, where moving fast to capture a large chunk of the market share in a new business or in a new type of product is key. It represents the ultimate way in the new economy, in which the logic of networks and partnerships manifests itself in organizational architecture and increased structural capital. Economic webs are clusters of companies that usually collaborate around a particular technology or platform. Economic webs are especially found in very knowledge-intensive and dynamic businesses like the software industry. It is the prerequisite for the success of many of its players.

SAP, the market leader in enterprise and inter-enterprise business software has been sharing its business with partners since the days of its mainframe product SAP R/2 in the 1980s. With the launch of SAP R/3 in 1992, which later became the market-leading ERP software product, SAP intensified partnerships with management and software implementation consultants, hardware vendors and smaller software firms. Eighty percent of the consulting business related to SAP software implementation was then carried out by SAP's consulting partners. Only the remaining 20% went to SAP's own consulting business. Since 1980 the number of SAP's partners has grown from a handful to several hundreds. At the same time SAP's revenues exploded. In the 1996 publication *Global Strategies of SAP*, Dietmar Hopp, SAP founder and then CEO and now chairman of SAP's supervisory board, confirmed that it was the leveraging of its partners that built SAP's growth. Hopp explained that key goals in building the SAP partnership web were to expand SAP's market through the relationship network of partners, via an increase in the range of SAP product and service offers through partner know-how.[19]

A McKinsey study stated that the most successful software companies in the world rated the importance of partners for their flagship product almost 30% higher than less successful software companies did.[20] In fact, partners help fill gaps in technology, speed time to market and increase market penetration. Software firms form new organization structures they call partner webs, which can consist of thousands of informal, yet highly performance-driven partnerships. McKinsey also found that successful software companies realize that they must not only have strong partners but they must have many of them as well.

---

[19] Dietmar Hopp (1996) "Globale Strategien der SAP AG", in Erich Zahn (ed.) *Strategische Erneuerungen für den globalen Wettbewerb*, Stuttgart: Schaeffer-Poeschel, p. 129.
[20] Hoch et al., *Secrets*, p. 181.

According to the study, successful software companies have on average four times as many partners as less successful ones. But the character of these economic web partnerships is very different and much more dynamic than what is known in virtual corporations. *How do these webs work?*

First there are the web shapers. The web shapers create the basic settings and the vision of the customer value that such a web will be able to generate. In the high-tech business they are also the ones who create the technology platform for the web, such as SAP did with "SAP R/3" and as Microsoft did with "Windows". Often the growth of the web shaper's company is determined by the growth of the web around it. In highly dynamic and fast-developing markets like in the software industry, market leadership cannot be built and sustained without the web. To generate this self-accelerating growth of the web, the web shapers have to give away a large portion of market share to partners in order to grow themselves much faster and build a much larger market than they would be able to do alone.

The McKinsey analysis showed that SAP received only about 20% of the revenues created in a typical SAP R/3 installation in 1998.[21]

Web adapters (follower companies) build on this foundation and expand the web. Follower companies are attracted to webs for a share of the web value pie. In the enterprise software business, not only professional service companies like Accenture, KPMG or PWC but also hardware manufacturers like Hewlett-Packard or IBM are web adapters, because they provide services or equipment in the software web to make the complete solution happen for the customer. If the value pie of the shaper's web is estimated to be potentially large at the later point, then the adapters are often attracted in amazing numbers even if the shaper is still small and its future unproven.

Economic webs create an environment that is extremely stimulating in terms of growth and innovation rates. They do not function through partner contracts but through incentives for partners to join, to stay and to act in the interest of the organizing player. Sometimes such webs consist of hundreds (like in SAP's partner webs) or even thousands of partners (like in Microsoft's web). When so many partners work together, they need a unifying force, which is the common interest on the part of the partners to succeed. The centre of such a web of software companies is usually a common technology platform. Partners can build their value proposition on it.[22]

---

[21] Hoch et al., *Secrets*, p. 205.
[22] Ibid., pp. 197–199.

SAP's R/3 (and now also mySAP.com) is such a typical web platform: SAP offers opportunities for complementary software product companies to link up their products to R/3 via standardized Application Program Interfaces (SAP named them BAPIs), which increases their market and business potential and makes R/3 for customers more attractive at the same time. In order to fully leverage the potential of the integrated R/3 software solution often a redesign of existing business processes is required. Because enterprises usually have not enough internal resources to do this, they need the help and support from consulting firms. This offers great incentives for professional service companies to join the SAP web. The more players joining the SAP web, the higher the value becomes for every other web participant, because it increases the attraction of the web's offering to customers and therefore increases the web's market in total. The partners build partner capital, which is owned by all of them together. But relationships between partners in such software business webs are typically very loose.

In the automotive industry, it would be almost unthinkable to imagine customers deciding who would make the brakes or the seats for their new automobiles and who would finally assemble it. In economic webs in the software business, many of the partners hold direct relationships with their customers. If a customer wants to implement a new ERP software solution, he or she can choose not only the software maker – SAP, Oracle, Peoplesoft and others – but also the software implementer – Accenture, Pricewaterhouse-Coopers, Cap Gemini, Ernst&Young, KPMG, CSC and others. If a customer chooses software from SAP and implements it with the help of Accenture, then both SAP and Accenture have established direct and largely equal relationships with the end-user. They both have built customer capital that is linked and depends on each other. Once again, that link represents intellectual capital, partner capital, without which customer capital would be of no value to either partner. If Accenture does not implement an SAP solution to the satisfaction of the end-user, then both Accenture and SAP have a problem. If SAP provides an inadequate software product, both partners will have a problem too, and customer capital and brand value will be destroyed for both of them. But when both partners have direct access to the customer, act relatively independently of each other and none has full control over the other, how do you manage the partnership, the partner capital, of such a company?

Partner capital in the form of value-adding communities, whether these are today more tightly controlled virtual corporations or much looser organized economic webs, represent – beside human, structural and customer capital –

an important asset on which the wealth-creation potential of any business depends in a new economy. Every company in the future will participate in such value-adding communities – either as a shaper or adapter. Often a company will participate in several in parallel – being the shaper in one and an adapter in others.

Enterprise culture and strategy as capital

We have now identified the different components of intellectual capital. But one important part is still missing. Intellectual capital is not just the sum of its components but is created from the interplay among them. If human, structural, customer and partner capital work together, the remarkable consequence of intellectual capital productivity occurs: the extraordinary economic value creation of today's corporate top performers. To do like them, its not enough to invest in people, processes and systems, customers and partners separately. The different intellectual capital components can support one another and can multiply the value of the sum of its components. But this is only possible with an appropriate culture and the right strategy at the right point in time.

Culture and the management style of a business is the greenhouse and the fertilizer that help intellectual, human, structural, customer and partner capital grow. The right culture helps people to grow personally and to build human capital, it helps to build structural capital by stimulating knowledge sharing and compilation of individual knowledge into structural capital and it helps to attract customers and partners and enrich relationships with them. But, much more importantly, the appropriate culture for a given business forms the foundation that allows a company to multiply the value of its different intellectual capital components by combining them.

For example, human capital and structural capital reinforce each other when a company has a shared sense of purpose combined with an entrepreneurial spirit; when management places a high value on agility; when management governs more by motivation than by punishment. Human, customer and partner capital grow when individuals feel responsible for their part in the enterprise, interact directly with customers and partners, and know what knowledge and skills customers and partners expect and value. Customer and partner capital grow when the company, its customers and partners learn from each other; when they actively strive to make their interactions informal; when customers and partners, for example, actively participate in new product developments of the company; or when employees and partners form professional communities. In the new economy, culture really represents economic value, because it is the basis to develop and nurture the intellectual capital growth of the corporation: it is culture capital.

But all the intellectual capital components described so far are of no worth for the corporation and are not capital at all if one thing is missing: that is, an overall concept for the corporation, a direction that gives meaning and value to the different "stocks" of the intellectual capital components and the flows, the interactions, between them.

Value is very relative. Things are only of worth to someone if they serve a certain purpose. So it is with intellectual capital. It is one thing to aver that intelligence is an organization's most important asset. Its quite another to turn that insight into plans and activities that lead to better performance and returns. To perceive intellectual capital as the Holy Grail for its own purpose will not work long for business executives, who need to make the mysteries of organizational brainpower serve material purposes, that is profit and sales targets.

An enterprise that can dispose of significant single components of intellectual capital has no real economic value if it has no *strategy*. Strategy, the mission, vision and objectives, is what gives organizations direction, which creates meaning and converts the means into value, which makes the mission and vision happen, which helps to achieve those objectives by setting the necessary focus in their activities. It bundles knowledge, skills and other in-tellectual assets of a corporation like customer and partner capital into a unique profile, which helps to exploit a company's total tangible and intangible assets to make more out of it than just its sum and to make it difficult to imitate by competitors, thereby representing competitive advantage.

This is why strategic enterprise management has become the cornerstone of corporate management and value creation in the new economy. But only the ability of an organization and its management, constantly to adapt strategy to changing market conditions will help to bring the full potential of the intellec-tual capital and intangible assets of the enterprise to light. Also important is the capability of an organization to execute a new strategy and to translate those new strategies into action faster than the competition is able to do. This repre-sents huge value for the corporation and its stakeholders. Strategy capital, which represents another form of intellectual capital, is exactly this ability to develop value-adding strategies, adapt them to technology and market changes, and execute them fast and successfully – again and again.

The economics of information and knowledge in intellectual capitalism

Information and knowledge have become in many cases more valuable than the original tangible business where this information and knowledge was gained. Earnings from stocks and options can exceed by far the corresponding earnings of the corporation itself if you have the right information and knowledge about the business perspectives of the firm. Knowledge about consumer buying behaviour, gained from credit card usage at the point of sales in a retail business, can be of more value than the value of the sales this customer has created at that retail store. If the credit card company sells the data profile of its customers, for example, to insurance, healthcare or financial service companies, these other companies would be able to address exactly the needs of individual customers, thus generating additional revenue, which often exceeds the original sales volume that generated this information. This is the reason that customer data have become so valuable and, consequently, subject to fraud and illegal transactions. Companies have to find ways in the future to exchange customer data with third parties only with the agreement of the customer – relying, for example, on the services of user and consumer communities who make sure that such data exchange is also of value for the user or consumer.

Today, the intangible portion of the world economy is probably of equal or greater size than the tangible one. But information and knowledge differ from cash, natural resources, labor and machinery. One radical difference is that knowledge can be used again and again without being consumed. The cost of producing knowledge is unaffected by how many people eventually use it. To write the code of a new software program costs the same amount of money, no matter if 300 or 1 million users will use it. The same applies to the cost of producing the knowledge to write a book. To be sure, the costs of producing CD-ROMs or the printing costs of a book depend on the number of copies produced. But these costs are caused by the "carrier" material (the material that transports the knowledge, such as paper or now CD-ROMs) and by the copying process – not by the knowledge itself.

Intangible knowledge assets behave very differently than tangible assets from an economic point of view. As a nonphysical asset, knowledge exists independently of space: the same knowledge can be sold as many times as you like without being worn out. The fact that you sold information or knowledge to someone does not prevent you from selling it to someone else. But knowledge and information can be extremely sensitive to time. It can outdate and depreciate faster than an accountant would be able to make the posting for an intellectual asset in the accounting system. But probably one of the most important characteristic of intangibles and knowledge is the more often you sell it and the more people use it, the more value it has.

The greater the number of people who use the same knowledge the higher is the probability that they can more easily work together in creating even more knowledge and value. This is the reason that user communities are so productive in creating intangible assets and value. It represents one of the most important success factors in knowledge-intensive businesses like the software business: if several persons or companies use the same software, it is much easier for them to share information and knowledge; for example, "Word" documents, "PowerPoint" presentations or business information, processed in an ERP system, because they can easily connect to each other's computer. This has important consequences. The more customers a software company like Microsoft has, the more customers it will get in the future.

This is why the law of diminishing returns is not valid in knowledge-intensive businesses. This economic rule, described first in the 18th century by Thomas Malthus and David Ricardo, says that there comes a point in any business activity where additional investment is less productive than prior investment. The classical example to explain this rule is the one of a farmer: if a farmer doubles the number of his staff, he may initially double his farm's productivity, because he is probably able to grow more crops with more people than with less people. But if he subsequently hires additional people, productivity will not necessarily increase at the same rate or even not at all. It may even decrease because additional workers generate additional costs but may not be able to grow more crops, because the resource "land" is not unlimited and can only be used, in contrast to knowledge assets, for one purpose at a time. And competition for scarce resources shrinks marginal returns on investment.

The parts of the economy that are based on physical resources (agriculture, mining, etc.) are still subject to diminishing returns. But the parts of the economy that are knowledge-based are largely subject to increasing returns. The reason is that the most important resource here – knowledge and information – is not limited to a single usage at a time like physical assets but can be used in parallel at the same time. If it can be – like software – copied and packaged, it can be multiplied easily. This is why for a software business, it is not the law of diminishing returns that is valid, but the law of increasing returns.[23]

---

[23] Hoch et al., *Secrets*, pp. 123–125.

The greater the number of people who use the same software, the greater the number of people who are attracted to use it. The more customers a software firm has the more customers it will get. This self-reinforcing cycle is the reason that product development *and* marketing are the key success factors in the software industry. The company that reaches market leadership first is not only able to cover the typical huge upfront R&D costs (for creating the "knowledge" represented in the software), but will be also in the best position to attract more customers and grow further, thus generating more revenue and greater profits, because it can distribute initial cost over more copies sold. Therefore, only the first players in the software business can win. Economies of scale matter in every business, but their power is exponentially greater in knowledge-intensive businesses with high upfront costs that have to be covered by sales revenue. Therefore, first copy costs are high and subsequent copy costs negligible (when upfront costs are covered). The more copies sold, the more profit grows exponentially.

But this is not only true for the software industry. The tendency of costs to accumulate at the front end of the value chain shows up in industrial goods, too, as their information content grows. For airplanes, automobiles, mobile phones, etc. the costs of design and R&D rises in relation to direct manufacturing costs.

The law of increasing returns makes it only logical for a company to give away its products free to customers on the way to reach market leadership. Netscape gave away copies of their software for free. End-users paid nothing to download Netscape's web-browsing Navigator from the Internet – and thereby created a huge demand for Navigator-based applications, which can only be written by people who have a version of the server-based software they have to pay for. Netscape's target was to create a community, a platform or economic web first and then generate profit out of it. It is typical of high-tech businesses to incur high initial costs for R&D or for network development. This has an important consequence on the way strategic enterprise management in such knowledge-intensive businesses should be carried out: if only the first mover succeeds, management has to place high bets early and has to make important and very costly decisions very fast. Corrections have to be made "on the fly" during execution if necessary.

Network effects (also called Metcalfe's law[24]) are based on the economics of communities. The more people use fax machines, the more the value of every

---

[24] Metcalfe's law goes back to Robert Metcalfe, the inventor of the Ethernet network technology. According to his rule, the value of a network increases exponentially with the number of its participants: network value $= 2^n$ ($n =$ number of network participants).

other fax machine increases because there are more opportunities for communication.

The more people use MS-DOS and Windows as the operating system for their PCs, the more valuable it becomes, because they can exchange data and files easily with other people and can use more software applications that run on MS-DOS or Windows.

Unlike the first form of increasing returns (those which tend to display a uniform exponential revenue or cost curve), this form of increasing returns in networks is often characterized by one or more inflection points: revenue will slowly ramp up until the inflection point is reached, and then revenue growth accelerates.

Take the World Wide Web (WWW) as an example: until a minimal threshold of professional hosts (information providers, e-commerce sites, etc.) was available, the WWW was of very limited practical value for the average end-user and therefore also for the company contemplating investment in e-commerce. But once the penetration threshold was reached, more end-users joined the WWW and the demand for additional hosts took off.

Companies that create virtual Internet-based communities function exactly according to these rules: first, initial investment is required not only to "build" the technical virtual community environment for the website but also to reach a critical mass of members. Second, substantial network effects accrue in virtual community initiatives given the value of direct or indirect interaction between members. The more parties join an electronic marketplace like, for example, eBay, the more value it will have for all members through creating a more efficient market by providing a broader offering and lower prices. Network-initiated growth therefore happens in two steps:

1. A first critical mass of users or customers has to be attracted by the company's product or service offering to create the foundation for the business – for example, through advertisements or freebies.

2. Market leadership has to be reached to become profitable. For this more customers or members have to be acquired. This can happen, for example, through the creation of a user community by facilitating inter-actions between the different customers/members. This increases the value to be a member for each customer with every new customer added. This provides incentives for each existing member to help acquire new members. As soon as the number of members is large

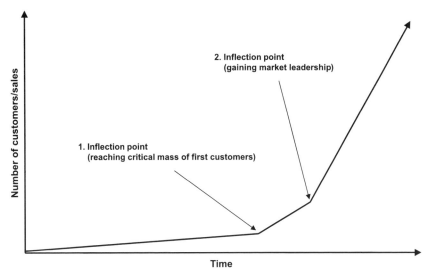

Figure 1.4 Typical growth of customer number and sales of a business with increasing returns.

enough, the community or marketplace becomes the standard and reaches market leadership (see Figure 1.4).

Only when the second inclination point has been reached will the marketplace organizer earn money. As the marketplace grows the organizer will get more revenue out of it via increased commission volumes or entry fees. Especially user networks but also consumer communities and subscription-based sales models follow the increasing returns model.

Another important economic characteristic of knowledge-based products is that the buyer cannot judge whether it is worth paying for a piece of knowledge or information until he or she has it. The value of a knowledge product is not predictable until it is on the market. This is why in the software industry the "first copy is free" approach works so well. Netscape got more and more users, because users had been able to test the software for free first. In knowledge-intensive businesses a new, much more close, but at the same time more open customer relationship plays a key role in becoming successful with new products and in new markets. User communities, through which a company provides its existing customers and potential new customers with a "test for free" environment and with the opportunity to exchange experiences with and opinions about the company's products and services, represent a good way of doing that. Such user communities help convince a potential customer in a much more effective way than any advertisement can do.

The failure of traditional accounting

Intellectual capital is nonsubtractive, can easily be multiplied, has to be created by large upfront investments (of time *and* money) and is often owned by several valid entities at the same time (for example, the customer and the company). Its value is unpredictable especially when using just the costs spent as a basis for valuation. It is no wonder that knowledge-intensive businesses like financial services or software are notoriously volatile. What is needed is a new model for accounting and corporate reporting, a new model to provide relevant information about a company's actual economic performance and future prospects. Management, investors and other stakeholders have to be able to assess timely the real value and economic prospects of a business. The high volatility of stocks of knowledge-intensive businesses is a clear sign that traditional financial reporting and accounting no longer represent results accurately and that a significant information asymmetry exists between insiders and outsiders.

The balance sheet only portrays the liquidation value of the enterprise. This was the original purpose of financial or general accounting: to provide investors and creditors with information about the value of the enterprise in the worst case scenario and when it should be liquidated. But the market value of a company today is far more than its "net assets" or "shareholder equity" on the balance sheet. In any business today, the portion of the company's assets that does not appear on the balance sheet is greater than the reported ones. In many new knowledge-intensive businesses, as we have already seen, the book-to-market value is 1:10 or even lower. This means that only 10% or less of the value of the shares of an investor in such companies is reported and can be explained and managed based on information from financial statements (see Figure 1.5).

Publicly traded shares of corporations are valued every day at the stock exchange. But the financial information published by the company does not

Figure 1.5   Traditional accounting and corporate reporting only help to explain and optimize a company's book value.

tell investors everything about the real value of the stocks they are buying or selling. The risk of a sudden loss through bankruptcy and subsequent liquidation of public corporations is usually so small today – due to the increasing quality of management, due to auditing and reporting duties, etc. and especially compared with the risk of losing money, due to sudden stock price volatility on the stock exchange – that it no longer justifies serving as the only basis for publication of relevant information about the corporation. It has also been shown that if a business is liquidated, even intangible assets like customer lists and in-process R&D can be sold.

Today, investors, especially institutional investors, require the same information as management. The only difference may be the level of aggregation or detail. The split between public financial information for investors and management information for internal purposes is no longer useful when the main objective of management, investors and all the other stakeholders is the same: to increase the value of the corporation.

This split is also not useful at a time when the legal borders of a company are no longer the confines for action for management. Now that economic webs with partners and virtual companies are becoming increasingly important, management has to extend its reach and needs relevant information about the entire web or virtual company in order to make the right decisions. Those new partners also require the same information. Therefore the split between internal management information and external statutory reporting is becoming increasingly irrelevant.

What is needed is a new model for accounting and corporate reporting, which serves both the needs of investors, other stakeholders and business partners, *and* management. It has to be able to report the actual value and performance of the corporation and has to enable people to interpret future performance and prospects on a more realistic basis. In order to understand what management and these other parties really need in the future, let us have a closer look at the limitations of traditional accounting in more detail.

Limitations of cost accounting and traditional management accounting

Even in the industrial age, financial or general accounting was not sufficient to provide useful and relevant information for management. This led to the invention of cost accounting at the beginning of the 20th century, mainly in the 1920s. Its main purpose was to allocate expenses and costs – which up to then had only been reported on a total basis for the entire company through the general ledger – to single products and to allow management to calculate more adequately product costs and to make appropriate pricing decisions.

Similar to management accounting, which was invented a little bit later, the main intention of management or responsibility accounting was to allow top management in the then more complex and greater corporate organizations to decentralize management responsibility. With the information provided by management accounting, which collected and reported both revenues and costs assigned to a management unit called the profit centre, top management was now able for the first time to assess and analyze profitability or return on investments on a profit centre basis; that is, for a part of the enterprise that does not constitute a legal entity on its own, but a unit with its own management responsibility.

The problem today is that cost accounting (as the name implies) and management accounting are purely cost-based. When ever larger portions of the business and single products are based on knowledge and intellectual capital, there is no meaningful correlation any more between input (costs, investments) and output (sales price, revenue, profits) as used to be the case in the industrial economy. The value of intellectual capital is not necessarily related to the cost of building it. The costs of producing knowledge products bears less relationship to its value or price on the market than it was with the costs of producing a ton of steel in the industrial age. The value of a pharmaceutical company's R&D pipeline could not be derived from their spending. The money invested for software development or to create a new movie does not tell us anything about future revenues generated by these new products.

The traditional industrial economy and its manufacturing businesses were based on cost-led pricing, where pricing started with costs, then put a desired profit margin on top and finally arrived at a price. There was a strict relationship between the costs of materials, labor and overheads of a product and its price on the market. This linkage has broken down. The value of a knowledge product for a customer – a software program, a movie, a drug, etc. – is not based on the number of software code lines, nor on how much money was spent to create the movie or to develop the drug compound's formula. It is purely based on the value its use creates for the customer. It is based on its quality, and in the final analysis on nothing but the market's valuation.

In knowledge-intensive businesses the concept to base prices simply on production costs and on the costs of other of resources consumed, for example, in marketing the product no longer makes any sense. When individual operations can no longer be tied to specific single end products, such as a CD with new software or a book, there is only one type of cost and it is fixed over any time period: that of the total system. Therefore the famous distinction between fixed and variable costs, on which traditional cost and management accounting is built, has become irrelevant.

What is needed instead is a new performance-measurement concept, which establishes a closer linkage between cost, market value created and time – that is, a performance-measurement concept that integrates the marketing view with the cost management view. Marketing can help to measure market value, which is the value a product has for a customer at a given point in time. Professional marketing can help to value the results of knowledge work, which is very hard to predict when management has to make investment decisions, for example, for new products or market segments. Therefore related measures and indicators have to be included in the new measurement and management system.

The value of fixed, tangible assets such as machinery is much more predictable than the value of intangible assets, which is why accountants agree that the price paid for equipment, minus accumulated depreciation, reasonably expresses its value. This relatively simple concept cannot unfortunately be applied to intangible assets. It is just not that easy to determine the value of intangibles. As a result, not only accountants but also managers tend to question the usefulness of investments in intangibles whose value cannot be assessed accurately. And this may become a real problem for enterprises, their investors and stakeholders: if they neglect the intangibles value chain of the company they may no longer be able to compete successfully for intangible asset-based competitive advantage positions. But even if management focuses on the intangible assets of their companies, one important problem remains.

You cannot manage what you cannot measure. Accounting does not provide the relevant management information necessary for management to effectively build intangible assets, increase return on total assets (including intellectual assets as well) and assess and improve the productivity of knowledge work. This has become one of the hottest issues in business management today. Purely cost-based management accounting systems, which try just to allocate costs and expenditures to management units and products, give no incentive for real value creation. Because the market value side is missing in the equation, it does not tell management anything about how much each single business unit or product contributes to overall value creation. On the other hand, pure market-driven decision making, for example, customer acquisition at any cost, is not the solution either, as the recent crisis with Internet start-ups has demonstrated. What is needed instead is a unique view on internal and external activities. Therefore, a cost-oriented view *and* a market-oriented view have to be combined to bring about the concept of a new accounting and management system.

Today, in the global marketplace, where businesses have to be present globally, decentralization of management power in these huge global organizations has become much more important than 80 years ago, when managers like Alfred Sloan at General Motors, who invented decentralization of management responsibility, split his enterprise, which had become larger and larger, into divisions with their own management responsibility. The prerequisite to do this successfully was the invention of management or responsibility accounting. Sloan had been able to increase profitability of the whole only by knowing exactly what the profit contribution of each of the units had been and how they performed compared with their individual targets. This was the basis of "management by objectives", and it is still the basis to unfold the capabilities and stimulate the productivity of a large business organization.

But today the target for public corporations is no longer pure "profitability". One reason is that profit, the net result after deducting all costs from revenue, is significantly dependent on accounting rules and standards. The profit of one business unit or one company cannot be compared with the profit of another business unit or another company, unless the underlying accounting rules are the same.

Do you capitalize R&D costs or not? The answer has a tremendous impact on profit if R&D expenditure is significant. Also, different inventory valuation methods have an impact on accounting results and on reported profitability. This has important consequences for managements that are under pressure to deliver value to institutional investors and other stakeholders: *profitability does not tell us much about the real value created in a business. Why is that?*

Profit does not correlate very well with development of the share price, as many empirical studies have shown. The question therefore is not whether a corporation is reporting any profit; that is, if it can report a positive result after deducting costs from revenues. The question is, rather, whether it is beating its cost of capital line – according to the shareholder management theory of today.

Cost of capital is the average return an investor expects when investing money in the shares of similar corporations. It is the average return an investor can get from the capital market – adjusted to the individual risk assigned to a specific investment. Only if the return of a company exceeds its cost of capital has it created value for shareholders, because shareholders could have obtained a return on the level of the cost of capital through other investments instead. This excess profit or return is called residual income, economic profit or economic value added (EVA). EVA is defined by Stern/Stewart, the American consulting firm that developed the concept, as net operating profit minus an appropriate charge for the opportunity cost (cost of capital) of all capital invested in an enterprise. As such, EVA is an estimate of true "economic" profit, or the amount by which earnings exceed or fall short of the required minimum rate of return that shareholders could get by investing in other securities of comparable risk. Because investments in intangible assets like R&D and brand-building are recognized as assets and added to the capital base (this is done through so-called "adjustments" of GAAP-based figures), the EVA concepts clearly represents a step forward and helps companies more accurately to assess the performance of their business units.[25]

Companies that started to measure performance using the economic profit or EVA concept were able – often for the first time – to link the internal performance management of business units to a capital market measure, something that financial analysts use to determine the market value of a corporation. It was the first time that it was possible to break down the overall value-added of the entire company into portions contributed by each business unit, often boosting the performance of business units and the value of the company's stocks, because the company was now able to focus on the value-creating activities.

While the concept of economic profit provides a more appropriate view on value created or destroyed than traditional accounting and represents a clear step forward in measuring and optimizing enterprise performance, it is not sufficient to capture the full value and the true performance of a knowledge-intensive business with large intangible assets. The reason is that this measurement system is still based only on financial and cost data. Even when R&D investments are treated as investments and are capitalized, this is done on the basis of costs spent on R&D. Assessing the value created by this investment and of the progress toward creating the intended value (for example, of a development project) cannot be achieved with this information – something that is

---

[25] For more information about the EVA concept visit the Stern/Stewart website at www.eva.com

essential in order to optimize a company's R&D portfolio and related investments.

Alfred Rappaport, the creator of shareholder value management concepts in the 1980s,[26] has described how the concept of calculating economic results by deducting actual return from the cost of capital of a business no longer reflects reality and should not be the basis for executive compensation.[27]

He gives the reason that the return expectations of investors, especially for the top performing companies (and these are typically the ones with larger intangible assets), are already reflected in the actual share price, and are usually much higher than the cost of capital, which represents just the average return you can get for stocks in general.

Rappaport quotes in his article that the expected return on capital Coca-Cola needed to justify its share price in September 1998 was 24.8%. But the cost of capital for the company at the same time was only 8.8%. Should a business unit of Coca-Cola then report a 12.8% return on invested money, in an EVA model the added value would still be 4%. But from an investor's point of view, this business unit would have destroyed value. Should the company as a whole only generate a return of 12.8%, the share price would drop immediately, because market expectations are much higher and a return of 12.8% would not justify the actual share price. Every return under 24.8% would destroy value. But under the EVA concept, a business unit manager who generates a 12.8% return would still look good and would receive a bonus. This would not be what investors want. The real threshold for an investor would be the 24.8% and not the cost of capital of 8.8%, because 24.8% are the returns for which he would have paid according to the actual share price, which reflects just this return expectation of the capital market.

Because the economic profit concept focuses on optimizing just one type of resource, financial resources – which clearly only takes accounting and financial data into account – it is not adequate as a management instrument today. Benchmarking the economic profit of companies or of business units can clearly provide a first indication of their economic situation. But because today in many companies human capital has become the scarce resource, rather than financial capital, and because often successful value creation is also dependent

---

[26] Alfred Rappaport (1986) *Creating Shareholder Value*, New York: Free Press. This book was later updated and published in a revised edition in 1998.

[27] Alfred Rappaport (March/April, 1999) "New thinking on how to link executive pay with performance," *Harvard Business Review*. For more information on Rappaport's shareholder value added approach, see: www.lek.com/ideas

on other, market-related factors (such as the successful realization of network effects), a management system based solely on economic profit is no longer appropriate. Because the economic profit concept is unable to reflect the specific economic characteristics of intangible assets, it falls short and fails to optimize economic performance in an enterprise that is based to a large extent on intangible assets.

So, companies, especially those in knowledge-intensive businesses, that own and use intensively intellectual intangible assets have to find new ways to measure and manage capital and its productivity. It is time to think about a new intangible performance monitoring and accounting concept, which could help management to value and report properly what it created, to control real-value performance internally and to use this as the basis for communicating with investors and other stakeholders. In Part 3 of this book I present a model and framework for such a new accounting, measurement, reporting and management system.

Economic webs and virtual enterprises: a challenge for accounting

Networks, economic webs and virtual companies represent another challenge for accountants. As explained before, economic webs and virtual corporations play an important role in growing new businesses in the new economy. Often partners in an economic web are co-owners of intellectual assets, which they have created jointly together with the company. Often the web itself is an asset for all its members.

These assets do not appear on the balance sheet nor in any financial report, but represent a major portion of the market value of a company that relies on partners on the upstream and/or downstream side. New knowledge-intensive businesses and Internet companies have to spend a lot of money to create a web of partners to generate enough potential customers to constitute a foundation for future growth. *How should such a company measure progress in web building and value created?*

As explained before, the costs incurred in building the network tell us very little about its value. The number of new web members may provide some information about its size and the speed with which it grows. But it does not tell us anything about the quality of the web, about the degree of commitment of its members. It does not give us any real information about its inherent value to management and to investors. Can the network be managed at all and how can its benefits for the enterprise be optimized without appropriate information? Traditional accounting does not help here as it is trapped within the confines of the legally defined enterprise.

Outsourcing of corporate functions can provide many benefits. Outsourcing noncore tasks to a specialist is usually cheaper than keeping them in-house. In addition, outsourcing allows a company to concentrate its forces and resources on the real value-adding tasks. If the information flow between partners is automated using IT such as e-business solutions, additional efficiency gains are possible. But outsourcing does not relieve management of the task of managing the entire value chain in order to keep its market position. Managing the costs of the entire economic chain, including all partners and suppliers, rather than just managing the company's own costs can yield a cost advantage of up to 30%. If a supplier who outsources to a second supplier, who then outsources to a third supplier and so on can all save costs, for example through processes that allow them to collaborate better, costs are not only reduced for each partner, but cost savings add up, so that the total cost of the value chain can be significantly reduced. Toyota is perhaps the best publicized example of a company that knows and manages the costs of its suppliers and distributors, resulting in it being able to realize such cost savings throughout its value chain that the costs of its end-product, cars sold, were significantly reduced.

Toyota was able to manages the total cost of making, distributing and servicing its cars as one cost stream, putting work where it costs the least and yields the most. Other such virtual corporations, such as Coca-Cola with its bottlers or other automotive companies with their suppliers and dealers went down the same route. But, increasingly, managing the economic cost chain will become a necessity for *every* business. *But how can accounting, the traditional source of relevant management information, support this task if it stops at the legal borders of the company?*

In the automotive industry, for example, car makers have forced their suppliers to provide them on a regular basis with cost information. The intention was to encourage suppliers to improve their business processes continuously in order to reduce purchase costs for the car maker. The car makers recognized the importance of being able to manage the total costs of the system, to collect and report in detail on all costs, even those incurred outside the four walls of the legally defined company.

But for many businesses it will be painful to switch to economic chain costing. Doing so requires uniform or at least compatible accounting standards applied to all companies in the entire chain and a common meta-language for describing the business processes to be documented. Each company does its accounting in its own way and may well be convinced that its system is the best possible, but economic chain costing requires information sharing across companies.

Car makers have been able to force their suppliers to cooperate, and it was easy for them to define the accounting standard, because it was usually their own internal standard. This will not work in other industries and in the new economy in general, where partnership is based on equality and no partner dominates.

Some recent technological developments, like the XBRL-based standard language,[28] in a new, unified, technical *and* semantic data format for the exchange of financial information between enterprises, analysts and regulatory authorities as well as via the Internet, may also provide new opportunities for the exchange of cost and control data. But there are still a lot of unanswered questions. The solution may not only be found in accounting itself. Especially for knowledge-intensive businesses acting in a highly dynamic market environment, the solution may be based on a combination of accounting, marketing and other data, which result from strategic planning and strategy execution processes. Executives of such businesses need to organize and manage not only the cost chain but also everything else – especially corporate strategy and product planning – as one economic whole, regardless of the legal boundaries of individual companies.

The end of traditional management

Every knowledge worker today is a manager of his or her own work and organizes tasks on that basis. But should knowledge workers become really productive for an organization, there needs to be a management system that links the work and activities of knowledge workers with those of other knowledge workers within their business unit, the entire corporation or the extended business network according to the enterprise's objectives. This should allow result-oriented business management at every level and in every area – inside and outside the boundaries of the company.

It will become the greatest challenge for managers to create an organization that can share knowledge. Networks connect people to people without the interaction of managers. In industrial capitalism the task of management was to plan, organize, execute and measure. The task used to be to manage pure

---

[28] XBRL = eXtensible Business Reporting Language. There is more about XBRL in Chapter 7.

financial goals, and so financial accounting was one of the most important management tools. Today, when costs alone are no longer the driving force, but results on the market side in the eyes of customers are (i.e., results based on costs *and* on market success, which represents the real economic value), the new workers, knowledge workers or professionals are not measured by the tasks they perform (that is, the costs they generate) but by the overall results they achieve. This requires a great deal of autonomy for them in their decisions. Knowledge workers are only productive when they, alone or in teams, plan, organize and execute many aspects of their own work. Traditional hierarchical organizations do not stimulate the productivity of knowledge workers. On the other hand, there has to be someone who makes the decision in case of conflicts or crisis. The question for any organization that wants to be economically successful in the new economy is not how to get rid of hierarchy, it is: *How to find the right combination of hierarchy and informal network structures to make knowledge workers productive and to enable coherent operatonal and strategic enterprise management at the same time?*

In an internal network organization, supervision is different. There is less supervision of the content of the work and more supervision of a person's overall performance and career. This definitely means that basic management tasks such as planning, budgeting and supervising must be done differently. It means that corporations need a new approach to and a new concept for managment. In terms of quantifying knowledge worker productivity we are today roughly where we were in 1900, a century ago, with industrial worker productivity, says Peter Drucker.[29]

Other challenges for management in the new economy will come from outside the organization, from its environment. The fact that any business today can soon become a global business has already been stressed. But still many businesses have not yet realized the full consequences of this development.

Globalization of markets means that companies have to reflect this fact within their internal organization structures. Companies, and increasingly many other institutions as well, can no longer define their scope in terms of national economies and national boundaries. They have to define their scope in terms of industries and services worldwide and have to organize their business into global business units.

But, at the same time, political boundaries are not going to disappear. National regulations will still affect businesses. And many companies have learned that,

---

[29] Drucker, *Management Challenges*, p. 142.

for national governments or national labor unions, the global "business unit" is a meaningless fiction. For them the country they live in is the only meaningful reality. And so only those businesses of the company that are based in the same country are the only units they perceive, accept and are willing to deal with. It will be very difficult for a company to differentiate, in advance, between decisions and actions it can take internationally or nationally. And this represents a real challenge for any management structure of a corporation today.

Another challenge that faces management from outside the corporation is how to define corporate performance and the purpose of the corporation in the future. In the last 50 years, the emergence of an affluent middle class of nonmanual workers, and the extension of life expectancy have led to the development of institutions such as pension funds and mutual funds. They are now the "owners" of the key property in a modern, developed society, that is, the publicly owned corporation. As a result, American institutions representing future pensioners now own at least 40% of all American publicly listed corporations. The future economic security of more and more people – that is, the people who can expect to live into old age – is increasingly dependent on their economic investments, that is on their income as owners. The emphasis on shareholder value performance for corporations will not go away. Immediate gains, whether in earnings or in share price, are, however, not what they need. They need economic returns 20 or 30 years hence.

But, at the same time, businesses will increasingly have to satisfy the interests of their knowledge workers – for example, with stock options – and will have to meet public expectations in the area of social and environmental performance, each of which are probably more short term compared with the interests of pension fund investors. Corporations have to learn how to balance short-term economic, environmental and social results with the long-range prosperity and survival of the enterprise.

Also, management will increasingly have to be based on the assumption that no single technology is a foundation for management policy. In the 19th century, each industry had its own unique technology on which it was based – the chemical industry was based on organic chemistry and coal mining had its own special technology, for instance. Nowadays these assumptions have become untenable. Today, enterprises have to be able to combine different technologies from an application and customer value point of view.

An example is the pharmaceutical industry, which has increasingly come to depend on technologies that are fundamentally different from the technologies on which the pharmaceutical research lab is based (genetics, for instance).

The same is true of software companies. In the business application software sector, development in the last few decades has largely been influenced by technology waves: first through the technologies optimized for mainframe computers (1970s and 1980s) and later through technologies for so-called client–server systems (1990s). However, today it is no longer a single technology that drives success in the business applications software market but the intelligent combination of different technologies in order to create as much customer value as possible. For example, a user might still want to run part applications on a mainframe computer, another part on a Windows NT-Server in a classical client–server environment and other application components on a web server outside the firewall. And this should happen in a way that all these different application components can communicate to each other in real time, independently of which platform they are operating. The availability of the right technologies is not sufficient today on its own in the business application software market for the market success of new products. It is the combination of industry-specific business knowledge and technology that counts. In designing new products, knowledge about business trends and about the future business requirements of companies has to be combined with knowledge about the possibilities and opportunities of new and old technologies and platforms, such as the Internet and the related communication and software standards. Only in this way can software solutions be created that are able to provide the high customer value and competitive advantage that is necessary for software companies to compete successfully on a global level.

Management will therefore have to be increasingly based on the assumption that technology is not a foundation for management policy and for corporate strategy. This is true even for the so-called technology sectors. This is because a successful strategy has to be oriented outside-in and focused on the potential value and benefit for customers and stakeholders. As production processes no longer dominate economic value creation and have been replaced by customer value creation – irrespective of how created – management has to make sure that any technology from whatever industry can be used by the company to create customer value, if its time has come.

In addition, we will have to accept that the scope of management is not bound by its legal confines. It has to embrace the entire economic chain, including the operations of partners and suppliers. However, as explained earlier, in economic webs – the ultimate form of business partnerships in the new economy – the economic chain bringss genuine partners together – that is, institutions in which there is equality of power and genuine independence. Management as a discipline has to be reinvented and new ways to manage performance and results across the entire economic chain have to be found – even if management cannot rely on ownership of assets and full control of partners.

2 New Corporate Success Factors

We are in enormous danger of losing our direction and flying straight into the ground without even knowing we are heading toward disaster. This alone should chill the soul of every investor, manager, or politician ... and it should be more than incentive to search for effective ways to measure and nurture Intellectual Capital.

Leif Edvinsson and Michael S. Malone[1]

Misunderstanding the nature of intellectual corporate assets can have terrible consequences for investors and stakeholders. One of the first cases that clearly demonstrated this was the Saatchi & Saatchi case, reported by Karl Erik Sveiby.[2]

The Saatchi & Saatchi case

In the 1980s Saatchi & Saatchi was the most successful advertising firm in the world with a 10-year story of uninterrupted success on the stock exchange – from 1976 to 1986, when market capitalization peeked and Saatchi & Saatchi became the largest advertisement group in the world. But the 1986 results also recorded the group's first-ever profit decline. The disregard of intellectual assets by management and by the London business community and Wall Street led to a continuous decrease of company value, from which it never recovered. The reason was that the two founders and the investment community did not comprehend how the management of intangible assets, such as knowledge, human capital, image and customer capital, create tangible profits. *What happened at Saatchi & Saatchi?*

Saatchi & Saatchi had its initial public offering (IPO) on the London stock exchange in 1976. It was the first advertising firm to overcome the city's perception of the advertising business as something without any tangible substance and worth. Thanks to the talent of the Saatchi brothers, the two founders, in what we would call today investor relations, the financial community began to see advertising as a business with reliable profitability

---

[1] Leif Edvinsson and Michael S. Malone (1997) *Intellectual Capital*, New York: HarperCollins, p. 14.
[2] Karl Erik Sveiby (1997) *The New Organizational Wealth*, San Francisco: Berrett-Koehler, pp. 13–18.

and good growth potential. But it was not only investor relations that created the success of the firm. It was the combination of continuously building up intellectual assets and of marketing these values to the financial community.

While delivering profits, growth and dividends to their new outside share-holders, the Saatchi brothers built up human and structural capital within the firm. They managed to preserve a creative spirit, which is the essence of good advertising, and attracted the best people in the industry. The disaster started to become visible in 1986, when Saatchi & Saatchi – after a second issue of stock – acquired the New York agency Ted Bates, and in doing so became the largest advertising firm in the world. In all prior acquisitions, the company was able to retain – other than the founders – nearly all the key people of the acquired businesses. But the Ted Bates deal was a turning point because of its size. A few key accounts were immediately lost after the acquisition because of conflicts of interests between the clients of Saatchi & Saatchi and those of Ted Bates – customer capital was destroyed.

By then a leakage of creative talent had also begun. Many Ted Bates profes-sionals were infuriated by the merger, and some said so publicly. The Saatchi brothers, due to the size of the firm and destroyed structural capital (the now missing pioneering culture and teamwork environment), were no longer able to retain key people. But, at the end of 1988, the group's market capitalization was still six times higher than its net assets; that is, its intangible assets were five times greater than its tangible assets. But it became harder to attract and keep good people and good clients – a clear sign of decreased human and customer capital.

This led to a financial crisis in 1989 which was accelerated by "crisis manage-ment" initiated by the banks: new managers cut costs and sold everything they considered noncore businesses. Then Charles Saatchi was persuaded to withdraw in order to decrease executive pay. A year later Maurice Saatchi left the firm and started a new agency with his brother and competed against his old company. He became so frustrated with the traditional way of "financial management" as run by the new executives the banks brought in that he wrote in a resignation letter that "for the first time in twenty-five years, I found myself in an agency where the term *advertising man* was being used as an insult."[3]

Traditional crisis management techniques destroyed intellectual assets at Saatchi & Saatchi. It is very obvious that the new management did not see

---

[3] Sveiby, *The New Organizational Wealth*, p. 13.

where the real value of the company was: in its human capital (value of key people and especially of the two founders) and its external reputation, its customer capital. With the traditional crisis management tools of cutting costs, they even accelerated the downward spiral by destroying intangible assets, which led to decreased financial results, which in turn led to additional "crisis actions" by management, which again destroyed more intangible assets.

But the tragedy of the rise and fall of Saatchi & Saatchi was not just the fault of the "professional crisis managers" the banks brought in. It was probably the fault of the two founders themselves, and the fall of their company started much earlier than was visible to the public. In the years before the IPO the company grew organically. This growth was generated by satisfied customers demanding more of the competence of the human capital of Saatchi & Saatchi. The firm employed a number of very skilled advertising professionals, had a collection of high-profile customers and had an image of being creative. With continuing financial success and growing profits, the brothers had been able to convince the financial community that advertising works like any other business – which was not true. The company's financial success was not based on tangible but on invisible intangible assets. This is an important fact, which was overseen by investors.

After the IPO, when the two founders used the money from the IPO to buy other companies, most of the growth came from acquisitions. The business community failed to recognize this important difference between organic growth and growth through pure financial transactions. The acquisitions meant that the firm no longer created intangible assets. In fact, it destroyed intangible assets – human capital, structural capital and customer capital – because the firm became so big with so many different businesses that efficient knowledge sharing was no longer possible. But from a purely financial point of view the company was still successful: it could report growing profit numbers, because the profits of the acquired companies were added to the profits of the existing business.

Good financial figures hide the decrease in value of its intangible assets. The firm's intangible assets were like a bank account that slowly depleted after it went public. After the IPO the two founders forgot all they had learned and became unaware of the damage the new strategy was inflicting on their key intangible assets. They should have adapted, instead, a knowledge and intellectual assets-focused strategy. They should have realized that their intangible assets – contrary to the belief of their financial advisors – were more important than their tangible assets and would have been a source for unlimited growth and subsequent financial returns.

It is these opportunities, based on the assets a company can dispose of, that define most of the company's value – not its historic profits and revenues from the previous year or quarter. For determination of the value of individual intangibles – a basic prerequisite for companies that really want to manage intangibles – the only reliable method available at that time was to estimate the future free cash flow or the residual income generation potential of these assets and calculate the net present value of this income stream. But "free cash flow" shows nothing other than the financial end results of intellectual capital productivity.

The problem is that such an approach sets the focus at the wrong position in the value chain – at its end, where intellectual assets had already been converted into financial results. With this approach, the underlying business assumptions and drivers are not known and cannot be managed. This does not help management to optimize sales, profits and cash flows from intangible assets nor to manage the effectiveness of the processes that create them. It also does not provide any incentives at all to create intangible assets – one of the most important tasks for enterprises in the new economy. But to create intellectual capital and intangible assets is the only way management will be able to create value in the future, when the benchmark in all industries are no longer profits created by tangible assets (which increasingly earn just their cost of capital and are thus not able to create value-added) but returns that can be achieved only with investments in intangible assets.

In order to be able to control not only the creation and exploitation of intangible assets but also to judge the performance of enterprises in total, a deep understanding of its intellectual capital components and of the related success factors is required. The following sections, which will provide insight into the necessary changes of important enterprise functions, are intended not only to help readers ask the right questions concerning the true future success factors of their companies but should also provide them with some ideas to get these new success factors under management control.

Managing human capital successfully

The most important thing for enterprises today is the ability to attract, grow, exploit and retain talent in the organization. *But what is it that really attracts talented people to work for an organization?*

It is not very easy to answer this question. Sure, there are the things usually mentioned, like a relaxed and informal culture and self-organized work, which should attract knowledge workers. But a company also has to be successful – nobody wants to work for a loser in the industry. *But how do you create such a culture and work environment that enables superior corporate performance? How does a company make sure that all its managers act in a way that nurtures this culture instead of destroying it?*

These questions have to be answered before management is able to create and leverage human capital. But corporate culture and working conditions are not everything that is needed to attract and retain key people. Knowledge workers and professionals only feel partly loyal to their employers. They usually belong to a community of practice of other similar professionals – engineers, software developers, marketing specialists, salespeople, consultants, etc. – whom they meet socially and in professional working circles. They exchange ideas and share and develop human capital in such a community. The bad news is that corporations cannot own such communities. And worse still: its key people's knowledge often flows into the community and then to other professionals who work for the competition. Nevertheless, such communities can be extremely valuable for companies, because professional learning and further development of an entire discipline can happen in such communities and often new ideas for new product development first surface here. If the company can make itself the heart of such a community, for which the best people in the community are proud to work, the community will serve the company – not its competitors. *A company that really wants to be successful in the long run, and wants to create superior returns, has to make its entire workforce more productive constantly. How can this be done?*

And not every employee has the same worth for a corporation. There are areas in every organization where people are easily replaceable and do not add value for customers, but who nevertheless do work that has to be done. And there are other, strategically relevant areas in product development, manufacturing, sales, marketing or customer service – dependent on the type of business and its strategy – where the core of the value proposition for the customer is created and through which the company is able to make a difference on the market.

First, companies have to create a "human capital map" that makes the following factors transparent: what the different functions and roles of the people in an organization entail, which are strategically important, how the current role and position holders are performing, if there is other talent available in the firm that may add more value in a new role or function.

Second, it has to try constantly to get more people to know more stuff that is useful for the organization. One possibility is to offer constant training to employees not only in areas they are actually working in but also in new areas, to create potential for further personal development. With these measures companies should continuously try to move their employees from low-value work to work that creates more value for customers.

Job rotation is another useful tactic: people who have gained the potential (for example, through training) to carry out another more value-creating job should change to it as soon as possible. A culture that makes job rotation natural within an organization is in itself an important intangible asset, which allows the company constantly to innovate and develop its human capital further. It is one of the major tasks of management constantly to enhance the human capital of the company by converting and developing lower value jobs and the employees who do them into human capital that is of more direct value to customers. They should outsource these lower value tasks to business partners who are able to generate more value out of them, because they specialize in these tasks.

To better exploit their most important asset – which is human capital, the basis of all its other intangible assets – corporations need to understand more about knowledge work. Managers have to understand the relationship between the personal aspects of knowledge that relate to individuals and the social aspects of knowledge.

Every item of knowledge depends on its social context. Socially conveyed knowledge blends with the individual's experience of reality. New knowledge and ideas brought into a community, a social structure, can either enrich the social system's knowledge (which is structural corporate capital if the social system is part of the company) or can be diluted or even rejected by the social system, dependent on its inherent rules. Intellectual tools are different from physical tools because they are based on a social context. They are used in interactions with other people. To use intellectual tools, a person must have confidence in the social context. External communities, which are created by volunteers, are therefore much more efficient at creating new knowledge out of individual knowledge, because the relationship between individual and social aspects of knowledge work better here than in typical hierarchical organizations. Hierarchies and the often unconscious rules of large organizations often represent a barrier to the free "flow" of knowledge.

Management has to be aware of this in order to make individual knowledge workers productive and to convert their individual human capital into corporate structural capital. For example, it does not make sense to train employees individually in new techniques and concepts if the organization in total is not yet able to accept these. If major changes need to be initiated, professional organizational development activities are required in addition to the individual training of employees, in order to prepare the organization for these changes.

Another important aspect of knowledge work is that humans rely both on conscious knowledge and unconscious or tacit knowledge in all activities. Probably every human being has experiences of this phenomena; for example, in learning to drive a car. When I learned to drive I thought I would never be able to control the brakes, gear and steering wheel at the same time when I had to take a bend. Today I never think about how to coordinate these tasks when I drive my car. The related know-how has become part of my subconscious knowledge and I am able to drive without using my conscious mind. Instead, I can think about the meeting with the customer I am going to visit. Why is this important? Because the subconscious mind is much more productive than the conscious mind.

Compared with our subconscious minds, our conscious minds are inefficient information processors. Studies show that the conscious mind can process between 16 and 40 pieces of information per second. But the subconscious mind can handle 11,000,000 pieces per second.[4] The insights into dramatically increased mind productivity by combining conscious and subconscious information processing are not new. For many years there have been techniques of management training whose mission it is to help executives and managers increase their intellectual productivity. And this is an important task for managers in the knowledge-based new economy, which generates not only more challenges for knowledge workers but also (and especially) for them. Managers are confronted by a dual challenge: they not only have to make their knowledge workers more productive, they have to make themselves.[5]

Much has been written recently about leadership. In knowledge-intensive businesses it is clear that a company will only be able to recruit and retain the top engineers, top software developers, top consultants, etc., if the key people in management can make a difference and can make those people enthusiastic

---

[4] Sveiby, *New Organizational Wealth*, p. 32.
[5] See the interview with Patrick M. Georges in Chapter 9.

about their future work and can meet their expectations. Leadership makes its impact on the individual – the human capital – by influencing the manner in which individuals choose to exercise their responsibilities.

The level of basic pay a company provides their top performers compared with what competitors pay plus provisions of stock options is important too. But money, while important, is not the be all and end all for these talented people. What they really require from the firm they intend to join is a motivating vision of the company, of the department in which they would work and an exciting project, things they would expect to contribute to their personal success and to the success of their organization. Visions can be given life only by real leaders. If you ask key people in successful firms why they joined those firms, you will often hear that, before they decided to work for that firm, they had been impressed by the personality of the founder or another strong leader, who got them so excited about the company and their future work there that they turned down other offers, even if the pay may have been better.

How can an organization create leaders from among their managers? Can it be done by a trainee program to form leaders or is it a question of selecting the right people? How can an organization nurture and stimulate important professional communities and make itself the heart of it? How can organizations make employees more productive and help them to understand themselves, where their strengths and weaknesses are, what the right place is for them to work and grow further – within the firm or even outside? Should organizations continue to invest in knowledge workers even if their future may not be with the company?[6]

It is likely that this will become the standard attitude in the future. Only in this way will the corporation be able to keep up a positive image in the labor markets, attract talented people and benefit from employees who have decided to go their own way or may only work for the company part-time. This will help them to grow their human capital and their market value and will at the same time still allow the company to benefit from their talent.

These are all questions that matter to every organization whose success is significantly dependent on the contribution of their knowledge workers. In Part 2 best practice examples for the management of human capital, employees and managers are presented, and we show how successful companies have answered these questions for themselves.

---

[6] It may be important to keep the relationship intact. A leaving talent may come back if this is the case, or may contribute to the company's ecosystem in the future (e.g. working for a partner or customer), if he or she perceives the company still as "a great firm".

Using structural capital to facilitate knowledge work

One of the most important questions for a knowledge-based businesses – may be even more important than human capital management – is how to convert individual knowledge into structural capital the company still owns when employees leave. In other words, structural capital is owned by the company and will remain even if individual employees leave. Enterprises have to get used to the fact that, despite having programs in place to retain key people, they can retain them for some time, but not for ever. Employees will have and must have their own agenda today.

Therefore, management has to make sure that the knowledge of key people is shared with others within the organization and with partners and customers. It also has to make sure that this individual knowledge will be structured and codified and will become part of the corporate common sense of the enterprise. By common sense I mean the common understanding within the firm of how its business works and how work has to be processed to realize its full value for customers. Codified knowledge – that is, codified individual know-how that can be shared – represents *first-order structural capital.*

Organization structures, communication, knowledge-sharing procedures and IT enable employees in an organization to use first-order structural capital efficiently to create more value in the form of partner or customer capital. Only by continuous recycling and creative utilization of shared knowledge and experience can the company systematically manage intellectual capital and create shareholder value. The means to create structures and procedures that enable the organization to do that and to manage its knowledge assets represent *second-order structural capital.*

It is not just the means to enable efficient knowledge work in business operations that represents structural capital; the processes and structures that enable management to guide the company in the right direction, to stimulate adaptation to changes in the marketplace and to manage the firm from a strategic point of view also represent structural capital. If an enterprise is able to combine intangible and tangible assets in a unique bundle and is also able to keep it through strategic learning processes *à jour*, which facilitate continuous feedback from the market side, it has at its disposal a powerful value lever that can be used to create sustained and superior competitive market positions.

Management can only manage for value by systematically managing the expectations of investors, customers and other stakeholders. Those expectations do not refer to historic performance, nor to last year's or the last quarter's earnings; they refer to future earnings capabilities and stakeholder value per-spectives. Management, therefore, has actively to manage the future of the company and has to share it with investors and stakeholders. Strategy plays an important role here as the tool to create a focus point and common destiny for the organization and its various stakeholders as well as the glue that binds its tangible and intangible assets into a unique whole. But strategy is no longer something that is defined today and remains valid for a long period. Companies have to put in place processes and systems that enable them constantly to innovate and learn at an organizational and strategic level. They have to be able to react nearly automatically to changes in the market environment or to new emerging technologies. What differentiates successful enterprises from their peers is the flexibility to redefine strategy quickly if market conditions change and the capability to adapt business structures, processes and internal targets instantly.

In successful business organizations, structures and tools have to exist that enable continuous planning and performance-management processes, linking different operations across business structures with each other and aligning them with strategy. Structures and processes are needed that help strategically to direct the organization and its partner network and that help management to adapt and implement strategy faster. As we will see later, strategic enterprise management processes and the underlying IT infrastructure play an important role in the new management system. These management structures and processes that enable the strategy-focused and adaptive organization represent *third-order structural capital*.

One special area in third-order structural capital management that global busi-nesses have to focus on more in the future is the size of the management and responsibility structure of the firm. Global companies face a very special challenge: they have to manage all their operations increasingly globally, each one as a single business unit, which also typically comprise third parties and partners. They need tools and management structures that help them to do that from a purely economic point of view. They need management tools that help them to perform collaborative strategic and operations planning, as well as transactions and performance management efficiently across the entire business structure – including partners and even customers. On the other hand, they still have to deal with national regulations, with national tax authorities and governmental agencies none of which share with them their global view. They also have to deal with regional cultural differences – for example, the more capitalistic "pure money approach" in America, the European "people approach" and the "spiritual approach" in Asia. An efficient means to solve the typical chronic conflict in global organizations between national, local and "political" thinking and activities, on the one hand, and global economic business management, on the other, also belong to third-order structural capital. Corporations that want to be successful in the future must build first-order, second-order and third-order structural capital and have to maintain and develop them properly.

Information technology (IT) to boost productivity of knowledge work

The availability of IT to support knowledge work exploded over the last two decades of the 20th century with the rise of the personal computer. Word processing, spreadsheet applications, personal databases and other personal management software tools were available for the first time to individuals and led to exponential growth in the productivity of knowledge work. The PC together with PC software provided the appropriate tools that enabled individuals to organize their personal work better and perform knowledge-based work and tasks much more efficiently without being limited by the restricted resources of a computer that is used by many people at the same time.

When I started my studies at a German university at the beginning of the 1980s, PCs were still not available for students. And what cumbersome work it was to finish an essay, at that time using a typewriter! If I wanted to make some changes to the text when I went through it at the end to effect some fine-tuning, I had to retype the entire page and often even the entire text. Today, writing this book for example, it would be unthinkable for me to do so without using a word-processing software program. It boosts creativity and helps you to concentrate on the tasks that are really important when writing.

Word-processing software constitutes one of the greatest inventions ever, it converted stupid typing work into real knowledge work. Secretaries trans-formed themselves into assistants who do not just write letters on behalf of their bosses (they still have to write a few letters – other messages are written by the boss himself and send off via email). Instead, they now perform self-organized tasks such as calling clients to evaluate their opinion about a new product or organize workshops with colleagues, customers or partners. Before the invention of the PC, computing power was only available for large corpora-tions that could afford the significant investment in expensive mainframe computers and the costs of employing an operator team. The use of these mainframe computers was restricted to purely corporate tasks such as accounting or inventory management.

Microsoft has built its success on the mission to make knowledge workers individually productive through IT. Microsoft's position today as the world market leader in PC software applications and operating systems is the consequence of the rise of the knowledge worker, who increasingly needed software tools and computing power for his or her self-organized knowledge work. But knowledge workers needed not only to be more efficient in their individual work, they also needed better tools to share their work and parts of it with other knowledge workers.

Client–server architecture was therefore the next logical step in the IT evolution. It allowed linking individual PCs – which at that time could only be used by individuals on their own work – into the corporate network. It was the time when local area networks (LANs) emerged, which linked PCs with each other and with central servers. This enabled several people to share one common database on the computer server and made exchange of data and information much easier for them. This was also the time when SAP came to market with its Enterprise Resource Planning (ERP) software system SAP R/3. It was the first true ERP system, especially designed to run within such client–server architectures, connecting for the first time the world of corporate computing, which is typically server based (or formerly mainframe based), with the work of individual knowledge workers, performed now mainly on PCs.

From a PC it was then possible to access the corporate ERP system, which supported back-end integration of business processes – for example, in supply chain management – or integrated accounting and purchasing, or integrated selling and production planning processes. Employees were then able on their PCs – without using a dumb mainframe terminal in parallel – to check open items in accounts receivables or the latest profit and loss statement and directly to use those data in a spreadsheet software application to perform analysis and create an individual report for their boss.

But the client–server world confronted the IT department with a real challenge. Deployment of personal computers was typically not the remit of central IT. IT had until then been exclusively occupied with "real" computing on mainframe computers and with the "big" business software applications running on those mainframes. Purchase of PCs and related software was very often done by end-user departments themselves. But now IT had to connect all those different, heterogeneous PCs with each other and with central servers and software applications. So, it became necessary for the IT department to extend its reach into the field of personal computing as well.

IT departments had to define common standards for PC configurations and operating systems, and had to establish a corporate IT strategy not only for the mainframe world, but also for the new and very dynamic PC and client–server world. For example, they had to decide whether they should invest in MS Windows or in IBM OS2 as the corporate PC operating system standard. This was not easy at the beginning of the 1990s, and the wrong decision could cost the company a lot of money.

Those people responsible for IT became increasingly aware that the main part of the costs for PCs and the client–server infrastructure was not represented by the acquisition costs of hardware and software (which was declining on a monthly basis) but by its maintenance costs. The challenge for IT departments was at that time not only to enable individuals to use IT, which was not fully centrally controlled (which is the idea of the PC), but also to try to control at least the basic frameworks, hardware and software technology in order to make connectivity between PC and servers possible at an affordable price. To manage better the total costs of ownership, which also means the maintenance costs, IT had to become more business-oriented, and not just technology-oriented. Implementation and maintenance of ERP software solutions required new skills from IT people: they had to understand business processes in order to be able to configure standard ERP software systems in the right way to meet the business requirements of their end-user departments and reduce subsequent maintenance costs.

The emergence of the PC in the corporate business world (initially the PC started as a device for private use only), the rise of client–server architectures and of standard ERP software represented a major change for the significance and importance of the IT function in many businesses. In the last six to eight years of the 20th century IT became a real business partner for other functions in the corporation. This was reflected by the fact that IT is now represented in many companies at senior executive level by a Chief Information Officer (CIO).

But, today, at the beginning of the new millennium, the IT function in any business faces three new challenges, which may represent not just a simple change but a major departure from corporate IT management:

1. The Internet is emerging as a platform for business computing and as an "operating system" to support business processes and communities that reach far across the borders of the traditional business enterprise. The

Internet combines the business processes of several companies into a highly efficient single business process, supports, on a unified access and communication basis, electronic marketplaces and facilitates communities of knowledge workers and external stakeholders. In order to make that happen for their companies, IT professionals have to manage the transformation from the traditional in-house IT platform to an IT architecture that supports those new collaborative business models, while integrating the existing system landscape and securing past investments.

2.   Standard business software and improved network technology now make it possible to concentrate corporate computing in regional shared service centres or to outsource it to external service providers without losing the integration of business processes or losing efficiency. With this approach not only are significant cost savings possible, but the corporation will be able to leverage its best IT people and best practice for all business units as well. The increased uncertainty of IT decision making, due to rapid technology changes, makes it even more meaningful to leverage specialist knowledge. This can be achieved by reorganizing IT into shared services or by outsourcing it to external service providers whose sole functon is assisting businesses with their computing tasks. The use of application service providers (ASPs) especially is increasingly interesting for organizations. These ASPs configure, integrate and maintain several complex business software applications, the related hardware and entire business processes. This can include, for example, the processing of the entire order-to-cash process of an enterprise in one region, say, in Europe. The ASPs leverage IT resources and the required IT and business process experts for several parties and are able to spread the often significant related costs over several organizations. ASPs are also well disposed to serve as an "exchange" or electronic marketplace that provides services for the different companies working together in an economic chain or value-adding community. ASPs can provide them with a common business computing environment, which they need to integrate their individual operations into seamless, digitized, collaborative business processes across the complete economic chain of all partners. IT professionals have to come up with a strategy that determines which IT services should come from in-house shared services, which should be outsourced and which should be kept at a department or business unit level.

3.   As information and IT has developed into an enabler for value creation, IT managers will have to change their attitude from a purely internal

reactive service orientation to a more proactive, strategic, IT management approach. The new focus of the IT function must not only improve support for existing business processes according to the needs of business units or end-user departments, but must also play a more leading role in business innovation and development of new business models. Internet companies are a good example of this. Their new business models became possible only through the Internet and new technologies. This will be the case in the future for any business. Strategic innovation will be much more driven by IT and not incrementally out of the existing business itself. Therefore the CIO may have to play in the future more the role of an internal strategy consultant than someone who is just responsible for supporting the existing businesses of the firm (more about this and about the new role of the CIO in Part 3).

These three challenges represent for IT departments the most significant change since IT became a corporate function in business organizations. IT departments must waste no time in leveraging the Internet for corporate business operations to enable new business models to help the business gain competitive advantage and reduce costs at the same time. They have to manage productivity and the costs of the IT function strategically, to outsource those tasks that can be delegated to external specialists, to examine application hosting or shared service centre strategies and to initiate and promote new business models based on new technology developments.

Managing economic webs and partner networks

Business diversification, which was a "fashion" in the 1970s in most industrial countries, has increasingly become a handicap in the new world economy. Being in the world economy means for nearly every business today operating geographic diversification. And, therefore, to be successful a business must focus economically and concentrate on a few areas that it truly knows and in which it has core strengths. This does not only apply to multinationals. Every business is in the new world economy today, even through it may not make, buy or sell outside a regional or national market. The global market is where every business's competition comes from. Therefore, it is in the world economy that every business has to be able to compete. This is the reason behind the many mergers, spin-offs and outsourcing activities of many companies today. These companies try to concentrate their activities on those areas in the value chain of their industry, where they possess most of the competencies required and where those competencies yield most return.

Whereas only mergers and de-mergers – that is, changes in ownership and control – attract interest from the public, it is in alliances that the real boom has been in recent years.[7] There are alliances of all kinds, such as partnerships, a large business buying a minority stake in a small one, cooperative agreements in research or in marketing, joint ventures or "handshake" agreements without any formal contract.

In order to capture the full value of their intellectual assets, companies have to concentrate their forces on those areas where they can create most value for customers and have to cooperate with partners to cover the other areas where they have decided not to act themselves. Because it is no longer rational to manage the complete economic chain by itself, the company has to give up control and rely on independent partners. Because management cannot give enough attention to businesses that do not belong to its own core activities, it would probably fail in a market environment that requires constant management attention and immediate action when changes occur. So it is better to free up management power in the shaper company and to use entrepreneurial power in the new partner company to fully leverage market dynamics for the complete economic chain or partner web by keeping these partner organizations independent or at least by owning only a minority share of equity.

In the past, it was believed that one management model, the corporate model, would serve every kind of business. Today, increasingly, we have come to accept that while the principles of management are universal, their application and execution are profoundly influenced by the different technology, different markets and different cultures of an individual operation. While corporations tended to acquire other businesses that acted in the same economic chain, they try to partner with them today.

In today's dynamic market environment it no longer makes sense to keep everything under one corporate roof and under one corporate culture. In the new economy similar rules also apply to corporations and individual knowledge workers alike: they are more productive in a self-managed environment, where they can determine themselves how to achieve a certain objective or task. While the model of the past for integration of a different business into a common economic value chain was controlled by ownership, the foundation of the new relationship was based more on mutual trust and looser partnerships.

But a lot of questions still remain. These partnerships and alliances are not "teams" – members act and work independently and with their own goals,

---

[7] Peter F. Drucker (1999) "The real meaning of the merger boom", in *The Conference Board 1999 Annual Essay and Report*, New York: The Conference Board, p. 4.

objectives and tasks. Nevertheless, in a partner network there has to be some common control over all partners, even if those partners compete with each other as is the case in economic webs, like the partner web of SAP, which has been already mentioned, where the professional service companies that provide software implementation services to SAP customers compete with each other. Otherwise, individual partners cannot plan their own operations and are not able to make the right business decisions. Probably this kind of control is based more on mutual agreements and on common targets between the web shaper and its partners than on control executed in a head office–subsidiary relationship, as is the case in ownership relations. In these new alliances, partnerships or partner webs, nobody commands. Therefore, the partners need to create "institutions" and management processes that enable each of them to perform their own task in the best way, from an individual perspective but within a common framework. The partners also need to set up, for example, collaborative business planning and performance-monitoring processes, to manage the network's overall performance from a customer perspective and to allow its members to coordinate activities. This requires an IT infrastructure that helps them integrate their operations and business transactions efficiently with each other and to optimize the costs of the total network.

Management of companies in all industries must learn to create, to manage and to restructure partner capital; that is, finding and if necessary refinding the right position in the economic chain of its industry. They have to create reliable relationships with other companies within that chain and develop management skills as well as a management infrastructure that enable its managers and knowledge workers to manage the entire economic chain. To do so, they have to work together with other managers and knowledge workers from partner organizations in order to create value for customers and other stakeholders in the most effective way.

Research and product development as the foundation for customer value creation

Contrary to common opinion, customers cannot really tell businesses what products to build. As product managers and engineers cannot rely on customer surveys to direct their efforts, they have to rely on their own competence and sometimes even on their instincts. This may seem strange, but it is really true: customers cannot tell you what they really want or how to design an excellent product, but they sure can tell you if a product does not meet their needs.

When we were developing a new software package for enterprise management at SAP, I set up with my American colleagues a customer advisory council in North America and then with my team in Europe another one for Europe. The intention was both to get input for software development and early feedback on concepts and to use the councils as a platform to acquire pilot customers. At the end, the two councils had been a resounding success, both for its members, most of them existing customers, and for us. But the expectations of colleagues from software development could not be met. They expected more precise input and advice from customers and potential customers about how to design the software in detail. The first council meeting was very disappointing for them. Instead of providing precise guidelines and answers about how to build the product, customers raised questions, articulated concerns and "imprecise" requirements.

I think that this is very typical. Customers are users of and not experts in designing products. The task of conceiving and designing a product will always remain the remit of product managers and developers. Customers very often do not know what their product-related requirements will be next year or in following years, or even when they are going to buy a new product. Discovering what this will be will still remain the unique expertise of product managers and engineers in the future. But user and customer communities can help to check that they are on the right track.

This is exactly what we did with our customer councils. We tried to raise the right questions at the first meeting, and then came up at the next council meeting with our product concepts and asked council members for their feedback. And it worked. When we presented the final version of the first release of the software product, feedback from council members was extremely positive. We came up with answers to their questions. And we incorporated their feedback from first product reviews into final product design, which brought about greater commitment from those council members to the company and our product than any advertisement would have been able to do.

As products become more sophisticated and knowledge intensive and intangibles begin to dominate in any industry, companies have to spend larger amounts of money for R&D and have to make sure, that they do not under-exploit the existing intangible assets for creating value in their R&D pipeline. The pharmaceutical, high-tech and movie industry are known for huge R&D

spendings required upfront to come up with new products. However, other industries are also experiencing significantly increasing R&D costs. There exist two main challenges for any organization looking for more value from their R&D investments:

1. The time from product specification to market entry – time-to-market – has to be reduced (meaning that efficiency needs to be increased and costs have to be reduced).

2. The relationship between short-term, changing customer requirements and preferences and more long-term-oriented product-development processes within the R&D organization needs to be managed actively (meaning that effectiveness, that is output, has to be increased).

A possible solution might be to differentiate, within R&D, much more between predevelopment that is oriented more toward basic technologies – sometimes called "platforms"[8] – and the development of the final product and its variants from a customer point of view, which is driven more by short-term customer and market needs. With this "platform strategy" companies will create bundled competencies (platforms) that represent "options" at the back-end for different products and services at the front-end. This allows us to tie one part of the development process more to long-term technology trends and research (the platform development) and the other part, the "configuration" of basic technologies – that is, the development of final products – more to marketing and sales.

But such new development processes also require a new type of management system and new measurement. For example, the company should measure how many products had been developed based on a specific platform and how fast new products have been developed compared with the existing market dynamic in order to track the results not only of final products but also of the platforms.

Companies today have to be expert at both marketing and technology/product design. The question is not whether the market should drive technology or whether technology should drive the market. It is usually neither. It is the combination of science- and technology-based organization units with organization units that are market based. Product development has therefore to be split into different teams, market and application experts on the one side and

---

[8] Hans Dietmar Bürgel (August 14, 2000) "Flexibilisierungspontentiale in Forschung und Entwicklung", *Frankfurter Allgemeine Zeitung*, p. 187. Bürgel is Professor of Business Economics at the University of Stuttgart.

engineers, scientists and technicians on the other. The market-based team will need to hire other people, a different working atmosphere and culture than a technology-based team. And then there has to be a structure and processes in place that facilitate the interaction between these different teams.

For example, 3M have tried to solve this problem by creating an internal market, where labs and marketing units can interact with each other more efficiently. But this requires new skills from both marketing and engineering people. The results concerning cost reduction, product quality and competitive advantage will be extraordinary, if the idea works in the marketplace. The winners and market leaders are going to be the companies that not only have the best scientific and technological know-how but also superior capabilities in understanding what a market's needs are and where it is going and which are able to integrated both into one product development process.

Another example, also from 3M, is the capability to anticipate market shifts faster in product development. This is the concept of the lead user or lead customer. Lead users are the advance guard, people who have needs way in advance of the rest of the market. The lead user tries to solve a problem that nobody else has yet. Let's imagine a firm is trying to test a new compound: they look at the spectrometers on the market, but none of them will do the job, and they can't find anybody to build one. So they build one themselves. If a vendor of spectrometers is able to identify such a lead user early enough and capture the lead user's experience and knowledge about such a new spectrometer, the company will be at the forefront with a new product at a time when all the other users in the market need exactly such a product because the lead user's technology has turned out to become the industry standard. Ordinary market research will never find these lead users. There might be only 10 in a thousand.

Both the product development and R&D function of the enterprise have to become more market driven and have to develop new methods to constantly monitor the market environment. Using methods such as the lead user concept the enterprise has to systematically capture new emerging needs in the existing customer base and in non-customer groups to remain at the leading edge.

Creating and using customer capital effectively

So far we have described the success factors for companies in the new economy on the resource and "upstream" side of their value chains. This included effective management of the basic resource – human capital – and the creation of organization structures, processes, and an appropriate IT infrastructure, which help to make knowledge workers and their companies more productive. We have seen, too, how organizations are able to make better use of their core competencies and reduce costs at the same time, by outsourcing noncore activities and managing their partner networks efficiently. By better linking R&D and product development with marketing and business development activities they can create sustainable competitive advantage. It is now time to think about how to convert the value of a company's human capital, structural capital, partner capital and its R&D pipeline into value for customers and into sales and revenue.

The customer side has become so important today because revenues and prices in a global free-trade economy are only dependent on the value the customer or a potential customer assigns to a specific product or service. One of the best examples of this development is the increasing number of Internet companies like eBay, who do nothing but provide consumers with a platform, where they can sell and buy via auctions. One method used in these electronic marketplaces is for a potential buyer to bid for an item. The market organizer then invites sellers to make the buyer a sales offer. The seller who best meets the buyer's expectations will make the sale. This ultimate way of buying and selling, also called reverse auctions, is turning the old industrial sales model upside down: the buyer determines the price not the seller.

The traditional link between costs spent and revenue generated has broken down. The main reasons are:

▶ The value and price of a knowledge product, in contrast to industrial products like steel or paper, is not determined so much by the cost it has consumed during its creation process, but mainly by the prospective value potential users and consumers attribute to it.

▶ A high portion of the total costs of companies today are "fixed costs", which occur typically before the first sale takes place and often even before the product is produced – for example, through product development or in creating a new brand through advertising.

But if a high portion of total costs are fixed and costs can no longer be linked to revenues generated, revenues and product profitability therefore can no longer be managed by mainly looking at costs. The traditional revenue and profitability management model has to be turned upside down, measuring and analyzing product value from the customer point of view and customer value first. In order to manage profitability and to manage revenues, we have first to value the existing customer base – customer capital – to which we can sell new products.

Customer capital is the total value of a company's relationships with the people or organizations to which it sells and it represents today an important key component of corporate value.

E-commerce companies like Amazon are very good examples of customer capital analysis. Market share and the number of registered users are here the key drivers for overall enterprise value. Consequently, these companies are often valued by the number of their active online buyers/users, whereby the intensity of the relationship between them and their users is a decisive factor for the price per user they can achieve in this valuation. The better this relationship is to a user and online customer the simpler it is for the company to sell to this customer additional products, increasing the value of this customer further. The better it knows its customers, the more it can offer them products or services that meet exactly their needs and can even sell them products of another vendor for a commission. The value of these companies is therefore often calculated by multiplying the number of users/customers by the possible future net returns per customer.

Internet service providers (ISPs) like AOL, where users have to pay a monthly fee and to register, have a stronger customer relationship and know their users better than "call-by-call" providers. Call-by-call providers know nearly nothing about their customers. The customer relationship is much weaker, resulting in much lower potential to generate additional revenues as they do not know their customer preferences and profiles. If financial analysts try to value those companies, they often take the number of customers they have and multiply it by a value per customer that is dependent on the intensity of the relationship with the customer. For the different market segments the average value for customers is determined by calculating the net present value of the possible future free cash flows or economic profits the company is estimated to be able to generate with these customers.

To bring the customer relationship to a level where it can serve as a competitive advantage, companies have to totally rethink how they develop new products or services and bring them to market. Increasingly, businesses in very dynamic markets and knowledge-intensive industries have started to integrate their customers into the product-development process. They let customers test prototype products, collect feedback in a structured way from partners and sometimes even from competitors. As a result they are able to go to market with new products faster, improve products while going to market and get customers more committed to the enterprise and its products. Customers have to become partners and management has to initiate the necessary activities and initiatives to make this happen.

Speed in winning new customers is often a critical success factor – especially in new business and market segments. This cannot be achieved without professional marketing. But marketing in a climate of intangible assets-based business works differently than did traditional marketing and sales in the industrial age.

Value-based marketing – the new marketing challenge

What is the difference between buying an intangible assets-based product, like a software package or a book, and buying a mostly tangible assets-based industrial product like a car?

Before you own and use the software package for the first time, or before you have read the book, you do not really know what you have bought and whether the money you paid for it was well invested. With the car it's different: at the car dealer's showroom you can sit in it, test-drive it, and discuss the car before you buy. Sure, after owning and driving the car for a certain time, you may not be convinced that you bought the right car. But, between the impression and level of information you can get about a tangible product before you buy it and the insight you can get into a more intangible, knowledge-based product before you own and use it, there is a significant difference.

Selling a tangible product is in most cases done by means of the product's identity – it is product-focused: the product speaks for itself. Potential customers are able to evaluate tangible products to a high degree during the sales process. In addition, products of the industrial age are less complex and product offerings from different vendors fairly equal. For potential customers it is therefore easier to evaluate and compare such products. In the industrial age, the most rational way of selling under such conditions was to present the product and let customers pick.

Salespeople therefore concentrated on product features and presented and communicated them to potential buyers. The task of marketing was, mainly, to extend this one-way communication to a broader scale by advertizing. The objective being to capture the attention of a large group of possible buyers, much larger than individual salespersons can reach, for a specific product. In such industrial age markets for "commodity" products, the buying decision of customers is mainly driven by price and – even more important – by the capability of the vendor to attract the buyer's attention. If products are more or less equal, the sellers who win are the ones who are first to attract the attention of potential customers.

Therefore, the marketing model of the industrial age was advertizing: one-way anonymous communication from the vendor to a market segment; that is, to a large group of unidentified potential customers. The ultimate goal was to generate as much (short-term) sales as possible. A marketing manager was perceived as successful when the campaign generated immediate results in terms of increased sales figures.

In the new economy, where all businesses and their products will become more knowledge-intensive, marketing will work in a different way. The reasons are twofold:

1.   For knowledge-intensive products, and even for traditional industrial products that have been updated with "software" components, complexity increases. The inherent value for the customer is not easy to explain in a two- to three-second TV commercial or through a colored one-page magazine advertisement. But it is the subjective value from the customer perspective that drives the buying decision and counts in determining the possible price and revenue the company is able to achieve in the market. The problem is that the customer knows the value of a product or the service it really represents only after buying and using it. Reliability and reputation – often materialized in brands – are today therefore playing a much more important role in the vendor–customer relationship than in the old economy. If you can't investigate the real value of a product before you buy it, you will try to buy from a reliable source, or you will at least try to get advice from someone who has already bought it, so as to reduce your risk as a consumer or professional buyer. Managing the individual customer relationship, on the one hand, and creating brands and sponsoring consumer and customer communities – where individuals and organizations help each other to evaluate value of products and services – on the other hand, have become the main marketing and sales instruments of today.

2.   Ever since businesses, especially through the influence of institutional investors, have understood that corporate value is not determined by short-term sales or profitability, but by its profitability and financial return generation potential for future years, marketing has played a key role. In order to create value from such potential, good, long-term, stable and profitable customer relations are essential. For example, in the mobile phone business today it is usual that a new customer will not become

profitable until the first contract ends. Only if the mobile phone company is able to renew the contract will the customer begin to become profitable. The task of value-based marketing is to manage customer capital; that is, the value of the long-term relationship with the customer. To do this successfully, marketing managers have not only to understand how to extend market share and sales but also to understand how to manage the entire life cycle of a customer relationship. This requires identification of market segments that are of value to the company, and others in which every new sale and every new customer destroys value. They have to understand the complete value chain: prospects, customers, customer turnover and customers they might win back. They have to know whether a customer is really profitable for the company and is contributing to its value-added. For this, marketing managers also have to know the costs generated by the customer through activities not assigned to the customer by the traditional cost accounting system – for example, extended handling costs through many small orders or many unusual hotline calls. They must estimate how long the customer will continue to buy from the company and under which conditions, how the customer affects other customers or prospects – for example, do they recommend the company's products or not – how often the customer does buy and how big is the cross-selling potential. For this, marketing needs new instruments not only to manage the new type of marketing activities and to improve customer relationships and community work but also to manage the entire value of customer capital by constantly optimizing the portfolio of customer relations.

Because sales figures do not tell us anything about the real value of an enterprise or about its potential for the future, the question is: does the company already live on its intangible assets (as in the Saatchi & Saatchi case)? Are good sales figures a sign of a fundamental change in the business that will favour competitors? Has the company really created customer capital?

Value-based customer management and marketing will therefore be the norm for how companies manage the market-facing side of their business in the future. Independent user communities will play a key role here. In a time when products are becoming more knowledge-intensive and when it becomes more difficult for customers to understand a product's possible value contribution to them, people turn more and more to communities of users to get advice before making a buying decision. This has been common practice in the software industry since its early days. So-called "user groups" (ASUG, the American SAP-user group, or DSAG, the German SAP-user group, are examples) play an important role in defining improvements to existing products or designing new ones. They also inform potential customers about companies and the experiences of customers using their products.

When I helped to introduce a new software product in the German market several years ago, several users – large, well-known German companies – spontaneously formed a "user group". The group also attracted companies considering using the same software in the future. When I visited some of those early customers, who had just gone "live" with this software package, in order to get feedback for product development and future marketing and sales activities, they asked me about other live users. I gave them names and contacts of other users. Some weeks later I received a call from one of them, who asked me if I would be willing to attend a meeting of the "user group" they just had set up and to channel their requests back to product development. They also told me they had received calls from other interested parties keen to attend the user group.

This user group was a success, both for us as the vendor *and* for the actual and prospective users of our software package. Members exchanged a lot of tips and tricks on how to use the software more efficiently and how to generate more value from it. They became so satisfied with the product they even persuaded other companies to use it, without any persuasion on our part, and offered to speak at our marketing events and conferences. But, on the other hand, they did come back several times with tough requests for additional functionality that they expected to find in the next release of the software and we had to take this seriously. The user group became a "co-developer" and helped us to identify and prioritize functional requirements for the new software release more efficiently.

Another example is provided by those World Wide Web communities for consumers managed by professional community organizers. Ciao.com in Europe, or dooyoo.de in Germany are communities of consumers that invite people to air their opinion about a new computer, car, movie or other type of product or vendor on the Web and receive an incentive if others read it and rate it as useful. These rated opinions can be very helpful if someone is looking for, say, a new Internet provider or power supply provider or wants to buy a new car and so on.

Such communities of users will become an important marketing channel in any business in the future. They are able to aggregate a dispersed group of people who share interest and expertise in a specific topic, no matter whether this is a professional topic, an interest in Roman history, in sailing or in a disease they suffer from. This compelling attraction for many people who otherwise might never have engaged with others in their area of interest has a momentum, and one that is of great value for vendors. Without the user community, vendors would never be able to reach people or organizations that are interested in a very special or specific topic. They never could be reached economically with traditional marketing and sales instruments. It is often the case that such a community will be the basis for a new, emerging, larger market segment at a later date.

But the more successful these communities are for their members – and for vendors as well – the more they become independent of vendors. In their relationships with customers, vendors have long held the upper hand. This has to do with information asymmetry. In most markets today, vendors are armed with considerably more information than their customers – especially if these customers are consumers. Markets have become very transparent for vendors due to this advantage. Vendors use this information to target the most likely customers to their products or services and often engage in price discrimination – the practice of charging one customer one price and other customers another, depending on what the market will bear.

Communities, especially virtual, Internet-based communities, will turn these market dynamics upside down. The value of a community for its members is that the community lets information flow. For example, information about achieved purchase prices and product and service quality between a larger number of members – that is, between customers and potential customers. Members, armed with a growing amount of information, search out vendors offering the best combination of quality and price tailored to individual needs. This ability to access more information and thereby extract more value from vendors will ultimately be one of the major incentives drawing members into virtual communities.

Communities also accumulate detailed information about their own members. Their preferences, their transaction histories, etc. are extremely valuable pieces of information for any vendor. But even members, assisted by the community organizer, sometimes have a significant incentive to provide selected vendors with access to this information, allowing vendors to make more appropriate offers to the member's actual situation and needs. Vendors could then offer – because they save marketing and sales costs – special discounts to those community members who share their data with them.

Successful communities cannot be controlled by vendors. On the contrary: user or customer communities will increasingly be organized as independent commercial enterprises, with the objective of earning an attractive financial return (for example, through membership fees and commissions from vendors) by providing members with valuable resources and environments through which to enhance their own power. *Should a corporation consider creating or sponsoring such communities, if the communities cannot be controlled by the corporation?*

This question is designed to assess risk. However, failing to act may be the riskiest act of all. Not only will companies risk losing the opportunity represented by communities, especially of virtual Internet communities, they will also incur increasing risk in that their core business will be exposed to attack by their competitors who might move more aggressively to build communities around their traditional business.

But, by encouraging user groups in this way means managers will have to develop new approaches. In contrast to the traditional corporate enterprise, the virtual community will require flexible and organic approaches and engagement by vendors, managers and knowledge workers. Seeding, feeding and weeding represent much richer metaphors for the evolution of community marketing than detailed blueprints and plans. This organic approach is driven in part by the need to be responsive to the emerging needs of community members but also by the necessity to run their own business and value creation model *à jour*, without being able to fully control the "ecosystem of the community" and of its sponsors. This requires from managers a set of new techniques and skills in working with prospects and customers – in this case with community members.

Venture capital managers know what differentiates successful start-ups from the failures: it is the capability of the management team to react to customer needs nearly automatically, to grow the business organically and to pull the right levers. The "management" of user communities requires similar capabilities from vendors and sponsors. Only this way is it possible to initiate the dynamics of increasing returns, and only this way the investments in communities generate value for an enterprise.

Even if communities cannot be controlled by vendors, getting communities of customers and potential customers to work in favour of your own enterprise can be done. If a vendor is able to make community members excited and create a momentum that helps to convince existing users that they are somehow part of a community of the best because they use the best product in their professional field, this community can serve as a extremely powerful marketing instrument.

But achieving this does require a fundamental redirection of marketing: marketing is no longer about "persuading" people to buy something that they may not really need, but it is about finding those people or organizations that value the companies' products most and are able and willing to spread this message to their own advantage. Users of knowledge products, in most cases, have an interest in others using the same product. The more users who use the same application software or use the same management or controlling technique the more valuable it is for existing users. It is then easier for them to find other users with whom they can, for example, easily exchange data from a software applications or just their experiences. Therefore, a natural incentive exists for satisfied users to help vendors to promote their product.

User or customer communities, especially those combining the characteristics of a virtual Internet-based community with a "physical community" – for example, a working circle or user group where regular meetings and conferences are held for members – will change the way companies manage business functions that operate at the customer interface; that is, marketing and sales. This requires especially a redefinition of the success factors that help to generate market advantage. It will favour the quality of individual customer and community relationship in preference to the scale and size of existing businesses.

How to value and measure intangible assets?

For top management tasks, IT has not been very helpful to date. Top executives have often not used the new technology, because it has not provided the information they need for their own task. The data available in business organizations are still largely based on the 19th century theorem that lower costs differentiate businesses and make them compete successfully. This theorem is the basis of traditional accounting, and ERP (enterprise resource planning) and MIS (management information systems) systems have taken data based on it and computerized them. These are the data needed to preserve financial and physical assets and to evaluate operational cost-efficiency. But neither preservation of financial and physical assets nor cost control is a top management task when the creation of value is largely based on intangible assets.

Much international research on measuring intangible assets has used financial metrics and tried to translate nonfinancial intellectual capital into balance sheet items that can be measured in monetary units. But little of the attempt to convert human, structural or customer capital into cash has proved useful for managers whose task it is to control and optimize the processes that create intangible assets or exploit them.

Large effects on reported profit figures are often due to unidentified changes in intangible assets. Many crises in both large and small corporations would have been detected earlier, if management and the investor and creditor community had been able to measure the value and development of intangible assets. Because profits are subject to accounting rules, which have not been designed for knowledge-intensive businesses and tend to focus on the costs incurred, they are simply not a good yardstick for comparing companies with large intangible assets. Profit, the residual result after deducting costs from revenues, is a measure that shows an organization's efficiency. It does not say much about its effectiveness – that is, how much value it has created and how well an organization is satisfying the needs of those it serves.

But this effectiveness, in contrast with pure efficiency, is what today decides the success or failure of an enterprise. Achieved revenues, which is part of the profit equation, may be a good indicator to how successful the company was *in the past* at creating value. Profit is therefore not a good indicator and measure for assessing the actual situation and economic "health" of an enterprise. The question that needs to be asked about recent performance is: *Has the company created or destroyed human capital, structural capital or partner capital, which helps to build customer capital?*

Traditional financial and management accounting does not help much in answering these questions. Measuring enterprise performance is not an easy task. Any measurement system is limited by Heisenberg's uncertainty principle. There is no possibility for absolute objective measurement at all. And in this respect there is no difference – contrary to what most accountants and business people think – between financial measures and other nonfinancial measures. The main reason why financial measures seem more objective is that they are founded on implicit concepts of what a company is and how it creates value and have been around for so long that they are guided by definitions and standards. The problem in taking only financial measures into consideration in assessing corporate performance is that many enterprise activities that create value today cannot be linked to a monetary value because they are not manifested through a sales transaction such as product sales. Most activities of knowledge workers, when they interact with customers or perform operations in the back office (e.g. in R&D) are not money transactions. Money as a proxy for effort invested comes into play only when that effort leads to a transaction where products and services are valued by monetary units through market mechanisms. But value creation often happens, especially in knowledge-based businesses, long before a transaction takes place – such as in the software or pharmaceutical industry, where product development, which creates future revenue potential, often takes years until it materializes in a product sale. The problem therefore is that as yet there is no comprehensive system for measuring intangible assets and the performance of their related enterprise activities that uses money as a common denominator and at the same time is practical and useful for managers. For this, a measurement system is needed. It must combine both financial and nonfinancial measures and compare actual measures with the ones from last month, last quarter and last year to track development of intangible assets and the success of an enterprise in creating and exploiting them.

Such a system, too, must make sense by comparing these assets and related enterprise activities with an industry standard to check how the company is doing when compared with its peers. Probably this is a much better indicator for management and for investors as to how the company is doing, both with its tangible and intangible assets, and how this will likely affect its future revenue potential. It will allow management to track creation or destruction of intangible assets and effectiveness in using them. It will be able to recognize bad performance early enough (before it becomes visible on the financial accounts of the company), giving the company a chance to do something about it. *So what should the task of such a new measurement system be?*

Consolidating the performance information of the entire economic chain

The new measurement system has not only to capture and represent the effectiveness of business operations and created value within the company but also across the complete economic chain, including the business operations of partners. Only in this way can an enterprise in today's climate manage all the important drivers and success factors for creating real customer and stakeholder value. It has therefore to team up with partners in collaborative planning and performance management – that is, in managing the output of the common value chain in the form of customer or stakeholder value. One challenge in designing and building such measurement systems is that different partner organizations usually have different accounting and performance-measurement systems. In order to be able to exchange information and discuss results, they have, first, to find common ground and reach an agreement on what the most important measures are, which ones are used by every partner to track performance, and how these measures are calculated and what their exact meaning is. Second, they have to agree on common performance management processes, how they set up plans and forecasts and how they define common targets. And, finally, they have to find ways

to link their accounting and IT systems to allow for the automatic exchange of data to support these collaborative performance-management processes.

The point-of-view principle in measuring performance and in reporting to stakeholders

A new measurement system will have to show how well an organization satisfies the needs of its different stakeholders. Because the needs of the various parties concerned may differ – shareholders are interested in dividends, customers in service levels and quality, to name but a few – different efficiency measures for different audiences will have to be employed. And each of them needs a different framework for interpretation of this measure, as their interest and knowledge about the company may differ. Management has to have a view on all these different perspectives in order to be able to manage expectations of various stakeholder groups. Within each perspective, it has to be decided which type of asset (financial capital, tangible assets, intellectual capital components or intangible assets) is important for the specific target group.

Balancing short-term performance with the creation of long-term business potential

Because time is an important economic factor, a new business performance-measurement system also has to reflect the dynamics of the business system in the time dimension. It has to track and to report not only short-term performance – that is, efficiency in using resources and existing intangible assets – and long-term effectiveness – that is, success or failure in creating intangible assets based on new business potential – but also has to make the dynamic relationships between both areas transparent.

The two most common concepts that attempt to support this system are: the concept of Kaplan and Norton of leading and lagging performance indicators brought together within the success driving perspectives of a "Balanced Scorecard"; and the concept of "System Dynamics" or "Systems Thinking" of Peter Senge and others, which helps to better understand the dynamics and interdependencies of various parameters of the business system in the time dimension and thus helps to optimize them toward a desired result and outcome.[9] Both concepts are very helpful today in managing a successful

---

[9] There is more about the Balanced Scorecard and Systems Thinking in Part 3.

enterprise. Also, the combination of both is possible in a comprehensive management and controlling system for strategic-enterprise management. Because time is a critical economic factor, and because the risk is often that short-term issues overlay or even hinder long-term value creation efforts, companies have to try and create a management and measurement system that helps to balance optimization of short-term performance and the more long-term-oriented creation of new business potential.

Measuring effectiveness instead of just efficiency

Operational efficiency has been measured at least since the birth of industrial organizations.[10] And there have recently been some significant advances in its measuring efficiency. With activity-based costing (ABC), for example, companies are now able to track costs of business processes and to improve their efficiency. Often, these costs had been summarized in a total item called "overhead", without any relation to customer service or product manufacturing processes that caused those costs. Today, ABC provides new opportunities to calculate costs of products and of serving customers more precisely. However, it does not solve the major problem of any knowledge-intensive business: to track the effectiveness of business activities; that is, value created compared with resources invested. While it is possible with traditional accounting or with ABC to optimize utilization of traditional industrial resources, which are captured in cost accounting by the collection and posting of the costs incurred through them, the problem is that all the other resources used are not taken into consideration and the output, value created, is not recorded at all.

On the resource side, consumption of resources is usually not reflected in the profit-and-loss statement, nor in profitability analysis if this resource is an intangible asset. For example, a happy customer used too often as a reference for other customers and prospects (prospective customers) may become an unhappy customer and one not willing to continue to serve you as a reference. Every prospect and customer you send to this reference customer withdraws customer reputation and customer value from an invisible "bank account". Such "depreciations" are not reflected in any financial statements today.

But the biggest challenge lays on the other side, the output side. How do you measure the value created by a management consultant in a customer project

---

[10] Cost accounting was the main tool that had been developed for it.

or the value created by a software developer who is involved in developing a software package? Sure, you can measure the day rates the consultant invoices and the customer is willing to pay. But still this is not a good measure because it does not track the intangible side. Has the consultant just invoiced and left an unhappy customer? Has he destroyed customer capital as a result, or has he added to customer capital through his work? A software company can easily calculate the resources invested in a large software development project in the form of "full time equivalent days". But it is much more difficult to find a measure to track the software developer's part in total value created.

New Internet-based business models have been established in recent years. Customers get specific products or services for free. For example, you can download Adobe's "Acrobat Reader" for free from Adobe's web page. This creates more demand for the company's other products – in Adobe's case for their software package with which you can create so-called PDF files. And for this other product, for the full version of Adobe Acrobat, customers have to pay. So Adobe gives away one product for free in order to boost demand for its core product.

Rapid market development, establishment of a de facto standard in the market and build-up of intensified customer relations is possible with such strategies. But they do not fit the traditional enterprise control and management accounting model, which requires a close link between activities and rewards – between costs and revenues. But these new strategies will become more and more common in the future. Revenues will flow from other sources and to business units other than to those that made the initial investments and where the largest portion of production, development or marketing costs have been incurred. *How do companies map those resources consumed for product development and marketing of "trigger" products to the generated revenues that originate from other products, other customers and consumers in other market segments or from indirect sales channels?*

Management has to continuously find solutions to track not just efficiency but also the effectiveness of business operations. It has to try and identify the flows that change or otherwise influence the market value of all assets, of intangible assets as well. It needs a measurement system that reflects the economics of its business in the light of its business strategy. The industrial paradigm of management, to manage for pure financial goals, is no longer appropriate. Financial performance is a result rather than the objective for management in the new economy. As the Saatchi & Saatchi case demonstrated, financial measures and objectives are too short-term-oriented and often hide the real status of the enterprise, which is the status of its intangible assets. A company can still perform financially, but may already be dead if intangible assets is what in reality counts.

Enterprise strategy and risk management

Unexpected success is often a problem for a business because it represents a first indication that the theory of the business is not in line with reality. Without a valid theory of its business, a company cannot tell what advance it has made toward desired results. It risks diversion and splintering of its resources to those business activities that do not help sustain competitive advantage. And every theory of a business, normally represented through the company's business model, needs a strategy to test this theory. Failure of strategy to produce the expected results is usually the first serious indication that the theory of the business needs to be thought through again.

Operational effectiveness means performing activities such as creating, producing and selling faster or consuming fewer resources. It gives companies an advantage over competitors, but the problem is that such best practice is easy to copy. The more benchmarking companies do the more they become equal in how they perform operations. In applying strategic effectiveness companies try to achieve sustainable competitive advantage by preserving what is distinctive about their own company. And this is what strategy is all about: the creation of a unique and valuable position that enables the enterprise to meet requirements and needs of a specific group of customers in specific market segments better than others. To achieve this, a company must focus on those areas where it has its strengths and where its main competencies are.

Strategy requires organizations to choose what *not* to do. And this is probably the most difficult decision – by the way – not only for businesses but also for individuals. Strategic effectiveness means checking and deciding all the time whether the former valuable competencies and activities still help to make a difference in the market. If this is no longer the case the company must discontinue these activities or develop them into a new business.

Such decisions used to be made every five or ten years. Today, in a fast-changing, dynamic global economy, such decisions have to be made constantly and very quickly. Strategic effectiveness means constant change management.

Successful strategic change management is the major prerequisite for corporate success. Businesses do not have time to build a competitive strategic position over a number of years. *They have to take what they have, their actual assets – which are mainly intellectual assets – and try to build from this fast, by leveraging new market developments and a new more powerful competitive position. What competencies does this require?*

With unavoidable and frequent changes in their usual environment today, enterprises have to become real change leaders. Often people understand that change is unavoidable, but hesitate to act. But instead of trying to postpone change, because it is painful and risky and requires a great deal of hard work, companies have to adopt a more active approach. Only this way can they preserve their competitive power in the future.

For this, organizations have to free resources from maintaining what no longer contributes to performance and no longer produces results. To maintain the status quo always commits a company's scarcest and most valuable resources and its ablest people, meaning they are not available to create the new businesses that are going to be the core business of the company in the future. Most managers are preoccupied with their existing businesses. Enterprises committed to change, instead, put every product, every service, every process, every market, every distribution channel and every customer on trial for its life on a regular schedule. They test its existing business against its theory of business and always ask if the existing management would start the same business again with the knowledge of today.

While constant change and abandonment of mature products and services is necessary, companies do need some stability. They have to define what their strength is, where they have their most important core competencies, and which are their most important intangible assets. And then, they have to try to grow those skills further while leveraging them to ride on the wave of new market forces and emerging, new business segments. The business must define its business theory, its mission and its strategy, test them regularly against market reality and adapt them from time to time.

Companies have to manage in parallel what Baghai, Coley and White called "three horizons".[11] Here, companies pursue: an operative strategy for the actual business (horizon 1); anticipate the next possible wave (horizon 2 with several options); and consider the unknown future by monitoring trends and start many "tries" to develop basic technologies and applications (horizon 3 with many options). To do so, companies have to constantly manage in a

[11] Mehrdad Baghai, Stephen Coley, David White (1999) *the Alchemy of Growth: Practical Insights for Building the Enduring Enterprise*, London: Orion Publishing.

systematic way the opportunities and threats in all three areas. For future options and tries – the pipeline of potential new businesses – they have to manage "alternative futures" and scenarios. Based on regular market analysis and risk and opportunity assessments they have to find the right point in time, when the choice for one of the "alternative scenarios" has to be made. And management has to establish organizations and processes that make sure strategic plans are consequently translated into real-world actions. Progress in implementing such a strategy has to be monitored constantly, both by managers and knowledge workers and, if necessary, corrective action taken fast. This requires an "adaptive" organization, which is able to adapt resource allocation to initiatives, projects and businesses, in order to react quickly to strategic changes in the markets or in technology.

Effectiveness and excellence in strategic enterprise management therefore requires both the capability to create compelling strategies – which are founded on corporate core competencies and take the expectations of important stakeholders into account – and their regular adaptation to market and technology changes. The capability to execute new strategies very fast but in a flexible way is necessary too. This requires an enterprise organization capable of learning on the strategy definition level *and* on the strategy execution and operational level. Such an organization will be enabled for double-loop organizational learning by integrating strategic and operational planning and performance management (see Figure 2.1).

Figure 2.1   Corporate strategic effectiveness requires a new management system.

Needed: new management tools and a new management system

All this has significant consequences for those who run an enterprise. Managers and executives need new tools and will have to use IT more intensively for their own tasks. This is because information, and especially timely information and the possibility to exchange it quickly and easily between managers within and outside the enterprise (e.g. at partner companies) is an important basis for new management processes and systems.

Several new techniques and tools are already available to help managers in these new tasks, but what has been missing so far is a concept that integrates different techniques into one consistent management system. A comprehensive concept is presented in Part 3 in the form of a comprehensive measurement system called a "Tableau de Bord" that integrates management processes linking the various enterprise activities into a coordinated strategy and perform-ance management process, and an external reporting and communication concept that links external stakeholder engagement and communication with internal management processes.

The management system and an enterprise's organization structure are inter-dependent. Before discussing and developing the new management system, we therefore have to consider the consequences of the discussed developments on the organization model and structure of the 21st century business enter-prise: What does the new model of an enterprise that meets the requirements of an intangibles-based economy look like? This is discussed in Part 2.

Part 2
The New Enterprise

3 Openness and Transparency as Success Factors

If we picture a company as a living organism, say a tree, then (...) half the mass or more of that tree is underground in the root system. And whereas the flavor of the fruit and the color of the leaves provides evidence of how healthy that tree is right now, understanding what is going on in the roots is a far more effective way to learn how healthy that tree will be in the years to come (...) That is what makes Intellectual Capital – the study of the roots of a company's value, the measurement of the hidden dynamic factors that underlie the visible company of buildings and products – so valuable.

Leif Edvinsson and Michael S. Malone[1]

In the mid-1990s, Germany and France were still perceived as underdeveloped capital markets. Open financial markets, a culture of free trade in company stocks and the possibility of investing in these markets easily from the outside had not been very much developed. For foreign investors not only was free access missing but it was also not possible for them to control their own investments as is usual today according to international corporate governance standards. Instead, in Germany "Deutschland AG" (i.e. corporate Germany) ruled, based on a network of cross-investments between major banks, insurance companies and other industry leaders with the CEO of one firm serving on the supervisory board of the other, making sure that they remained under German ownership. In France a large "old boys network", who had studied at the same "haute ecole" and were forever changing between industry and public administration jobs, made sure that the economy remained under the control of the French state bureaucracy.

In this environment it was no wonder that German and French companies hesitated to expose themselves too much to the "rude" global capital markets. Also, the private investor preferred to put money in a bank's savings accounts with low interest yields rather than risky corporate stocks. On the other hand, it was nearly impossible for start-up companies to raise venture capital; banks were not willing to finance these new businesses with bank loans. The consequence was that the German and French economies,

---

[1] Leif Edvinsson and Michael S. Malone, *Intellectual Capital*, New York: HarperCollins, pp. 10–11.

when compared with that of the USA – which created an open capital market and favours the culture of equity investments – continued to produce low economic growth rates. Good ideas for new businesses and for the creation of wealth remained dormant, or at least underexploited.

Today, at the beginning of the new century, the financial market landscape both in Germany and France, although perceived so far as insider events, have totally changed. In Germany, starting with the initial public offering of Deutsche Telekom in 1996, a real new stock culture was created in the second half of the 1990s. Millions of private households put their money in at least a few shares. The "Neuer Markt" in Frankfurt listed several hundred innovative new companies. Similar things happened in France at the "Nouveau Marché". Interestingly, most of these new players at the stock exchange were start-ups in knowledge businesses. By 2000, more than 50% of the "Neuer Markt" companies were either Internet companies, IT-software, IT-hardware or IT-service companies. The rest was made up mainly of media, telecommunication, financial services and biotechnology companies.

The rise of the "Neuer Markt" in Germany and of similar stock markets in other countries was a clear signal that things had changed. Whereas people in Germany and France traditionally put their savings into bank accounts – like most private investors in the USA some 15 years ago – they invested throughout the late 1990s, like their American counterparts, in stocks – hoping to participate in the value increase of these stocks and especially in the underlying intangible assets. Money was now available to support new ideas and innovation to a degree hardly seen before.

Consequently, the French and German capital markets opened up in general. In 2000, the unfriendly takeover of Mannesmann by Vodafone clearly marked the change: foreign investment and this takeover of a large traditional German company were, in contrast to previous public opinion, not only accepted but also became normal phenomena, as in other developed economics.

New tax laws in Germany, passed through the Bundestag in 2000, gave companies the opportunity to sell their investments in other companies without having to pay any taxes for the book gains – a major incentive for banks and insurance companies to sell large share packages in major German companies. This led to more foreign investment in large German companies.

In its January 2001 issue *Manager Magazin* speculated how this new taxation regime would affect matters: "Deutschland AG will be dissolved. Managers are desperately looking for ways to save their firms being broken up. The good news was that a more open, more efficient form of economy was emerging with more flexible capital allocation – without traditional chains. With the end of the so far typical German governance model based on large investments of banks in major corporations, the German economy will gain more efficiency and become more dynamic."[2]

But this positive development has recently experienced a step back. Through the new enterprise takeover law, which was passed by the German Bundestag, the executive board of a German corporation is now entitled to start defensive action when faced with a possible hostile takeover with just the approval of the supervisory board. Investors are not intended to be involved in the decision. This represents not only a step backwards in the direction of the old "Deutschland AG", but also represents "bad practice" according to international corporate governance standards.

But, it is unlikely that this will stop new economic developments. In December 2001, Gerhard Cromme, former CEO of Thyssen-Krupp and chairman of a German Ministry of Justice-initiated corporate governance commission, presented the draft version of a German Corporate Governance Codex. According to the *Frankfurter Allgemeine Zeitung*, this Codex is a reaction by the German government to the international criticism of German corporate governance practice.[3] Through the new law ("Transparenz- und Publizitätsgesetz"), German executive and supervisory boards are obliged to declare in the annual reports of their companies, whether they are acting according to the recommendations of the German Corporate Governance Codex. If they are not, no legal consequences are foreseen, but it is expected that these companies will be punished by capital markets. In this way Germany is trying to catch up with international corporate governance standards.

The situation has also changed in France in recent years. Mergers and acquisitions are driven in France today mainly by economic reasons – not political ones. The French governement and also French entrepreneurs and executives have changed their attitude in light of the growing pressure of global capital markets and the public.

This has created an economic environment that favours innovation and value creation from new ideas in a way not seen in those economies at least for

---

[2] Dietmar Student and Thomas Werres (January, 2001) "Treuloses kapital", *Manager Magazin*, p. 59.
[3] Werner Sturbeck (December 19, 2001) "Wer sich nicht an den Kodex halt, den straft der Kapitalmarkt", *Frankfurter Allgemeine Zeitung.*

decades. Entrepreneurs had been able to choose which venture capital firm they would take money from – not the other way round. Innovation has become the foundation for growth and wealth creation in today's economy. France and Germany have therefore tried to create a new basis for economic growth and for participation in the wealth of a global, more intangible-based world economy.

But in 2000 the Western economies were hit by "the Internet bubble bursting". The Nasdaq in the US, the Neuer Markt in Germany, the Nouveau Marché in France – all these new stock markets in which people had put a lot of money broke down, leaving many private investors who for the first time had invested in stocks with huge losses. What started as the rise of a "New Economy", with stocks rising almost endlessly and lots of big gains for everyone, ended for many as a nightmare of capital destruction.

Was what happened in the second half of the 1990s in Germany, France and other developed economies all wrong? Should these countries go back to the old days of protected economies? The answer is: they cannot. The global world economy is forcing country after country to open itself up to world trade and global capital markets if that country wants to get its share of economic growth. Only an open economy can provide the basis for the realization of growth opportunities and also for social development that the knowledge-based new economy is providing.

But the new economy is not dead. On the contrary, after the actual consolidation phase new economic growth in most countries is very likely within the next few years. However, the so-called new economy hype caused markets and in the end people simply to overreact faced with the prospect of a limitless, wealth-creating new economy. People were blinded by sublime visions without any real substance. Since then, institutional as well as private investors have woken up to this fact. The danger now is that we are going too far in the opposite direction and not seeing the fundamental economic changes taking place. Behind all the hype and subsequent crashes on the stock exchanges, new values, intangible assets and intellectual capital have developed into sustaining the production factors of value, which can be more powerful than anything seen before. For, indeed, a new type of economy has developed, almost unnoticed, over a period of several years, and it is constrained by different rules from those of the industrial economy of previous years.

Intangible assets are the drivers for value in this new economy. But they are at first hand invisible. So, companies based on large intangible assets (e.g. on business options founded on a new technology or the personal competencies of their founders and managers, as is the case with many new economy start-ups) are always subject either to over- or under-valuation. Because the real value of their intangible assets is not visible to outsiders, investors or potential business partners are not able to estimate the potential in these companies for generating new business in the future. So they either miss an interesting investment or business opportunity (if they underestimate it) or they accept too much risk, without being aware of it (if they overestimate it).

This is becoming increasingly a reality for every type of company, as knowledge and intangible assets will play an even larger role in the future in all industries. And because potential reward and risk associated with businesses based on intangible assets are extraordinarily higher than with businesses based on traditional tangible assets, everyone interested in a specific company or who is participating in its success or failure, whether as shareholder, employee, business partner, citizen of a community or where this company operates, is looking for answers to the following questions:

▶ How does value creation happen in the new economy and how well is a specific enterprise prepared for it?

▶ What is the role companies play in society, what can the public expect from them, and how and in which ways can companies want and fulfil their new role?

▶ How can companies better organize themselves, both internally and in their relations with business partners, in order to better leverage intangible assets and the value creation potential of the new economy?

▶ What type of management systems do companies need in order to gain more transparency of the status of intangible value and of the related value creation processes, and enable management, employees and other stakeholders to see where the value of the company lies and how they can contribute to extend it?

These topics are covered in Part 2 and in Part 3. In this part and this chapter the new economic conditions from a macroeconomic perspective are described and how an enterprise is able to create value under these new conditions is explained. In Chapter 4 we discuss the topic of companies becoming much more dependent in the future on acceptance from a broader basis of constituencies, such as employees, trade unions, business partners, customers, investors and financial analysts, consumer communities or environmental groups, in order to be able to achieve their own goals. This is important because the way a company acts in the eyes of the public has a significant impact on its ability to do business.

Then, taking two case studies, ABB and Cisco, I describe how companies can leverage organizational structures to create intangible assets, to exploit them and to create value with them. The example of ABB will demonstrate how a more traditional, centrally organized, group of companies with a local basis has successfully changed into a global business that can leverage knowledge on a global level and stimulate local entrepreneurship at the same time. The example of Cisco will show how a company has developed from a start-up into a networked e-business enterprise that is able through product innovation and through the intensive use of information technology and of new e-business concepts to act successfully in an extremely dynamic market and thereby create significant value added for business partners, customers and investors.

The economic environment for enterprises in a new economy

> *"The Long Boom" starts with the recognition that the world is faced with a historic opportunity. What we call the Long Boom – the years from 1980 to 2020 – is a period of remarkable global transformation. No other age ever possessed the tools or the knowledge to do what we can do today … With the right choices and actions, this economic boom can take off on a global level, and we could be entering another couple of decades of vast economic expansion – a boom to rival all past booms.*
>
> Peter Schwartz, Peter Leyden, and Joel Hyatt[4]

In its July 1997 issue *Wired Magazine* published "The Long Boom" an article that explored a future history of the world from 1980 to the year 2020.[5] It was seen as the kick-off for the idea of a "new economy". The two authors, futurist Peter Schwartz and the journalist Peter Leyden, track the trends of the first 20 years and carry them through into the next 20 years – the future.

Schwartz and Leyden see the "Long Boom" – the years from 1980 to 2020 – as a period of remarkable global transformation. Since the 1980s, a new computer and telecommunication infrastructure has been built that significantly increases the productivity capacity for the global economy and promises to deliver much more. Through the 1990s, Americans restructured their economy to take advantage of these technologies and sustain high levels

---

[4] Peter Schwartz, Peter Leyden and Joel Hyatt (1999/2000) *The Long Boom: A Vision for the Coming Age of Prosperity*, Cambridge, MA: Perseus Publishing, pp. 2–3.
[5] Peter Schwartz and Peter Leyden (July, 1997) "The Long Boom: A history of the future, 1980–2020", *Wired*.

of economic growth. Corporations are reorganizing, essentially shifting from centralized hierarchies to more entrepreneurial, decentralized structures and finally to flexible networks. And a veritable revolution has transformed the world of finance, bringing a hyperefficient use of capital. In addition, the end of the Cold War spurred increasing integration of what is becoming a truly global economy as well as the emergence of many new democracies, all of which has formed a more efficient market economy.

The two authors believe that, with the right choices and actions, this economic boom can take off on a global level and that we could be entering another couple of decades of vast economic expansion. This "Long Boom" will not happen on the basis of a natural law, but represents a historic opportunity for the world and one that will be turned into reality only if the actors understand it and act accordingly. Technological change and global integration and a new ethos of openness are the main driving forces that will transform the economy and the world in total.

Schwartz and Leyden start to compare the post-Second World War period with the situation today and with the possible future. In this 40 years, from 1940 to 1980, the US economy was flooded with an array of new technologies the development of which had been interrupted by the war effort: mainframe computers, atomic energy, rockets, commercial aircraft, automobiles, and television. In addition a new integrated market was devised for half the world – the so-called free world – in part through the creation of institutions like the World Bank and the International Monetary Fund (IMF). With the technology and the enhanced system of international trade in place by the end of the 1940s, the US economy boomed through the 1950s, and the world economy joined in through the 1960s. From 1950 to 1973, the world economy grew at an average 4.9% – a rate not matched since.

According to Schwartz and Leyden, strikingly similar forces are in motion today. The end of the Cold War was the triumph of the free-market economy and liberal democracy. This cleared the way for the creation of a truly global economy; that is, one integrated market. In the 1990s, the United States experienced a booming economy much like it did in the 1950s. In the next decade, parallel to the 1960s, we may as the authors believe enter a relentless economic expansion, a truly global economic boom – the long boom.

At the end of the millennium the two authors construct a scenario for a long boom until 2020. They insist that it is not a prediction, but a scenario that's plausible and one that does not rely on a scientific breakthrough. The basic science for the long boom is already in place for five big waves in technology: personal computers, telecommunications, biotechnology, nanotechnology, and alternative energy.

The symbiotic relationship between these technology sectors leads to a major economic discontinuity around 1995, generally attributed to the explosive growth of the Internet. It's the long boom's Big Bang – immediately fuelling economic growth in the traditional sense of direct job creation (first in the US), but also stimulating growth in less direct ways. On the most obvious level, hardware and infrastructure companies such as Cisco experience exponential growth, as building the new information network becomes one of the great global business opportunities around the turn of the century. The new media industry is entering the scene to take advantage of the network's unique capabilities, such as interactivity and individual customization. The development of online commerce quickly follows and new types of intermediaries, like electronic marketplaces arise to connect buyers to sellers.

Leveraging the new opportunities provided by IT, enterprises begin to shift from hierarchical organization, first to decentralized and then to networked structures. Nearly every facet of business activity is transformed in some way by the emergent fabric of interconnection. This reorganization leads to dramatic improvements in efficiency and productivity.

Fundamentally new technologies generally do not become really productive until a generation after their introduction, the time it takes people to really learn how to use them in new ways. Despite the productivity wins in recent years, the biggest chunk is still due. For example, in the USA the largest part of IT investment went in the past decades into support functions in the back office, such as accounting, order processing, etc., where 29% of the service sector's white-collar workforce are employed. By contrast, 71% of America's white-collar workers can be classified as "knowledge workers" – the managers, executives, professionals, and sales workers who perform more cerebral functions.[6] The real synergy between IT and white-collar workers has still to be created by knowledge-based IT applications. It will add another tremendous growth opportunity for every business.

---

[6] Stephen Roach (1997) "US: The boom for whom?" This answer to the article by Schwart and Leyden, by Morgan Stanley analyst Stephen Roach, is published in the archives of the Global Economics Team of Morgan Stanley. See:
www.msdw.com/GEFdata/digests/19771217-wed.html

Globalization as the catalyst

But the waves of technology rippling through the analysis by Schwartz and Leyden are, according to them, only half the story. The other half has to do with an equally powerful force – globalization.

Globalization began around 1980 with the idea of the open society. Mikhail Gorbachev helped to bring about some of its most dramatic manifestations: the fall of the Berlin Wall, the end of the Cold War. To kick it off, Gorbachev introduced two key concepts. One is "glasnost" – openness, the other "perestroika" – restructuring.

While "glasnost" means opening up, creating free trade and free markets, making a large global impact, "perestroika" creates a challenge for most former communist countries. Through massive restructuring they had to create the basis to successfully compete in global markets, to which they have opened their own economies through "glasnost". This was not only the case for former socialist countries, but also for Japan.

Japan had in the 1980s nearly perfected the industrial age manufacturing economy, but was not very well prepared in the 1990s for the new economy that favours more nimble, innovative processes, rather that meticulous, methodical economies of scale. Many of the attributes that favoured Japan in the previous era, such as a commitment to lifelong employment and protected domestic markets, worked against the country this time around. Japan was forced into greater restructuring work during the 1990s and at the beginning of the new millennium.

By the close of the 20th century, the more developed Western nations are seen to be forging ahead on a path of technology-led growth. The path for the rest of the world seems clear to Schwartz and Leyden: openness and restructuring. Individually, nations begin adopting the formula of deregulating, privatizing, opening up to foreign investment, and cutting government deficits. Collectively, they sign on to international agreements that accelerate the process of global integration.

Through most of the 1970s, all of the 1980s, and the early 1990s, the real growth rate in the world's gross domestic product averaged 3%. By 1996, the rate tops 4%. By 2005, the two authors forecast, it will hit 6%. Continued growth at this rate will double the size of the world economy in just 12 years, doubling it twice in just 25 years. This level of growth would have the potential to surpass the rates of the last global economic boom, the years following the Second World War.

Grady Means and David Schneider, both managing partners and leaders for strategic change consulting at PricewaterhouseCoopers, support the thesis of Schwartz and Leyden pointing out that the Internet revolution, built on these developments, has already generated tremendous economic value in recent years, but only within a very thin slice of the overall economy in the business-to-consumer (B2C) area.[7] They believe that tremendous additional value will be generated, by the improvement of business processes, if major industrial enterprises extend these new conditions of a more intangible networked economy to the business-to-business (B2B) sector.

To estimate the volume of the additional economic wealth to be created, Means and Schneider recommend keeping in mind the expansion of the worldwide capital markets in the past 20 years, a reflection of the economic developments over the period when global capital market value has increased tenfold from $2 trillion to $20 trillion, yielding an annual growth rate of between 13% and 14%.[8] According to Means and Schneider, this period may prove to be only a prologue to the economic and wealth expansion brought about by the e-business revolution in the B2B area; that is, by improvements of business processes between enterprises. They estimate that this could result in, again, a tenfold increase of economic value and wealth creation over some eight to ten years, from $20 trillion to $200 trillion (see Figure 3.1).

As for how large economic growth and the effect of a "long boom" might be, several experts agree, independently of each other, that an opportunity for a significant economic growth period over the next years for the world economy does exist. But where does this economic value and growth come from when looked at from an individual company point of view?

All authors more or less agree on the fundamental factors:

▶   New technologies allow companies to become more productive and to create new products and services with a higher value for customers.

▶   Global and open financial markets allow capital to flow into those markets, companies and products that provide the best prospects for value creation and innovation.

▶   Global markets allow businesses to sell into them products and services in

---

[7] Grady Means and David Schneider (2000) *Meta-Capitalism – The eBusiness Revolution and the Design of 21st-Century Companies and Markets*, New York: John Wiley & Sons, p. 130.
[8] Ibid., p. 131.

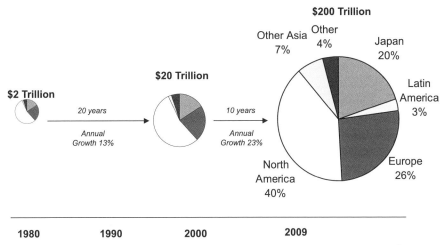

Figure 3.1 Unleashing global value through the new networked economy.[9]

much larger numbers, leveraging capabilities across more customers and gaining economies of scale.

▶ New, more efficient, networked organization structures allow companies to concentrate on their core competencies and outsource non-value-added tasks to partners without losing the necessary degree of business process integration for an efficient enterprise organization. This reduces costs and also allows a closer interface between customers and the supply chain, thus driving additional revenue.

The new economy favours economic value creation from intangibles

The value creation potential of the new economy is based mainly, beside globalization, on the deployment and intelligent utilization of intangible assets. Physical and financial assets no longer represent a competitive advantage and earn just their costs of capital. Value-added can only be created today on the basis of intangible assets. This also has something to do with the economics of intangibles.

Physical and financial assets are ''rival assets'' in the sense that alternative uses compete for the services of these assets. In particular, a specific deployment of rival assets precludes them from simultaneously being used elsewhere. Thus, for

[9] Grady Means and David Schneider (2000) *Meta-Capitalism – The eBusiness Revolution and the Design of 21st-Century Companies and Markets*, New York: John Wiley & Sons, p. 134.

example, if Lufthansa assigns an aircraft to the Frankfurt–New York route, that aircraft cannot be used at the same time on the Frankfurt–Tokyo route.

In contrast, intangible assets are, in general, nonrivalrous; they can be deployed at the same time in multiple uses, where a given deployment does not detract from the usefulness of the asset in other deployments. For example, software can be copied many times without any or sometimes only negligible opportunity costs and can serve at the same time a potentially unlimited number of customers. Stated differently, nothing is given up (no opportunity forgone) when the software is used by an additional user. Once the software has been developed, its usefulness is limited only by the potential size of the market and, of course, by competitors' actions, but not by its own use. This characteristic of intangibles is the major value driver in the new economy, whereas physical and financial assets can only be leveraged to a limited degree, by exploiting economies of scale or scope in production.

If an enterprise is able to sell products to the global market based on its intangible assets, using its own global corporate business operations, a large partner network, or the Internet, it can grow significantly faster, leverage larger scale effects and generate more value than any business based on physical or financial assets, because growth and value creation are not restricted by scarce assets.

Products based on intangible assets typically generate large upfront ("fixed") costs and often insignificant variable costs, thus generating with each additional copy sold exponentially more value, especially as soon as the initial investments are covered.

This is reflected in the market dominance of many intangible-intensive enterprises. As of the end of 1999, Intel Corp. had a 77% global market share in PC microprocessors, Cisco Systems had 73% of the router market, while 78% of Internet users accessed it through America Online, and eBay conducted 70% of online auctions.[10] Such market dominance is unheard of in traditional, capital-asset-intensive sectors, where even the most efficient and well-managed enterprises (like GE in appliances, Exxon, etc.) have market shares of less than 25%.

In addition, intangible-intensive enterprises are subject to large network effects as – surely – network effects are present in tangible-intensive industries too. Transportation networks (railroads, trucking, airlines, shipping), fixed-line tele-

---

[10] *Forbes* (November 29, 1999), p. 54.

phones, car rental companies are a few example of tangible-intensive industries in which network effects can be exploited. In recent years, however, intangibles are at the core of most industries/sectors characterized by network effects. Networks are increasingly characterized by product-related intangibles (unique products/services protected or not protected by intellectual property) at the core and alliance-related intangibles at the periphery.

Because the limit for businesses based on intangible assets is only the market, everything that helps to turn assets quickly into products and applications and helps to market and distribute them to as many customers as possible is working much more in favour of such businesses. This is why globalization and IT have become important catalysts for the new economy, especially the Internet, virtual corporations and e-business networks. They broaden the market (globalization), increase productivity and facilitate fast distribution and market share gains (IT and the Internet) and reduce time-to-market for new products (virtual corporations, e-business networks). Therefore, globalization and investments in IT have a higher positive effect on enterprises that are based on intangible assets than on enterprises that are based on the industrial model; that is, on physical assets.

Of course, intangibles existed before the 1980s and 1990s, dating back to the dawn of civilization. Whenever ideas were put to use in households, fields, workshops, intangibles were created. Breakthrough inventions, such as electricity, the internal combustion engine, the telephone, and chemistry and pharmacy, have created waves of intangibles. But what is new today, driving the new (since the beginning of the 1980s) economic productivity, is the unique combination of three forces. These three form the foundation of the new economy: *knowledge-based products* that are characterized by increasing returns; *intensified business competition* that is the result of globalization of trade and of the deregulation of key economic sectors (e.g. telecommunications, electricity, financial services and capital markets in general); and the *development of information and communication technologies*, most recently exemplified by the Internet, that enforce the effects of the two other forces.

Many people still see new economy businesses – that is, business models based on intellectual capital and information technology and traditional businesses – as two separate worlds: new economy and old economy. But today *every* company has to become aware of its intangible parts and has to manage and increase efficiency of intangible assets as has been done traditionally with tangible assets – otherwise companies will risk their future. A growing number of companies from traditional industrial and service sectors will start to concentrate on their strengths and will try to outsource other activities. The latter require physical assets and "commodity" resources that specialist businesses have decided to build as their own business model. This development will lead to a general transformation process, in which today's physical assets-intensive enterprises will migrate to a much "lighter" highly flexible and intangible asset-based enterprise that is able to create more value for customers.

It will be the main task of general managers in the years to come to convert their traditionally managed corporation into a corporation that can survive in the new economy and that can create sustaining value for customers, investors and other stakeholders. To do that, they have to grow their intangible assets systematically and use them effectively to create benefits for customers and stakeholders. Understanding the intangible assets of their companies and learning how to use them to generate value is of essential importance if these managers are to be successful. A gardener who understands what's going on at the roots of an apple tree today will be able to grow a satisfying amount of fruit the following year (see Figure 3.2).

But the very conditions that favour economic value creation and wealth generate fear in the eyes of many people. Globalization has run into considerable resistance from a coalition of labour, environmental, human rights groups and non-governmental organizations (NGOs). This coalition has mounted large

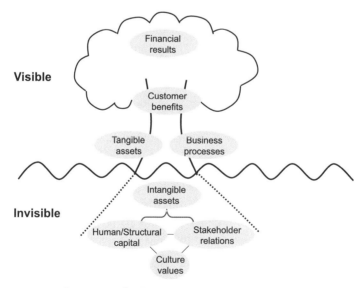

Figure 3.2 The "enterprise tree" and its ecosystem.

protests at World Trade Organization (WTO) meetings around the globe, including those at Seattle in December 1999 and Johannesburg in 2002. These groups represent constituencies who truly fear the effects of increased global integration and who could do much to undermine it. Their concerns are understandable and must be dealt with.

At the same time as businesses are adapting to these new conditions economically, they also have to open a dialogue with such coalitions – the voice of those people who are especially concerned about social and environmental consequences. To harness new productivity based on a combination of technological advances and global free markets and to convert it into economic *and* social value, companies and public institutions have to work together in new ways, so that they have the opportunity to address major global, economic, and societal issues that have resisted solutions in the past.

This dialogue affects the common understanding of the role corporations play in society and how business organization should behave. Taking into account that companies have become more and more dependent on the quality of their relationships both with existing or potential business partners, employees and customers, on the one hand, and that those relationships are increasingly becoming dependent on the public reputation of the company, on the other hand, enterprises can no longer close their eyes and turn away from what the public expect from them. They should treat this as an opportunity to boost their public reputation and strengthen their corporate brand and both create value for the societies in which the operate and for themselves.

Creating value through public reputation

> In today's post-Cold War world, trade, commerce and technology have reconfigured the global balance of power equation. Market forces and large corporations in many ways have a bigger impact on people's lives than government or regional and international institutions. Against that backdrop we need to widen the focus of business and embrace a new civic role for large corporations, globally and locally.
>
> Göran Lindahl, former CEO of the ABB Group[11]

The purpose of the business corporation of the old days, built on the foundation of industrial capitalism, was simply to ''make money''. Everything that did not obviously fit that scheme was not worth the attention of management.

---

[11] Göran Lindahl (January 31, 2000) ''A New Role for gobal businesses'', *Time* (European edition).

Employees were perceived as a cost factor and treated as such rather than as lively valuable assets to be grown and used, thereby creating more value for all stakeholders, including employees themselves. This attitude created many tensions and conflicts between corporations and society.

Economists, politicians and citizens distrust corporations that collectively create an amoral philosophy of management premised on a highly instrumental relationship between the company and its employees, its customers/consumers and its suppliers with the sole aim of maximizing shareholder value at the expense of these other groups. This opinion is supported by current economic theory, which is based on the assumption of a zero-sum game and that the profit of one player is the loss of another. According to this theory, a company finds itself in the midst of a set of competing forces that pit it not only against its direct competitors but also against its suppliers, customers, and its employees. This situation has been described by Michael Porter. The essence of his highly influential strategic theory[12] is that the objective of a company is to capture as much as possible of the value that is embodied in its products and services. The problem is that there are others – customers, suppliers, and competitors among them – who want to do the same. As the economists point out, if there is genuine, free competition, companies can make no profits above the market value of their resources. The purpose of strategy, therefore, is to prevent such open and free competition by building "unique selling positions" (USPs): to claim the largest share of the pie while preventing others from "eating your lunch". Implicit in the economists' model is the assumption that, by preventing open and free competition, the company impedes social welfare.

The problem with Porter's theory, which has shaped the thinking of a generation of managers, is that it is based on a static view of the world, in which the size of the "economic pie" is given. In this zero-sum world, all that is then left to be decided is how the pie is to be divided up, and corporate profits must indeed come at a cost to society. But the truth is that companies create new value for society by continuously creating innovative new products and services and by finding better ways to make and offer existing ones.

Such innovations provide companies with a competitive advantage enabling them to charge higher prices – that is, capturing the value-added themselves. Competitive markets, on the other hand, relentlessly force the same companies, over time, to surrender most of this value to others (and then

---

[12] Michael E. Porter (November–December, 1996) "What is strategy?", *Harvard Business Review*.

having to create value-added again through a new innovation). In this symbiotic coexistence, companies and markets jointly drive the process of creative destruction, which Joseph Schumpeter,[13] the Austrian economist, showed to be the engine that powers economic progress in capitalist societies. This kind of economic dynamics has become obvious especially today in our networked new economy and is reinforced by it:

▶ Through the Internet, markets of all kind are becoming transparent and much more efficient on a global level – competition can no longer be avoided, traditional "Unique Selling Positions" are quickly destroyed. This is creating room for new innovations and business models.

▶ Under the law of increasing returns, knowledge and intangible assets-based value creation systems can grow the "economic pie" as soon as it is shared with business partners, employees and customers (which, for example, induces network effects) – leading to exponential growth and value creation for all stakeholders.

The relationship an enterprise has with its stakeholders and its reputation in general – which are all-important success factors for an enterprise in the new economy – therefore also represent value-creating assets that have to be well treated in order to sustain the value creation potential of the company. If this does not happen, and if the company forces a stakeholder into an unfavourable position for a short-term advantage the enterprise will be weakened. Its capabilities to acquire, for an acceptable price, the necessary resources needed to create value for shareholders, such as talented employees, reliable business partners and satisfied and profitable customers, will decrease.

Schumpeter's view of companies is based on a dynamic analysis of how the pie gets bigger in a positive-sum game in which there is more for all to share. In this view, instead of merely appropriating value, companies serve as society's main engine of discovery and progress by continuously creating new value out of the existing endowment of resources and intangible assets.

During the 20th century, corporations earned an enormous amount of social legitimacy, both a cause and a consequence of their collective success. Amid a general decline in the authority of other institutions – political parties, churches, the community, even the family unit – corporations have emerged as perhaps the most influential institutions of modern society, not only in creating and distributing a large part of its wealth but also providing a social

---

[13] Joseph A. Schumpeter (1949) *Theory of Economic Development*, Boston: Harvard University Press.

context for most of its people, thereby acting as a source of individual satisfaction and social succour.

Yet, at the beginning of the new millennium, corporations suffer from a profound social ambivalence. On the one hand, they have given huge material benefits to society and, on the other hand, corporate managers are in most countries among the least trusted constituents of society. Perceived as agents, acting under the theory of a zero-sum world exclusively in favour of their corporations and their shareholders, corporate managers are increasing corporate profits and their own huge salaries by cutting costs, laying off employees and destroying social welfare. This perception is potentially one of the greatest risks that corporations face today. The clear lesson from history is that institutions decline when they lose their social legitimacy, as has happened to monarchy, to organized religion, and to the state. This will also happen to companies unless managers accord the same priority to the collective task of rebuilding the credibility and legitimacy of their institutions as they do to the individual task of enhancing their company's economic performance.

Corporate reputation is highly and quickly at risk in a world where multinational corporations influence a growing part of the daily life of every citizen in potentially every country of the world. A fundamental distrust of corporations by citizens and NGOs is the consequence. Citizens are becoming aware that only a few companies are in control of a large part of the total assets of some countries. For example, in the USA alone just 100 corporations control $1.5 trillion of assets and a third of foreign investment.[14] Therefore companies carry a proportionally greater degree of accountability than in the past.

Because many people still believe that business is essentially antisocial and that shareholder interests always come first before everything else – like safety, education or human rights – large, stateless global business organizations have become targets of NGOs and activist groups. Greenpeace brought the Shell oil company to its knees some years ago over the sinking of a North Sea oil platform – quite undeservedly when you look at the technical analysis in retrospect. Nonetheless, Shell's reputation was severely damaged. When Greenpeace started to attack British Petroleum, now BP Amoco, and wanted BP to get out of the oil business within 10 years, BP's CEO John Brown decided to take this seriously and offered Greenpeace a plan. He promised to create a

---

[14] Glen Peter (1999) *Waltzing with the Raptors: A Practical Roadmap to Protecting Your Company's Reputation*, New York: John Wiley & Sons, p. 8.

$1 billion business in solar power over five years. Brown was the first oil company CEO to address a major Greenpeace conference.[15]

Most managers of global corporations do not see them as agents for destroying social welfare. Their belief is that their primary role is to create value for all constituents. But they don't consciously articulate what role their companies play in society, leaving this task to those who shape the public perception of themselves and their institutions, notably economists and representatives of NGOs. Yet a new generation of corporate managers is starting to pioneer a new corporate model that increases value not just for their shareholders and investors. In a new economy founded on intangible assets, created by the interplay between employees, business partners, customers and society in general, they know that companies will have to incorporate into the economic chain all corporate stakeholders including public institutions and NGOs, and that the companies will have to share created value with them. These managers have confronted the question of what role their companies are to play in society and championed a corporate philosophy that explicitly supports the view of companies as value-creating institutions of society. And, they have reshaped the organization and management processes of their companies around this new philosophy.

Companies as social institutions

As businesses became global, companies encountered intensifying competition, and organizational, governing, and technological challenges across national and business cultures. As a consequence, companies increasingly began to consider how best to balance demands for growth against demands from society that widen the primary economic mission of the business enterprise into new areas. These societal demands from governments and communities as well as from NGOs had been particularly visible in areas like the environment and social responsibility, where the theme of "sustainable development" is gaining attention among global firms.

For more and more businesses therefore it became a must and a duty to accept their new social responsibility role – and also for the sake of their business. In response to the new contexts for conducting global business, companies such as BP Amoco, Monsanto, Royal Dutch/Shell, ABB and others, are implementing programmes that recognize that their economic, environmental, and social behaviour have a powerful impact on communities worldwide. Seeking to

---

[15] Glen Peter (1999) *Waltzing with the Raptors: A Practical Roadmap to Protecting Your Company's Reputation*, New York: John Wiley & Sons, pp. 5–6.

strengthen business ties and preserve their "license to operate" from communities, governments, environmentalists, and other stakeholder constituencies, these companies are placing greater emphasis on corporate citizenship activities that do not depend exclusively on philanthropy, but on fundamental business interest. Through citizenship initiatives, leading companies are seeking to better integrate employees into the communities in which they work, to demonstrate responsiveness to consumers as well as to investors, to build employee and customer loyalty, to earn community trust and credibility, and hence to be rewarded by investors' confidence. A good corporate reputation is therefore seen as a source of better economic performance and competitive advantage.

According to a survey of 1,000 consumers in the USA conducted by the Conference Board, a global, independent, public-purpose membership organization, which conducts research and knowledge-sharing in the area of management,[16] companies are already judged more heavily by image and reputation, brand quality, and business ethics than by economic or financial factors or size. Consumers agree that the goal of making a profit and obeying the law are necessary, but insufficient for business success today. They say that they hold firms accountable for doing business in a way that does not harm the physical environment, promotes worker health and safety, and ensures a fair and non-discriminatory work environment. A large number of these consumers also say that their perception of a company led them to consider rewarding or punishing it by purchasing or not purchasing its products, or by speaking up for or against it. An equally large number say they actually did take action. But not only consumers and citizens of the USA share this new notion; it is a worldwide phenomena. People expect more social responsibility from corporations.

Newspaper reports of the case of a French sheep farmer, who was sentenced to jail in September 2000 for an attack in the year before on a McDonald's restaurant, appeared worldwide, making Jose Bové in the eyes of many French people a hero in the battle against rampant globalization. At his two-day trial in the small French town of Millau, which was attended by 15,000 people, Bové was accused of dismantling, using farm equipment, a McDonald's restaurant under construction. His $17,000 bail was paid for by farmers and activists around the world. After the trial, Bové said that prison would not stop him from continuing his battle against multinationals and the World Trade

---

[16] David J. Vidal (1999) *Consumer Expectations on the Social Accountability of Business*, Research Report 1255-99-RR, New York: The Conference Board.

Organization, which he claims pose a threat to small farmers, good food and a way of individual life according to people's regional culture. Bové, nicknamed "Robin Hood", said the attack was ultimately against the "McDomination" of the world. Later, in an interview, he said that his Farmer's Confederation, linked with movements in other countries, would continue to act against multinationals producing what they see as standardized, unhealthy food.

From the beginning it was clear that Jose Bové's attack on the American fast-food giant had tapped into a deep well of public discontent and a feeling of powerlessness on subjects ranging from genetically modified (GM) foods to the powerful influence of American culture on French culture. In the interview, Bové also said that he would be going to Bangalore, India, to take part in a protest against genetically modified grain.[17] This affair demonstrates that such protests and public dissatisfactions do not have just purely local effect and cannot be ignored by any multinational large business nor by national governmental institutions. Companies that pursue just their economic goals may be in trouble in the future. A purely economic justification of a company's actions may cause damage to its reputation, because public opinion often equates it with abuse of public welfare in favour of shareholder earnings. How far public mistrust has developed is demonstrated by the often violent protests of NGOs and individuals at meetings of the WTO and IMF or of other international organizations promoting free global trade and commerce. For the protestors, economic globalization in favour of shareholders and other "capitalists" is achieved only at the cost of ordinary people and destroyed public welfare.

In the UK, government reacted to this trend by installing in April 2000 the government's first minister for corporate social responsibility Kim Howells. He set up a ministerial committee designed to ensure that the values of corporate social responsibility (CSR) are injected into all sectors of government activity. Howells sees his task as chiefly being a persuader and "celebrator" of the best practice of companies with a good sense of CSR. Among his ideas is an awards scheme for those firms with the best CSR records, marked by an "Oscar-style" ceremony each year. But he also intends to use the job to highlight companies with a poor record and to pressurize businesses to change their approach. The intention of Howells is not to force business to adopt social responsibilities by law, but to convince them that such activities will pay off for them. He believes that the reputation companies build up can be fragile, but they are more

---

[17] See, among others, the report of Zuzanne Daley (September 13, 2000) "French farmer is sentenced to jail for attack on McDonald's", *New York Times* (International edition).

robust if people trust them and understand what they are about.[18] Because corporate social responsibility works in favour of corporations, consequently he also saw no role for financial incentives from the government.

Other public institutions, too, have started to rely on corporations to assure public welfare and social standards. UN Secretary-General Kofi Annan has called upon the international business community to enact nine principles in the areas of human rights, labour standards, and the environment. In July 2000, representatives of 50 companies met with Annan and representatives of NGOs in New York to sign a "global compact" that commits them to support free trade unions, abolish child labour and protect the environment.[19] Among the 50 companies were DaimlerChrysler, Deutsche Bank, Shell, ABB, Ericsson, BP Amoco and Nike, as well as Dupont, Crédit Suisse First Boston and UBS. In the meantime over 400 companies have joined the initiative. Annan seems to rely now more on the power of such international global business organizations to pursue his goals of new, global economic principles as member states of the United Nations seem to be increasingly reluctant to support such new initiatives. His argumentation in front of the business community is that globalization could face a backlash because global rules for protecting corporate interests had become far more robust than those for safeguarding social standards. If those issues were forced on the WTO, he warned, they could become a pretext for protectionist policies that would hurt the world economy in total and especially the interests of developing countries. From his perspective, global corporations have to get used to their new role as global citizens taking care of human rights, labour conditions and environmental standards in order to protect their reputation and their basis to continue to do business successfully in a free market environment.

In addition to the multinationals, the global compact initiative is also supported by non-governmental organizations. The initiative will require companies to post a yearly update on their progress under the compact, and they will be subject to criticism by NGOs on their performance.

Large corporations have in many ways a bigger impact on people's lives than government or regional and international institutions, writes Göran Lindahl,

---

[18] Robert Shrimsley (May 4, 2000) "Minister to reassure business over civic duty", *Financial Times*.
[19] Details about the United Nations' global compact initiative can be viewed at: www.unglobalcompact.org

former CEO of ABB.[20] Against that backdrop Lindahl thinks that companies like ABB need to widen the focus of business and embrace a new civic role for large corporations, globally and locally.

Therefore, big companies like ABB train local people and transfer technology and business know-how into emerging economies. ABB treats employees and local communities everywhere with respect and tries to set examples of decency, fairness and solidarity, as well as of performance and competitiveness. This is done partly because such behaviour reflects the ethical core of a company and partly because to behave responsibly and to exercise good social practice also help the company's bottom line. Just as companies discovered that reducing their impact on the environment can also improve their competitive position by lowering costs and meeting the expectations of the consumer, Lindahl recognizes that tackling broader social responsibilities also furthers commercial goals. Companies that are good local citizens will find it easier to hire and keep talent, obtain good financing and gain societal approval, political support and regulatory consent.

A firm like ABB can use its strength – a global presence, a multicultural perspective, the proven ability to get things done quickly – to complement the actions of others, like the United Nations, and to fulfil its larger civic role, and to improve its economic performance at the same time.

The result is a win–win equation. By getting corporations to act as co-guarantors of human rights, the UN gains an ally. Businesses improve their reputations by becoming more a part of the societies they work in. In tandem with efforts to promote their corporate citizenship values, leading companies are increasing the transparency of their business and social practices. Today, the largest bloc of "social reporting" practitioners is located in Europe, particularly in the United Kingdom. There, a significant group of companies have adopted the so-called triple bottom line of reporting, through which firms commit to report not only on their economic but also on their environmental and social performance. They have become the lead examples for other Continental European companies that have followed this initiative.

---

[20] Lindahl (January 31, 2000).

The Shell report – an example of effective public relations

A good example for these pioneers is Shell. In 1999 the company published a report seeking to portray a balanced picture of the impact Shell has on society in economic, environmental, and social terms.[21] The report also reflects Shell's commitment to transparency and what it calls sustainable development. Earlier, in 1998, the company presented a road map of how it planned to integrate sustainable economic, social and environmental development into how it did business over the next few years.

Shell had foreseen the need for a management structure to help it to achieve these aims and, eventually, they evolved into Shell's Sustainable Development Management Framework (SDMF). The framework is built on Shell's values and principles and brings the necessary structure and consistency to the company's efforts to balance economic, environmental, social and other stakeholder expectations.

A diverse team from across the group designed the SDMF to include best practice and adapted existing systems to minimize the need for new procedures. It is essentially a classical management system adapted to embody sustainable development. It consists of eight steps. Key features include: integration of the economic, environmental and social elements in the company's everyday business; engagement; open reporting and verification. The framework can be applied over any time frame and to everything the company does, including business planning, project management and daily activities. For example, the framework makes it clear that for project proposals to succeed they must take into account environmental and social considerations as well as financial ones.

The new system provides a structure systematically to identify all areas for improvement at the same time stimulating new relationships and opportunities. Supporting the SDMF is an extensive toolkit of best practice and procedures to help users apply it in their own activities. The Sustainable Development Council exists to steer the implementation of the SDMF across the group. The Council comprises senior business executives from each of Shell's five core businesses and the heads of the corporate centre directorates. The Council is accountable to the Committee of Managing Directors. The SDMF has been distributed to over 3,000 senior managers worldwide and has been brought actively to employees' attention through the business line in 121 countries.

---

[21] Royal Dutch Shell Group of Companies (1999) *Shell Report 2000 – People, Planet and Profits: how do we stand?* See: www.shell.com/shellreport-en

The SDMF is designed to help Shell achieve necessary integration and to create the conditions for building long-term value and a strong brand in line with its business principles and society's expectations. Four key elements have been identified:

1. *Reducing costs* – in the short term by becoming more eco-efficient (doing more with less) and in the long term through better collaboration with business partners and other parties in order to save further resources.

2. *Creating new business options* – anticipating new markets driven by people who want a more sustainable world, and evolving business portfolios and supply chain relationships to match.

3. *Gaining customers* – enhancing the brand by providing services and products built on sustainability thinking to create customer loyalty and market share.

4. *Reducing risk* – managing risks better by understanding what represents responsible behaviour. Focusing on managing risks in existing assets in the short term and managing risks of the entire value chain and of the entire business portfolio longer term. Achieving recognition from financial institutions for success in this area (e.g. through reduced cost of capital attributed).

Critical to showing commitment, according to Shell, is establishment of a real dialogue with stakeholders. Such a dialogue must be a two-way conversation. The company must listen, engage and respond to its stakeholders and the company will be judged by its actions rather than by its fine words. Therefore, an integral part of transparency and confidence-building is the publication of data and information that is verified by respected, independent organizations. Beyond assuring accuracy and reliability, verification increases stakeholder confidence that what is being reported is a fair picture of performance.

With *Shell Report 2000* the company went further, publishing it on its website and continuously adding information and news. Mark Moody Stuart, Chairman of the Committee of Managing Directors at that time, stated in the report's "message from the chairman": "My colleagues and I are totally committed to a business strategy that generates profits while contributing to the well-being of the planet and its people. We see no alternative."[22]

---

[22] Royal Dutch Shell Group of Companies (1999) *Shell Report 2000 – People, Planet and Profits: how do we stand?* See: www.shell.com/shellreport-en

The company reports in the section "economic performance" about financial performance. In the section "environmental performance" the company reports about progress in reducing emissions to air, water and land and how it has achieved its improvement targets in this area. In the section "social performance" Shell reports how the company contributes to the welfare of its staff and the communities in which it operates and how it supports fundamental human rights and fights to improve safety.

Ever since 1998 Shell has been verifying, with the help of auditors, all health, safety and environmental performance data and parameters reported to it. The verification process has extended from data collection at the individual sites to final consolidation at Group level, where data from all contributing companies were reviewed.

In the meantime Shell has also started to verify social performance data and has asked its verifiers to look at the reliability of selected processes and data.

In each performance section relevant issues and present case studies are discussed to illustrate some of the challenges the company faces – and successes it has had – in striving to make sustainable development part of daily business. But Shell also shares its view forward with its stakeholders. In the section "Shell's view on the way forward" Shell explains the scenarios that help it to plan its strategy and look at some future challenges and opportunities.

But proving the reliability of data is only half the story. According to Shell it needs to be supplemented by independent views of what the data mean in terms of good or bad performance. Shell is working with industry groups to agree standard benchmarks and is exploring ways to gather independent views. Shell's ultimate ambition is to achieve a level of public trust and respect that will reduce the need for formal verification.

Like Shell, many other companies have come to believe that corporate citizenship enhances corporate reputation and increases trust in a company. Research is also shedding new light on the actual or perceived conflict between corporate pursuit of shareholder interests alone, as opposed to the pursuit of societal as well as shareholder interests. Research in the USA, by the Corporate Governance Research Center at the Conference Board, reveals that with respect to shareholder value and corporate citizenship there is no conflict between shareholders and stakeholders. According to this research, corporate citizenship on business economic performance is not harmful to shareholder value and, in specific instances, is actually helpful.[23]

Executives will utilize corporate citizenship effectively to manage their company's economic, environmental, and social impact on the communities where they operate, and on society as a whole and this will help them to enhance their corporate reputation. This will increasingly be accomplished through strategic alliances between businesses and external nonprofit, public-sector partners and non-governmental organizations, as well as through the extension of corporate relationships with stakeholders and shareholders, suppliers and distributors, and other business partners. For example, non-governmental organizations might serve as informal consultants to businesses.

The result:

► Positive corporate images will influence consumer choice.

► Employees will be more attracted to socially responsible companies.

► Investors are more likely to invest in companies that care not only about economic but also about social and environmental performance.

► Superior corporate social performance will help reduce or avoid regulatory costs.

But it is not enough just to behave responsibly. Such behaviour must happen in the context of the actual enterprise environment and must pay attention to the enterprise's own stakeholders. This means enterprises have to find out what their different constituencies want from them (customers, investors, society, business partners, etc.), how they are judged by them, and what they need to do to be believed. They have to develop consistent ways of monitoring, measuring, and reporting performance in a manner aligned to the expectations of investors, other stakeholders *and* society at large as well as with their own business principles.[24]

But companies are able to provide benefits to the public and fulfil their new societal role only if they can generate sustainable economic value. "Only a profitable corporation can think about being a social enterprise, too," as Jürgen Schrempp, Chairman of DaimlerChrysler put it.[25]

---

[23] Sophia Muirhead (1999) *Corporate Contributions: The View from 50 Years*, New York: The Conference Board.

[24] The ultimate trend is that private retail investors will bundle their shareowner votes with others via the Internet to exert pressure on companies. This will create in the future even more challenges for companies in the field of social and economic performance.

[25] Jeffrey E. Garten (2001) *The Mind of the CEO*, New York: Basic Books, p. 14.

Management in the new economy needs to build great institutions that generate profits for shareholders, provide customers with superior products and services, create high-quality jobs, and in the process make life better for the population at large. For this, companies need to be a "knowledge factory" gathering information and insights from all corners of the world, applying them in various combinations in other locations – in short, a company must become a truly global institution. At the same time it has to be local, stimulating entrepreneurial actions for its employees and has to create and maintain valuable relationships with its customers. A company has to be "connected" internally, and with its business partners and outsourcing service providers it has to be a networked enterprise. To make all this possible and to fulfil their new role as societal institutions, enterprises have to create new structural capital and invest in the enterprise organization.

4 Value Creation through Structural Capital

Industrial value chain processes no longer dominate value creation. Today it is innovation, it is seeking new ways of meeting market demands, that is yielding the highest return on investment – much more than improving incrementally a company's existing production line. And that means that you have to invest [...] in new structures that help you to innovate and to make a difference.

Leif Edvinsson[1]

Leif Edvinsson is one of the world's leading experts, and also, regarded as the father of intellectual capital (IC). As former vice president and the world's first Corporate Director of Intellectual Capital at Skandia in Stockholm, Edvinsson has been a key contributor to the theory of IC. Under his leadership, Skandia has pioneered a new system for visualizing and developing intellectual, intangible and organizational business assets and he also oversaw the creation of the world's first corporate Intellectual Capital Annual Report, published as a supplement to Skandia's annual report.

Edvinsson is today CEO of Universal Networking Intellectual Capital, (UNIC),[2] a conceptual company for intellectual properties management, such as patents and trade marks, based on the theories of intellectual capital. In addition he is a visiting Professor at the University of Lund in Sweden.

I met Edvinsson for the first time in April 1999 at a controller conference in Frankfurt. He gave a very inspiring speech about Intellectual Capital Management and how this can boost shareholder value. Later, I invited him to give a keynote speech about Intellectual Capital Management and to join myself and SAP executives at a panel discussion at the "mySAP Financials" conference in Basel, Switzerland.

The following interview, or "knowledge sharing exercise" as Leif Edvinsson preferred to call it, was conducted in July 2001.

---

[1] Edvinsson has more to say on this subject in his latest book. See Leif Edvinsson (2002) *Corporate Longitude: Navigating the Knowledge Economy*, Stockholm: Book House Publishing.
[2] For more on UNIC, see: www.unic.net

Interview with Leif Edvinsson

Juergen Daum: The subtitle of your book *Intellectual Capital* which you co-authored with Michael Malone in 1997, is "Realizing Your Company's True Value by Finding its Hidden Brainpower". What is this invisible brainpower of an organization and why is it important?

Leif Edvinsson: It is intellectual capital or intangible assets; the word *intellect*, derives from the Latin words *inter*, meaning "between" and implying relations, from *lectio*, meaning "reading" and "acquired knowledge", and from *capital*, meaning "a sum total". Intellectual capital is a concept of condensed, relations-based structured knowledge and competencies with development and value-generating potential. And it is important because it has become probably the most powerful value generator in the economy of today.

Juergen Daum: Can you explain that in more detail please?

Leif Edvinsson: In 1929 approximately 70% of the investment in the US economy went into tangible goods and some 30% into so-called intangibles. However, by 1990 this pattern was inverted and today the dominant invest-ments, both in the USA and Sweden, where I live, go into intangibles, such as R&D, education and competency creation, IT and software, and customer relationship building. In 1992, $200 billion had been invested into intangibles in the USA alone. If you multiply that number by 9, for the number of years passed since then, you end up with $1800 billion that has gone in the in-tangible economy of the United States since 1992. And that number is probably too low, because the investments have increased over the years. This is also reflected in stock prices.

According to the research of Professor Baruch Lev,[3] the average ratio between market value and book value in the late 1970s was 1:1, in the mid-1990s it had increased to an average of 3:1, and now it is more than 6:1. For some companies, like America Online (AOL), Microsoft and SAP, around 90% of their market capitalization value is in intangibles. So also the capital markets and investors are recognizing the value of intellectual capital and intangibles and are investing into intangible assets significantly by buying the shares of these companies.

Juergen Daum: But why are companies and shareholders investing more in intangibles today than in the past? Why have intangible assets or intellectual

---

[3] See the interview with Baruch Lev in Chapter 7.

capital become the most important value generator in the economy of today, as you just said?

Leif Edvinsson: The reason is that industrial value chain processes no longer dominate value creation. Today it is innovation, it is seeking new ways of meeting market demands, that is, yielding the highest return on investment – much more than improving incrementally a company's existing production line. And that means that you have to invest in systematic innovation. You have to invest in R&D. You have to invest in knowledge upgrading. You have to invest in new structures that help you to innovate and to make a difference. Unfortunately none of those investments are actually recorded as assets in the accounting system and are therefore not visible.

Juergen Daum: Why is this a problem?

Leif Edvinsson: As I said before, the US economy has invested more than $1.800 billion in intangibles during the last nine years. Because it is not accounted for, the danger is, and this happens every day, that this type of investment is regarded by traditional financial analysts as something without fundament – a bubble. Because we lack a deeper visualization of the components of the values created through these investments, of the intellectual capital created, nobody knew for example if the investment in an Internet company was worth the money or not. You did not have the information in order to know, if you invested in an asset, in something which will generate a return in the future, or if you have put your money in a bubble. And this is bad from an overall economic point of view. If the systematized information is missing, there is no market mechanism available which makes sure, that money flows in productive investments.

Juergen Daum: And volatility of stock prices will increase. You can see this with technology companies, which own large intangible assets. If you take for example SAP, which is a company with a track record of success over decades. But SAP stocks had been always very volatile. Why? because people can't really understand what the true value of the company at a certain point in time is.

Leif Edvinsson: And if you have that kind of volatility, based on sentiments instead of fundamental accountable data, at the stock exchange, then the cost of capital goes up. And then consequently it becomes more expensive to fund the future. And that is why we were in Skandia looking into: how do we develop another logic?

Juergen Daum: Before we come back to Skandia, I would like to finish on our first topic. So what are the components of intellectual assets or intellectual capital?

Leif Edvinsson: There are two major dimensions to make it very simple: one is people. The other is what is surrounding people in an organization, that is what I call structural capital – all those intangibles left behind, when people go home, and in that I include internal processes and structures, databases, customer relationships and things like that. So it is very simple. You have financial capital, human capital and structural capital, that can be refined into subcomponents. The last two are components of a company's intellectual capital. But human capital, cannot be owned by the company. Structural capital can.

Juergen Daum: One could argue now, that there is nearly no difference any more from an economic point of view in handling human capital and financial capital. Financial capital is scarce, therefore you have to pay a price for it – the cost of capital which is the average return an investor expects from a similar investment with the same level of risk associated. In the software industry there is a scarcity of good people. So you have to pay a software developer, like investors, enough money to satisfy him or her and let this person stay with your company and not go to the competition. It is like with the cost of capital: employees are only happy if they earn money at least at the level of, or better above, the cost of their human capital, which is their actual market value.

Leif Edvinsson: But there is a big difference! And the big difference comes into place when you start to look at it more specifically. If you treat people as you treat finance then you have what nowadays is called de-personalization. One person does not equal to another like one dollar does equal to another dollar. If I fire people, hiring later somebody equal if it turns out that my business is growing again, will probably not work: first, there is not someone equal, and second, if you fire a critical mass of your employees, you will destroy also your structural capital and you will be unable to recreate it by just hiring new employees. Several hundred thousand people have been fired in the telecom industry in Europe during the last six months. And those telecoms lost a lot of structural capital. They actually destroyed structural capital.

Juergen Daum: OK, I see your point. But what I mean is the following: if you get money from an investor, you have to pay him at least the real costs of capital. If you want to keep him as investor, it has to be more. That means that the financial value you create as a company has to be larger than the average return on financial capital. So you can't make it with the money itself, by investing this money in the usual way. You have to create additional value. So you have to get this additional value from somewhere else – not from financial or traditional asset investments. With human capital it increasingly becomes the same. You have to pay people really the value they are producing, otherwise they will walk away. So you have to create additional value out of the other components.

Leif Edvinsson: Yes. I totally agree. What we saw at Skandia, when we started to develop the new logic, was that it was something beyond human capital. You could express it as follows, which is very close to what you just said. When we opened a new market the first foreign operation took us about five years, now it's down to five weeks. And it's not that people work harder. It's that people work smarter with structural capital. So the reason why you could decrease the process time from five years to five weeks is not people, it's structural capital. And that is the point. This is what represents really the value of an organization. Not financial capital, not human capital, but structural capital.

Juergen Daum: And with structural capital you mean ''packaged'' individual knowledge, internal processes, computer systems, you mean the relationships you have created with your business partners that allowed you to do the same thing, to open a new subsidiary, again and again and very fast.

Leif Edvinsson: Yes. And once you realized that this is the leadership focus, then you have a 180 degrees of leadership transformation from human capital to structural capital! This is exactly what we tried to do at Skandia.

Juergen Daum: Yes, let us come back to Skandia. You worked at Skandia in Sweden – once a Nordic insurance company and now a global financial service company – as the world's first Corporate Director of Intellectual Capital. What did you do there?

Leif Edvinsson: I worked at Skandia for nine years. And I was hired to see if we could develop a new model, to move from the old insurance logic to a new financial service logic. At Skandia we did not believe anymore in the so far existing life insurance model and had been convinced, that we have to do something new to be a successful insurance, or now, a successful financial service company in the future.

Juergen Daum: What was wrong with the existing model?

Leif Edvinsson: The traditional insurance company does not make money on operations. It makes money on money. Which means, if you then have a lot of people devoting their time, life and energy to become better and better (in making money from money, that is from financial investments), and suddenly Mr. Greenspan changes the interest rate, their whole business model might collapse, because the rules for capital gains have been changed. And with that, things which have nothing to do with your internal operational efficiency, have a significant impact on your earnings, which go up and down with the external developments in the capital markets. Therefore, we wanted to change the game and asked: how do you create sustainable earnings? And looking for sustainable earnings, you come up with other perspectives than the ones that were predominant in the "old" insurance business, where the main value driver was financial investments.

Juergen Daum: And what was this other perspective? What was the new business strategy at Skandia?

Leif Edvinsson: The new business strategy was not to focus so much on financial investments, but to find a new way to create more value out of the operations. And to create more value out of the operations for a service company means that you have to look for new ways to create customer value. So Skandia decided to focus on the customers who where looking for an alternative to the traditional "death policy", which usually was called "life insurance". The original idea of a life insurance is that the payment from this insurance is going to those who survive the policy holder. Which means that it is not the policy holder who is benefiting. It is the survivors of the policy holder. So therefore we said, rather than asking "What if I die?", which is the key question asked by those who are selling life insurances, we should ask "What if I live?". So we shifted the focus and asked: how do you create value for a customer, who intends to survive and wants to enjoy his retirement? This is the idea of financial services instead of life insurance. And from a sustainable earnings perspective, it is the idea of a development of long-term customer relationship contracts.

Juergen Daum: This change at Skandia was obviously very successful. The IC value of Skandia has grown from a very minimal value in the early 1990s into some $15 billion at the beginning of the year 2000. What has changed within the company?

Leif Edvinsson: First of all the thinking. Secondly the reporting system, and third, how we were managing or better cultivating innovation.

Juergen Daum: Can you explain how you did this?

Leif Edvinsson: If you want to change something, you first have to change the thinking of people – the mind set. And if you want to change the thinking, you need to develop another taxonomy, another language. And this language has to be understood by your counterparts. You can use a lot of words to try to convince your CFO. But his mental model is not focused on words, it is focused on numbers. So if you want to communicate with people who are number trained, you have to develop numbers. So that is why we developed a number language for intellectual capital.

Juergen Daum: And with those numbers, you made the value drivers of the business and the value created or not created, for example on the customer relationship side, transparent to various stakeholders.

Leif Edvinsson: Right. This reporting of accountable data is essential. Both transparency and useful data are crucial for understanding future earnings potential or, in other words, the capital in waiting. And that is where you are coming in to what I call the cultivation, which is traditionally called "innovation management" or management at all. The cultivation is focused on the drivers and enablers for a future harvest, in contrary to financially oriented management, which is focused on the harvest. This is a mind shift of focus from past to the future earnings potential.

Juergen Daum: What do you mean by cultivation?

Leif Edvinsson: I mean that you get people to break out of the box to reach their and their company's full potential. You connect human capital with structural capital, and structural capital with the opportunities surrounding the structural capital, that is in the outside world, in the market. You invite the future and you immigrate to the future by opening the eyes of individual people but also of the organization at large for the opportunities that are captured in its intellectual capital and in the surrounding markets.

Juergen Daum: Why are financial numbers, which are serving as the basis for traditional corporate management, not the right tool to manage a company's opportunities and "to break out of the box", as you said?

Leif Edvinsson: Financial accounting and cost accounting is looking at the historical transaction dimension. Which means that you can explain the harvest by looking at the historic and actual cost and revenues. But if you do a forecast based on just financial information, the probability is very low that you will have the same level of accuracy. In fact, without any information about your potential, about the status of your intellectual capital, you have no chance to make any forecast with substance.

Juergen Daum: So the problem is that financial numbers represent only the result of your past effort to turn your potential, your past status of intellectual capital, into a harvest, into financial value.

Leif Edvinsson: Right. It tells you something about how you achieved it. But it does not tell you anything about the future. So therefore the challenge for us was to change from looking at the past to looking into the future. Which means that you have to develop and nurture a new thinking that is focused on new perspectives, which is a kind of mental training. We called it "knowledge navigation".

Juergen Daum: How does knowledge navigation work?

Leif Edvinsson: The overall objective is to cultivate innovation. And determined innovation normally starts with an analysis of available options. You go for best option before best practice. This presumes that you take nothing for granted. Openness is crucial. You must ask and listen to what you do not know that you do not know. You have to open your eyes to see, here and now, at this very moment. This is knowledge navigation. You don't have to be an expert to do this. On the contrary – expert knowledge can be a blinding frame of reference. The important thing is to cultivate a sensibility for events around you and what can be renewed. Innovative business concepts are generally based on a small shift that makes a big difference. In today's competitive world, that small difference might be the whole secret of a company's power of attraction, which is the basis for any economic success.

Juergen Daum: And how do the facts, usually communicated through "reporting", relate to that?

Leif Edvinsson: You should not let yourself be distracted by facts and numbers, but you should use them as a starting point for innovation. You use facts as rear view mirrors, you don't let them block your view ahead, but you take it as useful information to make better decisions when you drive ahead to generate new ideas. At Skandia, we used the "Navigator", a kind of Balanced Scorecard, to do that. The Navigator consists of five value-creating fields (see Figure 4.1). If we picture the domain of IC as a building, our financial focus would be the roof, the top triangle. External customer relations and the internal processes would then serve as the supporting walls. The foundation and basement of the Navigator "building" is the renewal and development focus. And the soul and centre of this home is, of course, the human focus. The financial focus is our stored past, our achievements so far. The company's people, customers, and processes are its very existence and its meaning. Its innovation and develop-

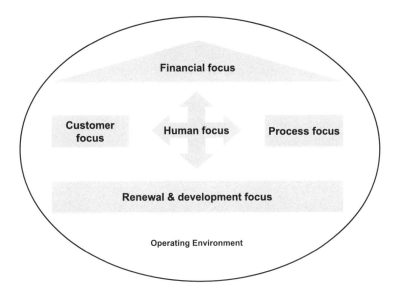

Figure 4.1   Skandia's "Navigator" to manage the company's financial and intellectual capital.

ment powers form the foundation, its future perspective, the new bottom line. The Navigator provides, beside financial results, ratios and measures on the status of Skandia's intellectual capital, such as *number of customer contracts*, which gives us a clue about the value we created for customers, such as *number of contracts per employee*, which gives us a clue about effectiveness of our processes and about our organizational effectiveness at large. Another example is *share of premiums from new launches (products)*, which gives us a clue about the success of past product innovation. We called it "Navigator" because navigation is much more close to weather forecasting than to explain the weather of the past.

Juergen Daum: But it is probably not enough that people think about the future. They have to be ready to take action and for this they need to communicate about it and they have to get a common picture of the opportunities and possible futures.

Leif Edvinsson: Right. And then you need numbers again as the tool for communication. If you look at weather reporting, weather reporting is done by numbers. It is done by satellites surrounding the globe. You measure every minute driving indicators for the weather. You summarize it in tremendous equations, and those equations are then translated into weather maps, which are then shown in the TV shows, which everybody can understand, where everybody can share a common picture and can act accordingly. Why is weather reporting important for companies?

Managing intellectual capital nourished new thinking, innovation and new perspectives. But to turn it successfully into action and value, you always need to shape the future. Any company which just looks on financials and has a historic and short-term perspective, won't last long. You need an economic weather report which provides you with an outlook based on the status of your intellectual capital. Otherwise you will act in the dark and you will not be able to realize your opportunities.

Juergen Daum:: How did you create your weather report at Skandia?

Leif Edvinsson: We did it first of all by the Navigator – a mean to enable us to manage intellectual capital internally. And then we did it by developing the annual report supplement, to let our investors and stakeholders understand the true value of the company. So actually we said, instead of having a report of the past – as in the traditional annual report we should have a report of the future.

Juergen Daum: So you gave an outlook for example on customer contract numbers which you expected and things like that?

Leif Edvinsson: Yes, by story telling. We used narratives about internal renewal processes. Because you have to balance that with the rules of the stock exchange. You can't predict with forecasts by numbers. But you can develop a little story. We did that in our annual report supplement, which is a combination of historic and actual numbers about value drivers for future results, like actual and historic customer contract numbers, and explanatory stories around them. This visualization of intangibles gives you a feeling about the future potential of the company.

Juergen Daum: So you say: give people insight into your business by sharing in how you see the world through story telling. Add some hard fact historic numbers, not only from the financial area but also about the status of important non-financial value drivers and prove with that, that you had been a reliable story teller. What will happen, if you do this as a company?

Leif Edvinsson: Look at Skandia! If you look at the structure of our supplement report, one piece of it is story telling, another piece is the same type of numbers you find in Balanced Scorecards. People are used to communicate the message about a company's status solely via numbers. This is why we added numbers about the status of non-financial value drivers, which give you a clue about the historical and future dimension of a company's intellectual capital. But also a story travels. To some extent it travels as good as numbers, if it is a good story, and provides you with the future dimension of a company's intellectual capital. So these IC supplements where communication devices that help to communicate the real status, past performance and future potential, of a company. But communication is only the starting point. The next step in this mental transformation at Skandia was to nourish the potential, which already existed, further. This is why we created the future centre.

Juergen Daum: What is the future centre?

Leif Edvinsson: It is actually a house, an old house. Skandia Future Centers (SFC) is a virtual networking organization based in Vaxholm, a small town near Stockholm, in an old villa built in 1860. It is a laboratory for organizational development. It is serving as an arena for knowledge safaris, strategic knowledge meetings and simulations concerts. During the first two years, when I managed it, the centre had almost 12,000 visitors who have come to, for example, test models of innovative knowledge enterprising in an en-vironment that encourages new ideas and creative processes. And it is not only a meeting place for those who work with Skandia. Gradually we expanded it to invite people from the future, thought leaders, as well as customers, and poli-ticians. So it became an arena where the future met the history.

Juergen Daum: So it is a forum where different people with different perspec-tives come together to think about the future.

Leif Edvinsson: Right. With that, you perforate the organizational border line. The future centre is a place, where people from Skandia meet with people they usually do not meet. And it is a place which is much different from the place at which they usually work. It is a prototyping space.

Juergen Daum: With that you stimulate people to get new ideas about the world as it exists and about the possible futures.

Leif Edvinsson: Yes. In fact it was the immigration into the future. And once you had been in the future, then you return to the present with the story which provides you and your organization with new perspectives and which is showing you new opportunities.

Juergen Daum: You mentioned that the organization often is a hurdle for innovation. What do you think is the role of the organization at all?

Leif Edvinsson: The role of the organization is to leverage the business opportunities. In our modern networked world, where nobody can achieve economic
success alone, the role of the organization is to provide the necessary structure
for individuals to collaborate in a way that leverages their talent and existing
market opportunities in order to create economic value. And if a company does
not take advantage of and realize its opportunities, it is not due to anything
else than its missing or weak organizational capabilities. And a company's
organizational capabilities can be measured and calculated. And we did
calculate that and expressed it as a leadership index.

Juergen Daum: That means, you can measure how productive an organization
is from an intellectual capital management point of view?

Leif Edvinsson: You can use a very simple proxy for it. And the proxy is what I
call the IC multiplier. It is structural capital divided by human capital. This ratio
shows that structural capital has to be larger than human capital. Otherwise
you have not a multiplier but the opposite of multiplier, which in turn will lead
to an erosion of human capital. If your structural capital is too weak, it will not
turn human capital into value and the value of your under-exploited human
capital will decrease as well. Which means that the largest component of IC has
to be structural capital or organizational capabilities. The focus is on getting a
higher leverage of the human capital through structural capital.

Juergen Daum: So the most important components of intellectual capital from
your point of view is everything which makes people for the purpose of the
company more productive.

Leif Edvinsson: Yes. And the financial number to score this is value-added per
employee, which opens the eyes for the main value driver today: to turn
human capital into structural capital which can be used to leverage market
opportunities.

Juergen Daum: What would you recommend to a company that want to start
to systematically manage its intellectual capital?

Leif Edvinsson: I see four phases in the IC management evolution of an organization (see Figure 4.2). Phase one is very much about the *visualization of
intangibles* from a reporting perspective. This is what we did at Skandia internally through the Navigator and externally through our supplement IC-report or
supplementary accounting how it is now called by some organizations like the
Securities and Exchange Commission (SEC) in the USA. Phase two is very much
focused on *human capital injection*, often labelled competence adding or
knowledge management. It is both the search for talents to be added and

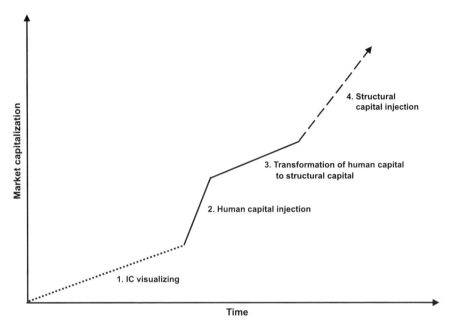

Figure 4.2 The four phases in the IC management evolution of an organization.

the implementation of structures, processes and IT systems which should increase the effectiveness of knowledge sharing between those talents. The third phase is the systematic *transformation of human capital into structural capital as a multiplier,* with much more sustainable earning potential for the organization. It is a refined approach based on the results of the second phase, but very much focused on the packaging of knowledge into recipes to be shared globally and rapidly across the organization. This it what we did at Skandia in packaging the knowledge of how to start an operation in a new country which allowed us to reduce the time to do that from five years to five weeks. It is a shift of leadership focus from human capital to structural capital as a multiplier for the human talents.

Juergen Daum: And what is the fourth phase?

Leif Edivinsson: The fourth phase is *structural capital injection externally.* Is has a turbo effect on the IC multiplier by combining different types of structural capital constellations for co-creation of new opportunities. One illustration of this is the recent merger between AOL and Time Warner, combining different organizational capital components with complementary customer capital potentials. Another example is the one you mentioned: Cisco, which combined its own structural capital – its customer relations and the distribution and manufacturing capabilities it commanded – with the structural capital of smaller acquired companies – their R&D capabilities – with the result of tremendous additional shareholder value created.

Juergen Daum: Are the efforts of each phase always reflected in increased shareholder value?

Leif Edvinsson: If you are successful in what you do and you report properly what you did through supplement accounting, so that the future potential for value creation from your intangible investment is clearly visible, then each phase often results in a stock market appreciation shift. These different phases of IC growth are gradually increasing the value creation potential of organizations. The challenge for the IC leadership, both on a corporate level and society level, is therefore both to shape the context for these growth phases, each of them being a huge challenge, and also to communicate these intangible value creation steps to the stakeholders in a repetitive, auditable and trustworthy way. Just as the old accounting system might be viewed as the first generation of economic knowledge management tools which have focused on financial capital – and in fact double-entry bookkeeping was a brilliant social innovation which coded all economic information in monetary measurable terms – now it is time for another generation focused on intellectual capital. Intellectual capital reporting will become a standard – both for companies and nations. But if you want to do it for nations, you first need to have it for companies. And it is starting already. In Denmark companies are obliged by law since the beginning of 2002 to report about intellectual capital in addition to their financial numbers. And in the USA it is now also recommended by FASB-financial accounting standards board.

Juergen Daum: Does the role of companies in society change under intellectual capital conditions when compared with their role in industrial capitalism?

Leif Edvinsson: Yes. In the industrial society companies, organizations were not just tools for value creation but at the same time institutions which you did not question. This is different today. The role of companies in society becomes extremely agile. Some people ask, do we need banks? Is there some kind of justification for having a bank anymore? Hardly they say, because you can do financial transactions over the Internet. If banks cannot demonstrate that they provide added value for society, they will probably cease to exist at a certain point in time. Today, companies do not exist in a social vacuum, where they can act just from their own point of view. They are under strong global economic, but also under societal, influence and have to change if the economy and if the society is changing. And for most companies today that means they need to get beyond the usual cognitive routines to speed up the organizational transformation. Because if the organizational transformation is too slow versus the market and society clock, you have a growing depth and a growing liability versus the stakeholders, which is very visible for Europe. The inefficiency in our organizations in Europe is rounding roughly on 40–50% at what it could be in other context. And who is paying for that? Well you and our kids.

Juergen Daum: So companies in Europe have to move faster, adapt faster to a changing world, become more open and more efficient at the same time. If they don't, the consumer has to pay the bill through higher prices. But in a highly competitive globally integrated economy, higher prices will not prevent those companies running into trouble and destroying as well value for share-holders, who increasingly are ordinary people who put their money into funds to prepare for their retirement.

Leif Edvinsson: And the third payer is the next generation. It is the opportunity cost of lower welfare and wealth. It is the same gap that you can see between East and West Germany ten years ago and still today as a result of the ineffi-cient economy of the former German Democratic Republic. So politicians, but also managers have a huge responsibility to society, and it is increasingly seen exactly that way by the public.

Juergen Daum: What are the major future challenges for companies and man-agement in the age of "intangibles"?

Leif Edvinsson: I think one of the big front lines and spaces for the future is knowledge care. And knowledge care is how you focus as a leader on the tacit dimensions of your workforce. Because if you have what I call the "HR" (human resources) approach, if you see and treat people as resources, you are squeezing out as much as possible of them. You are using the capabilities of the individuals up to the point that they become burn-outs. And burn-out is the most rapidly growing disease among knowledge workers around the world. And it is counterproductive for the organization as well, not just only for the individual. Burned-out talents are no talents any more and will not be able to contribute in value creating innovations. It is a waste and destruction of capital, of human capital.

Juergen Daum: And what do you recommend instead?

Leif Edvinsson: Focus on structural capital! So actually that means, that you have to find new work regulations, work environments, and work set-ups where you have knowledge nomads coming into your enterprise for two to four hours a day working with your structural capital and then leaving.

Juergen Daum: So you recommend that knowledge workers should work for several companies at the same time?

Leif Edvinsson: If you have only one buyer on the market, that is called monopsony. If you have only one seller on the market, that is called monopoly. Both of them are illustrations of very inefficient market situations. So if you are a full-time employee: how many buyers do you have of your knowledge? Just one, and that is inefficient. You should go out and sell your knowledge to more than one company instead of being in a full-time role.

Juergen Daum: But traditionally companies try to "own" their best employees because they fear sharing their knowledge with a competitor.

Leif Edvinsson: It could be even better for these companies if they share. Because in this case they make sure that this employee is up-to-date with his knowledge, much more than someone, who is just working for one company. And anyway, it is not human capital that counts in the end for the enterprise. It is the structural capital as springboard for the human potential. It is the quality of its structural capital that determines what a company is able to create from its human capital, with its talented people, what a company is able to make out of individual knowledge. And this is hopefully something different than what a competitor is able and willing to make out of it.

Juergen Daum: That is a very different approach for so-called "modern" human capital management, where you try to retain your talented employees as long as possible. If you are right, most companies and most economies are under exploiting their human capital.

Leif Edvinsson: Right. And just imagine the implications of your statement for a knowledge-based business and company like SAP. Just imagine the implications of your statements for the economies of Europe, with their restrictive labor market regulations. Methods and initiatives to unearth this hidden potential of knowledge productivity is what I summarize under "knowledge care". So part-time is the work style of the future. This trend will change the way value-creating interactions are done. New organizational rules will emerge, such as much looser organizational structures. Take UNIC, the company for which I serve as a CEO: actually UNIC has zero employees. Not even myself is employed there. So what is left in a company with zero employees? Structural capital. So it is a tremendous power shift that will take place, challenging traditional management of both corporations and societies to a transformation policy – to see the options to reshape the existing to something new and better. But that means that intellectual capital, IC – "I see", has to become visible. A growing proportion of good policy and political initiatives, both at the company and society level, often are distorted due to the lack of relevant map of statistics, the lack of a relevant weather map related to intangibles. So there is a lot of work to do, both for managers and for politicians.

Juergen Daum: Leif, thank you very much for this very interesting interview, or better: for this very interesting knowledge-sharing exercise.

The new enterprise organization structure

Probably the most visible changes that companies are obliged to make today are those concerning their organization and their culture. In the next few years companies all over the world will reinvent their organization structures and their culture and will start large reorganization projects to enable them to better leverage the economic drivers of the new economy: globalization, information and communication technologies, and intangible assets and intellectual capital.

One example is the Ford Motor Company. Ford announced in April 2000 that it was returning $10 billion to shareholders, capital that would not be needed by the new, leaner Ford.[4] The company was already in the process of spinning off most of its parts plants into Visteon, the newly founded independent parts supplier, which would be just another supplier to Ford from now on. While shedding physical assets, Ford has been investing in intangible assets. In the past few years, it has spent well over $12 billion to acquire prestigious brand names: Jaguar, Aston Martin, Volvo and Land Rover. None of these marques brought much in the way of plant and equipment, but plant and equipment is not what the new business model is about. It is about brands and brand-building and consumer relationships. The Internet facilitates these changes and helps Ford in two big ways: by the substitution of an outside supply chain for company-owned manufacturing, and by a contiguous interaction with consumers that offers myriad ways to enhance the brand value.

Ford is restructuring itself, in particular de-integrating vertically by spinning off the manufacturing of automotive parts. The increasing significance of intangibles – in Ford's case mainly of its brands and customer relations – as the major driver of corporate value is thus the direct result of new economy forces. This

---

[4] *Forbes* (July 17, 2000), pp. 30–34.

finally culminates in a global competition-induced corporate restructuring wave facilitated and supported by new, emerging information technologies.

Therefore, Ford is not an exception. Driven by severe global competitive pressures, rapid product and service innovation, and deregulation of key industries, companies started in the 1990s to restructure themselves in a fundamental and far-reaching manner and created the foundation for success in a more intangible assets-based new economy.

Vertically integrated industrial era companies, intensive in physical assets, were primarily designed to exploit economies of scale. However, these production-centred economies were sooner or later exhausted and became commoditized. They could no longer be counted on to provide a sustained competitive advantage and growth in the new environment. Positive results based on supply-side economies of scale ran into natural limits, at which point negative results took over. These limits often arose out of the difficulties of managing enormous organizations. This is the reason that companies like Ford responded by "de-verticalizing" themselves; that is, adapting their organization structure and business model by outsourcing activities that do not confer significant competitive advantage and strengthening the emphasis on innovation as the major source of sustained competitive advantage.

While less vertically integrated than its predecessors, an enterprise in the new economy is much more connected than in the industrial era. Traditional economies of scale (industrial, large, vertically integrated enterprises have been the consequence) are complemented and sometimes substituted by economies of networks, where the economic gains are primarily derived from relationships with suppliers, customers, and sometimes even competitors. For example, several competitors from the auto sector have created the Internet-based electronic marketplace Covisint, in order to procure auto parts and supplies at the same time and thus increase efficiency in procurement and save costs. So, how do companies create these new structures and cultures?

The evolution of organization structures

Changes in the economic environment have forced many companies in recent years to adapt their organizations, to invest in structural capital, such as global business structures and processes, and to support information and communication technology. While no reliable data on corporate investment in structural and organizational capital are available, it can be assumed that the size of these investments and their contribution to growth have been very substantial over the last two decades. One indication is the relatively small size and slow growth of R&D expenditures compared with the explosive growth in the market value of corporations (and that also means in their total intangible assets) since 1980.

For example, R&D expenditures in the USA, as a proportion of nonfinancial corporate gross domestic product (GDP), increased from a mean value of 2.3% in 1980–1989 to 2.9% during 1990–1997, which represents a modest increase indeed. Fixed tangible investment (as a percentage of corporate GDP) in fact decreased from 14.1% in 1980–1989 to 12.6% in 1990–1997.[5] In contrast to these relatively small changes in R&D and tangible investment, the S&P 500 index, reflecting the market value of the major US corporations, surged during the last two decades from 135.76 at the end of 1980 to 1342.62 on November 20, 2000 – a tenfold increase. This imbalance suggests that other investments, besides R&D and tangible assets, have created the bulk of the growth in corporate value over the past two decades. Organizational and human capital are prominent among those value creators. And, indeed, since the mid-1980s corporate restructuring – which is a prime creator of organizational capital – became a major managerial activity in the industrialized countries of the West.

In the last 20 years companies have passed through several steps in the evolution of new organization structures (see Figure 4.3). Whereas at the beginning of the 1980s the predominant internal organization structure was still functionally oriented (the enterprise was organized in functional departments such as production, sales and marketing, finance, etc.), businesses started to go international by opening up, first, sales and marketing subsidiaries abroad and, later, production sites. The management paradigm was oriented on production and physical asset management. The focus of the management system was cost and profitability management.

Growing globalization and emerging open international markets enabled companies to take advantage of these developments by integrating in a second stage their business processes across single group companies and national markets and by sharing knowledge on a global level, while stimulating entrepreneurship through decentralization at the same time. This also included optimization of the usage of tangible assets. Where it made sense, utilization of tangible assets was centralized (e.g. one computer centre per region). In other

---

[5] Leonard Nakamura (July/August, 1999) "Intangibles: What put the *New* in the New Economy?", *Federal Bank of Philadelphia Business Review*, p. 4. See: www.phil.frb.org/econ/homepages/hpnakamura.html)

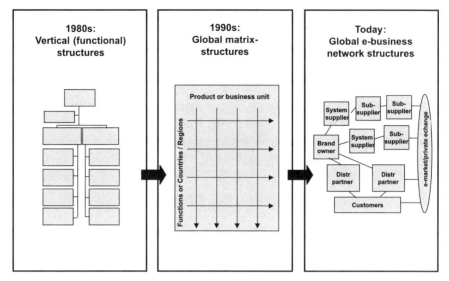

Figure 4.3 The evolution from functional organization structures through global matrix organizations to e-business network structures.

cases it was transferred to the markets, where the products go (such as production facilities).

But globalization also brought tougher international competition that required companies to become more customer-focused instead of production-focused. Integrated business processes promised more timely deliveries to customers by organizing the supply chain backward from the customer side: from the customer order to production planning, purchasing, production execution and delivery. Business re-engineering together with integrated ERP systems emerged as new concepts and tools that made it possible. And through the integration force of IT, companies have now been able to decentralize business operations into more independent business units while integrating operational processes across national boundaries at the same time. This was the advent of the true global business organization, modelled by ABB with its famous global matrix organization and of the first wave of value-based management (VBM), which means aligning enterprise targets with shareholder value.

Such a global, integrated, but decentralized organization structure will be the foundation for any successful corporation in the future. Some pioneers, like Cisco Systems, have already gone one step further: they created a networked organization that integrates business processes and operations across the borders of companies, creating a single networked e-business organization, consisting of different business partner companies, but which can act as one "single enterprise". Investments made by companies in organizational capital, processes, structures, and IT have been significant in the last two decades. But probably much more important is the knowledge and experience gained by organizations as they move through these transitions.

For a start-up, it is easy to adopt new business models and organizational structures fast. An established business, which is able to evolve from one stage into the next by building on existing organizational capital and on its experience with major change management initiatives, has another, more long-term-oriented advantage: as soon as the world changes and the start-up has to adapt itself for the first time to new market and economic conditions, the traditional company is in a much more favourable position. For the latter it is just another organizational change, and it has already developed the capabilities to master it.

Changes experienced in the past and new corporate structures and processes that have been created represent an important foundation for "old economy" enterprises for their next organizational transition to a networked e-business enterprise. Traditional companies that have not yet taken the first step (moving to a true global organization structure) will not be able to take the second step properly and quickly. Changing from a functional "international" to a true global organization that can share knowledge and intangibles and facilitate innovation and entrepreneurship therefore represents the foundation for the transition to the fully networked e-business enterprise. Taking examples from the pioneer companies, the following case studies should demonstrate the principles for successfully implementing both global and networked business structures, which represent the basis for successful enterprises both today and in the future.

From the functionally-structured "international" company to global corporation

In the 1970s and 1980s many companies changed their philosophy to what they called at the time "going international". They opened foreign offices or acquired local subsidiaries of foreign companies, mainly to support local sales and marketing. These "bridgeheads" developed later into larger subsidiaries, comprising additional manufacturing and production facilities as well. At the time these companies called themselves "international enterprises" and, in the

1990s, with a large corporate head office and "satellite subsidiaries" abroad, developed into true global corporations, which tried to leverage the advantages of global purchasing markets. In order to do that they relied on new organization structures, on a new global enterprise culture and on new business processes, all founded on new IT and global communication networks. The latter enabled the new enterprises to plan and to optimize resource allocation globally and to set up global reporting systems. This allowed management to coordinate efficiently their activities and functions that were scattered around the globe.

The model that evolved was that of the global corporation based, on the one hand, on a matrix organization structure that provides controls and guidance globally across boundaries and business units and, on the other hand, on a culture that stimulates local entrepreneurship and gives front line managers a great degree of freedom. The pioneer company here was ABB, which created an organizational model for the global corporation that was later applied by many other companies.

Case study: ABB

The ABB Group (Asea Brown Boveri) is the world's largest electrical engineering group, with revenues of over $23 billion and with 161,000 employees in more than 100 countries and a history that spans more than 100 years.[6] ABB, in serious trouble today, was throughout the 1990s one of the best examples of how the creation of structural capital enables businesses to become more innovative and adaptive and to leverage intellectual capital on a global scale. ABB was for three years running in the 1990s voted "Europe's most respected company" in a poll of executives by the *Financial Times*.[7] In 1997 President and CEO Göran Lindahl started an initiative to convert ABB into a knowledge-based and stakeholder-oriented corporation.

Jörgen Centerman, ABB's President and CEO from January 1, 2001, has built on the work of Lindahl and further reorganized the ABB Group. In a difficult economic environment the new restructuring – the first in its industry – is oriented around customer groups, aligning ABB with the requirement of

---

[6] These figures refer to the ABB Group as at the beginning of 2002. See the ABB website at: www.abb.com

[7] Jay Branegan (March 3, 1997) "Percy Barnevik, Chairman, ABB Asea Brown Boveri; Zurich", *Time Magazine*.

the more customer- than product-oriented new economy. ABB, currently struggling with some major difficulties and now with a new CEO at the helm (Jürgen Dormann came on board in September 2002), is still a good example of a traditional industrial company that has transformed itself, in a major effort at the beginning of the 1990s, into a truly global enterprise, creating significant organizational capital, which it can now use as the basis for the next step in migrating to a knowledge- and intangible-assets-based, constantly innovating, adaptive, networked and customer-oriented enterprise.

It all started in 1988 with Percy Barnevik, the CEO of the ABB Group, which had just emerged from a merger between Asea and BBC. Barnevik completed this merger – Europe's biggest cross-border deal in 1988 – in only six weeks, following his rule: "Act fast, even at the risk of making mistakes." He started immediately to convert the organization, which originated from two traditional industrial enterprises, into a totally new corporation with the famous global matrix organization. By doing that, he turned the traditional management model, where most management decisions were made at head office level, upside down.

Barnevik treated each of the more than 1,000 ABB companies as a distinct business and, whenever possible, as a free-standing legal entity. Each front line company was quite small – on average employing about 200 people and generating about $50 million in revenues. Barnevik's basic objective of creating such a large number of small entities was to ensure that employees would lose "the false sense of security of belonging to a big organization and will develop the motivation and pride to contribute directly to their unit's success".[8] The whole architecture was designed to work "with the grain" of individual identity, pride, commitment, and anxiety, thereby shaping people's behaviour at work. In contrast to the eight or nine layers of management that many company managers were used to in their former corporations, in ABB there is only one intermediate level between the Group Executive and the more than 1,000 front line company managers. As ABB's philosophy is decentralization – expressed by Barnevik through the famous term "Think global, act local" – the function of the headquarters in Zurich is only to give general guidelines, manage some very few global tasks, and to coordinate the global strategy.

---

[8] Sumantra Ghoshal and Christopher A. Bartlett (1997) *The Individualized Corporation*, London: William Heinemann/Random House, p. 184.

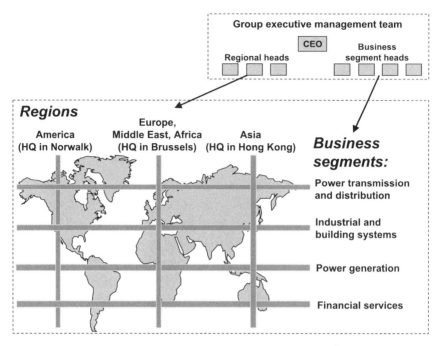

Figure 4.4   ABB's matrix organization from 1998.[9]

The structure of ABB: the global matrix

Structurally ABB was built around a global matrix (see Figure 4.4). At the top of the company is the Group Executive Management, which at the time of Barnevik consisted of seven executives besides himself. Three of the seven headed the major regions, North America, Europe and Asia Pacific. The other four executives in this group had each been head of one of the four "sectors" in which ABB's more than 50 Business Areas were grouped. Regional head quarters, located in their respective regions, had been responsible for financial performance, human resources, treasury, tax and infrastructure. Business segment headquarters in Zurich had worldwide responsibility for their core business (i.e. mainly for R&D, engineering, production, project management of both customer projects and group projects and management development) and they are part of ABB Holding in Zurich. Under the Group Executive Man-

[9] Sumantra Ghoshal and Christopher A. Bartlett (1997) *The Individualized Corporation*, London: William Heinemann/Random House, p. 184.

agement Level, in one dimension of the matrix, had been the global business area headquarters (also located in Zurich) and, in the other dimension of the matrix, the regional sector headquarters located in the corresponding region.

And, in keeping with the principle of radical decentralization, staff support at the corporate level was very thin. Under the rigorously enforced 90% rule, Barnevik trimmed corporate staff from more than 2,000 to only 150–200, with most human, technological, and financial resources being transferred to the operating companies. For example, this leaves a business area manager, responsible for a $300 million global business, with a staff of only three persons.[10]

How does such an organization function? How can you run a large global corporation, with a broad portfolio of technology-intensive and mutually inter-dependent businesses, with 1,000 highly autonomous companies, a central staff of only 200, and only one intermediate level of management? Percy Barnevik described it in his vision for ABB: "We have to be global and local, big and small, radically decentralized with central reporting and control. Once we resolve these dilemmas we will achieve real organizational advantage".[11]

Resolving these dilemmas required not only a new structure but also a new organizational philosophy that would minimize internal competition by stimulating overall growth and generate new opportunities for everyone in the organization, that would break down geographical, functional and cultural barriers, and would enable people to think and act entrepreneurially within the boundaries of the company.

The ABB management and enterprise culture

The foundations of Barnevik's success were vision and concentration. He concentrated ABB's business activities on those markets where he and his management team believed the company could reach a leading position, where the business was not out of touch or aging and where the market was still growing. Barnevik was convinced that the decade-long downturn in demand for power plants in the industrial world would disappear with the advent of a large group of industrializing countries focused on building the infrastructure for their own entry into the twenty-first century. This repeatedly articulated vision prevented ABB front line managers from perceiving their business as

---

[10] Sumantra Ghoshal and Christopher A. Bartlett (1997) *The Individualized Corporation*, London: William Heinemann/Random House, p. 185.
[11] Ibid., p. 26.

something in which the company would invest and made them believe their initiatives were worthless.

A lean head office with relatively few staff forced front line managers to be self-sufficient, to make their decisions themselves, and to act in their business and market in an entrepreneurial way. They concentrated on ways of creating opportunities and introducing innovations rather than finding ways to circumvent internal barriers or manipulate data to survive another corporate review.

Barnevik made the small, local, and radically decentralized elements the new organization's core, and the big, global, and central reporting and control characteristics the overlays. His main objective was to create an environment that enables people to think and act in an entrepreneurial way within the boundaries of the company.

The role of front line managers was not to be an effective part of a massive corporate machine, but to be entrepreneurial initiators with full responsibility and accountability for the development of a front line company. Such managers, because they headed a separate legal entity created by ABB, assumed full responsibility not only for their profit-and-loss statement but also for their balance sheet. They had to focus on managing cash flow, paying dividends to the parent company, and making wise investment decisions with their retained earnings, typically about 30% to 40% of total earnings. They could borrow locally and they inherited results from year to year through changes in equity. In sum, their job was not simply to implement the latest corporate program but to build a viable, enduring business. The task of their immediate superior, the global business area and regional segment manager, was to support and guide these front line managers in their decisions.

And Barnevik and his top executive colleagues were constantly present at the front. Barnevik travelled 200 days a year and estimated that he personally met more than 5,000 ABB managers. Again and again, he and his executive colleagues talked with local managers about their vision of the future of the power industry, where ABB wanted to be and how it was going to get there. Along with this clearly articulated vision, Barnevik also conveyed a strong sense of the company's core values and about the contribution that ABB could bring to the quality of life in the markets it served. As Barnevik explained it, ABB was not just in the business of selling power generation, transmission and distribution equipment, it was in the business of improving living standards worldwide, bringing free enterprise and economic development to China and the countries of eastern Europe, and improving the environment by making smoke-belching, coal-burning power plants relics of the past. In doing so, he wanted to inspire people to connect with the company's broad mission in a very personal way, to see the company as the means by which they could have a personal impact on issues of major importance in the world. Barnevik and his senior management spent an enormous amount of time representing an operating approach and style that reinforced the organization's belief that individual initiative and personal responsibility were at the heart of the company's philosophy. It was reflected in the respectful and thoughtful way they communicated within the organization and in their constant urging of individuals to question assumptions, propose solutions, and take action.[12]

The muscles of ABB: individual initiative and entrepreneurship combined with self-organized management councils and specialist teams

By giving front line managers a great degree of freedom and by encouraging them to take the initiative, Barnevik and his executive colleagues succeeded in generating an entrepreneurship that is typical of a small organization, but not one for a large global business. As Barnevik constantly reminded his management team, it was an organization designed to encourage individual initiative and ensure personal responsibility. And they combined the entrepreneurship style of smaller companies with the possibilities of a large global business organization to leverage best practice and ideas on a global level.

At ABB a company manager could rely in his decisions on the expertise of management colleagues in other organizational units. He had access to a steering committee that met three or four times a year and acted as a small local board for his front line company. With membership drawn from the corresponding worldwide business area headquarters, the regional sector head office, and colleagues running related front line companies within ABB, such a steering committee was a front line managers' sounding board for new ideas (how to reorganize his unit, for example) and decision forum on key issues (such as approval for strategic plans and operating budgets). In such a challenging management framework, a company manager was stretched beyond a preoccupation with his own operating unit. He was also invited to serve on the steering committees of the other companies reporting to the same regional sector head office like him. Some of the front line managers – those of the largest and most strategically important companies – also had a seat on the

---

[12] Sumantra Ghoshal and Christopher A. Bartlett (1997) *The Individualized Corporation*, London: William Heinemann/Random House, pp. 30–31.

worldwide business area board where global strategies and core policies were hashed out for the global businesses operations.

Looking from the top, the management style of a business area manager was not to steer and control his business through a large head office staff, but to motivate his front line managers, provide them with strategic guidance, convince them about new strategic directions and rely for the rest on the steering committees: that is, on other front line managers and their collaborative intelligence and common experience.

The radical decentralization of resources and responsibilities also penetrated deep into the formal structure. Most of the ABB companies had been structured into four or five profit centres, pushing responsibility and accountability down deeper into the organization. Managers who historically had thought of themselves primarily as engineers began to focus on market needs and became concerned about financial performance. The philosophy of moving people and ideas beyond their traditional boundaries also touched staff groups.

Many local specialists were finding themselves on global functional councils through which they were expected to contribute their expertise to improving the company's worldwide performance. This structure allowed ABB to stimulate individual initiative by managers and employees while leveraging, at the same time on a global level, best practice and intellectual capital. New ideas for organizing internal work processes or for services (e.g. those invented and created in one company) became available quickly to other ABB companies as well.

In many large corporations the divisional hierarchy has been accused of killing entrepreneurship. But, as ABB confirms, it is not the size and structure of an enterprise *per se* that is to blame. The real causes are the assumptions about the role and tasks of different management groups that are implied by that structure. Traditionally, top-level managers acted as chief corporate entrepreneurs, setting corporate strategy and implementing it through their control over the resource allocation process. Middle-managers had been focused on the proper fulfilment of the demands from above, playing the role of administrative controllers, and front line managers had been assigned the role of operational implementers, responding to the demands of internal organizational processes rather than focusing on external opportunities.

At ABB this model was turned upside down. The entrepreneurial process at ABB converted front line managers to the primary initiators of entrepreneurial action, creating and perusing new opportunities for the company. Middle-managers (the heads of business areas and regional segment headquarters) are no longer preoccupied with their historic control role, but have instead become a key resource to the front line managers, coaching and supporting them in their activities and developing them personally. And, finally, top management's task at ABB was – after having decentralized resources and having delegated responsibilities – to focus much more on driving the entrepreneurial process by developing a broad set of objectives and establishing stretched performance standards that front line initiatives must meet. Expecting the business area heads and company managers to take the leadership in developing their business strategy, top management – mainly the segment heads – saw their role as questioning and challenging.

This was not practiced in a remote way. Central measurement of goal achievement of all operative units gave them at any time an overview of the performance status of a business unit, of a company or a profit centre. If problems occurred, they interacted directly – at ABB this was called "fingers-in-the-pie-management" – and contacted the responsible manager to inquire about their business, encourage their initiative, or to offer help when performance was slipping off track instead of threatening and punishing. Top management saw their role as the one of a coach for front line managers.

The strategic enterprise management process at ABB

"In business, success is 5% strategy, 95% execution", said Percy Barnevik.[13] That is, the focus of Barnevik's new structure was not on inventing the best strategy, but on executing it fast and adapting it on the fly through the close collaborative work of the management teams.

Barnevik has been deeply involved in leading the company's key strategic commitments: to stay focused in electrotechnical products, for example, to execute a major shift of resources from Western Europe to North America and Asia, and to bet on the growth of developing markets like India and China. The analysis and decision making involved in reaching such conclusions have been far less demanding than the huge time commitment Barnevik and his group executives have made to the task of embedding broad corporate purpose and shaping a set of values to guide behaviour. Barnevik did much to ensure that the organization understands and was aligned around his vision. For example, he tried to meet the operational managers wherever possible. Equally important, he emphasizes the "how to" – the management policies

---

[13] Branegan (March 3, 1997).

and principles that are vital for effective implementations. Again and again he expounded on his 7-3 formula: "It's better to decide quickly and be right seven out of ten times than postpone. The only unacceptable action is to do nothing."[14]

At the middle level of the organization, the actions of business unit and regional sector managers had been far from control-dominated. While each of these managers had a primary responsibility for achieving results – the business area manager's focus being global strategy and the regional segment manager's emphasizing financial performance – they achieve them through non-traditional methods. Most key decisions for each of the operating companies are made in the steering committee that had been constructed for each front line company. Through the effective use of this forum, both the operating budget and strategic-planning processes became a constructive dialogue rather than a process based on imposed objectives. In addition, the usual matrix problem of front line managers being squeezed by the conflicting interests of their superiors was avoided. If the thrust of top-level management's action was to offset top-down processes with bottom-up initiatives, then the impact of those in the middle was to supplement traditional formal vertical linkages with new horizontal ones.

With so few staff members to engage in traditional control activities, business area managers became responsible for global strategy and cross-market policies in the worldwide relays business. They were forced to create shared supervisory forums like the business area advisory board, consisting of the manager himself, his three person staff of finance, technical and business development directors, and the presidents of the four major relays operating companies including the one in the US. These management units, the business segment management, business area management, local management and local advisory boards, as well as regional management, had been interlinked and balanced through an ongoing institutionalized management dialogue between them (see Figure 4.5). At the operating level they formed functional councils that linked R&D, purchasing and quality managers with their counterparts in other companies, using their quarterly meetings as a way of capturing and transferring best practices. This benchmarking was reinforced by an internalized control mechanism called the "performance league", which consisted of the distribution of the ranking of all business areas companies on key performance criteria.

---

[14] Ghoshal and Bartlett, *Individualized Corporation*, p. 187.

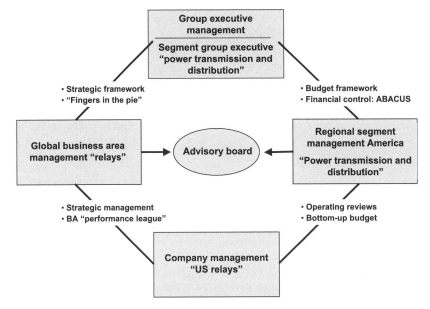

Figure 4.5   The ABB management system.[15]

Nowhere was the new openness of communication more clearly evident than in the contrast between the strategic management process at companies which managed their business in the traditional way and at ABB. Where at other companies the strategic management process was a top-down, staff-managed, financially driven model that focused managers on short-term operating performance under threat of divestment, ABB relied on an interactive, bottom-up/top-down process that was designed to engage managers at all levels in an ongoing dialogue about how to build and defend long-term sustainable competitive advantage.

The strategic enterprise management process at ABB was organized as follows.[16] Key financial targets – long-term and short-term – are defined at the group level for each business segment with the responsibility of the CEO. The task of the business segment and business area head offices was then to track new strategic opportunities and to analyze and constantly check if the business is still located at a place in the industry value chain where it can earn money in order to meet the CEO's key financial targets.

[15] Ghoshal and Bartlett, *Individualized Corporation*, p. 187.
[16] Based on notes taken by the author at a presentation given in Germany by Stephan Rademacher, VP Business Controlling ABB Power Generation Segment. See also Stephan K. Rademacher (March 30/31, 1998) "Controlling bei einem Global Player", Frankfurt: Controller in Dialog Conference '98, p. 3.

This is also where strategic three-year financial planning was executed. ABB used simulation models for different scenarios to track in financial planning changes of external conditions and parameters of the different business segments and business areas. The most probable scenarios became through timely defined action-trigger points part of the strategic plan. Starting off from this strategic financial plan business segment management made a breakdown of the overall segment targets and figures down to business area level. Then business planning on business area level started from a development/ production/market perspective.

The planning results are then passed on to the segment head office for final approval. After the budget was released, operative units (companies and business areas) had to provide forecasts of a few basic key figures to the segment head office on a regular basis.

Several times during the fiscal year, the segment management and controllers met with business area management to review performance and forecasts. This included also planning of further activities which had become necessary due to changes in the market or in other areas in order to reach the previously defined financial targets. A detailed analysis of business risks and new opportunities, the result of changed market or business conditions, made sure that they are detected and appropriate action taken. This not only includes consideration of business risks that may make it impossible for the company to reach its targets if they materialize, but also of new business opportunities that have emerged due to this change and that represent options to generate additional business and revenues. Based on this information, decisions on new activities and subsequent changes in resource plans and forecasts are made during this meeting.

With this planning and performance monitoring process ABB achieved a high flexibility in resource allocation and ensured that the whole organization was better able to meet financial targets. This was important, because these targets had been communicated at the beginning of the year to financial analysts and investors. And the expectations of the capital market about ABB's ability to meet these targets represent the foundation of ABB's future share price development.

The segment management saw its key role not as aligning, integrating and blessing the plans of various business area and regional managers in a ritualized annual review but of questioning, probing, and challenging them in bimonthly meetings. The developed scenario exercises forced them to think about how they might change their strategic postures or priorities in response to various unplanned political, economic, or competitive developments. The managers in the middle, the business area and regional headquarters managers were playing the anchor role in the management process at ABB, of which one tasks was to integrate and link the company's diverse tangible and intangible assets and resources into broad corporate capabilities and to leverage those capabilities to create distinctive advantages that support existing businesses and help the company enter new businesses and markets.

Also, the role of top management was crucial: its task is to create a sense of shared organizational identity – what Barnevik calls the "glue" – and to build organizational norms that value collaboration – the "lubricant" in Barnevik's terminology. This enables ABB to overcome the centrifugal forces driving independent entrepreneurial units and to avoid too much fragmentation, isolation and inter-unit competitiveness that create barriers against the internal flow of knowledge and expertise. Top management recognizes and rewards those who are seen as "givers" in ABB terminology – managers able to attract and develop talented people who become internal candidates for other parts of the organization.

While the top-level context setting and the front line personal networks can provide the enabling conditions for this vital process, it is the middle managers who are the ones to encourage cross-unit linkages – which is a major challenge in any traditional divisional organization which has at the middle level the highest barriers to horizontal transfer of knowledge and expertise. This is what at ABB was done by creating functional councils designed to transfer best practices developed by leading-edge operative companies, and by creating steering committees structured to provide front line managers with advice and support from their colleagues.

As top management's task is to take the lead in inspiring and energizing the renewal process (that is, the strategic enterprise management process), Barnevik has not accepted the logic of incrementalism, whereby the organization's aspirations are determined by the goals of the individual managers according to their perception of the past. Instead he has focused ABB on a very stretched, future-oriented corporate mission. As part of ABB's strategic enterprise management process Barnevik translated the broad mission into strategic objectives and further operationalized the broad vision by expressing the goals in financial performance terms: operating profit at 10% of sales and a 25% return on capital employed by the mid-1990s. This balance between, on the one hand, "soft factors" in the ABB management system, like the management culture and the emphasis on management dialogue and, on the other hand, between "hard factors", in the form of defined financial targets and performance figures, was the basis for the success of the company. Another component of the ABB management system playing an important role is the financial reporting system ABACUS, which is providing essential services in the area of the "hard factors", that is performance measures.

The nervous system of ABB's organization: the ABACUS financial reporting system

Another of the major foundations on which the ABB management processes are built is the ABACUS financial reporting system, which serves as an integration tool for financial discipline in the group. ABACUS is a central business data repository – which would be called a data warehouse today. To this data warehouse data is transferred automatically and regularly from decentralized transaction and management information systems at ABB's operations. With ABACUS, financial data is consolidated and converted into an US-GAAP format[17] – ABB's standard financial reporting scheme worldwide, which is used both for management reporting and external reporting.

ABACUS allows managers to run reports on consolidated financial data on any dimension. ABACUS is also used to assist the strategic planning process at ABB, such as the set-up of a three-year strategic financial plan of all business areas, and to support worldwide budgeting and periodical forecasting based on basic key figures. With this one system, managers have a reporting and planning database which allows them to interact and communicate with colleagues around the world on consistent data. It serves therefore as an important integration tool in ABB's management processes.

But ABACUS was not only designed to provide uniform, fine-grained measurements of all key dimensions of the company's operations. It was designed also to democratize information by making reports available in the same format and at the same time to everyone throughout the company. The objective was, first, to serve the needs of operating-level managers in identifying and diagnosing problems and, second to provide senior management with a means of monitoring performance. With a style described as "fingers-in-the-pie" management, those at the top never hesitated to reach down to the front lines if they sensed a problem. But the objective was to help rather than interfere.

---

[17] Corporations with shares listed at a stock exchange in the United States, must report according to the US-GAAP. For reasons of consistency, ABB uses US-GAAP not only as a basis for external reporting but also for its own internal reporting.

Göran Lindahl, a later CEO of ABB and in former days the group executive for the power transmission and distribution segment, always asked: "What's the problem? What are you doing to fix it? How can we help?", and in that sequence.[18]

The advantages of an entrepreneurial culture and open dialogue

Sumantra Ghoshal and Christopher Bartlett have described their visit to ABB's relays business in the USA at Coral Springs as one of the most influencing of the hundreds of visits they made in the course of the research for their book *The Individualized Organization*. The reason is that they studied a very unusual turnaround story at ABB's relays business:[19]

ABB's relays business at Coral Springs was historically part of Westinghouse's Power Transmission and Distribution business and the unit had a record of modest profitability and almost no growth. But after it had been acquired by ABB in 1989, its revenues had grown by more than 45% in four years, while its profitability had improved from 70–99%, cycle time had been cut by 70%, and inventories had been slashed by 40%. Overall, a mature operation in a mature business had developed, almost overnight, the performance profile of a young growth company. This might have been just another impressive but otherwise unremarkable turnaround – except for one thing. The transformation was accomplished by the same management team that had previously delivered the flat sales and break-even profitability.

On acquiring the business, ABB, to its surprise, had invited most of the key people to stay on, even after purchasing the remaining 55% of the business the following year. The company also asked the former company manager to run the whole relays business – even the Allentown operation that was ABB's own facility in the United States. Within weeks after the acquisition, Percy Barnevik and the, then, executive vice-president responsible for ABB's power transmission sector, Göran Lindahl, flew to the United States to express their confidence in the US-based managers. The two senior ABB executives also sent a strong message that the acquisition would not follow the traditional takeover model in which the parent immediately establishes restrictive strategic and operating boundaries around the acquisition. Moreover, the former Westinghouse company manager was amazed by the fact that Barnevik and Lindahl approached his team as colleagues rather than as superiors and that, as engineers, both of them really understood the key business issues of the

---

[18] Ghoshal and Bartlett, *Individualized Corporation*, p. 189.
[19] Ghoshal and Bartlett, *Individualized Corporation*, p. 17.

relays technology and marketplace. Unlike his old bosses, they believed that the power transmission industry was about to enter an era of growth and were willing to invest in that future.

This, together with the unique management culture which encouraged entrepreneurial behaviour, bottom-up–top-down open debate, global knowledge and best practice sharing, allowed a management team which was used to traditional corporate top-down management for decades to excel and to convert themselves into "young" growth managers.

Many people think that, to manage such a turnaround as demonstrated at Coral Springs, requires an overhaul of personnel first. That this assumption is wrong, and that people who spend their careers for 30 years in a traditional hierarchical corporation are able to convert to a totally different and new model, proves that the new organizational model, for which ABB stands, does makes a difference.

The new ABB

ABB was one of the first corporations to come up with a new model for a modern organization and corporate culture. After more than a decade of experience with a matrix organization it was time in 1998 to renew the system. When Percy Barnevik moved to the supervisory board as the chairman and Goran Lindahl took over as the new CEO in 1998, he decided to push ABB even further and to leverage what his predecessor has created and to transform ABB into a new economy company. Lindahl's mission was to transform ABB from a multinational industrial group – which already had created a foundation with its internal organization to manage change, to leverage globally knowledge and best practice and to unleash the entrepreneurial and innovation potential of its employees to a much more agile knowledge-based company able to better compete under new economy conditions. He called this change project Project Alpha which was to focus on five key areas.[20] These are discussed below.

1. The corporate brand name. Goran Lindahl believes that brand names for non-consumer companies are growing more and more in importance. A corporate brand can serve as a symbol of identity, identity for customers, shareholders and employees. The brand can unify all the stakeholders of a

---

[20] Goran Lindahl described his vision of the new ABB in a speech at the CEO/CFO summit meetings held at the World Economic Development Congress, September 22–24, 1999 in Washington, DC. See: www.abb.com

company and is thus a key to the long-term success in today's stakeholder dominant markets. ABB is now moving to become a supplier of smart solutions, moving away from a dependence on heavy assets toward a dependence on intellectual assets – brainpower. A brand will serve to communicate to stakeholders what the company stands for.

2. To develop a clear idea of where ABB wants to be in 10 years. Lindahl believes, that globalization has entered another phase in a world without boundaries, where not only technology and management know-how is shared globally, but also values. This requires expanding ABB's values beyond northern European ethics and values and US business school thinking, to adopt values that motivate the people ABB want to attract from the global talent pool. At the same time the company has to attract not only young people who have mastered the new technologies which are a cornerstone for the future development – like the Internet – but also to find a way to combine their ideas with the experience of older managers, those who know the business inside out, and who know what ABB's customers need. In Lindahl's eyes, ABB needed to become a lighter, faster company less dependent on heavy assets.

3. Lindahl's change program was based on the realization that ABB's core competencies represent intangible assets, assets that can be used to generate value in the future. He put it into the following words: "What ABB does best today can take the company to new strength tomorrow."

4. The project was dedicated to understand the need for change within the company. For the latter, Lindahl undertook a five-month process of surveying top managers and discussing what was wrong with the company. What started as an anonymous critique developed into a rich analysis and learning experience.

5. The final and fifth area is leadership through action. Lindahl says that at ABB management sets and share goals in the organization and let their entrepreneurs find their way.

Since 1998, when Mr. Lindahl took over from Percy Barnevik, ABB has taken a number of actions. ABB's business segments are realigned into six business segments: Automation, Building Technologies, Financial Services, Oil, Gas and Petrochemical, Power Distribution, and Power Transmission. Also, the balance in the management structure, the famous matrix organization, was shifted towards a more global business segment and business area structure. The new slogan was "Think more global and act more local." ABB acquired

Esag Bailey Process Automation to take market leadership in the automation industry. ABB also launched a major value-creation initiative with management focus on value drivers such as volume and margin growth, reduced working capital, and the elimination of non-performing assets. The company evaluates all of its investments to ensure they bring a return that is significantly higher than the average cost of capital in that particular business. Inside the decentralized group, new IT-based tools and shared processes – such as administrative, finance and IT services – are being introduced worldwide to drive deeper efficiency gains and to exploit economies of scale and scope.

Generating value through intangible assets in R&D

But much more important is the new focus especially on value creation from R&D and product innovation. Value-creation principles also drive ABB's research and development. ABB spends worldwide some $2.5 billion a year for R&D, some 8% of its revenues, a high level for this type of industry. The goal is to grow ABB's intangible assets and intellectual capital and leverage it for its customers on a global level. ABB is expanding in businesses where it can combine its knowledge of the markets with its latest technology to provide its customers not simply with a product, or a system, but with greater competitiveness. ABB's executives believe that only by cultivating outstanding ideas, focusing them on the needs of its customers, measuring their impact and protecting them as a source of value creation, can they be sure that ABB will continue to be successful as it grows in what they call the knowledge and service economies of the future. Markus Bayegan, Executive Vice President Group R&D and Technology Member of the Group Executive Committee, writes at ABB's website:

> We make this [large] investment [in R&D] because we believe it is the foundation for our future growth and profitability. Through it we keep our products and systems competitive, develop innovative solutions for our customers and make technological breakthroughs that change the rules of the game in our industry, while creating value for our customers and, ultimately, our shareholders.[21]

Exciting as such breakthroughs are, they can't be planned. Bayegan believes that a company needs to create the kind of environment in which new ideas have room to grow. But management plays a vital role in guiding the thinking

---

[21] For Markus Bayegan's comments, posted in 2001 on the "Technology" section of ABB's website, see: www.abb.com

of researchers, sets ambitious goals, and stimulates people to go for leapfrog innovations. Bayegan's opinion is that it is a must to make funding available for original research or high-risk research that has the potential to produce a high reward. That is the reason, why 20% of ABB's corporate resources are allocated to exploration, experimentation and pre-studies. But other incentives are also key: setting targets that stretch imaginations; understanding the valuable lessons to be learned from making mistakes; and recognizing people with both financial and nonfinancial rewards when they succeed.

Because the global market is changing rapidly, in part because the frontiers of technology are expanding so quickly, ABB believes that successful companies are those that are fast and flexible, that know their customers' markets and needs better than the competition, that focus on building and protecting their intellectual capital so that they can deliver complete business solutions. This is the strategic approach that guides the direction of R&D at the new ABB.

While ABB aims to deliver world-class R&D, the company's ultimate goal is to add value. That, in turn, means that it must be able to measure this value. Its continued attention to value creation through R&D is supported by several measurement systems. Obvious in this regard is the number of patents and invention disclosures. Since January 1999, ABB has looked at the intensity of innovation in its business areas, measured as the proportion of each area's annual sales derived from products developed during the last five years. In addition, return on investment is measured and underlines the significant role R&D plays in creating business for ABB and value for shareholders. ABB claims to have established a systematic approach to creating protected positions within important technology areas which lays the foundations for future growth. And, finally, ABB's entire R&D organization is goal-oriented, resulting in fast-acting R&D teams made up of thousands of dedicated scientists and engineers who make it all happen.

Creating value from intangible assets in the customer base

At the probable dawn of a recession in its core businesses, Jörgen Centerman became ABB's new President and CEO on January 1, 2001. He was continuing with the transformation started by his predecessor Göran Lindahl, by making ABB much more customer-oriented and combining better product innovation and solutions with the customer side to increase customer value.

With this second restructuring of ABB, the company was again the innovator in organization structures in its industry. It was first in its industry to organize itself fully around customers instead of products. ABB was starting to transform[22] its worldwide enterprise around customer groups, aiming to boost growth by helping its customers become more successful in a business environment of accelerating globalization, deregulation, consolidation and eBusiness. This is intended to avoid the problem of various parts of the group trying to sell different products and services to the same client.

ABB replaces its previously product-oriented business segments with four new business segments which are oriented on customer industries: Utilities; Process Industries; Manufacturing and Consumer Industries; and Oil, Gas and Petro-chemicals. Because new technologies continue to be a key driver in the growth of ABB, its R&D organization therefore remains critical. But, in addition, ABB is setting up a new division, New Ventures Ltd., to identify, invest in, to accelerate and to act as an incubator for, the development of new business opportunities.

Jörgen Centerman stated that this new customer-oriented structure, was ABB's response to what he calls the silent revolution in the market that is completely changing the business landscape. He names globalization, deregulation, privatization, industry consolidation, the environment, new technologies, e-business and collaborative commerce as the portents of this revolution, which results in faster changes and increasing complexity. Faced with increasing complexity and speed – much of it driven by the Internet – ABB's customers want clarity and simplicity, Mr Centerman believes. He believes that the Internet has created new opportunities for companies to collaborate with and deliver value to their customers. "Instead of the mass marketing of the past, the Internet allows us to interact with our customers one-on-one and deliver customized information, products and services on a massive scale," he said.[23] He believes that highly flexible mass customization will require common business and management processes worldwide:

> "Common business and management processes are essential in a truly customer-driven enterprise. This will over time provide a single interface between ABB and our customers and free up our people to focus on creating greater value for our customers. This is what our customers request today to capitalize on technology advances and rapidly changing markets in order to be more competitive. This, in turn, will fuel growth for

---

[22] ABB (January 11, 2001) "ABB realigns organization around customers". See: www.abb.com
[23] ABB (January 11, 2001) "ABB realigns organization around customers". See: www.abb.com

> *ABB. At the same time, it creates value for our shareholders and for the communities and countries where we operate.''*[24]

ABB perceives information and knowledge in a fast moving, increasingly globalized world as the new currencies of success. To remain a leader, ABB wants to reduce its dependence on heavy assets and build its combined intellectual wealth – ABBs brainpower. This is named the company's second revolution. ABB should become a lighter, faster, smarter company acting in real time, all the time. ABB's global resources, local market know-how and technology provide the company with a unique platform for building new value. The company aims to work so closely with its customers that it becomes part of their business and they part of ABB's.

Jürgen Dormann who took over the CEO position from Jörgen Centerman in September 2002 during a severe crisis (the company was confronted in the US with huge claims for asbestos-related damages), not only had to face managing this crisis but also continuing with the reorganization started by his predecessor – a dual challenge.

Lessons learned

The main lesson from the ABB case is the importance of the organizational capital and culture for the productivity of a business corporation. Any large organization tends to suppress personal initiative. The organization structure and culture created by Percy Barnevik at ABB has proven that large global organizations can go together with small local entrepreneurship, which is typical for small organizations. The key to this has been the matrix organization, which allows a high degree of decentralization and empowerment of front line managers while keeping some central controls. But it has been also ABB's unique management culture that enabled collaboration and knowledge sharing between those units and that inspired people to connect to ABB's mission in a very personal way.

Another important success factor is the existence of a strategic enterprise management system which is based on a central reporting and planning system (at ABB the ABACUS system). It pulled the different parts of the organization and the different management processes together, provided uniformed fine-grained measurement of all key dimensions of the group and enabled the company to democratize information by making reports available to everyone. The traditional hierarchy of management processes has been turned upside

---

[24] ABB (January 11, 2001) ''ABB realigns organization around customers''. See: www.abb.com

down: the role of front line managers is to serve as primary initiators for entrepreneurial action, the role of middle managers is not to control but to coach and "lubricate" collaboration and knowledge sharing between different front line units, and the role of top management is to define objectives and stretch targets and to constantly challenge and question. Since the merger between Asea and BBC in 1988, the reorganization task at ABB consisted in converting two very traditional industrial companies into one global organization. This latter can serve as a model for what companies will have to do in the new economy both internally and within the broader network of business partners. They have to build a virtual organization which creates at the same time a sense of shared organizational identity for all constituencies and that shares organizational norms that value collaboration.

Only organizations which have gone through an evolution and change process of their internal organization and management structures like ABB, will be able to move on to the next step which is to establish a similar system to manage the extended enterprise which includes the network of partners.

The new ABB, with its latest restructuring, is therefore also an example of how companies are able to leverage created structural and organizational capital to become an externally networked, customer and stakeholder-oriented enterprise, which is able to innovate constantly. It is not by accident that the new ABB emphasizes so much its R&D organization and customer orientation. As we will see in the next case study, customer and market-oriented innovation and fast development of new products has become the cornerstone of value management in the new economy.

From the global corporation to an e-business network

Many companies have been through a dramatic restructuring in the past few years. Through business process re-engineering and standardization, their efforts have created cost efficient structures and synchronized supply chains. Decentralization of responsibility has helped them to make managers and employees more productive and to harness their entrepreneurial potential. Through the implementation of integrated global business processes, tangible and intangible assets can be used and shared globally. But these efforts have tended to be more inward focused on the company itself rather than on markets and customers.

This has become a major problem for today's top managers. The organization in general, and specifically executives and managers, is still more focused on product development, manufacturing, process optimization, margins, working capital and fixed capital improvement – and less on customers, markets and brands. According to a survey of 506 CEOs in the USA, Europe and Japan carried out by the Conference Board,[25] the top management issue for CEOs for the year 2001 was customer loyalty and retention.

Customer relations have become much more important than in the past. Serving customers as a "trusted adviser" is of more value than the production of goods and services. Companies that have strong relationships with customers are often valued more highly on stock markets than companies that focus more on production. CEOs are therefore concerned to re-orient their companies from an inside-out- to an outside-in-focused organization. They want to move away from concentrating on production and sales – "the push principle". Instead, the reverse principle and view is needed: concentration on customer needs and the creation of structures that help to supply customers with products and services as and when needed – the "pull principle".

The change of the enterprise model: from physical asset dominance to customer capital dominance

The prevailing model for business enterprises in the 20th century was to own all those physical assets needed for economic value creation, which was perceived as "production of goods". Managing these assets effectively has called for a tremendous focus of management capacity. Streamlining supply chains, integrating with supplier bases and distribution networks, standardizing and improving business processes, installing related technology, generally improving operative performance and efficiency, trying to achieve scale economies by leveraging assets across a bigger market through, for example, mergers and acquisitions that allowed a reduction in the sum of assets of the new entity, tied up most of managements time and energy.

This production and fixed asset-based focus influenced also the other areas of "corporate capital": human capital. Employees tended to focus on the factors of production rather than on external relationship management with customers and on developing those skills which are not valued in the same way as those related to customer interaction.

In short, the business model for most companies has been based on a concept of the enterprise as a physical asset-based pyramid organized to produce and sell products (see Figure 4.6).

---

[25] Esther Rudis, Melissa A. Berman and Chuck Mitchell (2001) *The CEO Challenge: Top Market-place and Management Issues*, New York: The Conference Board.

During the late 1980s and 1990s initiatives to improve and synchronize the supply chain assumed that there was great advantage in having many of the factors in the supply chain under company control, within its "four walls". Companies used ERP systems which helped them to apply a consistent process model to specific industries. Today, many companies are still working hard to organize their supply chain and install ERP systems and SCM systems to better link with suppliers.

However, a rapid and dramatic revolution is well under way. Some e-business companies, such as Cisco Systems, are proving to be more nimble, and achieving greater capital leverage and much higher share prices than traditional companies. What has happened?

Companies like Cisco relied less and less on an internal base of physical capital and tried to better leverage their financial and human capital by concentrating on customer and solution-oriented core competencies, while outsourcing noncore activities across the supply chain. The traditional concept, based to a large degree on physical assets, was turned upside down. As with the Ford

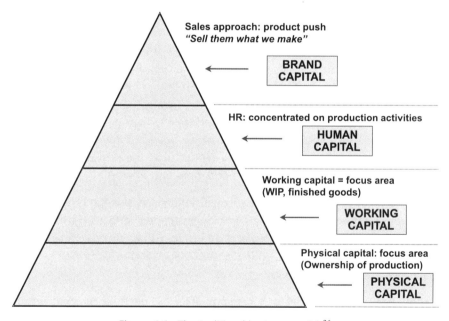

Figure 4.6   The traditional business model.[26]

---

[26] Grady Means and David Schneider (2000) *Meta-Capitalism – The eBusiness Revolution and the Design of 21st-Century Companies and Markets*, New York: John Wiley & Sons, p. 2.

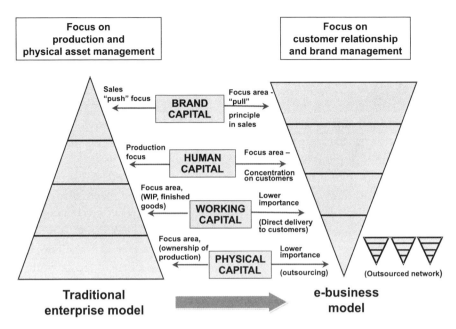

Figure 4.7   The transition to a much nimbler and a more intangibles-based business model.[27]

Motor Company example, companies were shedding physical assets in favour of intangible assets – like customer capital, which "infected" other previously undervalued intangible assets like human capital and R&D and boosted overall corporate value. By focusing human capital more on value-adding customer interaction activities than on internal-oriented production and manufacturing tasks, the value of human capital increases (see Figure 4.7). In addition, with strong customer capital in place, a company can buy new products and technologies from the outside through acquisitions, even at a significant price. This, rather than developing them itself. Such a strategy can boost the overall value of the corporation to levels unseen before, as the case proves.

With this concept, companies are creating customer and brand capital, human capital and financial capital and all at the same time. Cisco systems was one of the innovators in this field and, despite the fact that the company was only 15 years old, Cisco became in late 1999 the third company in history (following General Electric and Microsoft) to burst past the $300 billion mark in market

---

[27] Grady Means and David Schneider (2000) *Meta-Capitalism – The eBusiness Revolution and the Design of 21st-Century Companies and Markets,* New York: John Wiley & Sons, p. 6.

capitalization. What is especially impressive about Cisco is how it has managed to achieve its growth and to dominate the networking industry even in the face of formidable competition. While companies like Microsoft or Intel had the advantage early on of being handed a near monopoly by IBM, Cisco had no such jumpstart.

Cisco did two things that kept it among the leaders of the technology revolution and created that much of intangible assets. First, it outsourced most of manufacturing, distribution, and logistics processes and focused its own activities on customer relationships while linking suppliers and distributors to in-house processes and to its customers through network technology. And, second, it developed a strategy of innovation by acquisition, overcoming the industry's not-invented-here syndrome and allowing the company to ride the wave of technology development that was moving that fast that no one company, no matter how big or inventive, was able to cope with it based solely on internal innovation. For this, Cisco created a networked enterprise model that uses information and network technology to link its key constituents.

Case study: Cisco Systems

Cisco Systems was founded in 1984 by two Stanford University students, Sandra Lerner and Leonard Bosack. Different networks at the university could not exchange information due to different network protocols. Their solution was the invention of the router – a special network device that connects different networks with different network protocols and which has formed the basis for Cisco's business success up until today.

The company is headquartered in Silicon Valley at San Jose California and employs over 38,000 employees worldwide, has 430 sales and support offices in 60 countries, and sells its products in approximately 115 countries.[28] Cisco, in contrast to ABB which has its routes in the traditional industrial sector, was a true technology start-up which developed in the meantime into a mature business and into the world market leader in networking and Internet equipment.

Since shipping its first product in 1986, the company has grown to occupy the No. 1 or No. 2 market share position in virtually every market segment in which it participates. Since becoming a public company in 1990, Cisco's

---

[28] Status as at October 2001. For further information, see: www.cisco.com

annual revenues have increased from $69 million to $22.2 billion (in its fiscal year 2001 which ended end of July 2001). Revenues and profits have increased for 44 consecutive quarters and its highest market capitalization of $485 billion in February 2000 made Cisco the second most valuable company in the world behind Microsoft.

However, Cisco had to admit in February 2001 that it had missed its earning target and in the following quarter it became even worse – as was the case for the entire industry. Despite the actual difficulties Cisco have encountered in meeting the high expectations of the investment community in a declining economy, it is still *the* model for a networked e-business company and it is still, in its market segment, one of the most successful. What made Cisco one of America's greatest success stories?

▶ First, it was the innovation power of the company and its early orientation towards the Internet. When networks became the backbone of corporate information technology, as more and more PCs have been available with their users wishing to connect themselves to other PC users via local area or wide area networks or the Internet, Cisco was able to put itself at the head of the development of innovative networking solutions. Based on the invention of the router by Cisco's founders, the company was able to innovate faster than its peers. This happened in recent years mainly through acquisitions of start-ups and other smaller network solutions providers resulting in Cisco's worldwide market leadership in networking technology for the Internet. Clearly, the invention of the router created an important building block for Cisco's success and for its actual market position after it captured 85% of the market for routers. But this was not the only reason for its innovation success. Cisco continued to innovate after the start-up times through concentration on core competencies, through high levels of R&D spending, and through targeted acquisitions of small innovators, which it integrated successfully into the organization.

▶ Second, Cisco's success was also based on its nearly extreme customer orientation and its specific organizational design. Cisco concentrated on what it can do best: understanding what customers need, to develop the right products and services, and to organize the company and relations to employees, suppliers and other business partners in a way that customers can be served in the best way. Cisco used its intangible assets in R&D, its intangible assets from its know-how in designing organizational structures – that is, its business network of suppliers – and its human capital to deliver value to customers through new technology. To make that happen, Cisco created a networked e-business organization and used information technology to link its employees and the organization itself with its customers and suppliers. Today, Cisco manufactures virtually none of its products, relying on a digitized network of suppliers, who are linked via Cisco directly to its customers and vice versa. Financially, this has led to an increased level of decapitalization, reflected in a lean balance sheet, much leaner than that of Lucent, Nortel, and Alcatel, which are all operating in similar market segments. Whereas Cisco's physical assets and working capital counted in 1999 for only some 3% of its total assets, the same ratio for Alcatel was 15%, for Nortel nearly 30% and for Lucent nearly 50%.[29]

▶ Third, Cisco's success was also based on its extensive use of information technology and Internet applications to increase efficiency and to leverage improved information flows between itself and its key constituents in order to tighten these relationships. By using networked applications over the Internet and its own internal network, Cisco is seeing financial benefits of nearly $1.4 billion a year. This has led at the same time to higher customer, partner and employee satisfaction, to competitive advantages in areas such as customer support, customer order management and delivery times, and to improved internal HR and training processes. Cisco is today the world's largest Internet commerce site, with 90% of its orders transacted over the Web. John Chambers, President and Chief Executive Officer of Cisco Systems says: "Cisco's success and our increased productivity gains are due largely to the implementation of Internet applications to run our business. The ability to harness the power of the Internet to create a New World business model is driving survival and competition in today's fast-paced economy."[30]

At the end of the 1980s Cisco grew fast, from a typical start-up into a mature "real" corporation. As Cisco's founders Lerner and Bosack left the company in 1990, it became clear that Cisco needed to become a more mature organization to sustain its growth rate and keep customers satisfied at the same time. This was the time, when John P. Morgridge was hired, first as the company's president and chief operating officer and later, until 1995 when John Chambers took over, as its CEO. John Morgridge set the tone for the Cisco culture that still exists.

---

[29] Means and Schneider, *Meta-Capitalism*, p. 14.
[30] See http://www.cisco.com/warp/public/779/largeent/why_cisco/john.html

Cisco's management and enterprise culture

Morgridge ran the company on trust and hard-nosed spirit at the same time. The culture he created was a combination of open doors and direct communication, financial discipline, and customer focus. Customer input has had an enormous effect on Cisco's actions.[31] Morgridge was known to say exactly what was on his mind – not only internally but also in negotiations with other CEOs and he was totally against elite executive behaviour.[32] With this philosophy, he was able to strengthen the culture of community at Cisco. Unlike many companies, Cisco's management hasn't rewarded itself at the expense of its staff. More than 40% of the 40 million options granted in 1997 were to employees below the managerial level. One former Cisco engineer estimates that the first 1,500 employees are now millionaires on their Cisco stock alone.[33]

When John Chambers took over from Morgridge in 1995 as the new CEO, it was a smooth transition. Chambers, from his beginnings at Cisco, had been prepared for the task by Morgridge. The new CEO emphasized even more the main drivers for Cisco's future success. Chambers believed in recruiting the best people in industry, making them productive and to be totally customer orientated and to innovate as fast as possible – if necessary through acquisitions.

And for Chambers team play was even more important than it had been for Morgridge. Chambers knew that proper exploitation of intangible assets, which often are based on the quality of relationships, needed team spirit. As a first course of action, he therefore established a compensation system tied to team success. Leaders at Cisco are now compensated – among others – on the quality of the teams they build. ''I learned a long time ago that in team sports or in business, a group working together can always defeat a team of individuals. Even if the individuals, by themselves, are each better than your team. But if you build the best team of people who play well together, then you have a dynasty'', said Chamber.[34]

Teamwork is paramount in an organisation whose size and growth rate demand it. The more decentralized Cisco became (which had been necessary

---

[31] For more details see David Bunnell with Adam Brate (2000) *Making The Cisco Connection: The Story Behind The Real Internet Superpower*, New York: John Wiley & Sons, pp. 22–42.
[32] ibid, p. 25.
[33] Geoff Baum (February 23, 1998) ''Cisco's CEO: John Chambers'', *Forbes ASAP*. See: www.forbes.com/asap/98/0223/052.htm
[34] Bunnell and Brate, *Making the Cisco Connection*, p. 55.

as Cisco grew up – see below), the more any semblance of management depended on empowered individuals working together under the benevolent command of Cisco's corporate leaders. Chambers wanted people who challenged him and his executives. But he was convinced that the mavericks must still work with the rest of the team – and this applies to the Vice Presidents as well as the staff.

To create team spirit at Cisco meant offering workplace conditions whereby employees feel at home and – by the way – spend more time at work. Employees do not need to worry about running errands to the drugstore or the car wash. All material needs are satisfied inside the Cisco campus and buildings in San Jose. They can go to the company cafeteria for breakfast at 7 a.m. and later to have lunch. And all types of goods can be purchased at a shop in one of the buildings at the campus. In each of the buildings employees have several break rooms with free sodas and popcorn at their disposal. The break rooms house dry-cleaning services, for pick-up and return the next day. TimeOut, the Cisco gym, offers Cisco employees the opportunity to use their bodies instead of their minds. For their cars, there are car washes and oil changes. With all these services, Cisco employees can spend as much time doing their job as possible – with the company becoming the new neighbourhood. The Cisco Employee Connection – Cisco's Intranet – helps Cisco employees to waste less time on administrative tasks and on information sharing and collection.

And Cisco has tried to make its managers as invisible as possible so that employees feel like they are in a small, dynamic company. But managers are reachable for every employee in the role of a coach. As Cisco grew, it succeeded in preserving an open atmosphere. Any employee can go into any manager's office, including that of John Chambers, to talk. They define their own objectives to review with their manager, rather than have the manager do it. Cisco wants the employee to take more ownership of their job, learning, and career. And employees are also allowed to establish their own flexible work schedules, or telecommute.

Cisco's obsession with customers

The second important characteristic of the Cisco culture – besides its team spirit, change orientation and productive work conditions - is the obsession with customer focus. In the mid-1980s the company had no professional sales staff or official marketing campaign. Cisco did not purchase its first advertisement until 1992. Until then, Cisco succeeded by word of mouth and contacts over the Internet. In the beginning, it was Cisco's engineers who pioneered the router protocols and serviced the customer and helped them to customize their routers according to their needs – a fact which made the company distinctive. Cisco learned what the marketplace needed by letting customers be partners. They didn't just sell routers; they let customers add code to the router source code – for example, to support another network protocol. Through these various evolutions and adaptations, the multiprotocol router that we use today emerged.

Another element of Cisco's unique customer relationship was, from the very beginning, that the company relied heavily on the Internet. Morgridge made it Cisco's priority to develop an innovative use of technology for customer support. With this, Cisco gained a reputation among potential customers by being a significant Internet presence when it was just being introduced to general users.

While Lerner and Morgridge already had a track record in customer orientation, Chambers went one step further. Every night he checks on what's known within the company as "critical A" accounts – those where a customer's network is unstable because of a failure of some kind. Chambers checks these accounts using voice mail, not email, because it allows him to hear the "emotion" of the sender. Again, perhaps most telling about Cisco's customer focus is the way Cisco's leaders are compensated: in addition to team success, every manager's compensation is directly tied to customer satisfaction. Cisco surveys clients extensively each year, polling them on approximately 60 performance criteria, from product functionality to service quality. If a manager improves his or her score, then a fair amount of cash is involved. But, if the scores go down, Cisco will take money out of the manager's pocket.

But the challenge for Cisco remains that of retaining the necessary speed to innovate fast enough in order to become the leader of the Internet networking market and to remain flexible – an increasingly difficult task in an organization that is getting bigger and bigger. Cisco must be cohesive and team-dependent on the one hand, yet progressive, adaptable, and cutting-edge on the other. Cisco must stay versatile in its technology and must move fast. The two means to reach this goal had been decentralization into entrepreneurial business units and acquisitions.

The muscles of Cisco: the entrepreneurial and acquisitions based innovation process

In 1993, Cisco's market capitalization hit $714 million. To make Cisco a multi-billion-dollar company in the mid-1990s and beyond, Morgridge required a business plan beyond Cisco's initial strategies. The primary goal was to move beyond the router market. And now large customers were showing interest in emerging alternative networking technologies, like switching. Morgridge's team, which included John Chambers, decided to provide a wide array of related products by diversification. This became necessary, because the rise of the Internet was upon the United States and the rest of the world and Cisco wanted to grab as much market share of this networking business as possible. For this, Cisco needed to be innovative and to grow and expand as fast as possible. New companies were sprouting up everywhere on the Internet and all threatened to beat Cisco at the networking game.

Cisco's management team wanted the company to move from a simple horizontal monopoly in routers to the vertical monopoly of providing the Internet's backbone, emulating IBM's success in computing. They recognised that Cisco's 80% router market share would mean little when companies moved to new technologies and that owning the customer was far more important than owning a specific technology. And for this, Cisco had to be able to provide a complete network solution for businesses, including all relevant technologies and products. The company realized that the external pressure to move beyond routers was an opportunity to expand its range of solutions, set standards for an array of networking technologies and to became a clear market leader in the Internet network economy.

In 1993, therefore, Cisco's management defined a business plan which consisted of four areas of focus for future development: provide a complete solution for businesses to be able to strengthen the relationship to customers as "trusted adviser", use acquisitions to add new technologies, define the industry wide networking protocols and set the standard for it, and form the right strategic alliances.

Consequently, Cisco has acquired since 1993 many companies and with that has transformed itself, away from its heavy dependence on routers. The company offers today the broadest range of networking products in the industry. The year 1999 was the first in which revenues from non-router products exceeded 50% of total sales.

Cisco's acquisition strategy

One of the first acquisitions according to the new strategy was that of Crescendo in 1995. A manufacturer of LAN-switches, a technology which was increasingly threatening Cisco's router-based market position because the new technology was cheaper and easier to handle, Crecendo's annual turnover was $10 million. Cisco paid $97 million for Crescendo, a figure that Wall Street analysts described as hopelessly overpriced. However, Cisco went on to gain a $500 million turnover a year later with Crescendo products. In the light of this, Cisco's acquisition of Crescendo was cheap. The analysts had overlooked the fact that the combination of Crescendo technology and Cisco's sales potential (the Cisco customer base) meant that Cisco was able to immediately gain a much higher sales volume than Crescendo would ever have had in the foreseeable future. This is an impressive example of a successful strategy where intangible assets are involved, one that is able to combine different assets to realize an enormous leverage of value.

Over the years, Cisco tried to identify every product its customers needed and then bought the leading company in each product category. Later, when Cisco needed new products for its customers and was not able to develop them fast enough, it bought these new technologies through acquisitions.[35]

From the beginning, Cisco's management understood the concept of "Internet time". It was clear that the only way for Cisco to master the market was to move faster than its competitors. Cisco became identified as the backbone of the World Wide Web. Silicon Valley was sprouting Internet start-ups by the dozen and Cisco needed a strategy to keep up with this pace of innovation hence the strategy of acquisitions.

This strategy was to mark a major shift in Cisco's character. The company was founded by bright technologists who invented something radically unique. But Chambers believed that in order to grow at the pace needed to remain a market leader and to extend the own market position into the Internet area, he would need to buy these ideas and their companies rather than rely on internal research and development. The equation was: if Cisco builds its business on its core competency, the company will be able to increase the value of acquired technologies and products very fast, far beyond the acquisition price, by combining them with its own intangible assets – its customer base and its knowledge about customer needs and how to serve them. Cisco was able to create far more value than by developing these technologies itself,

---

[35] Bunnell and Brate, *Making the Cisco Connection*, pp. 35–36.

because it could concentrate all its management power on the more lucrative activities and competencies: on developing new markets, customer relations and in understanding customer needs.

The challenge, however, was that technology acquisitions are notoriously difficult to pull off and are not always successful. For this there are two main reasons: acquired and existing products and technologies are not necessarily perfectly complementary and may not be compatible, and the larger the acquired company, the more likely the danger that the post-merger integration will fail due to cultural incompatibilities. Cisco solved these problems through two means:

1. Cisco developed Internet Operating System (IOS) that enabled both integration of the new acquired technologies fast into the existing technology platform and delivery of an integrated *one* solution to customers. While different networking technologies emerged, Cisco saw the necessity to develop a unique protocol, which enabled it to integrate, for example, routers and switches into one network solution. The IOS connected different Cisco technologies, such as routers, hubs, switches, PCs and workstation file servers. One of the first things Cisco did with technology from acquisitions, was to add IOS code to the new platform so that it could work with Cisco's existing product line.

2. Cisco developed a structured acquisition process. Following formal criteria, acquisition candidates where carefully evaluated, for example concerning their cultural compatibility. Cisco decided not to continue with the process if its criteria were not met. But once a candidate matched the criteria, Cisco proceeded in three major phases: sell the idea to the CEO of the prospective acquisition candidate; apply Cisco's appraisal process; and, finally, put in place the integration and retention process. In phase one, the Cisco team approaches the CEO in a friendly way, tries to "sell" an acquisition by Cisco and tries to get the CEO to commit personally at least until the end of the integration phase. Hostile takeovers are not considered because of the integration problems they cause. In phase two, the appraisal phase, Cisco's acquisition team perform due diligence by drawing from every major department of Cisco. Not just legal and business issues are examined, but also cultural issues and human resources – issues concerning all its personnel, not just the managers. The mandate is to ensure that Cisco have a chance to retain all the new employees. Another important condition in the appraisal phase is to investigate if a quick win from a shareholder value

perspective is possible with the prospective company having to immediately deliver a positive return. The last phase, once an acquisition is negotiated, is deployment of Cisco's integration team to integrate as fast as possible all important functions of the new company including its IT infrastructure. The goal is to present the acquired company to its customers as part of Cisco as soon as possible, usually within 100 days.

In the datacom industry, leave rate of acquired employees can be as high as 40%. At Cisco, employees were, in fact, less likely to leave after an acquisition than if they had been directly hired. This was important for Cisco, because the primary asset of Cisco's acquisition, beside the technology, was the people who brought in their know-how.

Chambers estimated that Cisco paid between $500,000 and $2 million per employee in an acquisition.[36] If Cisco could not keep those people, the company would have made a terrible investment. So, during the integration process, Cisco focused first on retaining the acquired employees and integrating them quickly and thoroughly and second on how to drive the business.

The structure and nervous system of Cisco: an IT/Internet enabled partner network

Another important principle of Cisco's organisational design is extensive partnering and networking with other businesses. In developing their 1993 strategy, to expand the business beyond the router and to grow the company fast, Cisco's management team realized, that partnerships with other companies were not only desirable but inevitable. Cisco started to create alliances in sales and marketing, product development and manufacturing – the last with the intention of outsourcing all manufacturing activities to partners. In order to be able to outsource important parts of its value chain to partners, and to be able to act at the same time still as one *single* enterprise towards its customers, significant investments in the company's organizational capital and in IT-based systems became necessary. These were able to link all partners in real time, in the areas of:

▶ Customer relationship management: In order to provide customers with better services and to optimise at the same time its own resources, Cisco

---

[36] Glenn Rifkin (1997) "Growth by acquisition – the case of Cisco Systems". For more on this interview with John Chambers, one of a series of case studies published by Booz-Allen & Hamilton, see: www.strategy-business.com/thoughleaders/97209/page2.html, p. 7 (interview with John Chambers).

based its customer interactions on network technology and on the Internet. It invested massively in a web-based customer portal, Cisco Connection Online (CCO). This enables customers not only to configure correctly network equipment online, but also to get immediately a price for the configuration, complete the whole ordering transaction online and to monitor the status of the order management process at any time. In addition, customers are able to access product information, obtain information about tips and tricks for handling problems, and can download software updates.[37]

▶   Supply chain management and supplier relationship management. A web-based supplier portal, Manufacturing Connection Online (MCO), links Cisco's business processes directly to those of its suppliers. Through this network, customer orders are electronically transferred directly to the supplier's production planning systems after the customers have completed the ordering transaction at CCO. Also, distributors who deliver ordered products directly from the supplier to the customer are linked into the MCO network.[38]

▶   Employee productivity. Sales people at Cisco are able to access the same information about the status of customer orders through their own web portal. As a consequence, the communication between sales staff at Cisco and the customer is no longer dominated by order processing, but by more value-adding consulting aspects. In addition, a web-based employee portal, Cisco Employee Connection (CEC), greatly facilitated administrative tasks. Employees can, for example, book their own business trips, report PC problems, or settle their travel expenses. Managers can call up reports for decision making at any time and so on.

An e-business system to support the "virtual corporation"

Cisco's philosophy of a global networked enterprise that strategically uses information and communication to build a network of strong, interactive relationships with all its key constituencies (prospects, customers, partners, suppliers, and employees) required it to invest in a flexible information system infrastructure. The result is a system scalable and easier to deploy –

---

[37] Bunnell and Brate, *Making the Cisco Connection*, pp. 138–141.
[38] John Flower (March, 1997) "The Cisco Mantra", *Wired*. See: www.wired.com/archive/5.03/ ff_cisco_pr.html

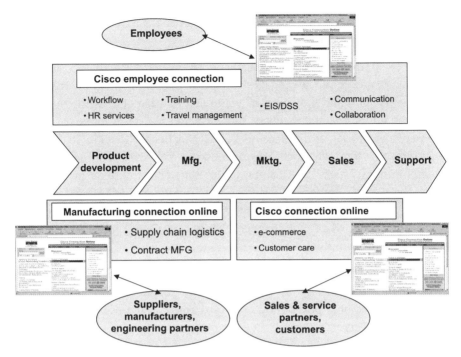

Figure 4.8 Cisco's e-business system with its three strategic solutions CCO, MCO and CEC.

for example, into new companies that either become a business partner or part of the Cisco organization through acquisition.

By using networked applications over the Internet and its own internal network, Cisco is seeing financial benefits of nearly $1.4 billion a year. Cisco became famous for its advanced use of IT and its extensive e-business system that supports three major relationships to stakeholders (see Figure 4.8).

▶   Cisco Connection Online (CCO) – an CRM portal to support interaction with customers.

▶   The Intranet for employees (Cisco Employee Connection – CEC) – an employee portal to facilitate communication between employees and to support them in administrative tasks and that delivers timely information to managers via and Executive Information and Decision Support System.

▶   Cisco's Manufacturing Connection Online (MCO) – a supply chain portal to support "virtual manufacturing" linking customers directly with out-sourced manufacturing at suppliers.

The strategic enterprise management process at Cisco

When Cisco changed strategy in 1993, attempting to achieve market dominance in the networking industry as Microsoft did with PCs and IBM with mainframes, it put a premium on speed as well as on growth. Having made the decision that the company was going to attempt to shape the future of the entire industry, the company looked at the market in Internet years, as opposed to calendar years. Because things had been changing so fast with regard to the Internet, each regular business calendar year equals seven Internet business years – as Chambers once stated.[39] So instead of looking at a one-year plan, Cisco began looking at every quarter and adjusting its plan up or down. At the same time the management team also began to think a couple of years out about what could happen. Before that, Cisco's management team never thought beyond a year.

So Cisco equipped itself to reach its ambitious goals by defining a clear strategy and strategic goals and by fast and anticipatory adaptation to changes in the market. This was only possible by making strategic enterprise management a continuous process:

► The management team began to evaluate company performance from a strategic point of view each quarter instead of once a year and checked whether actual performance is in line with plans and strategic targets. Accordingly, the company changed its plans up or down and readjusted resource allocation.

► Regularly the management team looked out several years ahead in a kind of scenario technique to evaluate where the market was probably heading and what the company's future position should be.

By linking these two processes together Cisco was able to achieve its goals in a highly dynamic and extremely competitive market environment.

An important piece of Cisco's strategic management system was the use of market segmentation, a philosophy based on what management had learned from Hewlett-Packard combined with the GE strategy of being either No. 1 or No. 2 player in each segment. Cisco divide the market into four segments and draw a matrix with the four segments on one axis and product, services and distribution on the other axis (see Figure 4.9). For each of the four segments they define market share objectives. They then determine the product, services and distribution needs for each segment – how these are developed, manu-

---

[39] Rifkin (1997) p. 5.

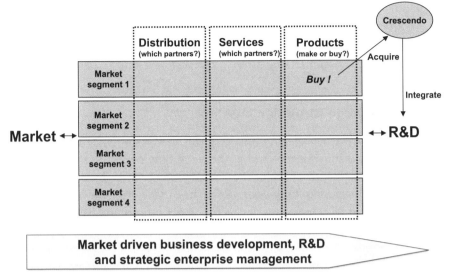

Figure 4.9 Cisco's strategic matrix at the basis for its strategic management and innovation process.

factured, sold, distributed and serviced – whether internally or through partnerships or acquisitions.

Using this approach Cisco was able to link a market-oriented strategic business development approach with more technologically-oriented product development. This enabled Cisco to drive product development from the market. And this outside-in bridging of usually two separated processes in R&D intensive firms helped, again, to concentrate forces and resources in R&D on the most critical areas and allowed Cisco to thrive on the Internet wave and grow faster than the market.

The challenge was to move fast enough. The management team saw that some smaller competitors were growing even faster than Cisco. They realized that they had to have some way to have the advantage of a big company while acting like a small company from a product development point of view. At that point Cisco's management team decided to break the company into business units for development while retaining big-company influence by leveraging the company's strength in manufacturing, distribution, and finance across the entire company. With that structure in place, the company was able to leverage intellectual assets in development in a way that is impossible for a smaller company. No smaller company would to go from $10 million to $500 million revenues in 18 months – what Cisco did with Crescendo after the acquisition. Smaller companies cannot scale in that way. They do not have the organizational infrastructure in place nor the resources that allows them to scale R&D capital in the manner of Cisco, with its distribution, financial and manufacturing strength extended and "boosted" by Cisco's partner network.

Cisco: advantage through e-business

Compared with its rivals in the multiprotocol networking systems equipment industry, Cisco is much leaner and at the same time generates more value for its shareholders. In an industry traditionally dominated by large, capital-intensive manufacturing businesses, Cisco has made its mark by being the first company to leverage e-business across the entire value chain. It was also among the first to demonstrate that e-business is more than selling products over the Internet. The company used the whole potential of the new technology for streamlining operations, building relationships with business partners to reduce costs, speeding innovation, providing improved service, and increasing customer satisfaction.

At the base of its success was its decision to adopt the model of an outside-in company, driven by the customer relationship and by brand-building rather than by the traditional role of an equipment manufacturer. And the company outsourced manufacturing in such an efficient way hardly seen before: Cisco linked suppliers and distributors closely to in-house processes using extensive network technology. As a result, Cisco pays 30% less than it would cost to assemble the products itself and is providing customers with improved service levels and faster delivery.

In creating an ecosystem that ties together chip manufacturers, electronic manufacturing services, component distributors, logistics partners, Cisco employees, and customers into a single information system, Cisco enables business partners to manage and operate major portions of the supply chain. Manufacturers act like adjunct Cisco manufacturing sites and the entire supply chain works off the same demand signal; any change in one node of the chain is immediately transferred throughout the chain. Cisco's supply chain initiatives have eliminated inefficiencies typical of traditional outsourcing, such as paperwork duplication and other labor redundancies that would have burdened both Cisco and its suppliers. This also generated benefits for Cisco's partners.

By managing all financial transactions for the exchange of goods through its enterprise system, Cisco has generated cost savings for its business partners and freed them from low value-added administrative tasks. With its global networked business, Cisco has not only created additional value for itself, but also for its business partners, tying them even closer into the Cisco ecosystem.

However, most value has been created by enabling unprecedented levels of customer service. It helps Cisco to achieve its main goal which is to build customer capital. Cisco's corporate culture emphasizes relationship building, speed, flexibility, and innovation – all key ingredients for Cisco's success. The openness and transparency embedded in Cisco's culture encourages Cisco people to share knowledge internally in order to build intellectual assets. It also inspires the company to team up with outsiders to acquire and retain intellectual capital – either in working closely together with customers, business partners and technology start-ups, or by smoothly integrating employees from acquired companies.

What really stands out is the rate at which Cisco has been building intellectual capital by acquisitions. Since its first acquisition in 1993, Cisco has acquired over 50 companies, averaging between seven and nine acquisitions per year. And even if Cisco, competing with other interested companies, was forced to pay a considerable price for an acquisition which exceeded the price based on traditional valuations of such companies, it was cheap in the end as it paid with the high-value currency of its existing customer base and its big marketing and distribution power. Cisco developed not only an intangibles based value creation strategy based on customer capital creation, but also developed the appropriate organizational structures, processes and the culture to make it happen.

Lessons learned

While ABB used its organizational design, culture, processes and structures to optimize productivity *within* the global company by stimulating entrepreneurship and facilitating exchange of knowledge and best practice across countries, Cisco went further and looked also at relations with external parties to create additional value and to support its intangibles-based strategy.

Whereas, for ABB, the big step was to become a global player and leverage its tangible and intangible assets on a global scale while still keeping an entrepreneurial spirit typical of smaller firms, for Cisco this was only the foundation to extend its reach and to optimize and manage the company from an outside-in approach – that is, to drive everything from the customer side. ABB is changing again with its reorganization announced in January 2001. The product-based business unit structure is becoming a customer segment-based business unit structure like that of Cisco. The key lesson in the Cisco case is that the customer relationship counts most in an industry characterized by complex products and fast innovation. It can serve as the cornerstone in an intangible assets based strategy to grow and create value for shareholders and all other stakeholders.

But the quality and intensity of the relationships a company maintains with its other constituencies like suppliers, distributors and employees is also important. If these relationships do not function well, the business processes which are based on them will also not work and the enterprise will not be able to satisfy customer needs through an outsourcing model. With the increasing need for companies to concentrate their forces on their core competencies and to outsource other activities to partners, the quality of the relationships to other stakeholders is of the same importance for success as choosing the right products and solutions for customers.

Cisco has shown that value creation from intangible assets can yield much higher returns, and can generate much more shareholder and stakeholder value, than the traditional manufacturing and tangible assets based model. But companies intending to take the same route have to stick to some important rules:

▶   They have to decide what their company can do best and how to create economic value by concentrating on its core competencies – they have to focus on the product or service they want to offer.

▶   They have to define a clear strategy on how to grow and how to target that market segment and what their exact objectives are. They have to decide on which upcoming customer needs they can second-guess and which not.

▶   They have to outsource other activities to business partners but still integrate them tightly into their ecosystem through well-designed collaborative business processes. The whole structure must be able to act as a single enterprise towards customers.

▶   They have to use advanced information and network technology to make the company more productive. Not only internally, but also in collaborative business processes with partners and customers, thus avoiding inefficiencies usual to outsourcing models.

▶   They have to define a clear strategy on how to make employees both individually and in teams more productive, because employees represent a company's most important resource to create value from customer relations and innovation.

▶   They have to maintain a unique relationship with customers and, for example, have to treat customers as partners and to let them influence product design, as Cisco has done. If this is not possible because the company does not sell directly to end customers, it has to focus on creating a strong corporate brand.

▶   They have to manage innovation as an outside-in process driven by customer needs. In this process "buy options" have to be taken into consideration as well. If the company has decided for an acquisition strategy it has to make sure through a structured approach that it is able to integrate acquired employees and technologies fast.

Virtual marketplaces and private exchanges

Cisco created a network that exclusively optimizes the relationships and processes between itself and its outsourcing partners. But when outsourcing of formerly internally provided services and operations is becoming a more common model, it will be of advantage for an enterprise to share outsourced services with other enterprises or ecosystems in order to benefit from even scale economies and cost savings in areas which are not regarded as core activities.

When more and more companies are moving to network-based structures, the logical next steps in the evolution of organizational models may therefore be the broader adoption of electronic marketplaces. Outsourcing of formerly internally provided services and of entire business processes is becoming a more common model as companies are concentrating on core competencies and are decapitalizing their traditional business models. Outsourcing is nothing new. But what is new is the level of performance that can be expected, if the outsourcing model is based on extensive use of information and network technology. As the outsourcing service provider is concentrating on its core competencies, it is also creating additional value. In addition, it is honing its business processes and human capital in the field of the services it is providing – building intangible assets. And, because it is managed, in contrast to an internal shared service unit, as an own business, it is setting free new market dynamics and redefining some important business rules.

With such e-business outsourcing models, a significant part or perhaps all of the supply chain may be outsourced. The remaining functions in the enterprise may be just product development, customer relationship management and general management. A company may decide to transfer many of its internal support functions, such as financial accounting, human resources administration, and maintenance, repair and operations procurement into outsourced networks. Some companies may also elect to outsource IT processes, legal counsel, and elements of marketing and sales, if management regards these functions as noncore to customer management or to the strategic growth drivers of the enterprise.

The new Internet and networked-based technologies, like electronic marketplaces, are playing an important role in such scenarios. Well-organized e-business networks of companies and their suppliers and service providers, tied together by orderly process models and technology, will offer ongoing optimization that easily exceeds the performance levels the company achieved through wholly-owned resources.

It is possible that B2B-marketplaces and Internet-based trading communities might become the great enablers of e-business. They may play a similar role in optimizing business processes within a network of businesses; that is, within an ecosystem of several companies, like the role ERP systems played in the 1990s in optimizing business processes within individual companies. Electronic markets bundle products and services of suppliers for buyers and vice versa, providing added value for both of them.

By providing a central platform for transaction automation, information aggregation, improved market liquidity, and extended market reach, the electronic marketplace can reduce the costs of product, process, and sales and more effectively leverage the financial and human resources of the participating companies.

Electronic markets form along two primary dimensions. They address either industry-specific processes or cross-industry functional processes. The former (vertical e-markets) are organized by specific industries to resolve specific supply chain inefficiencies that lower margins. The latter (horizontal e-markets) cut across industries to automate functional processes such as financial accounting, IT, generic supply chain processes, procurement, and human resource services. So-called meta e-markets combine different horizontal and/or vertical e-markets for and integrated offering to customers. Private exchanges are internal marketplaces that provide collaboration internally within a group of companies and represent their trading interface to both suppliers and customers.

A vertical e-market for the automotive industry: Covisint

Covisint is one of the most well-known electronic marketplaces. Founded by General Motors, Ford, and DaimlerChrysler in March 2000, Covisint (Cooperation, Vision and Integration) is a kind of purchasing community. The French PSA-Group (Peugeot and Citroen) and Renault as well as Nissan have joined in as well. The software vendors Oracle and Commerce One, where SAP holds a minority investment, are also investors. But as CEO Kevin English has said, Covisint is more than just a purchasing aid. It was created to make the entire automotive value creation process from the first screw to the final product more efficient and faster. "Today you still have to wait months for your new Mercedes-Benz. We will make it possible, that this will happen in the future in only two to three weeks."[40] Manufacturers will be linked to suppliers over the Internet and the market will become more transparent, decisions can be taken more quickly when it is clear if, and at which point in time, how many units of a specific item can be obtained from which supplier. More than 4,600 companies are registered at Covisint. Ford's online exchange "AutoXchange" and General Motor's online exchange "TradeXchange" will be folded into Covisint. Despite the huge initial investments, Covisint is expected to reach profitability in 2002.

Even more interesting than the size of Covisint are the benefits it plans to provide to its members. According to Ford research, it costs roughly $150 to process the paperwork involved in a single purchase order; the same transaction online costs only $5 to $15. So Covisint is expected to cut the total cost per car by at least 10%. The Automotive Consulting Group Jupiter Media Metrix estimates that participating carmakers and suppliers could save $174 billion in 2005 through Covisint, which would represent a cost saving of roughly $3,000 per vehicle.[41] First experiences are demonstrating that it is possible to save up to 17% in purchasing costs through Covisint.[42]

The Covisint project, which represents de facto a cooperation between competitors, will have consequences far beyond the car industry. It is seen as a major test for a cooperation between enterprises that are competitors on the sales and marketing side. It is viewed as a model of how e-markets can increase the efficiency of B2B relations and can generate more value. If the experiment

---

[40] "Covisint sieht sich auf der Erfolgsspur" (December 17, 2001) *Frankfurter Allgemeine Zeitung.*
[41] Racheh Konrad (November 15, 2000) "Head-on collision – old and new economies clash in auto industry marketplace". See: www.news.cnet.com/news/0-1007-201-3412381-0.html
[42] (December 17, 2001) *Frankfurter Allgemeine Zeitung.*

succeeds, electronic marketplaces might become a central element of the new B2B-economy.

The future of e-markets

Many companies are actually working to better link themselves with suppliers and customers and to outsource noncore tasks to service providers. In doing this, e-business models provide unique advantages in cost savings, efficiency gains and tighter relationships with business partners, but the greatest technical challenge is to make real inter-enterprise integration happen.

Now that hype about electronic markets, meta e-markets and the like is less intense, most companies are, as a first step, concentrating on improving internal processes using e-business scenarios to link themselves with their suppliers more readily. This creates the basis for participating in a second or third step in e-markets. Most likely is, after a first "testing phase" of one-to-one e-integration of some selected internal processes with those of business partners, that companies will start to create a private exchange that serves as the e-business integration hub for all internal transactions and as the gateway to suppliers and customers and later to e-markets.

This process of "setting up the infrastructure" for the e-business network will take a few years for most companies. It will yield, beside the strategic benefits of a better integrated ecosystem and improved customer services, significant cost savings of up to 30% of overall cost, according to the estimation of experts. But it is not just to establish the e-business network via a web browser. Most important is the quality of integration of the underlying transaction systems on the back end between business partners. As soon as this has been finished in a critical mass of companies, the time of e-markets will have arrived. But no matter how quickly these new concepts develop on a broader scale, the message is clear: in the new economy, the network will be the business.

Basic rules for building organizational capital

Taking the experiences from the ABB and Cisco case studies, six major rules can be defined. These are the rules that companies should stick to when they want to build successful organizational structures and processes to cope with the challenges of a more intangibles-based new economy.

1. There is no one way to do it right! Be creative and design a organization that fits to your company's culture, to its business, and its strategy.

2. Start with your theory of business and strategy first, that is with the definition of core competencies and market targets, and design the organization accordingly.

3. No organizational design is the right one forever. Be prepared that the organization has to be adapted to changes of your business strategy reflecting the changes in your market. Your organization needs to be enabled for constant change management.

4. Your organizational design has to support and stimulate creation of explicit knowledge and intangible assets in the form of rules, processes, descriptions and best practice.

5. Your organization also has to make employees individually more productive and motivate them to take over more responsibility in an entrepreneurial style. Your organization has to facilitate constant information flow between all management levels and enterprise areas and has to offer a fast access to common and process specific knowledge for individuals to ensure the necessary coherence in the company.

6. The most important part of your organizational capital are not processes, IT or structures and also not even individual people. It is your unique corporate culture that facilitates productive interactions between people – employees, customers and business partners. Social dynamics are the key to human capital and business relationship productivity and will gain even more importance in the future. Design an organization that supports your culture. To create a new culture is much harder and takes much longer than to create a new organizational design.

Part 3
New Management

5 New Value Drivers Require a New Management Approach

Twenty years ago we had the tools that were needed to manage strategy based on tangible assets. The management toolbox was filled with financial tools that were designed to manage tangible things. Now we have a different world. Strategy and value is being created from intangible assets. We need a new toolbox for management. Organizations understand strategy and how to compete in the new economy. But they do not have the management tools that allow them to do this. As a result we find that 7 out of 10 organizations fail to execute their strategy.

David P. Norton[1]

Globalization, emerging new technologies, and the deregulation of key industries resulted in severe competitive pressures which forced companies to restructure themselves in a fundamental and far-reaching manner. Therefore companies have invested significantly in organizational capital in two major phases (see Part 2).

In the first phase, companies tried to develop organizational structures to help them to leverage and exploit economies of scale of knowledge-based assets. The latter include business process best practice, expert know-how, R&D investments and also procurement capabilities and physical assets such as production facilities, on a global level (see the ABB case study in Part 2).

When value was created increasingly through new product development and through the creation of sustainable customer relations and when production activities, intensive in physical assets, became commoditized and failed to provide a sustained competitive advantage, companies responded in a second phase by de-verticalizing (see p. 140) and de-capitalizing themselves. They started to outsource activities that do not provide significant competitive advantages, and concentrated on the more lucrative customer dimension; that is, on customer relations (see the Cisco case study in Part 2). The focus was now to create structures that help to leverage better human capital and relationships with business partners. These create more productive collaborative business processes, such as in the area of supply chain management which

---

[1] David P. Norton is co-creator of the Balanced Scorecard concept. For more information, see the author's interview with him later in this chapter.

should help to create customer value, gain new competitive advantages and reduce costs at the same time. Actually, we are at the beginning of this second phase, where most companies have just started to invest in new organizational structures and related e-business infrastructures.

But organizational innovation was not the only area of intangible investments in the last two decades. A second important area of investments in intangibles was product innovation and R&D. A clear indicator is that from 1980 to 1999 the absolute number of professional creative workers in the USA has more than doubled, from 3.7 million to 7.6 million.[2] Therefore, at least as important as organizational innovation was product innovation.

A survey conducted by PricewaterhouseCoopers among more than 800 CEOs and board directors in the UK, France, Germany, Spain, Australia, Japan and the USA revealed that companies that generate 80% of their revenue from new products have typically doubled their market capitalization in a five-year period. High-performing companies – that is, those which generate annual total share-holder return in excess of 37% and which have seen consistent revenue growth over the last five years – average 61% of their turnover from new products and services. For low performers only 26% of turnover comes from new products and services.[3] And innovation provides returns far above average costs of capital. According to a study of the after tax profits of biotech and software companies[4] that depend on innovation-related knowledge assets almost to the exclusion of any others, the return on equity of these companies – and that means the return on intangibles – was 50% larger than return on physical assets and more than 130% larger than return on financial assets. The study presents a direct comparison between returns in traditional investments (in securities and physical assets like production facilities) and the returns of innovation capital or intangible assets as follows.

▶ *Financial assets*
   Ten-year average return on U.S. Treasury bonds: 4.5%

▶ *Physical assets*
   Average ROE for all companies with physical assets and inventories: 7.0%

---

[2] Leonard Nakamura (July, 2000) "Economics and the new economy: The invisible hand meets creative destruction", *Federal Bank of Philadelphia Business Review*, p. 17.
[3] Frank Milton and Trevor Davis (February, 2000) "Innovation and growth: Thriving beyond 2000". See:
www.pwcglobal.com/Extweb/industry.nsf/docid/C80F5245FE5866B38525 6A1F 001AE541
[4] The study was conducted by Baruch Lev and was mentioned in Thomas A. Stewart (April 16, 2001) "Accounting Gets Radical", *Fortune*.

▶   *Intangible assets*
    Average expected return on equity for biotech and software
    industries: 10.5%

The value creation potential of innovation-related investments in intangible assets can be even greater. Looking at 83 companies over a span of 25 years another study[5] revealed that their R&D investments returned 17% after tax return, whereas investments in fixed assets earned just 7% after tax, a rate which nearly equals the cost of capital of chemical companies today.

Investments into intangible assets such as in R&D and in organizational capital – for example, in IT-based applications that help to improve the quality of relations to business partners and customers – have evolved into the role of the major value driver of businesses in developed economies. So the urgency for systematic innovation management is on the agenda of every corporate executive today. But investing more in product innovation and in IT alone will not be enough in the future.

Successful growth will come from those businesses that harness all of their capabilities and people in the pursuit of future market needs. Companies are leaving behind a period in which new ideas were associated exclusively with individuals (such as the invention of electricity and the telephone), or with specialist functional departments (R&D or marketing). Now *all* levels of management and employees have to be involved in corporate innovation processes, including the most important external stakeholders of the corporation.

Innovation as the key driver for value creation of today has to happen on the operational level, where companies have to deal on a day-to-day basis with customers and other business partners – for example, through new processes and structures. It has to happen on the product and market development level, where new technology is discovered, new products developed and commercialized. And, finally, it has to happen on the strategic level, where companies define how they will invest to create value in the future and where they decide how they will combine different intangible assets to create growth – like by combining a new organizational design with an innovative new product which is either homegrown or acquired. All these innovation activities on these

---

[5] David Aboody and Baruch Lev (March, 2001) "R&D Productivity in the Chemical Industry".
See: www.stern.nyn.edu/~blev/chemical-industry.doc

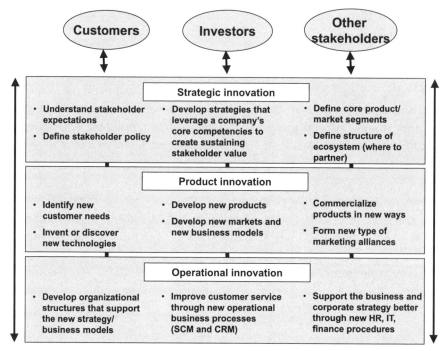

Figure 5.1   The company as an innovation system.

various levels have to be interlinked so that companies are able to renew themselves fast and successfully as a whole (see Figure 5.1).

This requires a new type of management system which guides the overall organization to constant innovation in all areas and on all levels but with a common focus in order to drive profitability and value generation. It has to help companies to measure effectiveness of enterprise activities, their efficiency, and business success under the conditions of the new economy. It also has to help them to better organize management processes and to improve external reporting and communication with the most important stakeholders, in order to be able to achieve optimized results in the new stakeholder-dominated environment of today.

In the near future, companies will start to invest massively in new management systems and in so-called corporate performance management systems. Many questions concerning a general concept for these systems are still left open, despite the fact that several new promising approaches have emerged as a result of academic research, consulting practice and from some leading companies all of which can be used as building blocks for the new system.

In this part of the book I provide readers with a conceptual framework for a new management system better suited to manage enterprises in the more on intangible assets-based new economy than traditional management tools. The goal is to provide a comprehensive overview of the new system, the relation to each other of its elements, and about the corresponding management concepts. But it is not intended that this is a final solution. The intention is to inspire managers, controllers, consultants, and others, to conceive the appropriate management system for their companies, or for those of their clients, required for success in the future. It is not the end but the start of a journey that will take many organizations and companies in the next couple of years into a new management world, with improved instruments and methods for successful corporate performance management.

The efforts and investments companies make to develop and implement such new management systems and tools could generate the next, and bigger, wave of productivity improvements. When companies act in a more forward looking way, when they are able to better estimate the consequences of risks and opportunities, and when they make better use of their real value drivers, they will be able to significantly improve their performance and their returns. The organizational operational renewals described in Part 2 form the foundation for this next step. They represent an essential basis for the new management system – from an organizational as well as from an IT perspective: they deliver the necessary flexible structures and processes, which enable companies to master the new value creation activities in the area of product innovation and relationship building with business partners and which can be managed and controlled with the management approach described in the following chapters. The corresponding operative information systems provide, as a kind of by-product, data and information required for the new management system as raw material. A well-organized, e-business system is therefore a good basis for the new management system.

Most companies will finish with the first phase of major investments in new organizational structures and processes within the near future. So it is time now to start with the implementation of the missing counterpart: with the conception and implementation of a new management system. But before we start to investigate the new management system further, we shall listen to one of the major experts and innovators in the area of the new strategic management system, David P. Norton, co-creator of the Balanced Scorecard concept.

Interview with David P. Norton

Harvard Professor Robert S. Kaplan and management consultant David P. Norton first introduced the "Balanced Scorecard" concept in 1992 with an article in the *Harvard Business Review* – presenting a management system which does not only rely on financial information but also on nonfinancial key performance indicators (KPIs).

Kaplan and Norton's system is based on extensive research into successfully managed companies. Their research revealed that these companies had developed a systematic approach to managing customer satisfaction, internal processes, innovation, and learning as well as financial performance in a balanced way. Therefore, they proposed to structure KPIs into four so-called "perspectives": financial, customer/market, internal, and innovation and learning. In the following years, the "Balanced Scorecard" evolved into one of the most successful management concepts ever attracting interest from corporate executives worldwide. Some 50% of major US companies have either already implemented a Balanced Scorecard-based management system or are about to do so.

Kaplan and Norton described their 1992 approach in more detail in 1996, when their first book was published.[6] Later, in 2000, they published an extended version of the Balanced Scorecard concept describing it as a strategy management system rather than a measurement system. They introduced a new approach that makes strategy a continuous process owned not just by top management but by everyone.[7]

David Norton is a co-founder and president of Balanced Scorecard Collaborative,[8] a professional service firm that facilitates the worldwide awareness, use, enhancement, and integrity of the Balanced Scorecard.

This interview was conducted with David Norton in February, 2001. I met David for the first time about two years before. At that time we worked together on a white paper that described a concept for such a new management system and how an integrated analytical software application can support it.[9]

---

[6] Robert S. Kaplan and David P. Norton (1996) *The Balanced Scorecard. Translating Strategy into Action*, Boston: Harvard Business School Press.
[7] Robert S. Kaplan and David P. Norton (2000) *The Strategy-Focused Organization*, Boston: Harvard Business School Press.
[8] See: www.bscol.com
[9] The white paper was for SAP's Strategic Enterprise Management solution for which, as its product manager, I was responsible at that time.

Juergen Daum: David, many people still think that the Balanced Scorecard is a measurement system. As *The Strategy-Focused Organization* states, obviously it is a strategy which is the focus of the new management system, which you call the Balanced Scorecard. But why has strategy become so important in today's more intangible-based economy?

David Norton: Strategy has always been important. But what is different is the rate of change in today's new economy. It's the fundamental changes that are important: the emergence of the knowledge economy and the knowledge worker. In the old world, strategy was based on using tangible assets, in industries such as steel, automobile, and manufacturing. Intangible assets such as the knowledge of your people, computer systems and software, your work processes, and the culture that allows you to innovate are driving the way in which value is being created in the new economy. These are all things that are all very difficult to put financial terms to. But these are the differences between success and failure today. 20 years ago we had the tools that were needed to manage strategy based on tangible assets. The management toolbox was filled with financial tools that were designed to manage tangible things. Now we have a different world. Strategy and value is being created from intangible assets. We need a new toolbox for management. Organizations understand strategy and how to compete in the new economy. But they do not have the management tools that allow them to do this. As a result we find that 7 out of 10 organizations fail to execute their strategy.

Juergen Daum: I remember something that you said at a conference, that one of the major differences between a tangible and more intangible-based business is that intangibles are more difficult to manage because they represent more a potential value than a value in itself. Therefore, companies need a strategic management system not only to react fast to changes on the market side in a structured way, but also to better focus and coordinate their internal activities, which are using these intangible assets to create tangible value. I also remember you saying that strategy is an organization's unique way, how it creates value.

David Norton: Yes, exactly. That's what strategy is. Strategy is the way that an organization creates value for its shareholders or for its stakeholders. If you are a private company, your goal is to create long-term financial value for your shareholders. If you are a hospital your goal is to create long-term good health for your patients. This is the measure of value. Your strategy then is how you create that value. The fundamental difference in this new economy is that there is not a direct one-to-one relationship between an intangible asset, like the knowledge of a worker, and a financial outcome. I cannot show that if I send my workers to training programs for a month, that sales will go up or costs will go down. Instead I have to make the case that training will improve something like quality, and if quality will improve, customer confidence will improve, and if customer confidence improves, then they will buy more. It's like a four-step logic, between training a person and getting a result. The nature of an intangible asset is that you have to describe the steps that are involved in the value creation. And that's what strategy is.

The other thing that's different in the new economy is that you cannot isolate the value of a single intangible asset like knowledge. How you create value is like a recipe. You have to put together several ingredients. Training your people is only one ingredient. You also have to give them computer systems. You have to give them incentives. You have to give them leadership. There are several assets that you have to combine, in order to get a result. It's impossible for a financial system to describe this process of value creation. Financial systems are always snapshots: they can't describe a time-based logic of cause and effect. Financial systems are always singular. They look at labor as one category, inventory as another. They can't integrate different kinds of assets into what I would call a strategic recipe. That's why you need something different. That's why the Balanced Scorecard has become so popular with organizations.

Juergen Daum: Let's come back to the title of the book. It not only says "strategy" but that the entire organization has to be strategy-focused. What are the major principles of such a strategy-focused organization?

David Norton: The basic idea starts with the word "focused". Every performance management system has a point of focus. Typically that point of focus is financial performance. Everything in the organization then gets tied to this point of focus. If it's the budget, everybody works on short-term financial goals so they live within the budget of that year. Some organizations introduce quality programs and become quality-focused. What we have learned from working with organizations, is, if you want to execute your strategy, then you have to put the strategy at the centre of your management system. You have to get everything tied to the strategy. That means, when you educate people about what the organization does, you should educate them about the strategy. When you set up compensation and incentives, they should be tied to the strategy. When you allocate resources in your budgets, then those should be tied to the strategy. With the Balanced Scorecard, organizations are able to describe their strategy; and once they describe it, they can manage it Those things seem to be obvious, but they do not happen in most organizations today. Instead of tying things to the strategy, most management systems are tied to some piece of the strategy, like quality, or budgets, or EVA. All of those are good things. But they are only a part of the strategy. You have to stand back and find a way to holistically describe each of the elements of the strategy and then put that at the centre of the organization. I think that the breakthrough of the Balanced Scorecard is that for the first time an organization has a way that it can describe its strategy because it allows you to deal with nonfinancial factors – the intangible assets – and to show how those are being tied to financial outcomes. And once you describe it, you can manage it. In the past, we have tried to manage something that we can't even describe, which is an impossible task.

Juergen Daum: But you also say that a Balanced Scorecard-based management system does not only describe strategy. It also makes strategy a continuous process. So this management system does not seem to be a static system but rather a dynamic system. Can you explain how the Balanced Scorecard makes strategy a continuous process?

David Norton: The Balanced Scorecard describes the theory of your strategy. It defines your hypothesis – that's the term that I use. You believe that, if you do A, B will happen. That's your strategy: do A and cause B to happen. Now you communicate that to your organization, so that they understand it: that they are supposed to do A and B will happen. But strategy is a complex thing. You are not quite sure whether B will happen. So you now have to start monitoring the strategy through your feedback systems. In effect what you are doing is testing the hypothesis.

A management team should come together every month, review how they are doing. They should always ask the question, if I am doing A, is B happening? For example, if I am training my people, is quality improving? And if quality is improving, is customer retention improving? Thus, you begin testing the strategy. You don't develop a strategy and go away for a year and come back to look at it. You do this on a continuous basis. I have seldom seen an organization that had a strategy that was all wrong.

One of the big New York banks, trying to consummate a merger, set a goal of retaining all customers. They found that they were losing customers in a certain area. When they studied the customers they were losing, they found that these were unprofitable customers. They had been spending money to try and keep them, when in fact they should have been happy that the customers were leaving. When they saw what was happening, they realized, that they made a mistake in their strategy and they modified their goals. Instead of retaining maximum customers, it was to retain maximum assets. As a result of the changes they succeeded. But it wasn't that the idea of retaining the customers was wrong, it was just that they did not quite get it all right. It was a question of which customers to retain. They went through a process of learning. They ended up retaining 95% of the assets. Five years later they had another major merger and ended up retaining 99% of the combined assets.

What you saw there was not only how they modified the strategy, but how they retained that learning within the organization as a core competency. That's the idea of continuous learning. It's a closed loop. When you start your strategy, it's a theory. Then you test it and modify it as you go forward.

Juergen Daum: So it's a kind of organizational learning.

David Norton: Yes, definitely.

Juergen Daum: Organizational learning probably has lots to do with communication between people throughout the organization. And as we have seen with the emergence of ERP systems in the 1990s, IT can help a lot in facilitating better communication around operational management processes, because it can help to provide the right information at the right point in time to the right people. How do you think an information system can help to support a Balanced Scorecard-based management system and related strategic management processes?

David Norton: Having a computer-based system is essential. Without one, you have no eyes. You have no ability to learn. And I think it extends in two ways. One is, it allows information to come back to you as a basis for learning. It also allows you to communicate out more broadly. In my experience you work at two levels. Level one is when the top executives first clarify their strategy, design a scorecard, communicate it to the organization. They communicate at a very high level. But it's a very important kind of communication because it simplifies the world for the organization. It says: these are the ten things that are important, these are the ten things we are going to do and that's what we want you to concentrate on. People hear that and then begin doing it. And you know on the first day, they don't need a measurement system or a computer system to do that. They need to know that safety is important. They need to know customer satisfaction is important. You get impact from simply communicating clearly what the priorities of the organization are.

Once you have done that however, you have to get to the next level. What the information system allows you to do, is get granular. It allows you to get sophisticated. For example, if you take the bank that tried to retain customers instead of retaining assets, they could not have executed the strategy if they didn't have an information system that could tell them which customers were unprofitable. They would have been stuck there with their head in the clouds. They would not have been able to say, "I don't think we should worry about losing those customers because all those customers aren't profitable." But then the question is, which ones aren't profitable and which ones are. The information system allowed them first of all to test the hypothesis, and find out that the fact that they were losing customers wasn't bad. Secondly it allowed them to do something about it. They could never have got that value without an information system.

You can also use the information system to cascade the scorecards down through the organization. One of the key enablers of successful strategy execution is having alignment from the top to the bottom. You can educate the bottom of the organization. But if you can get them to internalize it and set their own goals and build their own scorecards in a way that they are linked to the scorecards at the top, then you have something powerful. And again, it's very hard to do that without an information system. Conversely it's very easy to do it with one. And so I think the information system allows you to work on both ends. It allows you to go deeper into the organization and executing, and it allows you to go deeper into the data and information so that you can gain more insights.

Juergen Daum: You mentioned that the leadership team plays an important role in the first phase of the definition of the strategy but also in the execution phase. So what exactly is the relationship between the Balanced Scorecard and the leadership team, keeping in mind that the Balanced Scorecard is not a measurement system but a strategic management system?

David Norton: The Balanced Scorecard is definitely not a measurement program. The Balanced Scorecard is a technique to describe a strategy. It uses the language of measurement, because measurement clarifies; measurement is not ambiguous. You can say that quality is important. But what do you mean by quality? Does it mean on time delivery? Does it mean rate of defects? The language of measurement forces you to be more specific and clear. What you are really doing is using the language of measurement to describe the strategy. That's what a Balanced Scorecard does.

First and foremost, strategy is the responsibility of the executive team. You can't even begin to describe the strategy, unless the executive team is involved in doing it. More importantly, strategy is about change. You are trying to take your organization to some place it has never been before. And in order to do that, you have to bring about fundamental changes. In today's economy, the nature of those changes are pervasive. You have to change everything; people's skills, organizational structure, new technology, e-commerce, new investments. The critical role of the executives in implementing strategy is to manage a complex process of change. And the Balanced Scorecard helps to do that, because it helps to communicate the vision of where they are trying to go; it helps to measure it; it helps to get feedback. But at the heart of it, the leaders are using the Balance Scorecard as a tool to manage change.

Unless the leaders are involved, you can't bring about the changes that are required. You can't reorganize. You can't make the investments in training and quality that are required. Only those at the top can do it. If an executive is not involved, you will not get the changes the strategy requires. And as a result, you will not get the benefits of a measurement system like the Balanced Scorecard. The number one question I ask, when people say they have a Balanced Scorecard is "Who is using it?" And if it's the executive team, I feel good that they are probably getting results. But if it's not, I know that they are wasting their time.

Juergen Daum: You once said that the Balanced Scorecard can also help the members of the executive team to better communicate with each other, and to come to a common understanding about what their strategy really is. To stimulate improved communication about strategic issues in the executive team is exactly the objective of the concept of a "Management Cockpit Room" (see p. 345) about which we talked once. Often the problem of executive teams from my experience with customers is that, for example, the VP Marketing sees only market share, the VP manufacturing only sees his or her production line, and the CFO only sees financial figures. If they want to better execute strategy, they have to come together and find a common understanding about what strategy means. Can you explain, how the Balanced Scorecard can help?

David Norton: Implementing strategy means, that every facet of the organization has to contribute towards a common direction. And this starts at the top. The typical leadership team has about 10 people on it. These people get to the top because they are the best within their niche. The chief financial officer, the human resource officer, the operations officer, the marketing officer, each has mastered a very complex discipline. And when they get to the top, they understand much about their discipline, but very little about the disciplines of others. One of the magical things that happens when they come together, develop their strategy, and use a tool like the Balanced Scorecard, is that they begin to learn about the other disciplines.

They learn about marketing and customer segmentation. Or they learn about the human resource skill development process. A huge amount of cross learning takes place. That enables them to appreciate how their piece of the organization is influenced by others. It creates a shared vision, if you will; a shared mindset that comes from understanding all of these pieces of the strategy and how you fit in it. That gets reinforced every time that management team comes together. What they are doing is focusing on this common model; their strategy. Suddenly you find that marketing is no longer just the responsibility of the marketing director. They now start working on it as a team and providing input. It's the common focus of the strategy. A lot of people are using the term cockpit to describe the way in which executives try to guide their organization using the critical performance indicators. But it's really getting them to work as a team and to all look at the same set of indicators, at the same business model and to understand, how they will make it work together.

Juergen Daum: Can you summarize the advantages of applying a Balanced Scorecard-based management system?

David Norton: We can now see the major advantages for companies that use the Balanced Scorecard in the results they have been able to achieve. Various studies that have been done indicate that 7 out of 10, or 9 out of 10 organizations that have strategies are unable to execute them. What we found with Balanced Scorecard companies is that they beat those odds and that they beat them quite dramatically.

We have a set of case studies of organizations that over the decade of the 1990s used the Balance Scorecard to help them to execute their strategies and they have succeeded dramatically. Companies like Mobil Oil, which moved from last in industry profitability to first. Or Saatchi & Saatchi who increased their shareholder value by factor five over a three-year interval. Or Cigna Property & Casualty with $3 billion increase of shareholder value. The executives of these companies will say that the Balanced Scorecard was critical to their success; that they could not have done it without the scorecard.

They all had good people, good strategies, good customers, but they were somehow unable to make it work. The Balanced Scorecard gave them a way, to get their organization focused. Most people want their company to succeed; they are well intentioned. But if they don't have any focus, they bump into one another. They sometimes cause more work than they perform. With the Scorecard you are able to get all of that energy focused in the same direction. And focus is what makes the difference. The bottom line for a Balanced Scorecard user is that they successfully execute their strategy.

Juergen Daum: If organizations want to introduce a Balanced Scorecard-based management system, what are the critical success factors or, conversely, what are major pitfalls they have to avoid?

David Norton: Number one is to get sponsorship from the executive level of the organization. Then secondly is to recognize that this is not a measurement program but rather this is a program to execute strategy. With the Balanced Scorecard you are creating a tool, which is going to be your navigation aid. Then I would say, get started! Don't spend too much time sitting there and analyzing it. Get the program designed. And then – in parallel with that – begin recognizing that you are going to need to tie it to an information system, you are going to need to communicate it to your organization, you are going to need to tie it to your budget. To get the benefits from a Balanced Scorecard, you have got to do these other things. And if you do those things, I think smart executives then see it as a tool and they learn as they go. There is no one right way to do it. But if they get committed, they support it, they understand it and end up changing the way they manage, then they learn how to shape it as they go. I think, if you have those three ingredients in place, then you will succeed.

Juergen Daum: You now have 10 years of experience in working with companies using the Balanced Scorecard, and it has really developed in that period to become the most successful management system in the world. My last question is what in your opinion will be the major challenges in the next decade for companies in this increasingly dynamic and more and more intangible-based economy, and what this will mean for the further development of the strategic management system?

David Norton: There are a couple of things that I see. One is external to the organization in the macro economy. Investors, regulators, employees are all demanding more insight into how the organizations are doing. And right now the only record of how organizations are doing is financial. So the first thing I think you will see emerge is that a Balanced Scorecard approach is going to become a standard way of reporting outside the organization to investors and shareholders. Today they ask for that information, but it's not done in any structured way. Just as the economy has moved from tangible to intangible, reporting on the economy will move from the tangible to the intangible. That's the migration from financial reporting to Balanced Scorecard reporting.

The second thing that I see happening deals with the discipline of management. If you look at the management textbooks you find there is a lot of rocket science in parts of the organization. People in financial management do derivatives. People run linear programs in refineries. Even statistical analysis of customer satisfaction is used in marketing. But at the executive levels of organizations, there is not a whole lot of rocket science. They push back on concepts like system dynamics and simulation. The intangible economy demands that you look at relationships between actions, investments, and their long term-impact. In other words, it requires that you do systems thinking. I think that you will see, at the executive levels of organizations, more and more commitment to systems thinking, and the analytical tools that are required to support it.

Finally, the third thing that I see is the concept of the balanced strategy. When we talk about the Balanced Scorecard, people think about the balance between financial and nonfinancial measurements. But the other thing that has become clear is that strategy itself is a balancing act. A strategy is not just doing one thing or having one theme like productivity management. A strategy requires you to create a balance between short-term activities, like operational effectiveness, and long-term activities like innovation. A typical strategy has to cover several points in a time spectrum. It has to focus on short-term productivity; it has to focus on the mid-term of shaping customer value and customer value propositions, and it has to focus on long-term innovation. These three things have to happen simultaneously. When they invest in an organization, shareholders are making judgments whether or not that is going to happen. They are investing for the long-term, but they also want to see short-term performance. Organizations will ultimately have to report out on their whole strategy. They will have to report out on their pipeline of new products. They will also have to report out on things like customer retention and quality as well as how they are doing with costs per transaction. I think you will see more maturity in the way in which strategy is managed and how companies will communicate outside of the organization as well.

Juergen Daum: This trend to report to the outside not just financial but also more nonfinancial figures in a structured way is very interesting. I discussed this recently with controlling experts here in Germany. And the fact is that controllers here are already required to be involved in this type of communication on the nonfinancial drivers, which provide external parties, mainly investors, with insight into the long-term value creation process of the company.

David Norton: Yes, I think you will probably see that happen faster in Europe than in the USA. The trend is happening in both places, but the USA tends to be much more reserved about communicating bad information to share-holders. There is a real reluctance on the part of corporate executives to com-municate anything they don't have to. I think that's less so in Europe. You tend to see more innovation that way.

Juergen Daum: David, thank you very much for this very interesting interview.

What is a management system and what should the new management system do?

In the knowledge-based new economy, where efforts and results are not that interlinked any more, successful enterprise management requires more than just resource and cost control. It requires risk-taking decisions to decide on why the company is in business, on its strategy, on the balance between immediate profitability and market share, on the balance between immediate profitability and investments into innovation and intangible assets. It requires control of efficiency *and* effectiveness.

While the efficiency of an organization (for which traditionally its costs are a proxy) is an important precondition for value creation, it is an organization's effectiveness (for which traditionally the proxy are revenues) that leads to com-petitive advantage and growth and generates, finally, value. Management has to start with the intended results and has to organize the resources of the organization to attain these results. And the management system is the tool to do that. It has to guide the organization on its way into new territories, to new improved results. It has to measure the actual status of the business and its value-creation processes, organize and institutionalize the necessary decision and management processes in order to allow the organization to realize fully its opportunities and manage associated risks. It also has to help to better communicate results externally and to engage an organization's stakeholders.

The new management system has to institutionalize the new cultural values that engage all relevant stakeholders, who are, by the way, also important "corporate resource providers" as employees, investors, and business partners – which means nothing else than, that a careful analysis of their objectives and requirements has to become part of the strategic management process. It has to provide tools, structures and processes that make sure, that all activities and initiatives are tied to the strategy so that a company can harness the full potential of its intangible assets and is able to manage product innovation as well as the operational business and customer relationships from a value perspective. The new system must help to make innovation a continuous process on strategic, product innovation, as well on the operations level. It must help to make a company more productive and to unearth its hidden values in its existing intangible assets and market opportunities as well as to enable it to build in a systematic way new intangible assets in order to create competitive advantage and sustainable returns for its stakeholders.

Intangible assets – what is important from a management system point of view?

Including information about nonfinancial success factors in management reports is a step in the right direction, but it is not sufficient in order to successfully manage and fully exploit a company's intangible assets. The intangible value-creation process is in most organizations a quite complex process. It therefore requires a good understanding of the nature and characteristics of intangible assets in order to know what really matters in designing the conceptual framework for the new management system.

Scalability, network effects, and increasing returns are the major advantages and benefits of intangible assets. But often overlooked is the fact that intangibles, like physical and financial assets, are subject to the fundamental economic laws of balancing benefits and costs. So both, benefits and costs or limitations of intangible assets, have to be considered in order to get the complete picture.

Benefits from intangibles

The three major drivers of benefits from intangibles are scalability or nonscarcity, increasing returns and network effects.[10]

Scalability or lack of bottleneck characteristics (nonscarcity)

Knowledge-based assets such as a software program or the manuscript of a book can be copied almost infinitely and can be made available to more than

---

[10] This explanation of the benefits and limitations of intangibles follows the argumentation of Lev. See Baruch Lev (2001) *Intangibles: Management, Measurement, and Reporting*, Washington, DC: Brookings Institute Press, pp. 21–49.

one customer at the same time. They do not possess bottleneck characteristics like the physical assets of a rental car, which can be rented at one time only to one customer, or machinery that can be used at one time to produce only one product.

Increasing returns

Due to the typical cost structure of knowledge-based products (high fixed costs in the form of product development costs, very low variable or marginal costs), profit usually increases quickly with the number of units sold. This is especially the case once the initial investments in product development have been paid off. This often leads to increasing returns.

Network effects

Since the positive effect for the existing users normally increases with the number of new users, these kinds of products can often also profit from network effects that trigger an exponential growth of the network, providing the new product can be established as a "standard" in the market. For example, the benefit for users of a software program increases with the number of total active users. This is because the probability increases that someone else, with whom a user intends to collaborate, is using the same program and the collaboration becomes easier (such as exchanging files, sharing the same logic, etc.).

Negative effects and characteristics of intangible assets

In addition, negative effects or limiting factors (negative value drivers) of intangible assets exist. These can eliminate any benefit and can even turn positive effects into an economic loss. The most important limiting factors are a too small relevant market and therefore missing growth potential, missing property rights and control over intangibles, the investment risk associated with intangibles, and the nontradability of many intangible assets. It is the task of the management system, to help to avoid or at least limit these negative effects.

A too small relevant market and missing growth potential

Intangible assets do not restrict the scalability of themselves, as physical assets do, and they can be used to serve many customers at the same time. But their scalability is dependent on the size of the relevant market. If the market is not large enough, the growth potential might not exist which is necessary to cover the often large initial investments. In such a case, a company will not be able to achieve the expected returns and might even generate a loss. Therefore, especially for companies which invest in intangibles, market research has become even more important in order to find out before they start to invest, if the market is large enough to enable the necessary growth level required for success.

Lack of a complete control over the benefits of intangible assets

The benefits of tangible and financial assets can be effectively secured by their owners. The well-defined property rights of physical and financial assets enable owners to effectively exclude others from enjoying the benefits of these assets without having invested in them. In the case of intangible assets this is often not the case. Knowledge-based assets are often characterized by "spill over effects" where competitors detract from the use of an innovation that its investors have, by copying it. Often, this is reinforced when employees with critical knowledge join a rival company or through other types of "knowledge leaks". This can be partially restricted by means of patents or protection of proprietary rights, but usually not completely. The often missing property rights and missing control over intangible assets is leading to a constant tension between the (often huge) value-creation potential of investments in intangible assets and the difficulties encountered in delivering on the promise through full appropriation of benefits. The problem can often only be solved by use of "time-to-market". Here, the investor is on the market with the product faster than the competition and rapidly increases own market share by use of network effects to reach as fast as possible market leadership (and large sales volume and scale effects) in order to realize the benefits from investments made in product development. The management system must help to quickly recognize and overcome growth limits in the strategy management and feedback process and to control output.

Investments in intangible assets are riskier

Investments in innovation capabilities such as in R&D, in organizational assets and human capital are much riskier than in other enterprise activities such as production. Only a small number of innovations accounts for the lion's share of realized sales and revenues. For example, the top 10% of patents both in

Germany and in the USA accounted for 81–93% of total patent value. Only a few products or processes are blockbusters, while the rest are worthless investments. But risk associated with investments into innovation-related intangibles is not equal. It is dependent on the phase of the innovation process. During this process, that typically starts with basic research and the new ideas phase, continues with the prototyping and then the implementation and product development phase, and ends with the commercialization phase, the level of risk concerning future outcome (revenue, profit) is continuously decreasing. Risk (that is, volatility), however, is not all bad as options models indicate, but can create value when the downside loss can be constrained. This is precisely one of the tasks of the new management and management accounting system.

Nontradeability

The absence of organized and competitive markets for intangibles leaves intangible assets often as not exchangeable and companies can only exploit them within their own organization. This results often in restricted risk-sharing opportunities; for example, for in-process R&D, which increases the risk of intangibles and restricts their growth. Internet-based markets in intangibles may provide the missing transparency, along with liquidity and risk-sharing. Web-based exchanges for intellectual property, like pl-x.com, offer valuation and insurance services as well as a trading platform. Such exchanges, however, are still in their infancy. Another solution to solve the problem, at least partly, is a phased approach for investments in intangible assets. Investments in product development will not be released in total at the start of the process but in phases after certain milestones have been reached. At each milestone it will be decided if the development project will be continued, abandoned, or a retrial of the last phase started. According to the real option valuation method the value of an investment can be significantly increased if management is consciously using the flexibility it has in such a process to limit risk and optimize reward. Over time, as the project is moving forward, new information, for example about future marketing and sales opportunities for a product under development or about technical feasibility, becomes available and allows management to make better decisions. A phased approach allows postponement of some important decisions until more information becomes available and also keep the options open.[11]

---

[11] The concept of real option valuation is explained in Chapter 7.

Managerial diseconomies

However, the major limitation on the use and growth of intangibles is managerial diseconomies. Intangible assets are, in general, substantially more difficult to manage and operate than tangible assets. The virtual nature of intangibles complicates their management and companies often do not have direct control of them. For example, identifying unused physical capacity in a production plant and taking corrective action by, say, changing work distribution between plants or by changing price policy, are straightforward tasks, whereas optimizing network effects from a new technology is a challenge. Diseconomies resulting from limited capacity to manage intangible assets are the major factor restricting the use of these assets and economic growth based on them. Overcoming such diseconomies systematically through an improved management system and related information systems promises enormous rewards. Companies which are able to leverage the benefits of intangible assets and to control their limitations and negative effects through a better management system will clearly have an advantage over their peers who still struggle to define an intangible-based strategy.

How to create value from intangible assets

The fundamentals of corporate value creation can be described in a generic way as: *invest* in business areas, that is in market and product segments and related assets, which yield the highest (financial and nonfinancial) return from a company's stakeholder point of view; *manage these investments* by maximizing benefits and overcoming limitations and negative effects; and *control operations and business processes* as efficiently as possible by generating maximum revenues and profits for the company.

The decision to invest in a specific business area, that is in a specific market segment, is a strategic decision. It is dependent on financial considerations – for example, on the expectations of financial return in order to create the highest shareholder value – and on nonfinancial considerations – for example, on the consideration for which purpose the company is in business, and what other important stakeholders – besides investors such as customers, employees, non-governmental organizations and the public at large – expect from the organization. And, it is definitely also dependent on the core competencies of an organization and on tangible and intangible assets available, on which it can build in designing a new strategy. The task of this strategic investment decision, which basically represents the core of a strategy, is to define the area of the enterprise's activities in the light of its core competencies and to define a desired result and through which type of investments the organization intends to achieve it.

The problem with intangible assets-based businesses is, and these are here in the focus, that there is no direct relationship between investments in intangible assets and a financial outcome. One cannot show that if a company sends its employees to a training program for a month, that sales will go up or costs will go down, as David Norton said in our interview. Instead, the company has to make sure that training will improve, for example, service quality and that the company comes up with new leading edge products, while reducing time-to-market (for example, through training which teaches development and research staff a more customer- and market-oriented approach). And if the service quality improves and the company comes up with more competitive products in time, customer confidence may improve. And if customer confidence improves, then customers may buy more from the same source and market share will increase as well. And if market share increases, the company will finally be able to generate more sustainable revenues and earnings.

It's like a multistep logic, between training a person and getting a financial result. Therefore investments in intangible assets that should produce the desired result, requires that an organization describes the steps that are involved in the value-creation process that builds on these intangibles assets (see Figure 5.2).

Since intangibles and knowledge, which constitutes the basis of many intangibles, are so hard to capture and turn into real tangible values for customers and shareholders and being subject to constant change they must be put into a generally applicable context and a framework that links them to a common target. And it is the task of strategy to provide such a framework and to combine assets, both intangible and also tangible, into a unique "recipe" which allows a company to make a difference on the market.

Another important characteristic of intangible assets is that their value is normally far more dependent on external factors, such as for example market perception, than are physical assets. An organization has therefore not only to try to get all steps necessary, from investment to return, under its control, it also has to be prepared to adapt strategy constantly. Unique competitive positions in the market based on intangible assets can only be retained, or even expanded, if the enterprise is always one step ahead in this kind of external development, and has already adapted its own strategy before a change occurs. Simply monitoring the implementation of a once defined

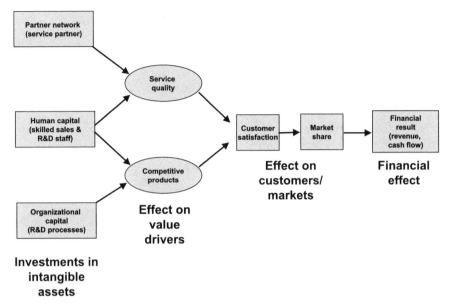

Figure 5.2 Successful investments into intangible assets require a multistep logic. How to do it – a strategic recipe.

strategy is not sufficient. Strategic learning processes must also be reactivated constantly, and the strategy itself has to be revised time and time again on the basis of the new knowledge from the "field". So strategy management should not just be a top-down process, where management is communicating the new strategy and expects its precise execution. It should resemble a closed loop and include a feedback and learning cycle which allows the constant adaption of strategy to reality (see Figure 5.3).

Strategy work becomes an important "production factor" for value and has to be organized as a systematic and continuous process. Intangible assets, and value-creation processes based on them, for example in product innovation and in customer relationship building, create financial value only through their intelligent combination. This has to be adapted constantly to changes in the market without losing sight of the initial objectives and of actual efficiency and performance.

Therefore, the new management system has to help to balance long-term oriented strategy and value management with the optimization of short-term

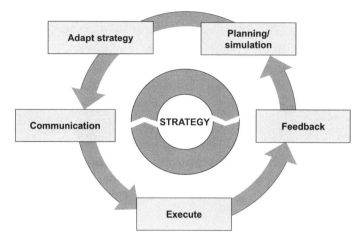

Figure 5.3   Strategy management has to happen in the form of a feedback loop.

enterprise performance by integrating the two processes for strategy and performance management.

Managing the product innovation and market development process

Patenting, cross-licensing, trademarking, moving first, or establishing an industry standard are ways to appropriate most of the benefits of intangibles in the area of product and market development. R&D and marketing alliances are examples of how companies try to manage the risk of the related intangibles. Furthermore, the formulation of appropriate exit strategies, such as licensing or sale on an Internet exchange, is aimed at mitigating the nontradability restriction.

Leveraging the benefits and control of the limitations of these investments is the objective. If we picture the process of product innovation, it requires at the beginning investments in R&D, then investments in means, that help to gain control over benefits of the initial investments made, and finally investments in commercialization or "multiplication" of a new technology in the market.

In order to constraint the limitations of the benefits, it is important to establish sync and decision points in the process in order to define if further investments still make sense (based on the success of R&D activities or concerning the actual market situation), to assess the actual risk exposure and to decide if risk could be further restricted (for example, through additional alliances). Because the outcomes of investments in product innovation and related intangibles are quite insecure, the only way to manage these investments successfully is to establish a separate process for product innovation that institutionalizes check points and makes sure that new markets and technology relevant information are systematically examined and that management asks itself if further investments still make sense and can be made.

Managing operations

Management of operations – that is, of the process that organizes how customers receive ordered goods and services (supply chain management) and how related financial (such as billing and collection), marketing and sales (promotion campaigns, direct marketing), and service tasks (consulting, installation, maintenance) are executed – stands also in close relationship with the other already described two areas, which the management system has to support. How a company should organize its operational processes is dependent on the strategic decision, where its core competencies are and how it intends to create value. If a company decides that owning the customer is more important than owning production, then it should outsource manufacturing and should concentrate on developing new methods to interact with customers more efficiently and with a higher value for customers, as Cisco did. But the organization of operations has to be also synchronized with the product innovation process. When a company comes up with a new technology and new products, a new model for distribution, services and sales may be required.

So all three management areas (strategy management, product innovation management, and operations management) are interlinked and together form *the value creation system* of an organization. Because the relationship between investments made and financial and nonfinancial results obtained in intangibles based-businesses is looser, companies have to try to get all steps necessary, from investment to results, on all three levels under its control through proper management. Only in this way are they able to leverage the opportunities and to constrain the downside and limit risks. This requires a management system that integrates and synchronizes the strategic management process, the product and market development management process, and the operational management process (see Figure 5.4).

This new management system has to facilitate insight in and understanding of the value creation system of an enterprise: of its value drivers and of the dynamic relationship between them. It has to provide a high degree of transparency and has to facilitate a continuous dialogue and communication

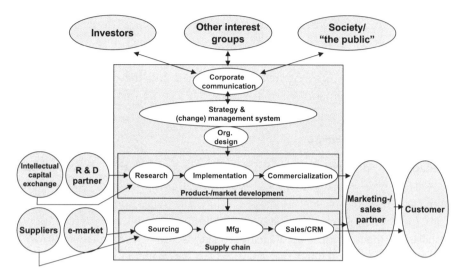

Figure 5.4   Example of a intagibles-based value-creation system.

process between all involved parties – both internally and externally. It has to provide a comprehensive view on the entire business and its value-creation processes: not only on activities within the enterprise, but also on activities taking place in the organizations of business partners, if they are critical for reaching corporate objectives. It has to provide more transparency of the intangible value-creation process, for example in product and market development, and has to enable management, employees and other stakeholder, to see where the true value of the company lies and how they can contribute to extend it. Therefore, it has to enable efficient communication with major stakeholders, who can significantly influence the corporations market value. This is especially important in the area of intangible assets, where stakeholder expectations, such as of financial analysts and investors, can represent a significant value lever.

6 Architecture and Elements of the New Management System

I sometimes feel like I'm behind the wheel of a race car. I need to keep my eyes on the horizon, but I need to keep my attention on the rearview mirror to see who is gaining on me. From the passenger seat, consumers are telling me where and when they want to be dropped off, and behind me my shareholders and business partners are engaged in backseat driving. One of the biggest challenges is that there are no road signs to help navigate. And in fact, every once in a while a close call reminds me that no one has yet determined which side of the road we're supposed to be on.

Stephen Case, Chairman AOL Time Warner[1]

Every organization has to define first what its "theory of business" is; that is, what it stands for and the reason it is in business. The theory of business represents the "constituation" of an enterprise and creates a firm foundation for its strategies and value-creation system design, which may change over time. Especially when internal and external rate of change increases, a company's theory of business becomes an important "anchor", providing stability and enabling sustainability. Therefore, successful enterprise management starts with a proper definition of the theory of business.[2]

The theory of business of an enterprise defines what its core competences are, for what business purpose they should be used, and for which stakeholders it wants to create value. Only when this has been determined can the strategy of an enterprise be defined or redefined; that is, how exactly can the intended value be created, through which measures, with what resources and objectives and how should the value-creation system of the enterprise be configured – in short, how its value-creation processes should be organized and what activities will be kept in-house or outsourced. As soon as the strategy and value-creation system have been defined, we can then determine the right measures for the measurement and reporting system and how management processes should be designed.

---

[1] Jeffrey E. Garten: *The Mind of the CEO*, New York: Basic Books, p. 38.
[2] Peter Drucker has described the idea of the "theory of business". See Peter F. Drucker (1999) *Management Challenges for the 21st Century*, New York: HarperCollins, p. 43.

The task of strategy is to convert the theory of business into performance. Its purpose is to enable an organization to achieve its desired results in an unpredictable environment. So the task of strategy also is to constantly reconcile internal efforts, activities, and initiatives with external broader market trends and changes in customer and stakeholder expectations with respect to the organization. The theory of the business and strategy are conceptual models, which are implemented in real-world business through what I call the ''value-creation system'' of a company, its business system represented through its value-creation processes that determine the company's operational activities, risks and opportunities. So, only when the business purpose and the strategy is defined can an organization name what are the most critical things for successful opportunity and risk management to be supported by the management system.

The management system itself consists of the elements accounting and measurement system, management processes, and communication processes with external stakeholders. The accounting and measurement system's task is to provide objective information on the process and market status of the enterprise activities. Management processes enable a fast and efficient knowledge exchange between the managers in the enterprise and in the broader ecosystem around the information provided. They institutionalize decisions on strategy adjustment and on optimizing short-term performance by adjusting operative activities and resource allocation. Well-organized communication processes with stakeholders should engage them for the enterprise on the one hand and should integrate their expectations and objectives into the strategic enterprise management process on the other hand. Such a management system enables an enterprise to continually control and optimize its short- and long-term success in a dynamically changing environment.

Before we start to investigate the different elements of the new management system further, I want to describe, first, how an enterprise and its management can get more clarity about how the process of strategy (re)definition can take place and how the operational design of the enterprise, that is of its value-creation system, might be set up.

Definition of the theory of the business

Any company has – either explicitly or implicitly – a theory of its business. In most cases this theory of business exists implicitly. It is not expressed verbally, but it does exist in the minds of the core group of executives and business managers in the form of common values and thinking of what ''our business is and what it is not''. In a period of rapid change and total uncertainty, it is worthwhile for any organization, new or existing, to think through its theory of business again, especially if it wants to manage and optimize its intangibles. A clear analysis and a clear picture of the theory of business is the basis for aligning successfully all involved parties in the business or value-creation system of a company and to exploit its full potential.

As outlined earlier, the two major characteristics of intangibles are: the upside, the opportunities are, due to their scalability, not limited, but the risk associated with investments into intangibles are often huge. Managers are trained to manage risks in all forms. But they are not so much used to manage suddenly occurring opportunities, which require fast decisions and action in total uncertainty in order to realize them. They can master this challenge through two means: through better knowledge about one's capabilities (of the enterprise), and by limiting the downside, the risks, through a better management system. If management knows the enterprises capabilities and strength, its core competencies, it is much easier to make good strategic decision fast and under time pressure.

Assessing an organization's core competencies

The assessment of an organization's core competencies is done in two steps: first they are systematically identified and second they are valued.

One way to identify an organization's core competencies is to study today's company management disciplines and functions and to check if the organization owns specific competencies and capabilities in these areas in comparison to similar organizations. The competencies and capabilities of an enterprise in all value-creating areas have to be examined. This includes an organization's strategic (change) management and corporate performance management capabilities, its product innovation potential, its operational and customer relationship capabilities, its competencies in support functions, and finally its capabilities to communicate effectively and in a value adding way with investors and other stakeholders. The second step comprises the valuation of the identified core competencies in comparison with other similar enterprises.

Both can be done through structured interviews of executives, managers and employees as well as of customers, suppliers, business partners, investors or financial and industry analysts, and of opinion leaders of the most important stakeholder groups. To develop such a questionnaire, the following list of evaluation items can serve as a guideline. But the topics on the questionnaire as well as the formulation of the questions have to be adapted to the individual organization and in some cases also to the individual target groups for the questionnaire. The list here should therefore serve just as an example:

Strategic (change) management and performance management capabilities

▶   Degree of awareness of and reaction speed to changes in the industry and market environment.

▶   Success rate in implementing new strategies; speed and quality of execution.

▶   Existence of a change-management-culture and degree of involvement of employees in the change-management-process.

▶   Accuracy of forecasts and results/earnings volatility.

Product innovation capabilities

▶   Effectiveness in discovery in relation to resources deployed: number of successful inventions / new product ideas in a specific period compared with investments made and number of people employed – benchmark with similar companies.

▶   Capabilities for successful implementation of new product ideas: number of patents and licenses, time-to-market in product development, increase of "coded knowledge" etc.

▶   Business development and marketing capabilities: speed in of multiplying the adoption rate of new products per market segment, capability to create "network effects" and their success rate.

Operational and customer relationship capabilities

▶   Effectiveness of Supply Chain Management: degree of "availability-to-promise", lead time, reconfiguration time, costs, inventory levels.

▶   Effectiveness in customer relationship management: customer satisfaction, customer retention rate, number of new customers per period, development of the average customer lifetime value.

Capabilities in support functions

▶   Capabilities in human resource management and employee productivity: development of skill levels versus requirements, leave quote, attractiveness for new hires, value added per person, etc.

▶ Effectiveness of finance: total costs of finance compared with total revenue, costs per transaction e.g. in billing and accounting, day sales outstanding (DSO), level of cash on hand required, return on financial investments, costs for preparing and disseminating business information, quality of prepared business information and decision support services.

▶ Capabilities in Information Technology management: number of "online-employees"/degree of IT support for business processes, server and network downtime, reaction time/speed in supporting new business processes, total IT costs compared with total revenue.

External communication capabilities

▶ General: number of positive/negative quotes in the press.

▶ Investor Relations: ratings of the quality of provided information and services through financial analysts, sustaining premium on stock price for good communication (benchmark).

▶ Stakeholder communication: rating of the companies information policy through the opinion leaders of the most important stakeholder groups.

On the basis of the results of these interviews, a company is now able to set up its core competency map/a scorecard of its specific capabilities, which shows its specific strength and competencies in comparison with its peer group. When the core competencies are identified and valued with respect to other companies in the industry, you can move on to define the business purpose of the organization.

Defining the business purpose

The definition of the business purpose happens it three steps:

1. In-depth analysis of the core competencies, which have been already identified, with respect to their combined value creation potential.

2. Identification of markets and potential buyers for products and services created on the basis of these core competencies.

3. Definition of the organization's value proposition or mission statement.

The objective of the detailed analysis of the core competencies is that management understands why and how the organization owns this specific strength and competencies, what its drivers are, which competitive advantage they provide, and what value they represent in their combination from an external perspective. It represents, therefore, an assessment of these core competencies from a market perspective and the identification of possible marketable products and services that can be created with them.

With the following step, the identification of possible demands and markets for core competencies, an organization can seek out possible business opportunities; that is, where and how core competencies can create value. Here, an organization has to find out for which market segments; that is, for which target groups and how it will create value on the basis of its top core competencies. And this can be an area where the company has not yet done any business.

This is why an assessment or (re)definition of the business purpose of an organization makes sense also for a company, where management thinks that it exactly knows its business purpose. It could be that the company has developed some competencies over the years that are very valuable in a totally different industry or in a business the company has not yet been in, resulting in new value-creation opportunities. The result of this step should be a mission statement and value proposition of the organization, which describes on a high level *how* the organizations intends to create value *for whom* using *which core competencies*.

The outcome of this phase is that an organization is either able to clarify and better describe its existing business purpose or that management has defined a new business purpose. In both cases the most important stakeholders, who have to be involved, have to be identified and the enterprise strategy needs to be defined in order to enable the organization to realize successfully its business purpose.

Identifying an organization's major stakeholders

What is a stakeholder? A stakeholder is someone linked with the economic, political or social destiny of the organization of which he or she is a partner and therefore has a vital interest in its success. Stakeholders can represent groups, organizations, or private persons, who hold a "stake" in an organization. This stake can either consist:

▶   of money that someone (an investor) has invested into the company with a specific return expectation

▶ of trust that someone (a customer) has invested into the company's product offering and into the capability of the company to create value through these products or services

▶ of mental or physical workforce, knowledge, creativity and lifetime that someone (an employee) is investing into the value-creation process of a company in exchange for a salary and with the expectation to increase his or her own intellectual capital and future career opportunities

▶ of investments in various forms in the ecosystem of the company, for example into the build up of product know-how in its own workforce or in the form of foregone opportunities to work with other companies, that someone (business partner) has made with the expectation for a profitable business

▶ of investments in infrastructure and education, which are exploited either directly or indirectly by the company, that public organizations (a state or community in which the company is doing business) have made with the expectation of creating economic performance and wealth for its citizens

▶ of trust and belief in the usefulness of the company from a general economic and social perspective (the public) or by putting its own reputation at risk by linking the own organization closely with the company (non-governmental organizations), forming the public image of an organization

Due to the increased openness and competitiveness of stakeholder related markets, stakeholders have gained an increasing influence on companies in the last couple of years. Global capital markets have confronted companies with more demanding investors and financial analysts, who have a huge influence on the management of corporations and can even force managers to resign if they do not perform.

Other stakeholder groups have gained more influence as well. The increase of choice for employees and business partners in a global and open market corresponds with a decrease in their loyalty versus the enterprise. Talents in the software industry can choose their employer today everywhere in the world. Customers can buy through the Web where they feel that they would get most for their money. Business partners, such as suppliers, are no longer dependent on single customers and are using their new power, for example, in pricing negotiations. In addition, multinationals especially are increasingly targets for non-governmental organizations who are trying to convince the public, through massive use of the media, that such enterprises increase their economic performance at the expense of social and environmental values. This can hurt a company's reputation and capability to do business in an environment where many people share the thinking of these non-governmental organizations – as the case of Shell, mentioned earlier, has shown.

Stakeholders are perceived increasingly as important resource providers and as strategic partners. A good relationship with them represents therefore an asset. A good relationship with investors makes it easier to raise new money to finance growth and new investments. A good relationship with business partners provides the opportunity to win additional companies as partners, to grow the own ecosystem and, for example, to realize network effects. A good relationship with employees makes it easier to win more talented people and to nurture growth of a company's structural capital, which helps to create value for customers and shareholders.

Companies – especially companies in an intangibles-based business that are generally much more dependent on good stakeholder relations and networks than traditional companies – increasingly have an active policy with regards to their stakeholders and are trying to establish an efficient communication process with them. But one precondition is that an organization identifies systematically its most important stakeholders.

Depending on the business purpose of the company and on its core competencies in action, it will have different priorities concerning stakeholders. For example, a company engaged in markets where business success requires constant technological innovation on the one hand, and a large customer base on the other hand has at least two major stakeholder groups: talented employees needed in product development, in sales and in customer service, and customers who represent the foundation and source of future revenues and growth.

At which level investors are chosen as major stakeholders depends on how a company intends to finance its future growth. If its intention is to rely on innovation by means of acquisitions (as Cisco did), then it is dependent very much on its own stock value, because stock is increasingly used as "acquisition currency". Therefore, capital markets, institutional investors and financial analysts will represent a first priority stakeholder group for such a company. But if it intends instead to grow more organically from within, and if the existing investors agree, investors may be a second priority under the assumption that good products and satisfied customers will, over time, create shareholder value almost automatically.

The decision as to which stakeholder group is attributed a first priority and which comes second is an important one. Companies are not able to treat several stakeholder groups in an equal way nor can they dedicate to all of them the same management attention. In part, the decision results from a company's defined business purpose and its mission statement which define for whom the company intends to create value. This needs to be complemented by the identification and analysis of the critical resources of the company, which represent another candidate for important stakeholders (such as employees). But this can be finally done only when the strategy has been defined. If a company, in order to achieve its strategic objectives, requires first and foremost talented employees, who are difficult to find and to hire, employees are definitely a candidate for the top stakeholder group. For a company in the oil business the relationships to environmental groups can be of the same importance as the one to investors, if it wants to retain its "license to operate".

In summary, companies will be able to identify candidates to become their most important stakeholders by analyzing which resource providers their core competencies in action require and by ascertaining who it is they intend to create value for. Both are candidates to serve as the organization's first stakeholders.

The ability of a company to support several first priority stakeholder groups is dependent on the degree of consistency of the expectations of these groups and of the availability of enough management resources to manage the relationships.

Concentration on only one or two first priority stakeholder groups does not mean that companies should ignore the other stakeholders in their partner role and should instrumentalize them – try to manipulate them in order to extract maximum value out of them regardless of their own intentions and expectations. If companies also view their other stakeholders as important resource providers and treat them accordingly by giving them a say in the design and further development of the common ecosystem, they might be able to increase value added and income significantly for all stakeholders in a positive self-enforcing sum game. SAP AG with its partner network, where partners can be seen in the role of secondary stakeholders, has already been named as an example for an ecosystem, that created value added for all its stakeholders. After having defined the core competencies and the business purpose of an organization as well as its most important stakeholders, the next step is due: the definition of the organization's strategy.

Defining an organization's strategy

As David Norton said in our interview, strategy is the unique way an organization intends to create value for its stakeholders. In contrast to the theory of business, which describes on a high level how a company wants to create value for whom, the strategy has to describe the target more precisely – what result or objective the organization wants to achieve in a specific timeframe. And it has to provide the "recipe" for it: that means it has to describe exactly how the organization intends to execute these objectives.

The definition of the enterprise strategy therefore has to start with the desired outcome from a stakeholder perspective. Once the first priority stakeholders are defined, an organization has to translate expectations into targets by considering its opportunities; that is, its core competencies and related market opportunities. In addition, objectives for second priority stakeholders have to be defined as well, if these stakeholders provide important resources for the company's business activities and are to be engaged by the company. Those objectives will then serve as "secondary conditions" or "constraints" for a company's strategy.

Here a simplified generic example. If a company's first priority stakeholders are defined as its customers, then the most important stakeholder expectations to be considered are those of customers; for example, to be served by the company with the best products in the market. And even complaints from customers about product quality can sometimes be an indicator for that – these customers have a high level of quality expectation concerning the product offering of this specific vendor, and only of this vendor. Management can now take these expectations from customers as an indicator that customers believe that the company is able to provide the best products in the market (but has not done it in their case – therefore the complaint). If management shares this belief, it can take it as an opportunity to grow by converting it into an intangible asset by nurturing and enhancing the company's product innovation capabilities and its relations to customers, who strongly believe in these capabilities – that is, by systematically using these capabilities as value drivers.

The number one target of the company's strategy could then be to increase market share within its existing customer base (by selling them new products) and to increase overall market share (by selling to new customers, into new market segments). In order to do that, the company builds on its competence in developing innovative products, in addition it may also try to improve customer relationships – for example, through a new service model, that provides better customer service and allows the company to better retain its customers. Because this company would then be dependent on finding enough talented employees to achieve its objectives in product development and customer service, a secondary condition would be not to exceed a certain employee fluctuation rate, increase employee satisfaction, to engage more leading experts from its industry or to hire a larger number of talented younger people. Another condition could be to generate a specific financial return for shareholders, at least above costs of capital at best above shareholder expectations, in order to present the company as an attractive investment to the financial community and to be able to raise the necessary money to fund the company's new strategy.

So, defining the strategy means taking the desired outcome as the starting point. This has been defined on the basis of the expectations of an organization's first priority stakeholders. It continues by taking the expectations of second priority stakeholders as a secondary condition into consideration, and by looking for opportunities to achieve the desired outcome on the market by leveraging the company's core competencies. How this should be done can be assisted by answering the following questions:

▶   What type of customers should be served with which products or services (definition of product/market segment combinations)?

▶   What marketing, sales, and financial targets should be achieved when in these market segments?

▶   How will the new products be developed, manufactured and delivered (for example, through in-house development or acquisitions, through own manufacturing facilities or through contract manufacturers)?

▶   How will the new products be commercialized and how should the marketing targets be achieved (for example, with or without marketing and distribution partners)?

Having defined the market-related strategic objectives, management has to define in a second step the means and resources necessary to achieve them. So it also has to define strategic objectives for important basic resources (employee development, financial funding, enhancement of IT infrastructure) and for other activities, such as in marketing, alliance management, and mergers and acquisitions.

The result should be a detailed list of strategic objectives for the various functional areas of the company that make sure the company will be able to achieve its overall strategic target. It is very important for a common understanding of the new strategy throughout the organization and for a successful execution later, that the management team agrees on the cause and effect linkages between these various objectives. Even if managers and executives agree on strategic (sub)objectives and on how to achieve them, they often disagree on the sequence of the means and strategic (sub)objectives and on the dependencies between them. If this important question is not clarified at the beginning, it will lead later on to unnecessary disruptions during execution and could result in a total failure in strategy execution.

For each of the strategic (sub)objectives, management will then define a target; that is, it will quantify it. For this, the management team has to agree first on how progress for a specific objective will be measured; that is, which measure will be used, and it will then define the target (value) itself. Then the management team has to agree which initiatives and major projects have to be established in order to be able to achieve the objectives. Often these represent a real challenge for an organization and require major change which cannot be achieved through the usual day-to-day activities. Then a major project or initiatives has to be kicked-off, which brings together a team of people from various areas within the organization that can act across organizational boundaries in the framework of such an initiative. Once defined, the cause and effect linkages can also serve as an excellent basis for assessing risks associated with the new strategy, because through such a linkage it becomes obvious if the overall strategic objective or several strategic (sub)objectives, which have to be achieved in order to be successful in total, are dependent on the successful execution of other objectives. As a starting point for strategic risk assessment as part of the strategic management process, and in order to clearly agree on the critical areas from the beginning, the management team should rate the probability of achievement and should agree every strategic objective on its major risk factor.

So the outcome of the strategy definition process represents a comprehensive description of the strategy as cause and effect linkage of strategic (sub)-objectives, including the related targets (on the basis of the defined measures), initiatives, and risk factors and their ratings (see Figure 6.1).

This example of a cause and effect linkage to strategic objectives is based on Kaplan and Norton's Balanced Scorecard concept. It represents a comprehen-

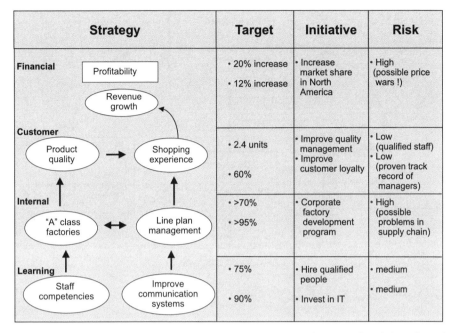

Figure 6.1 Example of a cause and effect linkage according to the principles of the Balanced Scorecard concept.

sive framework for describing a strategy and measuring the progress of its implementation. Once a scorecard has been developed, it serves as the organizing framework for the strategic management process and allows an organization to systematically translate a strategy into action.[3] And it forms the basis for the strategy management part of the management system I propose in this book.

But the classic Balanced Scorecard with its four perspectives – financial, customers/market, internal business processes, and growth and learning (see Figure 6.2) should be adapted in a flexible way according to the individual requirements.

For example, the first priority, and also the important second priority stakeholders, should be represented through an own perspective in the scorecard – if necessary in addition to the four named perspectives. The sequence of the

---

[3] For a detailed discussion of the concept, see Robert S. Kaplan and David P. Norton (2000) *The Strategy-focused Organization*, Boston: Harvard Business School Press. A shortened version is also described in a SAP AG white paper, co-authored by David Norton and the author of this book: SAP AG (1999) *SAP Strategic Enterprise Management – Translating Strategy into Action: The Balanced Scorecard*, White Paper, Walldorf, Germany: SAP AG.

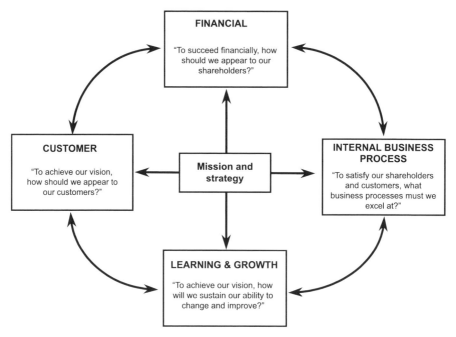

Figure 6.2 The four Balanced Scorecard perspectives as proposed by Kaplan and Norton.

perspectives for the cause and effect linkage should start with the perspective that represents the first priority stakeholder group. The other perspectives should follow, according to the priority of the related stakeholder group and/or according to the importance of the respective perspective for achieving the strategy's main objective.

So the intention is not so much to present a "balanced" view on all perspectives, but to clearly state what the first objective is and to define other objectives that have to be achieved. It is by taking these other objectives into consideration, as constraints, that we can attain the main objective. Only this way will it become clear to every employee involved what the main objective of an organization following a given strategy is.

However, stakeholder-related transparency of corporate strategy is also necessary and this requires that corporate objectives concerning the various stakeholder groups be clearly communicated. This is the precondition for productive relations to all stakeholder groups. Often managers publicly say, for example, that the company's main stakeholders are customers and then employees. In many cases they are not even aware, that the fundament of

Strategic perspectives

Strategy map
(Strategic objectives, cause & effect linkages)

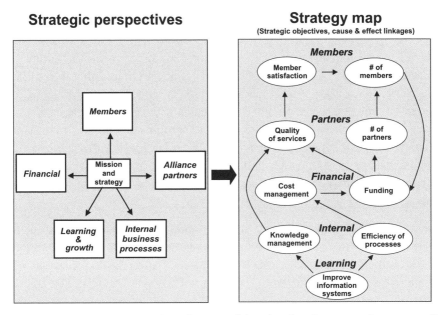

Figure 6.3 A five perspective Balanced Scorecard that describes the strategy for a non-profit organization.

their business may be a different paradigm (for good reasons). If they make public statements and stakeholder know that they are not true, that can hurt a companies reputation and stakeholder relations over time dramatically. Therefore priorities concerning stakeholders should be consciously decided and should be communicated to all stakeholders.

The concept, for a non-profit organization, is presented in graphical form in Figure 6.3. This organization has defined its "members" as its most important stakeholder group. As paying members they are the main source of the financial resources the organization needs to fund its non-profit activities. In order to acquire new members, the organization is relying on alliance partners providing various services for members.

So, the outcome is a detailed "strategy map", which describes the cause and effect linkages of strategic objectives and in addition, related quantitative targets, initiatives, and risk rates as depicted in Figure 6.1. It therefore describes, how an organization intends to achieve which value target for it's most important stakeholder groups.

If strategy definition and redefinition follows a structured and systematic approach, it enables an organization, subject to fast changes in the value of its intangible assets because it acts in a highly dynamic market environement, to achieve sustaining business success. In addition, an established strategy definition and redefinition process is also an important mean to capture the individual managerial knowledge of executives and to transform it into sustaining structural capital, if it takes place on a regular basis. If the individual human capital of different managers (their managerial knowledge and experiences) is translated into corporate structural capital through competency, market and strategy maps, the successor of an executive who has left the company not only is helped to start easier and faster, but the organization too will also accumulate management know-how and the ability to learn faster on a strategic level.

One outcome of a new strategy and an important strategic objective for the internal perspective could also be to overhaul and change the organizational design, structures and processes. This enables an enterprise to achieve its new strategic targets and is related to the design of an organization's value-creation system.

Definition and design of the value-creation system

Only through the right configuration of a company's value-creation system will it be able to execute successfully, over time and under intensive competitive pressure, a new strategy. The design of the value-creation system is therefore dependent on its theory of business and its strategy. If a company is changing its business theory or its strategy, it has to check whether the actual configuration of the value creation/business system is still in line with it.

The value-creation system of an organization is the complete set of processes through which it creates value for its stakeholders: strategy management and corporate performance management processes, product innovation and commercialization processes, operational and customer relations processes, and communication processes with major other stakeholders. Finally, it comprises also the way an organization is sourcing, developing, deploying, exploiting, and managing its basic resources such as human capital, financial capital, alliances, and IT.

So, after the strategy has been defined, take a careful look at the value creation system on the basis of which the strategy has been implemented and use it as a final check to see if everyone in the management team agrees on and understands the new strategy and its translation into the day-to-day business in the same way. But it is also necessary to clarify and to define the things that have been left open during the strategy definition process. These are usually things that have been perceived as "execution details" and put aside. Often it is these "details" that have a large impact on the outcome; that is, whether the company is able to function successfully against the backdrop of the new strategy in its day-to-day business or not. Often their importance is not seen by the people who decide "ad-hoc" on them in their day-to-day work, especially if they had not been involved in the strategy discussion. Also changes made to single value creation processes in implementing of a new strategy should not lead to the result, that they do not fit any more to other value creation processes and that the company risks the success of the overall strategy. So the management team itself has to have this final critical and systematic look on the entire value creation system.

For example, the management team has to agree on how it will organize its product innovation and commercialization processes. Will it develop everything in-house or will it work with R&D partners or even license intellectual property from others? How will it organize its internal R&D activities and the implementation and commercialization phase of the product innovation process? Will it work with sales and distribution partners downstream, which it has to include very early into the product innovation process?

In addition, how the company will organize its operative business processes according to the actual strategy has to be clarified. How does the company intend to organize its supply chain, that is, how customers will get products or services? Will it rely on in-house manufacturing and in-house service resources or will it work instead with alliance partners and outsource all or major parts of manufacturing and focus just on customer consulting and customer care management activities?

What also has to be defined and what is a major component of an organization's value-creation system, is how the organization intends to source, develop, exploit and manage its basic resources such as human capital, alliance partners, financial capital, and information technology. That is, the management team has to define, as part of the value-creation system, its human resource, alliance, IT, and financial management policies. This can happen by answering, for example, the following questions:

▶ *Human Resources:* Should the company work in specific critical areas, for example in R&D, with freelancers or not, should it outsource certain services, such as hiring?

▶ *Finance:* How does the company intend to finance growth? Only internally through free cash flow or does the company accept new shareholders or the dependency on banks? In the first case, the company has to make sure, that specific cash flow goals are defined in the scorecard. Should the company outsource certain tasks in core finance to external service providers, such as the collection process?

▶ *IT:* To which of the IT operations will the management team dedicate the company's management resources, or is it better to outsource certain IT services? The more the task becomes strategic, the more management probably will try to retain the service in-house, as it then often represents a differentiator and a competitive advantage. Few companies will outsource their entire business intelligence competence centre; it provides management and knowledge workers with the most critical information for the success of the company and its design is heavily dependent on the individual company. On the other hand, it could make sense to outsource even here certain services such as basic data collection tasks or in the area of preparing rolling forecasts – that is, in areas where repetitive tasks are executed which do not add much value to the business.

▶ *Alliance Management:* Management also has to decide if it will manage alliances only decentrally or does it want to establish, in addition, a central alliance management competence centre? In such a competence centre the company could pool competencies to establish, develop and manage alliances. It would be responsible for providing contractual, legal, tax and business development services, for establishing a common alliance policy and for the training of decentral alliance managers. If working more with partners is new for the organization, then such a central unit could be more appropriate. As the organizations alliance management capabilities are further developed, many of these tasks may be delegated back to operational units.

Typically, these policies concerning basic resources both play the role of constraints for the overall strategy and form important components of a company's value-creation system (see Figure 6.4). Therefore, they have to be taken into consideration during the final check of the strategy and of the related value-creation system. But which resources really represent basic resources for an enterprise is dependent on its theory of business and its strategy.

As soon as this last step – the final agreement of the management team on the organization's value-creation system – is concluded, the foundation to define a comprehensive performance measurement system that will serve later as the basis to support the management processes is in place.

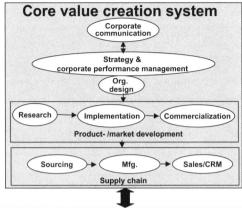

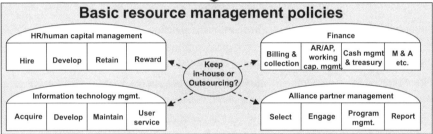

Figure 6.4 The value-creation system and the management policies for the basic resources.

Performance measurement and accounting

How can an enterprise, especially one that uses intangible assets, measure its performance and value created? Financial measures may be sufficient to measure business performance related to tangible assets, but these measures fail in evaluating business performance related to intangible assets and especially in valuing these intangibles itself. The result is that there is a growing disconnect between what a company reports through its financial statements and between the value it created. Earnings and cash flows from tangible and financial assets amount to just a fraction of the value of companies. The rest is due to future cash flows and earnings potential of its intangible assets.[4]

---

[4] A part of the market value of a company is definitely due to speculation. Improved transparency concerning the intangibles of a company and the related value creation processes enables investors and managers to isolate the residual, speculation-based part of corporate value and thus to minimize it.

Companies must shift their focus from being exclusively concerned with their tangible assets and their current financial performance to finding the right balance between maximizing the value of current performance and the creation of business options that create earnings and free cash flow in the future. This requires companies to establish management processes for creating and exploiting in a systematic way intangible assets: on the strategic level through new combinations of existing or acquired intangibles, in R&D through new inventions, and in commercialization through the creation of productive partner networks and customer relations. As a basis for these new management processes a performance measurement and accounting system is required, one that provides the necessary performance measures and performance database.

Financial measures are lagging indicators, they give delayed information about a company's reality. Therefore, proactive managers need to balance the focus on both actual short-term financial performance (which is a proxy for the efficiency of an organization) and on intangible assets that will drive value in the future. So monitoring nonfinancial measures and reports on measures related to the most important value-creation processes that create and exploit intangible assets, while giving details at the same time about short-term performance, are important tasks of the new management system.

It is no longer a matter of debate that nonfinancial measures are important. The question now is: How do companies use them and, in addition, how can financial accounting be improved for reporting overall enterprise performance, including the performance of intangibles?

About this important topic I have spoken with one of the leading experts worldwide on intangible assets-based reporting and accounting, Professor Baruch Lev.

Interview with Professor Baruch Lev: A new accounting model that recognizes intangible assets

Baruch Lev is the Philip Bardes Professor of Accounting and Finance at New York University, Stern School of Business, the Director of the Vincent C. Ross Institute for Accounting Research and the Project for Research on Intangibles. He earned his MBA and Ph.D. degrees from the University of Chicago. He has served on the faculty of the University of Chicago, University of California-Berkeley (jointly at the business and law schools) and Tel Aviv University, where he was dean of the business school. Lev is a permanent visitor at

Ecole Nationale Des Ponts and Chaussees (Paris) and City University Business School (London) and a consultant to numerous corporations and investors and lectures internationally, conducts executive seminars on finance, accounting and intellectual capital issues, and works closely with such institutions as the US Securities and Exchange Commission and the Financial Accounting Standards Board, OECD, the European Union, and the Brookings Institution in the US. His research concerns the optimal use of information in investment decisions; business valuation issues; corporate governance and, recently, intangible assets and intellectual capital, in particular, the measurement, valuation and reporting issues concerning intangible investments.

Based on his extensive research and consulting, Baruch Lev is proposing a new model for accounting that recognizes intangible assets, one of the major value drivers in today's knowledge-based economy. Such a model provides managers as well as investors with more useful information to manage and to assess in a much better way today's intangible assets-dominated business corporations. Baruch Lev recently published his concepts of "management, measurement, and reporting" of intangibles.[5] With this interview, conducted in August, 2001, I wanted to know more about the new accounting system for the new economy.

Juergen Daum: Mr. Lev, you are a Professor of Accounting and Finance and a recognized expert for "intangibles" or "intangible assets". What has raised your interest for intangibles?

Baruch Lev: The task of finance and namely of accounting always was to capture and report the performance and results of business organizations, but also to provide information about the drivers of future revenues and growth – the assets. And financial accounting, based on the principle of double entry, did a reasonably good job in doing exactly that since its invention 500 years ago – until recently, when intangible assets increased in importance. It's not that intangible assets are something totally new. Intangibles have existed always. But with the arrival of the new information technologies, the structure of enterprises has changed dramatically within the last decade, and intangibles represent today often the major assets of these corporations. Physical and financial assets are rapidly becoming commodities, yielding at best an average return on investment. Abnormal profits, dominant competitive positions, and sometimes even temporary monopolies are achieved by investments in intangible assets such as R&D, advertisement or new

[5] Baruch Lev (2001) *Intangibles: Management, Measurement, and Reporting*, Washington, DC: Brookings Institution Press.

business models and processes. Empirical research demonstrates, that companies with high levels of investments in R&D and advertisement for example, show far better earnings and stock performance than companies with lower levels of spending in those areas. But unfortunately traditional accounting is not able to capture, measure and report on intangible assets. Companies are investing huge amounts of money in intangible assets but are not able to report on them and manage them properly. This is forcing investors, but often also managers, to act in the dark. One consequence for example is increased stock price volatility in knowledge-based industries such as software and pharmaceuticals. This is why intangibles raised my interest.

Juergen Daum: Why is accounting, as it is done traditionally, in our knowledge- and information-based economy of today an outdated model?

Baruch Lev: One of the major problems with today's accounting systems is, that they are still based on transactions. Anything which is not related to a legally binding transaction with third parties such as sales, purchases, borrowings etc., will not be registered in the accounting system. In the industrial and agricultural economies, most of the value of business enterprises was created by such transactions – by the legal transfer of property rights. You purchased for example for 10 and sold for 12. The accounting system registered both transaction, and computed the result – profit of 2. In the current, knowledge-based economy, things are more complex.

Much of the value creation or destruction precedes, sometimes by years, the occurrence of transactions. The successful development of a drug, for example, creates considerable value, but actual transactions, such as sales, may take years to materialize. Until then, the accounting system does not register any value created in contrast to the investments made into R&D, which are fully expensed. This difference, between how the accounting system is handling, or better not handling, value created and is handling investments into value creation, is the major reason for the growing disconnect between market values and financial information. Even now, after the stock market declines, the average market value of the S&P 500 company is six times the value reported on the balance sheet.

Juergen Daum: But financial information is still the only reliable information investors and the public have about companies. Financial analysts, who are analyzing the performance of corporations and who provide investors with investment recommendation, are using nearly exclusively financial figures in their reports. And those financial figures are based on information and data provided through financial statements, through accounting.

Baruch Lev: Yes, and this is exactly the problem. The financial statements are insufficient to assess properly the performance and the value generation potential of today's companies, where intangible assets are the major drivers of corporate value. Evaluating profitability and performance of a business enterprise, by say, return on investment, assets or equity (ROA, ROE) is seriously flawed since the value of the firm's major assets – intangible capital – is missing from the denominator of these indicators. Measures of price relatives – for example, price-to-book ratio – are similarly misleading, due to the absence of the value of intangible assets from accounting book values. Valuations for the purpose of mergers and acquisitions are incomplete without an estimate of intellectual capital. Resource allocation decisions within corporations require values of intangible capital. I am often asked by executives, how much should we invest in R&D, employee training, or brand enhancement. Managers don't have the tools for intangibles' resource allocation. These and other uses create the need for valuing intangible assets, in practically all economic sectors, old and new.

Juergen Daum: And why does this not happen? Why do companies and their accountants not account for their intangible assets?

Baruch Lev: Intangible assets, such as new discoveries like drugs, software programs, brands or unique organizational design and processes that provide a competitive advantage like, for example, Cisco's Internet-based supply chain, are by and large not traded in organized markets, and the property rights over these assets are not fully secured by the company, except for intellectual properties, such as patents and trademarks. The risk of these assets – for example of drugs or software programs under development not making it to the market – is generally higher than that of physical assets. Accordingly, many, particularly accountants and corporate executives, are reluctant to recognize intangible, or intellectual capital as assets in financial reports, on par with physical and financial assets. And under GAAP, expenditures made to increase brand awareness, to foster innovation, or to improve the productivity of employees cannot be capitalized.

Juergen Daum: If you look at the phenomena of the Internet companies, which represented probably the most condensed version of "intangibility", the concerns related to intangible assets that you mentioned, such as nontradability and high risks, are valid if you think about the large amounts of money which have been lost by investors. At the beginning you never knew if the "dotcom" you selected, would make it or not. And when it got into trouble, there was no asset left which could be sold to compensate shareholders, at least partly.

Baruch Lev: What happened with the Internet is the same as what happened with any other revolutionary invention. Always people become overly enthusiastic with new technologies. That happened with electricity, with railways, and with automobiles. In the first moment when the phenomena takes off, everybody fears missing the train to wealth and invests significant amounts of money in the new stocks. Later they realize, that it costs them a lot of money to make money with such investments, even if the company will be successful. And doubts will come up, if all that will work out. In a competitive economy it is not clear which one of these many new players will survive. At the beginning of the 19th century there had been over 200 car manufacturers in the US alone. People had been enthusiastic about these car companies and share values skyrocketed. Today, we have only three left, basically two, because Chrysler is part of DaimlerChrysler.

So I think with the Internet it is the same. Among the many Internet companies you will find some which will be successful, probably America Online, e-Bay, and Amazon. One or two, not more, in each small market segment. So the Internet is a special phenomena related to a new invention, a new technology. You cannot compare it with established markets and companies, which by the way will become now also "Internet enabled". And many so-called "old economy" industries are rich in intangibles. In a recent study which I conducted together with Feng Gu from the Boston University, where we analyzed data for 2,000 companies for the period 1990–1999, we found that the intangible capital on average in aerospace and defense companies exceeds by far market value, and in food/beverages the intangible capital to book value ratio was more than 7. This is the type of information investors need. If investors would have had more reliable information about intangibles of these Internet companies, it would have been easier to assess their true value. The absence of reliable information about intangible assets represents a major economic and social problem today.

Juergen Daum: Why?

Baruch Lev: For a company which possesses a larger amount of intangible assets, GAAP-based financial accounting and reporting produces insufficient information, with the result that investors are in the dark and managers operate by guessing. For example, it has been shown that the expensing of intangibles results in an understatement of profitability for high intangibles growth companies. With coauthors I examined more than 1,500 R&D intensive companies. And we found that companies with a high growth rate of R&D expenditures – but relatively low growth rate of earnings, typical to young, intangible-intensive enterprises – are systematically undervalued by investors. This increases cost of capital for these companies and the costs to finance future wealth of economies at large, which are increasingly dependent on investments in innovation to create economic value. And it reduces prosperity by distorting flows of investment capital, which should go where it can be most productively employed.

Juergen Daum: So companies should report on their intangible assets. Often intangible assets are calculated as the difference between their market value and book value. Is this the right approach?

Baruch Lev: No, this approach is unsatisfactory because it is based on two flawed assumptions. First that there is no miss-pricing of stocks in capital markets – which is not true as you have seen with the burst of the Internet bubble – and second that balance sheet historical values of assets reflect their current value. The market-minus-book approach to valuing intangibles is also unsatisfactory because it is circulatory. One searches for measures of intangibles value in order to provide new information to managers and investors. The market-minus book measure is derived from what investors already know and represents no new information. There is obviously a need for a different approach to estimating the value of intangible assets.

Juergen Daum: What do you recommend instead?

Baruch Lev: First we need an operational objective for designing an improved information system. And the objective of the new accounting or information system I propose is the facilitation of two major forces characterizing modern economies: the democratization and the externalization of the decision-making process both within organizations and in capital markets.

Juergen Daum: What do you mean by democratization and externalization of the decision-making process?

Baruch Lev: The democratization of the capital markets is reflected in the increasing role of individual investors in these markets. While professional financial analysts still play a central role in capital markets, millions of individual investors are becoming their own analysts. A large number of financial websites attempt to cater the need of these new "analysts". But most of these sites basically compile and manipulate publicly available information such as financial statement data, analysts' earnings forecasts, and so on, which are devoid of relevant and meaningful information about intangible or knowledge assets. While analysts may obtain some such information from management, individual investors cannot.

The externalization of managerial decision making is related to the changes of the structures of enterprises. In the industrial-era vertically integrated corporations, decision-making authority was largely centralized and confined within the boundaries of the organization. Managers had in-house most of the information they needed. In contrast, in the modern corporation an increasing number of important decisions are shared with entities residing outside the legal confines of the corporation: customers, alliance partners, suppliers of outsourced services, and so on. The networked corporation needs timely information about its partners and is called to provide information about itself to network partners. So the democratization-externalization process creates new constituencies and enhances demand for relevant information.

Juergen Daum: And what is your new accounting model for the new economy? How should companies report about their intangible assets?

Baruch Lev: The most relevant information to decision makers – either managers or investors – in the current economic environment concerns the enterprise's value chain, or business model as it is often called by analysts. By value chain, I mean the fundamental economic process of innovation that starts with the discovery of new products or services or processes, proceeds through the development phase of these discoveries and the implementation stage and establishment of technological feasibility, and culminates in the commercialization of the new products or services. Successful knowledge-based companies, operating in high-tech, science-based, Internet and service sectors, but also in traditional industries like aerospace and defense, chemicals, consumer products, oil and gas and retail sectors, engage in systematic, carefully planned and executed processes of innovation.

And this innovation process is where economic value is created in these firms. Current accounting does not convey relevant and timely information about the innovation process which is critical to the survival and success of business enterprises. Investments in the discovery phase are immediately expensed in financial reports and the value-creating implementation stage of the innovation chain, where an FDA (Food and Drugs Administration) drug approval, a patent grant or a successful beta test of a software product takes place, are not even reported separately to investors. And even the commercialization stage, which generates recordable costs and revenues, is generally reported in a highly aggregated manner, defying attempts to evaluate the efficiency of the firm's innovation process, such as the assessment of return of R&D or technology acquisition, the success of collaboration efforts, and the firm's ability to expeditiously bring products to the market. So what I recommend as one important element of a new accounting system is a Value Chain Blueprint, an information system for use in both internal decision making and disclosure to investors.

Juergen Daum: A Value Chain Blueprint, is it something like a Balanced Scorecard?

Baruch Lev: Yes it has something in common with a Balanced Scorecard. The Value Chain Blueprint focuses, like Balanced Scorecards, on both financial and nonfinancial value drivers. But in contrast to the Balanced Scorecard, where the main intention is to better manage strategy and implementation of new strategies by describing the strategy, the Value Chain Blueprint's mission is to better report on performance and to help to better manage performance by describing how a company is creating that performance. And as performance of companies today is dependent on their capability to innovate and to bring successfully new products to market, a performance reporting and management system has to focus on the innovation value chain. This is exactly what the Value Chain Blueprint does.

Juergen Daum: What it is exactly a Value Chain Blueprint? What does it look like?

Baruch Lev: A Value Chain Blueprint consists of nine sets of measures that provide information – mainly nonfinancial measures – about the lifeline of innovation of successful business enterprises (see Figure 6.5).

These nine sets of measures are assigned to three main areas of an innovation value chain: discovery and learning, implementation, and commercialization. For the discovery area, three sets of measures depict information about *internal renewal* – such as R&D activities, about *acquired capabilities* – such as technology purchase, and about the status of *networking in discovery and learning* – such as R&D alliances or communities of practice. For the implementation phase, another three sets of measures report about *intellectual property* created – such as patents, trademarks or licensing agreements, about *technological feasibility* – such as the status of clinical tests for a new drugs or beta tests for software programs, and about *Internet activities* – such as degree of online purchases Web traffic, etc.. For the commercialization phase, again, three sets of measures provide information about *customers* – such as customer turnover and value, brand value, or the status of marketing alliances, about *commercialization performance* – through revenue figures such as innovation revenues,[6] patent royalties and knowledge earnings,[7] and about *growth prospects* by reporting on the product pipeline and launch dates and expected break-even and cash burn rate. The Value Chain Blueprint's task is to provide information about innovation capabilities and their consequences. Therefore, it is an information system aimed at capturing the links between resources and outcomes. The intention is to provide with the Value Chain Blueprint concept a comprehensive representation of relevant information items. For specific companies not all information mentioned may be relevant. For example set 4 is irrelevant for companies without patents, and the Internet-related information in sets 6 and 7 will be missing for companies without online activities. In such cases companies would just use a subset of the comprehensive Value Chain Blueprint I am proposing. I want to make clear that my Value Chain Blueprint is different than most other proposed information systems in that it is scientifically-based. Each of the proposed measures and

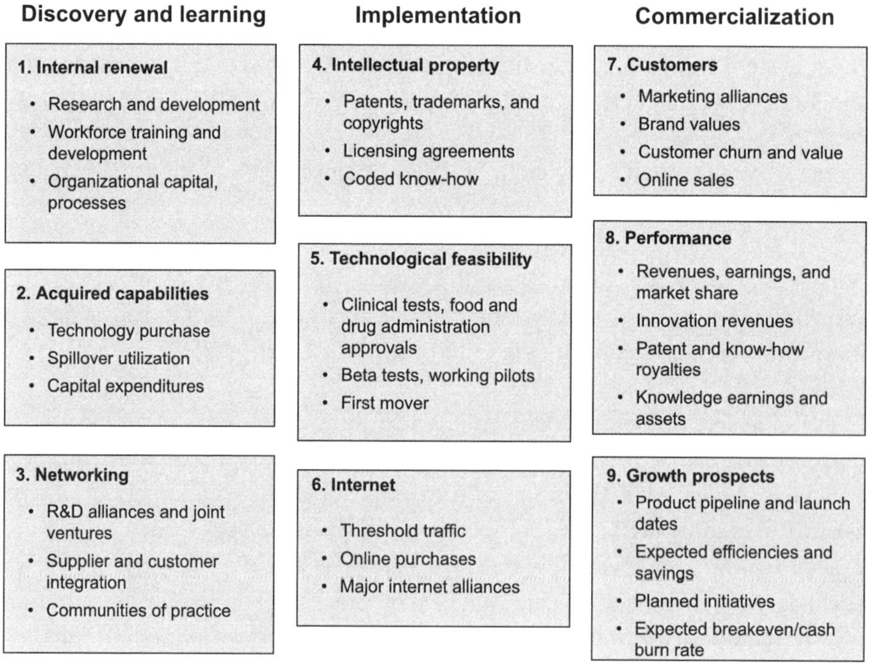

Discovery and learning	Implementation	Commercialization
1. Internal renewal • Research and development • Workforce training and development • Organizational capital, processes	**4. Intellectual property** • Patents, trademarks, and copyrights • Licensing agreements • Coded know-how	**7. Customers** • Marketing alliances • Brand values • Customer churn and value • Online sales
2. Acquired capabilities • Technology purchase • Spillover utilization • Capital expenditures	**5. Technological feasibility** • Clinical tests, food and drug administration approvals • Beta tests, working pilots • First mover	**8. Performance** • Revenues, earnings, and market share • Innovation revenues • Patent and know-how royalties • Knowledge earnings and assets
3. Networking • R&D alliances and joint ventures • Supplier and customer integration • Communities of practice	**6. Internet** • Threshold traffic • Online purchases • Major internet alliances	**9. Growth prospects** • Product pipeline and launch dates • Expected efficiencies and savings • Planned initiatives • Expected breakeven/cash burn rate

Figure 6.5   Baruch Lev's Value Chain Blueprint.[8]

---

[6] "Innovation revenues" is Baruch Lev's term for a measure of the percentage of annual sales generated by recently introduced – in the last three to five years – products.

[7] "Knowledge earnings" is Baruch Lev's term for a measure of the return for knowledge assets in contrast to returns from financial and physical assets. The calculation of this measure is described in Chapter 7.

[8] Lev, *Intangibles*, p. 111.

indicators was shown by economic/finance research to represent a value driver, namely to be statistically linked with the value of the firm.

Juergen Daum: How should companies select the right measures?

Baruch Lev: Specific scoreboard indicators or measures should satisfy three criteria to ensure maximal usefulness. First, they should be quantitative. Second, they should be standardized, meaning that they can be compared across business units and across firms for valuation and benchmark purposes. Third and most important, they should be confirmed by empirical evidence as relevant to users. This could be done by establishing a significant statistical association between the measures and indicators of corporate value such as stock return and productivity improvements. These three criteria for choice of the specific scoreboard indicators ensure that the proposed information system satisfies the needs of internal and external users. A typical company will have about 10 to 12 key value-chain indicators that should inform both managers and investors – at different levels of detail and frequency, of course – about the company's innovation activities, with special emphasis on investment in intangibles and their transformation to tangible results.

Juergen Daum: What will motivate managers to use the Value Chain Blueprint to publicly disclose this information in a systematic and consistent manner?

Baruch Lev: Firstly, an important use of the Blueprint is also to assist managers in their decisions. Regarding disclosure to capital markets, I strongly believe that if a coherent, well-defined, and decision-relevant system is developed to reflect the major attributes of intangible assets and their role in the overall value-creation process of the enterprise, most managers will respond by disclosing voluntarily some or all of the information. The reason for my optimism is that the availability of a new disclosure structure, endorsed by the major accounting policy-making institutions and perhaps by other influential parties, such as the large accounting firms, will initiate an information revelation process.

Enterprises with good news will start disclosing, motivating others to join them. Because no news is bad news in capital markets, the silent enterprises will be penalized. So I propose that an appropriate accounting policymaking body, in the US preferably the FASB with strong encouragement and oversight by the SEC, take up the major task of standardizing intangibles-related information, creating a coherent structure of information and a comprehensive set of interrelated reports on value-chain development, with special emphasis on intangible investments and assets.

Juergen Daum: You mentioned before, that the Value Chain Blueprint is one important element of a new accounting system. What are the others and what especially happens with the current accounting system?

Baruch Lev: The Value Chain Blueprint does not replace accounting. It precedes and complements accounting-based information with additional information about the fundamental phases of the value chain, which are not reflected in financial reports. Financial information is still useful and is needed to provide a final reality check on the value creation or destruction as products, services, or processes move along the value chain. So the second element of a new accounting system is an overhauled version of financial accounting and reporting.

Juergen Daum: What do you think has to be changed with our present financial accounting?

Baruch Lev: The most significant and urgent change required in the present accounting system relates to the recognition of assets. Current GAAP essentially rules out practically all intangibles from being recognized as assets. This includes both internally generated intangibles and most acquired intangibles, such as in-process R&D for example. Such a broad denial of intangibles as assets detracts from the quality of information provided in the balance sheet. Even more serious is its adverse effect on the measurement of earnings. The matching of revenues with expenses is distorted by front-loading costs by the immediate expensing of intangibles and recording revenues in subsequent periods unencumbered by those costs.

What is required is a significant broadening of the recognition of assets in financial accounting and reporting. I am fully aware of the fact, that the high risk associated with investments in intangibles is one of the main reasons why accountants resist capitalizing these investments. But it makes sense to recognize intangible investments as assets when the uncertainty about benefits is considerably resolved. And now, as for example R&D projects advance from formulation through feasibility tests such as alpha and beta tests of software products, to the final product, the uncertainty about technological feasibility and commercial success continually decreases. Accordingly, I propose the recognition as assets of all intangible investments with attributable benefits that have passed certain pre-specified technological feasibility tests. Such recognition will improve the periodic matching of costs and benefits, particularly for firms with high growth rates of intangible investment. The recognized intangibles will be reported on corporate balance sheets, thereby placing intangible assets on a common footing with physical assets.

The amortization and write-offs of intangibles will convey valuable information about managers' assessment of the expected benefits of intangibles. To limit possibilities of earnings management and manipulation, intangibles' recognition should be separately disclosed in financial reports, allowing skeptical investors to easily reverse the procedure.

Juergen Daum: This broadening of current asset recognition rules you propose is indeed a major overhaul of accounting. How likely is it that this will happen?

Baruch Lev: I strongly believe that a significant change in the current accounting system is called for. Such change, however, will require regulatory intervention – changing current accounting rules and regulations – which is bound to raise significant managerial antagonism. I therefore altered the priorities to enhance likelihood of success. I recommend to start with a voluntary yet well-defined and structured reporting system, which is the Value Chain Blueprint, and proceed later with changing the accounting system itself. I think with this approach, antagonism to the latter will be reduced, when managers and accountants gain experience with the disclosure of intangibles-related information and observe its successful dissemination in capital markets.

Juergen Daum: With the actual economic slowdowns, people may think that "new economy", "Internet bubble" and "intangibles" are the same and are not that relevant and important any more. Are you concerned about that?

Baruch Lev: Yes, I am concerned that intangibles – to which I have devoted much of my research and professional activities in recent years – will be swept by the tide of disillusionment surrounding the new economy. That people will lump together the permanent phenomenon of intangible investments as the major source of corporate growth and value with transitory economic downturns, stock market volatility, and the financial difficulties currently encountered by certain technology sectors. That it will overshadow real and fundamental economic developments in which technological change and innovation, ushered by intangible investments, play such a major role. But economic slowdowns and capital market conditions do not change these fundamentals: that an enterprise's competitive survival and success will primarily depend on smart intangible investments leading to innovation and effective commercialization. The central role intangible investments play in corporate success, economic growth, and the enhancement of social welfare remains unchallenged.

Juergen Daum: What do you recommend to managers concerning intangibles in the actual economic situation?

Baruch Lev: In the booming economy and capital markets of the 1990s crude measurement and valuation models could be tolerated, at least for a while. In today's slow-growth economy and stagnant capital markets, on the other hand, more attention to corporate resource allocation is required from managers. So managers should develop the capability to assess the expected return on investment in R&D, employee training, IT, brand enhancement, online activities, and other intangibles and compare these returns with those of physical investment in an effort to achieve optimal allocation of corporate resources. Managers should also continuously monitor the efficiency of intangible asset deployment. While licensing patents and know-how, for example, may not be a top priority when earnings are ample and speed-to-market is crucial, it is an important source of income during periods of slow growth. Today, most business enterprises do not have the information and monitoring tools required for the effective management of intangibles. So investing in these new type management systems may become an important task especially during an economy slowdown. In a challenging business environment I foresee a need for increased, rather than decreased, attention to intangibles – the major driver of corporate value and growth – by both managers and investors. It is now time for the full incorporation of intangible capital in the managerial strategic and control processes as well as investors' analysis of securities and portfolio performance.

Juergen Daum: Baruch, thank you very much for this interesting interview.

7 The New Performance Measurement and Accounting System

Investors need a variety of information to project future profits and cash flow. Historical financial results are a starting point, but are rarely adequate by themselves. Investors need to understand the company's business model, the market for its products, the specific tangible and intangible assets that provide its competitive edge, and the quality of its management team. They also need to understand the key milestones for the development of the company and its progress on achieving key operating performance measures.

An SEC-inspired Task Force[1]

The major objective of an accountng system is to capture, store and prepare data in such a way that can be used to provide investors, other major stakeholders, and management with a true, fair and consistent view on the actual economic status of the enterprise. This is done by reporting on actual performance of the past reporting period, and on created, acquired or destroyed options for the future value creation, that is on net assets. Traditionally this happens through the profit and loss statement and the balance sheet. By reporting on investments made in future business options, that is on assets, and on what the company will have to pay back to third parties and has to deduct from its future income stream, that is on liabilities, investors can estimate the potential of the company to generate future earnings and free cash flows, which can be used either for new investments in order to grow further, or to pay dividends to shareholders.

This basic accounting framework has to be extended into the areas of intangibles-related enterprise performance and value creation. As much of the value of today's companies is created before any sales transactions take place, the new accounting system has to capture all values created from processes, activities, and events that happen before any transaction takes place – in addition to those in manufacturing, that are usually captured through traditional cost and work in process accounting. It has to report on

---

[1] This extract is taken from the report produced by an SEC-inspired task force. See Securities and Exchange Commission (2001) ''Strengthening financial markets: Do investors have the information they need?'', p. 4, which can be accessed at:
http://www.fei.org/finrep/files/SEC-Taskforce-Final-6-6-2kl.pdf

the value potential of future options created through a new strategy and provide insight into values created in product innovation through a FDA approval of a new drug or through a successful beta test of a new software. In addition, it has to report on further business options and value created in operations, for example through the implementation of a more adaptive supply chain network or through improved customer retention. And it also has to provide insight into the productivity of basis resources such as human and financial capital.

So what is needed is a comprehensive measurement system that spans the entire value-creation activity of an enterprise and an underlying accounting system that is able to capture, process and document information on a company's investments and on its value-creating activities that are relevant for evaluating its actual performance and its future value creation capabilities. Therefore, such a measurement system has to include indicators and measures about all value-creating processes – no matter if these are backed by tangible or intangible assets, no matter if these are financial or nonfinancial measures.

Standardization of the measures for the new enterprise measurement system

Because a larger number of the constituencies of an enterprise need timely information that can be compared with information about other companies, it is desirable that the elements of an enterprise's or business unit's measurement and reporting system are standardized. Only then can they be used to compare performance for valuation and benchmark purposes.

Through legally enforced GAAP rules and strong international agreement on best practice, there is generally accepted framework of accounting procedures, measures and calculation schemes in the financial world. One of the main challenges in using nonfinancial elements in performance measurement systems is that no comparable standards are available and too many options exist for selecting and using such elements. Even in the financial area, where measures come close to a standardization and allow comparisons across companies, the situation today is often unsatisfactory, because individual companies calculate, for example, their gross margins and operating income in different ways.

The major difficulty in defining a common and standardized reporting framework is that the most useful nonfinancial information for investors, for example those related to intangible assets, are specific to the industry and company. It is probably not practical for any regulatory body – such as the FASB in the USA – which publishes binding accounting and disclosure rules for corporations, to define precisely for hundreds of different industries, which performance data and measures have to be disclosed. Even if regulations could be set up that cover such a multitude of industries, the pace of change is so rapid that it is unlikely that regulators could actually change the disclosure rules quickly enough to keep up with the needs of investors. But what such regulators could do is to establish a framework for disclosure of financial and nonfinancial corporate performance data that describes the broader principles, and create a common language showing how it has to be done. This is what an SEC-inspired task force in the USA is recommending.

This task force investigated possibilities to improve corporate reporting, by taking especially the increasing importance of intangible assets into account, and recommended in its final report of May 2001 creation of a framework for voluntary supplemental reporting on intangible assets and for operative performance measures.[2] Companies should report on measures related to intangibles that help investors to assess the impact of the intangibles on future profits and cash flow. The framework should not prescribe specific measures (because the relevance of these measures varies across industries and companies), but should provide a structure, language and process to help companies explain in a consistent way how their business creates value and help improve comparability across companies in the same industry. So this framework should define a common, generic approach that companies could use to describe their business system and value-creation processes (in my terminology: their value-creation system). Companies could then select and focus their disclosure on those components that are most relevant to their business.

In addition to such a standardized common reporting framework, the specific measures, indicators and reporting schemes for an industry may be defined and regularly updated in the future by industry groups, which issue comprehensive lists of standardized industry-related performance measures, including their description and calculation rules, and a set of rules that describe how performance reports should be structured. Each firm has to select from these lists the measures that are relevant to its business according to the actual strategy and according to its existing value-creation system.

Because the relevance of specific measures for the evaluation of a company is often relative and subjective, it should indeed – as Baruch Lev in our interview

---

[2] Ibid.

has proposed – be confirmed by empirical evidence as relevant to users. Third parties could do this in a similar way as auditing firms provide opinions on financial statements. Probably third-party verification and auditing of nonfinancial measures will emerge on a wider basis, as companies seek to establish credibility in the eyes of their investors, the public and other important stakeholders, and because they want to make sure, that their new extended reports are in line with established standards and best practice.[3]

Triggered by the spread of the Internet, considerable advances have recently been made in setting up the necessary standards for disclosing and exchanging of even complex business data. The main building blocks are XML-based standard languages[4] that serve as a catalyst for the development of a standardized measuring and reporting framework for nonfinancial business information. Because such a technology enabled standard allows companies to publish and exchange information with others very easily via their website, it is likely that such new techniques for business data exchange become quickly and widely used.

One example of this is XBRL (eXtensible Business Reporting Language), an XML-based language that supports the extraction, manipulation, exchange and analysis of financial information. Despite common practice and standards, often financial data from different companies was non-comparable, because each company used its own standard of structuring and aggregating financial accounts into financial statement items and reports. XBRL is providing now common XML-based definitions of financial statement items, thus enabling business organizations to exchange financial and performance information more easily with their stakeholders. The XBRL standards are defined by the XBRL committee, a group of more than 70 members that represent the major accounting companies, software companies, and other organizations.[5] XBRL is supporting US-GAAP based and IAS-based financial reporting as well as a growing number of other country's GAAP and is therefore likely to become

---

[3] An example of this emerging practice of auditing nonfinancial KPIs for external reporting is Shell with its "Shell report" described in Part 2 of this book: Shell started to let third-party auditors testify nonfinancial measures the company reports as part of its "triple bottom line reporting".

[4] XML-based standard language is specifically designed as a mark-up language to deliver information over the Web. An XML-based standard language – such as XBRL – is an application that consists of a set of elements and a structure that can describe documents of a particular type. The elements in an XML document contain the actual document information and indicate its logical structure.

[5] For more details, see the XBRL committee homepage at: www.xbrl.org

XBRL code

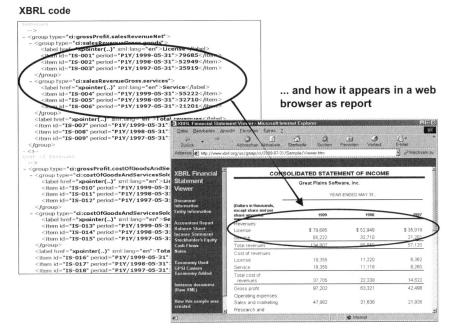

Figure 7.1 Extract of an XBRL-based profit and loss statement based on the XBRL taxonomy for Financial Reporting for Commercial and Industrial Companies according to US-GAAP (publicly available example at the XBRL Commitee's website at www.xbrl.org).

the new worldwide standard for exchanging and reporting financial data. Figure 7.1 shows a XBRL scheme according to US-GAAP.

While XBRL is focusing on financial statement data, there are similar initiatives on the way to use XML-based languages to report and exchange nonfinancial business data. For example, the Balanced Scorecard Collaborative Inc., the company of Kaplan and Norton, has established a Balanced Scorecard XML Standards Committee with its members drawn from all major Balanced Scorecard software application vendors. The BSC XML Standard includes, for example, standardized elements for measures, strategic objectives, perspectives and targets in order to establish a common language around the Balanced Scorecard. This standard should facilitate the seamless integration of Balanced Scorecard-related applications over the Internet, enabling organizations to easily exchange performance- and strategy-related information between different software applications and across enterprises.

These developments, in establishing standards for the use of financial and nonfinancial performance measures across enterprises, are quite promising. However, it will still take some time until the new technologies are applied on a broader basis and a critical mass of users are committed to their use. While these XML-based languages provide a valuable syntax and semantic for the standardization of measure catalogs, the content of these catalogs is still not defined. Even with today's urgency, that companies report more nonfinancial business information to analysts, investors and other external parties, it will still take some time for regulatory bodies, industry organizations, consultants or specialized service providers and data aggregators to come up with a generic performance measurement and reporting framework and with a standardized list of industry specific relevant performance measures that will be accepted and applied by a critical mass of enterprises.

Until this happens companies must work their own way through. The framework described in the following section is intended to provide organizations with guidelines to define their own improved measurement, accounting, reporting and management system. It is based on the results of relevant expert discussions of recent years about these topics, both in the USA and in Europe. And while this discussion is still continuing, I am sure that companies that create such a measurement system now will be able to adapt it easily in the future as new standards are available. And they will benefit already today from increased transparency through improved business performance and better recognition of their intangibles by investors and financial analysts.

Conceiving the new measurement system

The task of the measurement system, as an important part of the new management system, is both to measure investments made in specific physical or intangible capabilities of a company and the related results; that is, to measure performance achieved through these investments, hence to measure input and output.

An enterprise today, especially when it comes to intangibles-dominated, knowledge-based businesses, is a much more complex economic system when compared with a simple trading or agricultural business. In the latter case, it was enough to measure input and output at the borders of the enterprise; that is, on the basis of external transactions such as purchase and sales that had been recorded in the general ledger. It is also more complex than the industrial enterprise that required, in addition to the general ledger, a sophisticated cost-accounting system to enable managers to optimize resource consumption and value-creating processes in mass manufacturing. Today, it is not only the efficiency of internal processes but also achievement of external effects like network effects that have become a major source for value created – often they are the most important critical success factors for companies, which have to act and survive in highly dynamic markets. Therefore, the bulk of the value created by companies today often results from new, successful strategies, introduced quickly and executed successfully, from the development of new products and their successful commercialization, as well as from improved customer relations.

These changes have to be reflected in the management system and its measurement tools. The new measurement system therefore needs to be oriented in its structure and content on the value-creation systems of today's enterprises. That is, on the system that represents the major value-creation processes and activities of an organization, that creates through constant innovation intangible value, which is then converted systematically into customer and financial value. And the tool to do that is a system of measures providing a concentrated view on all mission critical areas of an enterprise: on its actual general performance and on its success in implementing a new strategy, on its performance in developing new products and improving time-to-market, on its performance in operations and in managing basis resources like human or financial capital or important information resources.

The Tableau de Bord: the enterprise control panel

Several concepts of how to measure nonfinancial value drivers and intangibles have emerged in recent years. Here are some examples:

▶   The concept of the Balanced Scorecard, proposed by Kaplan and Norton, provides an excellent framework for reporting on the status of the implementation of a strategy and about general performance as well as for selecting the appropriate measures.

▶   The concept of real option valuation (ROV)[6] provides a valuation scheme for future "real" business options created through new strategies, that can serve at the same time as decision support tools to manage these options, the corresponding investment projects, and related opportunities and risk.

▶   The concept of the Value Chain Blueprint, proposed by Lev, provides the, so far, missing standard to account for and measure productivity and value creation in the product and market development process of a company and provides a measure system to control and optimize this important value creation process.

---

[6] See later in this chapter for more discussion of real option valuation (ROV).

▶   The SCOR model proposed by the Supply Chain Council enables
    companies for comprehensive benchmarking in the area of supply
    chain management.[7]

▶   The concept of customer lifetime value, that enables a company to
    measure the value of a customer across the entire life cycle of the
    enterprise-customer relationship, provides the possibility to value intangi-
    bles created in customer service organizations.

▶   The concepts of value-added per person provide a scheme to value the
    productivity of a workforce.

These are concepts that are already widely accepted and which are used in
practice. What is missing so far is a comprehensive framework for performance
measurement and reporting that comprises all important value-creation areas
and activities of today's enterprises – including those based on intangible
assets. It has to include measures related to strategy management and
corporate performance management, to product innovation, to market and
business development, as well as to operations and to support processes that
manage the enterprise's basis resources. These measures have to be integrated
into one comprehensive measurement system in order to provide managers
with the necessary big picture on the status of total corporate performance *and*
with insight into all value-creation processes.

Therefore, the new monitoring and measurement system has to be based on
the value-creation system of an organization and has to use it as a kind of
reference, if it is to provide relevant management information. I call such a
indicator-based performance measurement system an organization's *Tableau de
Bord* (see Figure 7.2). It is a concept for structuring indicators and measures in
a way that enables internal and external constituencies to inform themselves in
the most efficient way about a company's general or total performance *and*
about the status of its most important value-creating processes.

The concept is based on the French Tableau de bord, the control panel of an
enterprise, that delivers to the ''chef d'entreprise'' indicators and measures
which he or she needs to run and control the enterprise successfully.

The concept of a Tableau de Bord was known and used in France long before
the concept of the Balanced Scorecard emerged. In its traditional form it was
based on financial data and included financial measures taken from the balance
sheet and the income statement. Because in France a mandatory chart of

---

[7] The SCOR concept is described in more detail later in this chapter.

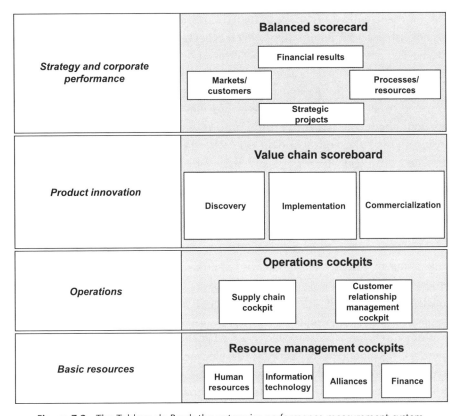

Figure 7.2 The Tableau de Bord: the enterprise performance measurement system.

accounts exists for financial accounting, it exhibits a standard which enforces not only a financial statement structure but also a structure of internal management reports that varied little between different companies. Therefore, it was possible to propose standardized forms of Tableau de Bord – each could be easily and quickly adapted to a specific enterprise. Having such a standard in place was probably the reason why the use of Tableau de Bord was a common practice in France for many years.

The concept was extended at the end of the 1980s to include also nonfinancial measures and was then named 'Tableau de Bord de Gestion''.[8] It's aim was to

---

[8] It was described in J. de Guerny, J. C. Guiriec and J. Lavergne (1990) *Principe et mise en place du Tableau de Bord de Gestion*, Paris: Masson S.A. The book provides a detailed description about how to set up a corporate measurement system. Unfortunately intangibles were obviously not of interest at that time and are not explicitly included in the concept.

inform management faster about negative developments than was possible by using just financial information, which reflects business reality always with a delay. The extended concept of the Tableau de Bord should therefore provide management with early warning indicators in order to enable anticipation of certain important events and more proactive action. But the Tableau cannot respond to all possible questions and provides only limited quantitative information about the status of the most essential value-creation areas of a company and the corresponding operative processes. These latter should be updated on a short-term basis and should be coherent with each other and allow top management to act directly.

This philosophy behind the Tableau de Bord is the key to manage and control an enterprise – especially in an intangible assets-based and highly dynamic new economy: top management should not only look at the general outcome and the status of strategy execution, but should also have an eye on the most important value-creating operative processes. This is important because value related to intangible assets is not created directly, but through business processes that either exploit intangible assets – such as in sales where customer relations are exploited – or which create intangibles – such as in product development or business development. If the status of all value-creating processes and activities as well as all investments in intangible assets are recorded and can be reported, a company has created the enhanced measurement system which is required as the foundation for the new management system.

This enhanced, more holistic, performance-measurement system has to complement management information originating from cost accounting and traditional management accounting. But, also, KPIs based on the Balanced Scorecard concept have to be complemented through additional and detailed information about those enterprise areas, that create or exploit the new intangible values. The concept of the Tableau de Bord de Gestion, that covers all important value-creation processes of an enterprise in a systematic way, is therefore the right approach.

The Tableau de Bord, as the new control panel of the enterprise and as its measurement and controlling tool, comprises four views:

1. A Balanced Scorecard with indicators focusing on strategy execution and general performance.

2. A product and market development view, oriented on Lev's Value Chain

Blueprint concept, which allows managers to measure effectiveness and efficiency in the product innovation and market development process.

3. An overall view in the form of "cockpits" for the control of processes in supply chain management and customer relationship management.

4. A view on the status of the most important basic resources of the enterprise, which enables managers to control the related support processes of the organization.

The comprehensive view, which the Tableau de Bord provides, makes it possible to immediately link Balanced Scorecard measures – that inform about the status of strategic performance (for example, in change management) and about corporate or general performance – to measures that inform about improvements or deterioration of business performance in the respective execution areas and in operative activities, in order to identify immediately causes of deviations. Because only the most important value-creation processes and their indicators are presented, information overflow is avoided. On the other side, the status of the most important operative processes remain visible in the Tableau de Bord without further drill down. Deviations of actual performance from targets but also sudden opportunities on the operative level can be detected immediately and management can act in a proactive way before these developments may affect total results in a negative way in the financial perspective of the Balanced Scorecard view, where indicators come up with a red light.

For example, the measures that inform in the Balanced Scorecard view about the status of strategy execution in an important product development area or that inform about the status of a strategic objective related to new business processes in the area of customer relationship management, can be related immediately to the respective operative measures: to the details about actual performance of the development project and of its corresponding commercialization processes, and to the performance details in the customer relations management area which are presented in the CRM cockpit.

For the selection and use of measures for the different views of the Tableau de Bord, a systematic approach and some basic rules are required which make sure that measures are consistent with each other and can be also reused in other views.

General rules for working with measures for corporate reporting

Work on the new measurement system should, from the start, be conducted in a structured way, in order to avoid double work during implementation and misunderstandings and misinterpretations in its later use. These efforts will pay off if one takes into account that the defined measures will form the basis for all future internal communications around strategy and performance (between managers and between managers and controllers) and later also for external communication (with business partners, investors, analysts).

Companies should therefore, first, create a framework for a measure library, before they start to define the measures for the various Tableau de Bord views. This makes sure that measures are defined in a consistent way and that a common understanding of measures between all involved parties in internal and external corporate communications processes exist. If this has been done, it will also be much easier later on to include new measures, when new needs come up, and also to "digitize" the measurement system; for example, by using analytics software applications, in order to better support management processes. The framework for such a measure library can consist of the following attributes. These attributes, which should be defined for each measure that will be used in the enterprise measurement system, are only a proposal. They should be enhanced and adapted according to the individual needs of an organization.

▶ *Description:* Each measure should be described as exactly as possible through a short text. It should explain what the purpose of this measure is, what it is measuring, what the advantages are in using it and also what the shortcomings and possible disadvantages are. This should include also a recommendation for the areas where it makes sense to use that measure and where it should not be used.

▶ *Calculation scheme:* The measure library should include for each measure a detailed scheme or formula, which describes how it is calculated

▶ *Update frequency:* The measure library should also include, for each measure, in which frequency it can and will be updated and what difference may exist concerning the quality and calculation method of that measure between the different update versions. It may happen that the same measure will be used, for example, for strategic purposes in a Balanced Scorecard view and at the same time to monitor operations in an operations cockpit. But the update frequency may differ – in the Balanced Scorecard it may be on a monthly basis, in the operations cockpit on a weekly or even daily basis. Sometimes the way to calculate the measure can differ depending on the frequency. For example, if operating profit has to be reported before the monthly closing in accounting has taken place, for certain cost items standard costs may be used, because actual cost data are available only after the monthly closing process has been finished. This has to be transparent for a user of that measure.

▶ *Data source:* For every basis measure[9] that should be used in the enterprise measurement system, the possible data sources for it should be defined. For each measure used later in a report, it should be possible to follow an "audit trail", by drilling down to the original data source and to either verify the actual value of that measure or to analyze it further. This is important, especially if professional auditors should verify corporate reports that include nonfinancial measures – as in the case of Shell. But also if a company intends to use measures only internally, this will be helpful. If a manager is questioning the reliability of the data in a report – a situation which is probably common to every controller – the availability of an audit trail will prove the accuracy of the data immediately and will refocus the discussion on the content of the report.

▶ *Owner:* For each measure an owner should be defined. He or she is then responsible for correct data collection and delivery as well as for consistency and correct calculation of measure values.

When the framework for the measure library has been defined, it is time to start to define measures for the various areas of the Tableau de Bord. All measure definitions should be stored in the measures library, to allow for their later reuse in other areas of the Tableau de Bord without the need to redefine the measure again (see Figure 7.3).

Strategic indicators and general performance measures

The measurement system should account for input and output – that is, about investments and their returns and about costs and revenues. It should also provide information that allows managers to better manage the process in between and enable investors to assess the actual performance of that

---

[9] A basis measure is a measure that is not calculated from other measures. "Sales revenues", for example, may represent a basic measure. "Operating profit", which is calculated by using, among other measures such as "Sales revenues", is not a basic measure, but a calculated one.

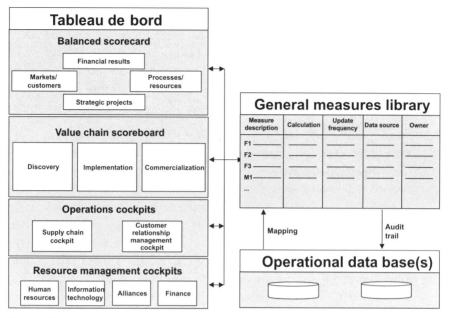

Figure 7.3 The measure library provides the measures for each view of the Tableau de Bord.

process. What does this mean for strategy and performance management system in an organization?

Input on the strategic level equals the investments in the different product and market segments of a company. It also includes investments into major change management activities, process innovation activities and in the development of major basis resources. Even investments made by alliance partners that are critical for the success of a company's strategy can be viewed as an "input" on the strategy and performance management level.

In the strategy and performance management view of the Tableau de Bord one should find therefore indicators and measures that allow top managers to get a picture on how successful a company is with its investment in its different product and market segments. In addition, the picture will show how success-fully the most important change management program is executed, what the status of the development of the most important basis resources, such as human capital or alliances, is and how actual total enterprise performance is developing; that is, what the actual overall results are and what business risks exposure and future potential looks like. A systematic approach to reporting on strategic and general performance provides the Balanced Scorecard concept.

The Balanced Scorecard

The Balanced Scorecard became known first as a measurement system and as a concept for grouping financial and nonfinancial measures in a report in way which allowed the reader to recognize how the organization was doing from a strategic point of view. This, not only concerning financial performance, but also concerning performance in customer interactions, efficiency of internal processes, and effectiveness of innovation and learning initiatives. While Kaplan and Norton have further developed the concept into a more comprehensive strategic management system, the measurement part of the concept, which focuses on the measurement of the status of various strategic success factors, is still an important part of the total concept. The quantitative evaluation of strategy execution, of general business performance and of risk exposure on the basis of objective information represents an important basis for effective strategy and performance management processes and management dialogues.

First and foremost, the Balanced Scorecard is a tool to support strategy execution. Secondly, it serves to monitor more short-term oriented general performance of an enterprise. Therefore, measures for the Balanced Scorecard should be derived from strategic objectives defined during the strategy definition process (see Chapter 6). Whether it is a financial investment, a change management initiative or a major project – without knowing the objective of an investment, management cannot define what the output, the desired result should be. And determining the right measures also helps to fine-tune the definition of the company's strategic objectives. Therefore, a company should early on try to define a first draft version of its Balanced Scorecard measures during the strategy definition process. After the definition of the measurement system has been finished, then strategic objectives and their measures should be carefully evaluated again. For selecting the right measures for the Balanced Scorecard, answering the following questions may be of help.

▶ Can we really tell from the measurement whether the desired objective is being met and is the measurement predominantly in the zone of influence of those responsible for the related objective? Or in other words: is there a direct correlation between the desired action and the change in the measurement or are there other influencing factors?

▶ Can we obtain easily the data for this measure? Can we provide an audit trail if necessary? Or are the data for a similar measure already available that could be used instead?

▶   Is the measure easy enough to be understood by managers and employees who are to use it? Is it able to trigger behaviour, especially if it should be used as a basis for an MBO and incentive system?

▶   Are measures consistent with other measures in the cause and effect linkage of the strategy? Are we measuring along our strategic value chain?

The procedure to define the strategic measures according to the Balanced Scorecard concept could start with a brainstorming and pre-selection session where possible measures are identified. Then these measures should be discussed in the project or management team and a plausibility check according to the questions listed above should be performed. The person, who is responsible for a strategic objective, should check whether it is possible to use the selected measure to track progress in achieving this objective. Once a measure has been finally selected, all the attributes for it have to be defined and agreed upon in the team. The result of the definition process for the measures for the Balanced Scorecard may look like as depicted in Figure 7.4.

Concepts for general performance management

Building on the Balanced Scorecard, how can a company, in addition to strategy execution, support more short-term oriented performance management?

Generally one can have two different views of an enterprise's performance: first, you can look "top down" *on* the organization, by analyzing its total or general performance or, second, look *into* the organization and analyze individually the performance of the processes that create total results. The Tableau de Bord combines both approaches within one concept. The strategy and general performance informs about total performance. At the same time additional views inform about the performance of the value-creating processes of the company – but only about the most important ones and only about their most important drivers and factors in order to avoid information overflow.

So, the question is how to measure total or general performance and how to present it in such a way that managers can further analyze it in more detail, for example, along the enterprise's organizational structure, and that enough insight is provided already at the top level in order to draw managers' attention to problem areas and to invite them to more detailed analysis.

One example is the portfolio concept. Its advantage is that it can combine strategic measures from various Balanced Scorecard perspectives in one

Balanced scorecard measures list

Perspective	No.	Strategic objective	Representative measure
Financial	F1	Increase value	Expected discounted cash flow
	F2	Increase productivity + 10% p.a.	profitability
	F3	Lower net working capital	NWC, DSO, cash to cash cycle
Markets/ customers	M1	Acquisition of new customers	% of customers < 1 year
	M2	Increase customer satisfaction	customer survey index
	M6	Improve customer retention	customer churn rate
Processes	P1	Improve order processing	order cycle time, costs
	P2	Improve forecasting quality	forecast quality, delayed orders
	P3	Improve inventory management	inventories/sales, stock turnover
Learning	L1	Increase sales from new products	% of sales from products < 2 years
	L2	Increase job expertise	actual expertise/required expertise
	L3	Improve employee satisfaction	survey index

Figure 7.4 Strategy measures are selected according to the strategic objectives defined during the strategy definition phase.

graph in order to enable managers to compare many different enterprise units at once (product profit centres, subsidiaries, regions, etc.). The measures that are included, usually two to three, could for example represent the most important measures from the Balanced Scorecards of these units. So it is an excellent tool to compare, from a strategic viewpoint, the different business units of an organization according to the most important strategic objectives of the enterprise (see for example in Figure 7.5). As an additional service a drill down could be offered from the portfolio graph to the individual Balance Scorecards of the various enterprise units to support further analysis.

The concept of knowledge capital earnings

A concept presented by Baruch Lev for measuring general performance – that is, the total performance of an enterprise – is to calculate its knowledge capital earnings and its knowledge capital in addition to earnings resulting from financial and physical assets.[10]

The calculation of knowledge capital earnings according to Lev's concept, starts with a company's or a business unit's reported results - with the profit reported

---

[10] This concept is described in detail in the study by Feng Gu and Baruch Lev (April, 2001) ''Intangible assets: Measurement, drivers, usefulness''. See: www.stern.nyu.edu/~blev/intangibleassets.doc

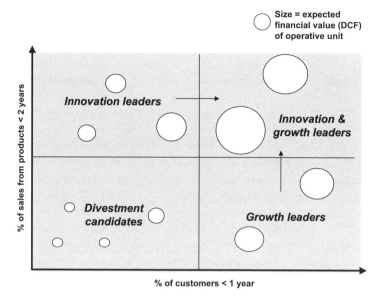

Figure 7.5 Portfolio analysis of the performance of the different operative units of an enterprise.

in its income statement – and continues with the analysis of the assets that produced these earnings. For example: a company earned $500 million. Its balance sheet reveals that it has financial assets of $1 billion and physical assets of another $2 billion. As was outlined above, according to Lev the average after-tax return of financial assets is about 4.5% and of tangible assets it is 7%. So $45 million and $140 million respectively of the total earnings can be credited to financial and tangible assets and $315 million must have been produced by other assets. Baruch Lev calls that residual "knowledge capital earnings" (KCE). This value serves as the basis to calculate the knowledge capital, by multiplying the calculated knowledge capital earnings by an expected rate of return on knowledge or intangible assets (10.5%). In order to produce $315 million in earnings, the company would need $3 billion in intangible assets. By reporting on knowledge capital earnings and on knowledge capital itself it becomes transparent which part of corporate earnings can be credited to other assets than the ones reported on the balance sheet.[11] This information could then serve as the basis to start a more in-depth analysis of the value-creation system using the Tableau de Bord.

---

[11] Ibid. I outlined here the basic principles of the concept. In reality it is a little bit more complex.

Together with Marc Bothwell, a vice-president of Crédit Suisse Asset Management, Baruch Lev has been investigating the implications, if one is benchmarking companies using this measure. They analyzed and ranked for the third time leading American companies in 22 industries by knowledge capital through a so-called knowledge capital scorecard. The result was published in *CFO Magazine* in April, 2001.[12] It indicates clearly the advantages of incorporating knowledge capital into investment analysis. For example, for companies like Dell Computer and Pfizer with their stocks trading at huge multiples of book value – Dell, 17.5; Pfizer, 18.2 – the ratio becomes far more reasonable when knowledge capital is added to book value (a sum named comprehensive value by Baruch Lev): for Dell the multiple is then only 1.26, for Pfizer 1.9.

According to Lev, companies with a ratio of market value to comprehensive value significantly above 1 can be viewed as overvalued. Those with a ratio below 1 are probably undervalued. The negative correlation between this ratio and the subsequent stock returns of the 105 companies evaluated in the scorecard was remarkably strong. Between the August 31, 2000, cutoff date for the scorecard analysis and the end of 2000, the average weighted return of 53 companies with a ratio of market value to comprehensive value below the median of 1.08 was 7%. For the 52 companies with a ratio above the median, the average return was −15.5%. Companies with some of the highest ratios, such as Broadcom (8.5) and Siebel Systems (5.8), have since experienced some of the most severe slides in the stock market. Broadcom was down 80%, and Siebel was down 60%. In contrast, companies trading at low multiples of comprehensive value fared far better. The shares of Rockwell International, for example, with a ratio of 0.62, and Georgia Pacific (0.35) were both up 15% over the same period. Lev's knowledge capital earnings and his comprehensive value could be added as a measure to the financial perspective of the Balanced Scorecard view and can serve as a basis for the portfolio analysis of business units or subsidiaries of an enterprise in order to benchmark them against each other concerning their created intangible values.

The concept of real options valuation

An interesting concept for valuing an enterprise's possible strategies or individual investment projects is the concept of real option valuation. It enables companies to value more precisely real (business) options, which might be created through a possible new strategy path or new investment project and

---

[12] www.cfo.com/Article?article=2415

to analyze them in more detail and to optimize therefore the overall value of such an investment. This becomes possible because the real options valuation concept takes explicitly the decision flexibility of management into account. This enables management to adapt decision over time, when new information becomes available. What are real options?

The real option valuation concept is based on the Black-Scholes model for valuing financial options. This model was developed in the USA by Fischer Black and Myron Scholes in 1973. Financial options are rights to buy or sell financial instruments such as stocks, bonds and commodities at a specified price (the strike price) before a specified date (the expiration date). Financial option valuation is first and foremost a risk and opportunity management instrument. It enables investors to estimate the true value of an investment and keep an option open, through which they either want to minimize risk or open up a future opportunity. It supports the investors in the decision, if it makes sense to keep the option open, that is to continue to invest in it.

The concept of real options tries to apply the same principles used to value financial options to real business options. Real options are opportunities to invest in, or liquidate the "real" operating assets of a business. Real options can therefore be perceived as options to invest in the potential of a company, to sell products or services in the future. This can include investment in new business areas or in new regional markets or investments in a development project. The value of real options is heavily dependent, in contrast to the value of financial options, on management's ability to change and optimize operative business processes and activities (such as in product development) over time as new information becomes available or as uncertainties are resolved; they are exercised through management's strategic choices.

Many strategies can be enhanced over time if they prove to be successful in ways that only become apparent as time goes by. Additionally, many investments can be made in stages, retaining flexibility to respond to future conditions. Flexibility is inherently valuable. It increases the upsides and limits the downside of strategies, enhancing their values. The concept of real options valuation tries to value this flexibility inherent in many especially intangible-based strategies. Real *put options* are options to abandon, contract, or switch operations. They become "in the money" when the value that could be realized by "selling" the real underlying assets at the strike price is greater than the value of the asset in the way it is currently deployed. Real *call options* are options to defer an investment, expand a current investment, or make a new investment (in a strategy, business area, or project). They go "in the money" whenever the present value of the new investment exceeds the present value of its costs (the strike price). They are most valuable for businesses that have many options to invest in new ventures as new market information becomes available. Because upsides are often less bounded than downsides (losses are often limited to 100% of the amount invested), real call options tend to be more valuable than real put options – the reason, why entrepreneurship pays off and entrepreneurs exist.

Several ways exist to value real options. One is the decision tree approach demonstrated for our purposes by the following example where it is used to help a pharmaceutical company in the USA decide whether or not to invest in a clinical trial of a new drug.[13] The decision at hand is whether to continue with the project, modify or abandon it. To do that, the pharmaceutical company first needed to forecast the possible product revenue. So the company was investigating the market in order to get information about the probable development of the number of customers – existing and new ones. It then estimated the total penetration as a percentage of the customer base currently being served by all available products that would be categorized with the new product. Then it forecast the product's share of penetration or market share, the possible price it believed it could get and which was in line with its marketing strategy, and the number of units sold per customer and year. Then the revenue forecast was calculated.

When forecasting product revenue over many years, one must also look at pricing issues that affect revenue such as lowering of technology entry barriers and issues that affect the number of units, for example, prescription behaviour of physicians. Because the interdependencies between various revenue drivers can have tremendous dynamic effects over time, to use a software-based system dynamic simulation can be very helpful in analyzing the sensitivities of such a model in order to come to a more realistic revenue forecast.[14] Once such a model has been set up, it can also be used to update a revenue forecast as soon as new market information is available. The result can then be used in the real option decision tree analysis that should provide information for management to help it to decide whether or not it makes sense to invest further in the development project and perform the clinical trial.

---

[13] This example has been described by L.E.K. Consulting LLC in its newsletter series "Shareholder Value Added", Vol. XVI, *Making Real Decisions with Real Options*. The newsletter can be obtained at www.lek.com

[14] The concept of systems dynamics or systems thinking will be described in Chapter 8.

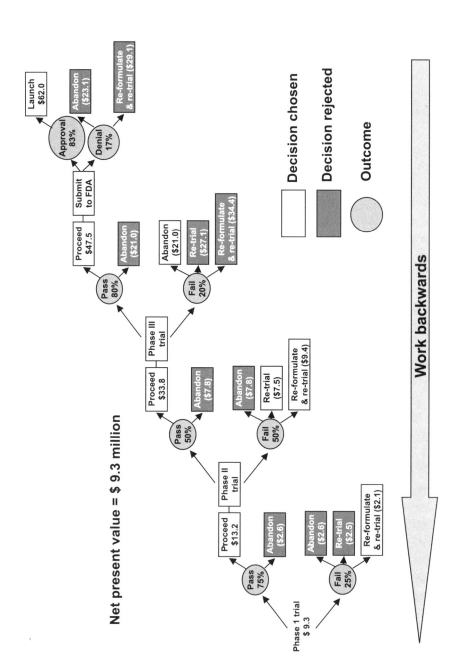

Figure 7.6 Example of a decision tree analysis according to the real options valuation concept.[15]

The clinical trial was the first in a series of three trials that would be necessary to verify the drug's efficiency. If the drug made it through the three clinical trials it would then have to be reviewed by the FDA for final approval. Based on scientific evidence and academic research, the probabilities of passing each of the three phases were 75%, 50% and 65% respectively. The FDA approval probability, assuming it had passed the trials, was 85%. The estimation of the costs of the entire trial and approval process would be $23 million.

A real option valuation, based on the decision tree method, can now use this information about risks and costs to evaluate such a project by taking into consideration the decision flexibility of management after each trial phase to continue, modify or abandon the project. This works as follows.

First, you create a decision tree incorporating all possible outcomes of future trials and all of management's decisions in each event. Then the net present value (NPV) of each possible "end state" is calculated using the standard discounted cash flow (DCF) model. Then, starting with the final year of the evaluation phase and working backwards, the assumption is that management chooses the highest NPV alternative at each decision point. This process clarifies whether or not it makes sense to abandon, re-trial or proceed if any of the trials fail. As Figure 7.6 shows, it turned out to be optimal to reformulate if the first trial phase failed, repeat the second trial phase if it failed, and abandon the drug if the third trial phase failed. To calculate now the NPV for the phase 1 trial, one has to eliminate the (un-chosen) lower NPV scenarios to arrive at an adjusted NPV of $9.3 million (75% × 13.2 + 25% × −2.5).

Compared with a simple DCF analysis, which is not using the decision tree[16] and is resulting in a negative NPV of −$1.8 million, the value of the decision tree valuation is significantly higher because it recognizes the value of the real options consisting in the flexibility of management to choose at each decision point – in the event of failure in the respective phase – the one of the remaining options that has the highest net present value.

Such a decision tree analysis is an interesting method to value staged investments with multiple options to abandon as it is typical for the product innovation process of a company. The value of these investments can only be

---

[15] L.E.K. Consulting LLC newsletter. And see: www.lek.com
[16] The calculation without using the decision tree goes like this: first you calculate overall probability of success (75% × 50% × 80% × 83% = 25%) and of failure (100%−25% = 75%) and then the DCF value itself (25% × $62 million + 75% × −$23.1 million = − $1.8 million).

understood and captured by considering both current and potential future decisions. By identifying optimal responses to future contingencies before they occur, management can gain clarity about how and when to make future investment decisions, which is greatly reducing the likelihood of making a bad decision. So the decision tree valuation is a good tool to value scenarios concerning investments decisions that refer to investments in product innovation. It should therefore be used to support the strategic management process and in the general performance management of an organization that is investing significantly in product innovation.

Other methods to value real options include the binomial model,[17] that is used when at each decision point exactly two options exists, and the Black-Scholes method,[18] which offers the most precise quantification of real options value for one dimensional decisions and options that arise from a single, market-priced source of risk.

As helpful real options are to demonstrate the value of flexibility, if the inputs remain too uncertain the output may be of no value. So, only if reliable forecasting data is available and/or can be updated over time, for example in the context of the strategic management process, this method should be applied to support managerial decision making. But even when the valuation does not result in precise values, there is another possibility to use the model. Companies can use real option valuation models to back-solve for what the inputs would have to be to justify a given value; that is, to calculate the amount of investments that have to be made in order to justify a given value. For example, such a model could be used to calculate the investment needed to justify the actual value of a business unit or an entire company that is engaged in constant product innovation.

But perhaps the main benefit from applying real options is the managerial mindset it creates. Understanding that flexibility is valuable does lead managers to identify options to expand, defer, switch, or contract operations that before would have expired unexercised. It also leads executives to move from putting all their eggs in one basket and fixating on ''most likely'' scenarios to pursuing several paths at once, investing in stages, and making decisions to increase flexibility going forward. This results in an enhanced ability to adapt to

---

[17] The binominal method is described in the above-mentioned L.E.K. newsletter, and see: www.lek.com

[18] A case study for a real options valuation for an oil company based on the Black–Scholes method is described in Keith J. Leslie and Max P. Michaels (2000) ''The real power of real options'', *McKinsey Quarterly*. See: www.mckinseyquarterly.com

new situations and opportunities and increased shareholder and stakeholder value.

We now have finished the discussion on how to select, use, and calculate measures that help to manage strategy and general performance of an enterprise, for example based on the Balanced Scorecard and portfolio concept. Taking the example of knowledge capital earnings, a method was presented which supports companies in measuring general or total performance and in valuing results of and return on investments – especially if they own significant levels of intangible assets. The method of real option valuation is standing for a valuation method, which makes the probable future total result of an investment (which can represent an entire business area or a large development project) more transparent, by taking into account all future options and risks, thus enabling management, to make better strategic decisions.

The product innovation cockpit

The product and market development view of the Tableau de Bord should inform about product innovation and commercialization capabilities and their consequences. In addition to information about performance of product and market development activities – that is, about the status of development of new products and new market segments – it should also provide information about the assets related to the innovation chain of a company (which are mainly intangible assets). The product innovation chain of an enterprise represents the systematic, carefully planned and executed process of innovation, as it is common today in R&D intensive companies. In many knowledge-intensive businesses this process is one of the main sources of value created. Each of the innovation chains – where an enterprise can be engaged in several in parallel (one per market segment or product group) – represents also a major investment.

The real option valuation method has been presented as a method that can help companies to evaluate, from a strategic perspective, if the investment in a product innovation can still create value or if the related project should better be discontinued. But the real option valuation method is not sufficient to manage the investment itself, that is the development project, and to make it a success. In order to leverage the benefits and to control the limitations in systematic way, it requires more – that is, a measurement system that allows monitoring of every step of the value-creation processes of the product innovation chain. And this is exactly the purpose of Baruch Lev's Value Chain Blueprint.

The structure of the product innovation cockpit is oriented on Lev's concept, that divides the product innovation chain into three main phases. The only difference is that measures for activities related directly to customers are grouped in the CRM cockpit and not in the product innovation chain.

Here, some examples follow showing measures for the product and market development view of the product innovation cockpit of the Tableau de Bord:

Phase 1: Research/discovery phase

Measures for the research and discovery phase should inform how good an organization is at acquiring new capabilities and at inventing new products – either through internal efforts, through acquisitions of externally developed technologies, by leveraging spillovers (i.e. using the ideas of others) or through alliances and networking activities.

1. Internal renewal:
   - Success in research and development
   - Workforce training and development in R&D
   - Institutionalized decision processes, knowledge management

2. Acquired capabilities:
   - Technology purchase (number and success)
   - Spillover utilization
   - Return/productivity of investments

3. Networking:
   - R&D alliances and joint ventures
   - Integration of suppliers and customers in research phase activities
   - Communities of practice

Phase 2: Implementation

To monitor the implementation phase, measures should be used that inform about how well a company is translating inventions of phase 1 into intellectual property or other options for commercializing them successfully. These options can include an FDA approval for a new drug, successful beta tests of a new software application, a working pilot of a new technical product, or realized first mover advantages. In addition, if a company is engaged in online activities and/or is creating new marketing channels through the Internet, the progress made in implementing Web activities based on inventions carried out in Phase 1 can also be an indicator for such options.

4.   Intellectual property:
     - Patents, trademarks, and copyrights
     - Licensing agreements
     - Coded know-how

5.   Technological feasibility:
     - Success of clinical tests, FDA approvals
     - Beta tests, working pilots
     - First mover advantages

6.   Internet/Creation of new marketing channels:
     - Threshold traffic
     - Online purchases
     - Major Internet alliances

Phase 3: Commercialization

For the commercialization phase, the product innovation cockpit should present measures that show how good an organization is in commercializing its discoveries and new products; that is, how good it is in translating these innovations into tangible (financial) results. A sign for this is when a company is making progress with marketing alliances – especially if it is relying on network effects – and positive developments in the area of brand value and brand perception. If it is using the Internet as a sales channel, online sales statistics provide insight about the development of this sales channel. The product innovation cockpit should also inform about commercialization success of specific products and innovations by presenting revenue figures, earnings and market shares for them. It should also inform about the potential for the future by providing data about possible product launch dates and about the status of development projects. This should include also information about planned (marketing) initiatives, their expected break-even date and about their actual cash burn rate – for example, for major market development activities.

7.   Market development:
     - Marketing alliances
     - Brand values
     - Online sales vs. total sales
     - Market share vs. competition

8.   Performance:
     - Revenues, earnings, and markets shares

- Patent and know-how royalties
- Knowledge earnings and knowledge capital

9. Growth prospects:
   - Status of new product pipeline; planned launch dates
   - Expected efficiencies and savings
   - Planned initiatives
   - Expected break-even and cash burn rate.

The product innovation cockpit of the Tableau de Bord provides a comprehensive view on the product innovation chain of an enterprise and enables managers and investors (if this information is included also in external reports) to accurately assess its product innovation performance and its product innovation potential. For this, the generic model (as presented here) has to be adapted to the specific company. Some of the listed items may not be relevant to one company while another company may find other information items, that are not included in the list, more useful. Therefore, it is recommended, before one starts to select and define measures for the product innovation cockpit of the Tableau de Bord, that a company first define the activities and events for each of the nine logical views that are relevant for it. Answering the following questions might be helpful to do this.

1. What do we do to renew ourselves internally and to develop new ideas? How do we invest in research and innovation?

2. Which technologies or components do we acquire for these innovations from external sources and how do we proceed exactly?

3. How do we use networks (to development partners, customers, user-communities, marketing partners) in the product innovation process?

4. How do we create intellectual property and how are we trying to retain and secure it?

Each identified major activity of a company in the three main phases of the innovation chain should be represented in the product innovation cockpit by at least one measure. And each of the selected measures should be tested, as if it has been described for the definition of the measures for the Balanced Scorecard view, concerning: its usefulness regarding its general relevance, if the data for it can be easily obtained, if it can be understood by the people that should use it and if is it able to trigger behaviour, and if it is consistent with other measures used in the product innovation cockpit.

So, the procedure to define measures for the product innovation cockpit is, in principle, very similar to defining Balanced Scorecard measures (brainstorming, pre-selection, detailed assessment and a plausibility check regarding its usefulness). Once the definition has been finished, these measures also will be stored in the measure library.

Very important for the selection of measures that really could tell later on something about the productivity of the product innovation process, is to take care that input measures related to the research and discovery phase, as well as to the implementation phase, can be linked to output measures of the commercialization phase. This also requires selecting such input and output measures, for which data on the same granularity level can be obtained. If, for example, success of product innovation should be monitored for each single product, this requires that data can be either directly or indirectly obtained for investments and expenditures as well as for related revenues or for other output measures, that should be used instead, on the product level. Otherwise, it will not be possible later on to compare investments into research and product development (person days, financial capital) with revenues generated through these products or with other output measures.

The operations cockpits

While the task of the product innovation process in the value-creation system of today's companies is to create options for future business and new revenues by developing attractive and marketable products (product development) and by preparing the related marketing and sales channels (market and business development), the focus of the so-called operations, of the operative business processes, is to translate those options that represent in essence intangible assets, into tangible products and services and to realize their value by generating revenues with them through sales transactions. The first task, producing products, is the task of supply chain management. It includes purchasing of raw materials, manufacturing of products that can be sold to customers, and distribution, that is the process, that makes sure that customers will get the products which they have ordered.

The second major task of operations is to execute customer specific marketing campaigns, to execute actual sales and service transactions, and to create, enhance, and maintain customer relations in order to enable the company to sell to these individuals or organizations not only today, but also in the future.

In an abstract form these operational value-creation processes can be described as follows: supply chain management has to satisfy a specific customer demand and has to execute on a claim of a customer by delivering a product to this customer at a specific predetermined time. It is the task of customer relationship management to make this demand conscious for a (potential) customer through marketing and sales activities, to guide potential customer to the products of the company, and to transform this demand in a legally binding transaction (sales), that is into business for the company. In addition to actual sales, sustaining customer relations has also to be created in the customer relationship management area of a company. Because supply chain management and customer relationship management are two different tasks with different objectives, they are represented in the enterprise value-creation system by two different processes, that are controlled via a supply chain cockpit and a customer relationship cockpit.

The supply chain cockpit

The task of supply chain management is to make sure that goods are available at the right time, in the right quantity and quality, and at the right location. So supply chain management become physical, even in knowledge-based businesses, enabling the company to correctly deliver goods to customers *and* to optimize its related resources (purchasing, production, distribution capacities, but also working capital in form of inventories).

While manufacturing became a commodity activity in many industries, supply chain management is one of the most advanced areas of expertise in today's enterprises and one of the most sophisticated. If a company wants to build outstanding and profitable customer relations it often has to rely on a world class supply chain management that ensures that goods for customers are available as promised to them (so that they will buy again) and that the company's purchasing, production and shipment resources are optimally used (so that production costs remain as low as possible, and the company is able to make a profit).

One of the major breakthroughs in supply chain management was to see it as a process. The concept of "business processes reengineering" arose in the 1990s and has led to the name "supply chain management". It was first focused on optimizing the supply chain within one operative unit or company: sourcing, manufacturing, and delivering. But because many enterprises developed during the 1990s into global organizations, supply chain management became a quite complex task. When a global enterprise wants to manage its supply chain not just within one operative local unit, but across different group companies and enterprise units, across warehouses, plants, and distribution centres scattered across the world, then that supply chain management process has to be based on a flexible and easily configurable supply chain network that can link these different locations and resources through an information system with each other in real time. Only in this way can the necessary transparency exist that allows an enterprise to optimally use its capacities and to keep delivery dates as promised and, at the same time, optimize continuously the flow of goods and materials within the entire network.

Consequently, building such supply chain networks was the investment focus in the area of organizational capital in many global enterprises during the 1990s. In many cases it is the same today, as many organizations have just entered the next phase in supply chain optimization. With the concept of the "decapitalized enterprise" that results in major initiatives to outsource assets in areas that are not perceived any more as the core business by delegating, for example, manufacturing or distribution tasks to other companies (see the example of Cisco in Part 2 of this book), and with the requirement to let customers "pull" products and services instead of "pushing" these to customers, things have become even more complex. The two major challenges in supply chain management today are to:

1. Integrate suppliers that provide, for example, outsourced manufacturing services into the supply chain network like an internal department. Customers should experience no difference and should not even be aware that tasks had been outsourced.

2. Enable the supply chain network for adaptive and fast reconfiguration when demand is changing. Fast adaptation of the supply chain network should be possible without creating bottleneck situations or to suboptimally use capacities. The same applies for the production of newly developed products. If they require a reconfiguration of supply chain processes, this should be possible instantly without considerable reconfiguration costs in order to enable the company to bring new products to market fast.

So the supply chain cockpit of the Tableau de Bord has to provide information about the efficiency of supply chain processes – within the enterprise but also within the entire ecosystem. It has to provide information as to how successful a supply chain process is in fulfiling customer requirements, for example concerning product quality and delivery dates. But it also has to provide information about the capability of the company to reconfigure quickly the supply chain network to meet changing customer demands or to bring new products to market fast.

To have an efficient, reliable, and adaptive supply chain network in place is an important competitive advantage and can represent an option for additional future revenues, if the company decides to offer its own supply chain network as a service to other companies. Its supply chain related organizational capital will represent then an intangible asset. The supply chain cockpit has to include measures about these three major areas:

1. Supply chain efficiency: capacity use, order cycle time, costs, working capital employed, quality and efficiency of collaboration.

2. Supply chain reliability: order fulfilment rate, number of delayed/wrong quality deliveries, reliability of supply chain network partners, percentage of disputed jobs/orders for top five partners.

3. Supply chain adaptability: supply chain response time at reconfiguration, impact on lead time and costs.

The selection and definition of measures for the supply chain cockpit follows basically the same principles as the definition of the measures for the product innovation cockpit and the Balanced Scorecard view of the Tableau de Bord. Defined supply chain measures should be included as well in the measure library for a possible later use in other areas (for example, in the Balanced Scorecard).

It is recommended that the number of measures for the supply chain cockpit be restricted to a maximum of 9 to 10 (three for each of the described measurement areas) in order to not overload it with information. The typical result will be that the supply chain cockpit will mainly include output measures. This is fine, because the task of the Tableau de Bord is not to provide information for managing the supply chain itself but on the overall status of supply chain management results.

In addition, it is possible to set up a comprehensive supply chain cockpit with more detailed information about specific process steps and tasks that support companies to manage and optimize their supply chain. An interesting option would be the ability to "drill down" from the supply chain cockpit of the Tableau de Bord, when it is implemented as a software-based management information system, to more detailed information of the operational supply chain cockpit and to execute directly detailed analysis. In order to avoid inconsistencies, measures used in the supply chain cockpit of the Tableau de Bord should represent a subset of the measures of the operational supply chain cockpit or should be calculated by taking these operational measures as the basis. A widely used concept for such a comprehensive supply chain cockpit is the supply chain operations reference (SCOR) model which has been proposed by the Supply Chain Council (SCC).[19]

The SCOR model is a cross-industry reference model for the description of supply chains. It includes a common terminology and a list of generally applicable measures and their corresponding best practice benchmarks. The SCC developed the model and is an independent, not-for-profit, global corporation, with over 400 company members and with chapters in North America, Europe, and Asia. The model describes supply chain configurations and supports their quantitative analysis. According to the model, a supply chain configuration is defined through four major processes.

1. *Plan:* demand/supply planning.

2. *Source:* sourcing/material acquisition.

3. *Make:* production execution.

4. *Deliver:* Order management, warehouse management, transportation and installation management.

Between these processes a "customer and supplier" relation exist, so that each process represents a customer for the previous one and a supplier for the following one (see Figure 7.7).

The SCOR model's objective is to provide a common language for communicating among intra-company functions and inter-company supply chain partners about the virtual supply chain. It allows companies to set up links between their internal processes and processes taking place within business partner organizations by enabling them to easier identify the linking points and to optimize the integration processes. This model also forms the basis for the supply chain scorecard proposed by the SCC to benchmark a company's supply chain with others or to use it for internal management purposes (see Figure 7.8) It therefore represents a good conceptual starting point for the definition of a company specific supply chain cockpit and for selecting the corresponding measures.

---

[19] The mission of the Supply Chain Council is to further develop and promote the use of the SCOR model. Its members are leading manufacturers, logistic and distribution service firms and supply chain software companies. See the SCC website at: www.supply-chain.org

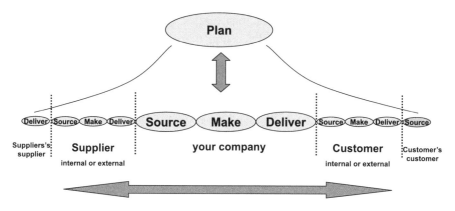

Figure 7.7 The SCOR model.

SCOR supply chain scorecard

Performance versus competitive population

Overview metrics		SCOR level 1 metrics	Actual	Parity	Advantage	Superior
Customer-facing	Delivery performance/ quality	Delivery performance to comm. date	50%	85%	90%	95%
		Fill rates	63%	94%	96%	98%
		Perfect order fulfillment	0%	80%	85%	90%
	Flexibility & responsiveness	Order fulfillment lead times	7 days	7 days	5 days	3 days
		Production flexibility	45 days	30 days	25 days	20 days
Internal-facing	Costs	Total logistics management costs	19%	13%	8%	3%
		Warranty costs	NA	NA	NA	NA
		Value added employee productivity	$122K	$156K	$306K	$460K
	Assets	Inventory days of supply	119 days	55 days	38 days	22 days
		Cash-to-cash cycle time	196 days	80 days	46 days	28 days
		Net asset turns (working capital)	22 turns	8 turns	12 turns	19 turns

Figure 7.8 The SCOR supply chain scorecard.[20]

---

[20] See "SCOR version 5.0! Introduction Web Cast" at www.supply-chain.org

The customer relations cockpit

Good customer relations are an important basis for a company's ability to sell and to generate revenues. Therefore customer relations represent a major intangible asset. Good customer relations can, for example, create additional value, if they enable a company to more easily sell to its existing customers new products and thus to generate additional revenues, profits and cash flows.

Whereas in the old days sales activities had been the major task of enterprises on the customer side, it is now customer relationship management (CRM). It is not any more about to just execute a sales transaction but to manage the underlying resource; that is, the customer relationship, which makes the sales transaction possible. Good customer relationships represent an option for future income and revenues and are an important basis for growth. In addition, they can serve a powerful market entry barrier for possible new competitors.

The traditional way management looked on customers was purely from a period perspective by reviewing actual sales figures and margins. Today, it is far more important to be able to look at the entire customer relationship from a life cycle perspective, in order to be able to optimize the total relationship across the life cycle in a proactive way and thus to maximize its total value for the enterprise. Customer relations are then treated more as an investment and asset (see Figure 7.9).

As with other investment projects, investments made in the initial phase, in customer acquisition for example, typically have a negative impact on customer profitability. Later, when customer relations are established and when customers buy again and again, revenues will increase and the profit curve will go up. Finally, in the last phase of the life cycle, it will flatten again. Therefore, if the aim is to optimize return on investment of a customer relationship across its entire life cycle, a periodic view on it is not sufficient, as happens in traditional management reporting. Instead, a company has to monitor the life cycle across periods in order to be able to plan the right marketing activities for the right point in time. Such a plan will help to either grow revenues and profits in the growth phase or to extend the retention phase. Only in this way will the company be able to maximize the net present value of its investment.

Individualized and personalized communication strategies are the key to building good customer relations. Companies must try to turn every transaction into a highly personalized, meaningful customer interaction and then build

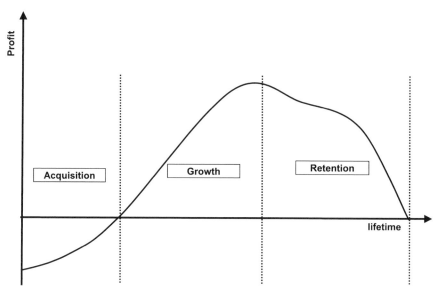

Figure 7.9 Phases of customer lifetime value management.

on the basis of these interactions a firm relationship that induces customers to make more purchases. But this has to be managed and optimized from a customer lifes cycle perspective. Successful customer relationship management comprises therefore several tasks. Some of these are shown below.

▶ Recognizing potential customers and converting them into (first-time) buyers.

▶ Executing transactions to the customer's satisfaction (here supply chain management enters the game).

▶ Providing customer care and service across all communication and inter-action channels used by the customer.

▶ Managing the entire customer portfolio of the company actively and maximizing return on investment across the entire life cycle of customer relations.

Whereas the first three topics represent more the operational side of customer relationship management – day-to-day activities in marketing, sales, and customer service the fourth is a more long-term oriented task that provides the framework for the others. It represents the strategic part of CRM, or the strategic CRM process, called also customer lifetime value management.

The strategic objective of customer relationship management is to create a customer portfolio that can serve as a basis, to maximize revenues, profits and growth of a company. The strategic CRM process, that optimizes customer lifetime value for individual customers but as well for the company's entire customer portfolio, is named customer portfolio lifetime value management (CPLVM). It should therefore play a coordination role for all operative CRM activities in marketing, sales and service. For example, through a statistical analysis of historic customer behaviour a company determines how customer retention for different customer groups may develop in the future. If it combines in the next step this information with information about the profitability of these different customer groups, it is able to identify those where the return on investment of certain marketing activities and campaigns will be the highest. The identified and selected customers will be then handed over to operational marketing campaign management. By concentrating marketing activities on the most valuable customers of the customer portfolio, the company will be able to further grow total customer lifetime value[21] of its customer portfolio. In order to continuously increase the average customer lifetime value of a customer portfolio, the CPLVM process has to play a centre role and has to set the targets for the operational CRM processes and activities.

Collecting in a systematic way data about customers and customer related activities and also the quality of the data collected is essential for successful customer relationship management and for the ability of a company to optimize customer lifetime value. Therefore, measures have to be included in the customer relations cockpit which provide insight about how successful the company is in collecting these data. So the customer relations cockpit should include measure for the following areas:

▶ *Customer value:* customer value added[22] per period, development of customer lifetime value per customer group over time – actuals and forecasts (calculated on the basis of retention rate and customer profit).

▶ *Effectiveness of marketing activities:* response rate, referral rate, conversion rate of suspects (suspected potential buyers – for example, identified on

---

[21] Customer lifetime value can be calculated by multiplying the retention rates with the expected customer profits and by calculating then the net present value of these future profits, which are weighted with the retention rate.

[22] Average customer value-added can be calculated for a business unit or for a customer group by deducting from total operating income costs for customer acquisition and retention and by dividing the result by the number of customers.

the basis of a profile analysis) to prospects (identified buyers), contribution margin per campaign, marketing costs vs. revenue.

▶   *Effectiveness of sales activities:* sales revenue, sales margin, conversion rate of prospects (identified buyers) to customers, size and development of sales pipeline (number of leads, identified opportunities, quotes, contracts), retention rate, sales costs vs. revenue, market share.

▶   *Effectiveness of services activities:* service revenues, resolution quotes, number of complaints and returns, customer satisfaction, service costs vs. revenue, workloads vs. capacity.

▶   *Effectiveness of collecting data about customers and prospects:* user recognition rate (at the company's websites), percentage of incomplete customer/user profiles, percentage of sign-ins/customer with customer card (user provides personal data) vs. total customers/users.

Also here the selection and definition of the measures follows the same principles as the definition of the measures for the other views of the Tableau de Bord. It is also recommended that the number of measures for the customer relationship cockpit be restricted to a maximum of 10 (two to three for each of the described measurement areas) in order to not overload it with information. Preferably a set of measures (that is, the measures per measurement area) should include as well input measures, like retention rate, and output measures, like customer lifetime value. More detailed information can be made available separately, for example through an operational CRM cockpit, as has been described already for the supply chain cockpit.

The resource management cockpits: human resources, alliances, IT, and finance views

Human resources, financial capital, alliances, and IT represent basic resources for the value-creating processes of the enterprise in order to enable it to create, for example, customer value in product development or in CRM. Therefore, information about the status of the related processes, such as sourcing, developing, and retention of these resources, is of importance for getting an insight into how healthy a company is. If the average employee's skill level is decreasing and those employees with the most critical skills needed to execute successfully new strategy or to bring new products to market are leaving, the future is at risk. If a company is running out of cash and is not able to finance investments, it will be an even more critical situation. If network effects play an important role in gaining future market share and the company has to rely for that on alliance partners, the status of the development of these alliances is also a critical success factor. And, finally, if the IT infrastructure is not able to keep up with business strategy and cannot support it, a company will not remain successful either.

The key to an enterprise's success in relation to the management of its basic resources is their intelligent enterprise specific use. An enterprise is able to create value-added for its stakeholders only if its returns are exceeding its costs for these basic resources. But because enterprises have to compete with other enterprises for these often scarce resources, their prices are continuously increasing as well as the threshold from which value is being created. For example, companies have to pay talented employees above average salaries. But before such a talent is able to contribute in corporate value-creating activities, the company has to invest significant time and money in training and development. The same is true for alliances and IT. A company can acquire and buy from the market IT components. But the company-specific solution needed to support its business has to be "developed" or at least configured and needs to be adapted to the company's actual requirements. Therefore, a company has to manage its basis resources not only efficiently but also effectively. For this, an enterprise has to select and acquire, develop and retain its basis resources according to its strategic objectives.

This is especially important, because the deployment of basic resources has only a very indirect impact on total enterprise performance. In order to be able to use basic resources in the most effective way, all important decisions and activities which are related to them, such as in hiring, development of human resources and skills, major decisions in alliance management as well as the IT and financing strategy, have to be aligned with enterprise strategy. Therefore, starting from the strategic objectives of the Balanced Scorecard, objectives and measures have to be deducted for each of the basic resource areas. These objectives then serve as guidelines for directing the activities and decisions in basis resource management in order to put them to the most effective use for the enterprise.

Each view in the resource management cockpit of the Tableau de Bord should include measures related to the objectives that have been derived from the strategic objectives of the Balanced Scorecard. The resulting objectives can be regarded as the strategic objective for Human Resources (HR), for alliance management, IT and for finance. In addition, each view will also include measures that capture the efficiency and effectiveness of the operational processes, such as hiring, employee development and payroll in HR, cash and working capital management in finance, development and deployment of new IT solutions, and acquisition and development of alliances in alliance management.

The definition and selection of strategic objectives for the different basic resource areas should follow the same principles as for the definition of the measures for the Balanced Scorecard view. Measures for operational activities should be oriented toward related processes. For each important process one measure should be added to the view of the respective basic resource.

In the following sections, some typical, basic resource aspects will be presented that should be considered when trying to select the right measures. This will also include examples of such measures. For each individual enterprise decisions need to be taken about which relevant basic resource areas need be represented by a separate view in the resource management cockpit of the Tableau de Bord. One criterion for this decision could be if a resource plays an important role in one or several value-creation processes but at the same time is scarce and/or requires large investment for its development.

The HR view

In the industrial era the HR department was primarily focused on administrative tasks, such as the hiring process, processing payrolls, and administering benefit plans. This has changed in the new economy, where HR tasks have become more sophisticated and complex. The major task of HR management today is to ensure that a company has the right people with the right skills in the right jobs and at the right time as it needs them according to its business strategy. HR has to manage a company's human capital and has to set policies in place that determine how to acquire it, manage it and optimize it.

In their most important value-creating processes, companies today employ so-called knowledge workers, highly qualified employees able to collaborate effectively with other internal or external knowledge workers and with experts in the customer organization using the processes and organizational capital of their company. The problem is that companies cannot hire someone from the street who can do that right away. Usually it takes a year or two for a new employee to become really productive. And this requires intensive company investment in the selection, acquisition and development of such knowledge workers. And then the company has still to retain these employees.

So, in the HR view, the measurement system has to provide information about how successful a company is in acquiring employees, how fast these new employees are integrated, if the company disposes of the required skills to support its strategy and how productive employees are, for example in working with other employees in value-creating constellations. The HR department should also develop procedures and instruments that support managers to monitor and systematically develop productivity in their teams. In addition, HR should also provide information about the efficiency of its own administrative processes.

In order to be able to develop its employees according to strategic needs and objectives, companies have to define for each function the required skills and competencies and have to assess – at least once a year – how actual skills and competencies of position holders match with these requirements. The outcome can then serve as the basis for systematic training and development activities. If this information is stored in a so-called skill database, management is able to aggregate these data and can use them to check when major strategic decisions have to be made, if critical skills required for a new strategy are already available or how big a possible skill gap is. On the basis of such a skill database HR management is able to systematically develop the enterprise's human capital according to its strategic objectives. It is also able to react faster to strategy changes that result in skill and competency gaps, and which can seriously damage a new strategy should they remain undetected. Here are some examples of what the HR department could measure:

▶ *Strategic HR performance:* vacancy rate of positions requiring critical skills or other measures related to strategic HR objectives (for example, development of specific skills and competencies in the organization).

▶ *Employee productivity:* value-added per person and period, development of value-added per employee over time, revenue and profit per employee.

▶ *Effectiveness of employee acquisition:* number of applications per period, hiring quota of applicants with the right profile, hiring costs, expected average value-added per person for new employees within the first three years.

▶ *Effectiveness of employee development activities:* job rotation rate; number of employees per period moving from low value adding to high value adding jobs; skills and competency gap per functional or business area (in percent ages).

▶ *Effectiveness of employee retention:* leaving rate per critical employee group, average years of service with the company.

▶ *Efficiency of HR administration tasks:* headcount in HR departments; administrative costs per employee; costs per transaction (per employee, per payment run, etc.), percentage of vacant positions.

The alliances view

Alliances can provide companies with additional resources in critical areas such as R&D, marketing and sales and can help them to multiply their own capabilities and to scale faster. This is especially important when time-to-market is critical and a company is not able to acquire or develop the necessary resources fast enough. Alliances are also a means to manage risk; for example, development risks can be reduced if a company share such risks with others. And alliances can be used to induce network effects. Depending on the degree a company relies on its alliances and on the areas in which it is doing so, the alliance view measurement framework will differ or will be relevant or not relevant at all. Here are some examples of what the alliance view could measure:

▶ *Effectiveness of marketing and sales alliances:* number of operating/ dormant alliance partners, average revenue per operating alliance partner per segment, average number of skilled persons (persons with knowledge about the company's technologies, products, or services) per alliance partner and segment.

▶ *Effectiveness of R&D alliances:* time-to-market for new products compared with similar product developments without alliance partners, value-added from R&D alliances (for example, saved costs and management time and reduced risk costs vs. costs of alliances).

The IT view

No enterprise today is able to create organizational capital that increases employee productivity, execute new strategies successfully, and organize its business processes efficient and effectively without making significant use of IT. The problem is that the contribution of IT to business performance is indirect and hence cannot be directly measured. However, some important success factors exist for efficient and effective IT management. These can be used as a basis for monitoring performance in an IT department. One success factor is how actively an IT organization is managing its maintenance workload and free IT resources. A problem for many IT organizations is that they are so busy keeping up and maintaining the existing system landscape and IT infra-structure, they are unable to provide active and timely support to a new strategy or improved business process. Resource consumption of maintenance tasks, also called costs of ownership, can be significant and can, at worst, consume all available resources, making it impossible for the IT department to develop and deploy new solutions. The standardization degree of the equipment may play an essential role here.

So, an important objective for an IT operation could be to ensure that a significant amount of resources is not occupied by day-to-day operations and maintenance activities. The resources are then made available to enhance the IT infrastructure and to adapt it to new business processes without increasing total IT resources and costs. Another important target is to keep IT costs and resource consumption as low as possible when compared with an industry average.

Other objectives include an assessment of how flexible a company is in reacting, on the basis of its existing IT landscape, to new business requirements and how reliable IT services and systems are. The more that companies rely on their IT – for example, by integrating outsourcing partners, providing support for customers, and selling online – the more they are dependent on a 24-hour 7-day reliability of web servers, application servers, databases, and on accept-able response times for users.

Here are some examples of measures that could be included in the IT view of the Tableau de Bord:

▶   *Total IT costs and resource consumption:* IT costs vs. revenue; IT costs vs. industry average or other benchmarks.

▶   *Flexibility:* percentage of total resources/headcount deployed in, or available for, new projects and not needed to keep the actual infrastruc-ture up and running, percentage of equipment per function/enterprise area that is older than x number of years.

▶   *Reliability:* server and network downtime, average web page download time, failed pages and server requests, response time for users that report a problem.

▶   *Standardization rate:* percentage of IT equipment that is standardized across the enterprise.

▶   *Effectiveness of new solutions implemented:* return on investment of new solutions and systems and amortization time, productivity improvements through corporate information resources (for example, productivity improvements for employees by reducing time spent on administrative tasks).

▶   *Strategic effectiveness:* performance and implementation progress of IT projects that are critical for successfully executing the company's strategy.

The finance view

The task of operational finance is to make sure that an enterprise is not running out of cash, that it is using financial capital as efficiently as possible (by keeping working capital low and by investing excess cash in the most profitable way), and that it is executing financial transactions such as collection, payment, cash management, financial investments, financing, and financial risk management processes (such as foreign currency hedging) as efficiently as possible.

So, financial management has very much in common with supply chain management: it has to make sure that cash is available in the right quantity, at the right point in time, at the right location in the enterprise to pay suppliers, employees and shareholders. At the same time, unnecessary "inventories" in the form of receivables and cash should be avoided or at least minimized. In addition, as in physical supply chain management, transactions, tasks and processes should be executed as efficiently as possible and at lowest cost. So it is no wonder that the concept of a financial supply chain has emerged recently.

The main advantage of this concept is the focusing of managerial attention. This is no longer restricted to optimization of single financial tasks alone but now includes the optimization of processes intended to reduce cash flow and working capital along the entire value chain. A large potential for optimization still remains untapped in this area. The principle is similar to that of supply chain management: replace information with working capital. When a company is able to receive at the time of billing the information, that a customer will dispute an invoice, it can react immediately and has not to wait for several weeks, when it occurs after several dunning rounds that something is not quite right with the invoice. This will reduce day sales outstanding (DSO) and working capital. A means to achieve this is electronic bill presentment and payment (EBPP); that is, the electronic presentment of an invoice and the possibility to pay electronically. An invoice is presented to a customer via a web-based portal on the website of the company or at the website of an outsourcing services supplier. The customer will receive an automated email message to indicate that an invoice has been issued and it includes a link to the invoice itself at the customer portal of the company. The invoice can then be approved and paid by the customer immediately (by authoring for example, a direct debit). Should any dispute arise, the company's automatic workflow processes can immediately react and solve the problem or issue a corrected invoice.

But with EBPP a company not only can reduce DSO and uncertainty in liquidity planning – that is, its working capital – but is also able to save significant invoice handling and collection costs. Consultants estimate, that EBPP can reduce the overhead associated with issuing invoices by as much as 70%.

At the other end of the financial supply chain, global corporations have started to implement "payment factories", that aggregate electronically payments to suppliers on a worldwide basis and optimize the routing of these payments through preferred banks and financial service providers. In doing so, the corporations have reduced dramatically the overall number of payment transactions as well as cross-country payments, leading to significant transaction cost savings and reduced bank fees.

The third interaction point to reduce costs and prevent locking up of a company's working capital is to organize cash management and treasury processes. These are methods utilized to invest excess cash and borrow cash from banks in a more efficient way by using electronic linkages, internally to all operative units and externally to financial service providers and public money and currency exchanges. They allow an enterprise to identify excess cash and financing needs within the entire organization in real time and to execute financial investment and financing transactions in the most efficient way. So, approaching operational financial management from a financial supply chain viewpoint has clear advantages over the traditional approach and provides ample opportunities for optimization (see Figure 7.10).

The second major task of finance, beside liquidity management, financial investment and financing management, management of cash flow and of operational financial processes, is to provide tools and information that help managers as well as investors to assess and optimize a company's performance. But this task, usually called accounting, controlling, and reporting, does not fall in the area of financial resource management. Therefore these tasks are not reflected in the finance view of the Tableau de Board. Measures that inform about the performance of accounting, reporting and forecasting processes may

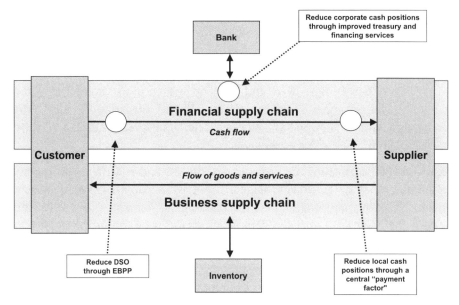

Figure 7.10   The financial supply chain and its three interaction points designed to reduce costs and prevent the locking up of working capital.

be added either as a separate view in the Resource Management Cockpit ("Business Information and Business Intelligence") or might become a sub view in the view "information resources" – a renamed version of the IT view.

So, the Finance view in the Tableau de Bord could include measures about:

▶   *Overall efficiency:* total amount of working capital employed in the financial supply chain compared with industry benchmarks, total finance costs vs. revenue and vs. industry best practice.

▶   *Collection and AR efficiency:* days sales outstanding (DSO), costs per outgoing invoice, accuracy of cash-in forecasts.

▶   *Payment and AP efficiency:* costs per incoming invoice, percentage of manual interventions in the payment factory.

▶   *Efficiency of treasury:* return on financial investments (compared with average market return), average interest rate paid compared with actual interest rates paid in industry, costs per transaction.

▶   *Cash/liquidity forecast and financial risk exposure:* cash on hand available in 3 months, in 6 months, in 12 months according to last business forecast available and planned treasury transactions, currency exposure and risk, and risk in financial investments.

A new model for accounting

After having finished the definition of the measures for the different views, the Tableau de Bord may now look like the example depicted in Figure 7.11.

What does it mean for accounting practice if companies use a Tableau de Bord or a similar concept to manage their business? Is it just enough to add such a measurement system like the Tableau de Bord that includes financial and nonfinancial measures and use a data warehouse or similar tool to produce the new measures – but leave accounting as it is?

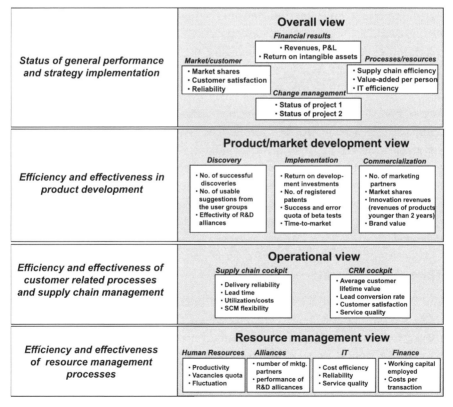

Figure 7.11 An example for a Tableau de Bord that provides measures for a holistic analysis of enterprise performance.

Focusing on the new measurement system and on making it available as soon as possible to managers is probably the right first step. But this will be not sufficient in the long run. Without the systematic recognition of intangible asset investments as assets in accounting, companies will not be able to accurately calculate the return of investments that should be presented in the financial perspective of the Balanced Scorecard and in the product and market development view of their Tableau de Bord.

Of course, it is possible to live for some time with improvisations and to do these calculations separately and to use some rough assumptions in doing so. But, as soon as the new concept of measurement the Tableau de Bord gains acceptance within the organization, and externally, not only will there be increases in requirements for timeliness, accuracy, reliability, and that the reported measures are auditable, but management and other constituencies will also ask for more relevant financial accounting and improved measurement of financial performance.

As an important basis for the new performance management system, in a second step, an improved accounting system is required, able to recognize expenditures for R&D, for brand-building or for creating customer value as investments. It must report more precisely on income and cash flow and has to provide insights into the risk status of the enterprise.

In the following sections some considerations and concepts for an improved approach to accounting are presented. These examples should enable companies to report through their financial statements in a systematic, auditable and more accurate way about their economic performance. All activities through which companies create economic value today have to be reflected in accounting; this in order to provide the necessary internal and external transparency managers and investors need to make investment decisions.

The balance sheet

The balance sheet provides a snapshot of what resources (assets) a company owns and has under its full control and where it got the money to buy or build them (from shareholders/equity or through borrowings from third parties). To date, under current accounting rules, the aspect of full control was considered as more important and relevant for considering an investment as an asset than the aspect of investment (an expenditure in order to obtain future benefits, not for the actual period). Therefore, traditionally, it was not possible to treat certain investments as assets and to report them on the balance sheet. This was because the future benefits cannot be fully secured for the company and are associated with a high risk – which is typical for investments in product and market development or in creating customer relations or brands. But this practice does not reflect economic reality. Increasingly, it is leading to problems in the area of external transparency of enterprises and in internal enterprise management and control – something which has been of concern to accounting experts and management consultants in recent years.

As one possible solution, the concept of economic value added (EVA) emerged. As already discussed (see Part 1), EVA recognizes investments in intangibles as components of capital employed; that is, as an asset on the balance sheet in management accounting through so-called adjustments that capitalize the related expenses. A second proposal made is to report intangible assets with their fair market value on the balance sheet; this, in order to close the growing gap between market value of companies and their book value and to increase the relevance of financial statements to investors and the transparency of corporations. Reported in this way, the market value of the enterprise is then explained in detail through the assets listed on the balance sheet.

The problem with such a proposal is that a company's intangibles assets do not translate directly into the value of the company as a whole. Instead, the value of a company is driven by its *perceived* ability to generate profits and cash flow, which must not correspond with its *real* ability.

Intangible assets help companies to generate profits and cash flow and are a key indirect driver of value. Reporting on them definitely helps investors; for example, to assess the true value of a company. But the intention of GAAP is not that the balance sheet of a company reflects its market value. Market value is too much dependent on market forces of capital markets (on offerings and demand, on speculation) and on market psychology, and is therefore only indirectly linked to the fundamental value of the assets of an enterprise. Instead, the financial statements of a company, especially of the balance sheet, are meant to provide information about the investments made in assets and changes in those assets and liabilities from one period to the next. This information, when combined with other information – for example, from the Tableau de Bord – helps investors assess the value of the company. Valuing investments made in intangibles with its market value is also hardly practicable, because for many intangibles a market does not exist and therefore it has no market value.

So, a better way to account for self-created intangibles on the balance sheet is to treat them as investments and to value them with the investment amount;

that is, with the related expenses incurred. The balance sheet should provide insight into the investments made by a company in its future value-creation potential – and not in the actual market value of these assets. An assessment, how successful a company is in developing these potentials further and how capable it is in realizing their value and in generating revenues and cash flows from them, must be based on other information sources. The income and cash flow statements of a company show how successful the company has been in turning past investments into income and cash flow. This may serve as an indicator as to the company's ability to repeat this performance. Information about the status of the different value-generation processes of the company, as it is presented in the Tableau de Bord, provides investors and management with information about how successful the company is in developing these investments into real future income and cash flow potential, what risk is incurred in the process, and how fast the company is making progress.

A valuation of intangibles on the basis of their market value would require a company to constantly revalue the balance sheet to reflect the actual market value of its assets. In this case a reasonably objective estimate of the perform-ance of the company would not be possible any more for its external con-stituencies (and probably also not for management). Valuing the company is not the task of accounting or management, but of the market, of financial analysts and investors. Management has to provide them with the necessary information to do that: through improved accounting and financial reports, but also through additional reports; for example, through supplemental reports based on the Tableau de Bord concept.

The new balance sheet would compare all investments with financings. These investments would also include, in addition to investments in working capital and fixed assets, investments in intangible assets. To reflect the increased importance of the effectiveness and capital requirements of processes (for example, of the supply chain) and the increased importance of relations to business partners for the economic success of today's enterprises, I propose a new balance sheet. This employs subdivisions for each of these categories in the balance sheet, where relevant. So, it might then look like this:

Investments (Assets)

▶   Investments in intangible assets in:

- Research and development
- Customer acquisition and retention
- Brand-building

- Structural and organizational capital/knowledge management
- Employee training

▶ Investments in tangible fixed assets:

- Land and buildings
- Machinery and equipment
- . . .

▶ Investments in financial assets:

- Shares in affiliated companies
- Shares in business partner companies
- Loans to business partners
- . . .

▶ Investments in working capital:

- Material supply chain (inventory, etc.)
- Financial supply chain (day-sales outstanding, cash, etc.) ...

In the notes, the company should also report on investments made by alliance and business partners, who are part of the company's business and ecosystem, and who are therefore extending the business capabilities of the company with their own investments (or reducing them, if they discontinue such investments). This may for example include investments in the extended supply chain infrastructure, which will affect the companies capability to serve its customers in a more timely and reliable way.

Financings (Liabilities)

▶ Equity

- Subscribed capital:

    – Shares held by institutional investor
    – Shares held by private investors
    – Shares held by employees
    – Shares held by management
    – Shares held by other major stakeholder groups
    – Own shares

- Capital reserve
- Retained earnings
- . . .

► Liabilities

  • Short-term liabilities:

    – Payables to suppliers and other business partners

    – ...

► Long-term liabilities:

  • Bonds (hold by financial institutions, by business partners)
  • Loans (from financial institutions, from business partners)

► Provisions:

  • for short-term expenditures
  • for long-term expenditures

► Others

But expenditures with an investment character – that is, investments in intangible assets – should not be capitalized mechanically. As Baruch Lev proposed in our interview, this should be done when it is becoming indeed obvious that an asset has been created. This is the case when the uncertainty about future benefits, which can be expected from such an investment, is considerably resolved; for example, through a successful beta test (for R&D expenditures in a software business) or through a successful test of a representative group of new customers that shows an increase in the probability that they will buy again (for investments in brand-building or in customer acquisition). Depreciation, based on the expected economic "life" of these assets, would start when first revenues are generated from these assets. These intangible assets, which are typically still associated with higher risks than tangible assets, will be subject to an annual – in critical cases even to a quarterly – "business test". Usefulness from a technology and market perspective will be assessed in such a test and, if expectations have to be lowered, extraordinary write-offs will be required.

The process of systematic capture, collection and documentation of information for the capitalization of investments/expenditures for intangible assets will provide a company with an additional benefit. Management can now dispose of valuable detailed, objective and auditable information about the programs in product development or in customer relationship management, that were intended to create these intangible assets and secure their future benefits. Planned amortization or exceptional write-offs on intangibles will then demonstrate how successful a business unit or the entire enterprise is in exploiting these assets.

The income statement

The traditional income statement highlights the most important cost of the production-orientated industrial era: the costs of goods sold; that is, direct product costs. When raw materials and direct labor made up most of a product's cost, this was important information for managers and investors. But today, many companies are engaged in intangible value creation and have very low variable costs or direct product costs, but incur high fixed costs. They have to invest larger and larger amounts in their capability to produce and sell new products, such as in R&D or brand-building. Such changes in the value-creation system should be reflected in the income statement in the right way and readers should be able to compare expenditures and investments with the revenues created by them.

As has been mentioned already, a major problem with actual accounting practice is that companies investing heavily in intangibles, and especially young and growing companies, report an incorrect income. It is too low (because investments in intangible assets, are totally expensed). Conversely, companies that live from existing intangible assets, and do not invest any more or under invest in new intangible assets creation and in future capabilities to perform, report too much income. This is because costs for past investments are not taken into consideration in the actual income statement, which reports only about the revenues generated by these past investment, but does not deduct any depreciation – not to mention that such an income statement obscures the fact that such a company is putting its own future at risk.

In addition, companies today have also much higher operational indirect costs. These are incurred in areas that have not been important in the past – for example, higher administration costs which are generated through a different practice in working with or for customers – through improved customer service. Often, these costs become obscured because the related expenses are not regarded as having any link with customer service and are therefore lumped in the traditional income statement with many other costs under general and administrative expenses. This, despite the fact that such costs can tell us much about operational efficiency. Activity-based costing tries to solve this problem for management accounting. But its results, too, have to be included in external financial reporting, in the income statement.

In order to provide relevant and useful information both for managers and investors, the new income statement has to focus on the real work of today's companies and on their real value-creation processes. To report on sales revenues, cost of goods sold and general and administration costs is not enough. Also, other activities which contribute to value-creation in today's companies – that is, in addition to efficient production and administration processes – have to be reflected in the income statement. These revenues should be broken down in separate items – one for each value creation area, such as one for product revenues, another one for service revenues and so on. Expenditures should be reported separately per value-creation area: cost generated in customer relationship management (direct marketing, sales, customer service); cost generated in product and market development; and costs for direct material and production costs.

The income statement should therefore, like the Tableau de Bord, be oriented on the value-creation system of a company. If the company is engaged in significant R&D activities and product innovation work, there should be a separate line item for it in the income statement. If the company does significant customer acquisition and relations work, these efforts and related resource consumption should be separately reported in the income statement as well. These items will then include also depreciation for capitalized intangible assets and should lead to much more accurate income reporting as expenses and revenues are now matching – one of the fundamental processes underlying any accurate earnings measurement.

If the company has created a significant network of alliance partners on the sales and marketing side, this network can also represent an important asset. It can be perceived as a source, or at least as an enabler, for new future revenues. With the help of a network, products can be marketed and sold easier and faster, a success critical market share can be reached earlier, and therefore first mover advantages can be realized with a much higher probability. An indicator for this capability could be the total revenue generated through the companies products by all its alliance partners including its own revenue – that is, the revenue generated by the total ecosystem. This type of information provides insight into the size and development of the ecosystem or partner network and therefore about the future capabilities of a company to generate new business and revenues. It should therefore be reported in the notes of the income statement. The alliance view of the Tableau de Bord might then provide further and more detailed information. Here is an example for such an income statement:

Revenues (according to product and customer groups)

► minus costs to produce products/services (including depreciation from tangible fixed assets and intangible assets, such as investment in the supply chain network)

▶ minus costs to develop products/services and to introduce new products/ service on the market (including planed depreciation and extraordinary write offs on capitalized R&D, brand creation, and business development expenditures)

Product Margin

▶ minus costs to serve customers (operational expenses)

▶ minus costs for customer acquisition and retention of the reporting period (including depreciation on intangible assets, such as investments in the creation of long-term customer relations)

Customer Margin

▶ minus costs to manage human resources

▶ minus costs to manage financial resources

▶ minus costs to manage alliances

▶ minus costs to manage IT

▶ minus other operative expenses and admin costs

Operating Income

▶ minus costs for general management (personnel and other expenses, for example for the corporate centre)

▶ other general and admin expenses

Income before tax and extraordinary income/expenses

▶ minus/plus extraordinary expenses / income or revenues not related to the core business

▶ minus tax

Net Income

The cash flow statement

Traditionally the purpose of the cash flow statement is to illuminate a company's liquidity status and show how management uses its financial resources. But the information the cash flow statement reveals about liquidity is of relative usefulness only as it is always a snapshot and is related to the past period. Much more important would be to have information about the probable development of liquidity in the future, based on actual information from operative business forecasts and planned financial transactions. For this, the finance view in the Tableau de Bord produces much better information, because it is directly taken from finance, where people act each day on the basis of this information. A report in the notes to the financial statement, based on forecasts on the basis of the measures of the finance view of the Tableau de Bord would therefore be the better solution to report on the liquidity status of a company.

But managers and investors must also know how much cash a company can produce over and above what's needed to operate it, and that is free cash flow. This information complements the information about earnings and shows how much a company is able to invest in its future and in future growth from current earnings and how much is available in addition to pay dividends to investors or to make important acquisitions. So a cash flow statement could look like this:

Net income

▶   plus depreciation for intangible and tangible assets

▶   plus/minus other operative non-cash operative expenses/income

Operative Cash Flow

▶   minus investments in working capital

▶   minus investments in tangible and intangible assets

▶   plus/minus other non operative investments or cash flows

Free Cash Flow

The risk statement

Enterprises that invest significantly in intangible assets usually represent for investors a higher risk than do other enterprises. The relationship between investments in intangible assets and their results is more loose and is dependent on many external and internal influences, and often not under the full control of management. The insecurity and risk about whether such an investment will generate a return at all is therefore significant. On the other hand, companies investing in intangible assets and knowledge-based products, can take advantage of several benefits. The created assets, for example in the form of coded knowledge, do not normally have the typical bottleneck characteristics that you might find in production facilities. This means that an enterprise with given marketing options is able to target economies of scale relatively quickly and can transform initial market success into market leadership. The main benefits are, therefore, that almost no limits to growth exist if the investment has been proven as successful from a market perspective.

We do know from option theory that if you can limit the downside – the risk of the underlying business of an option – and keep the upside open, the option value will increase. So successful management of intangibles-based businesses means two things: first, to grow the upside by leveraging increasing returns and by inducing network effects through fast action and reduced time-to-market; and, second, to limit the downside. In order to do this a company has to reduce the "cycle time" of management decision, so that it is able to react faster to threats and changes in its environment. Also, a company has to monitor in a systematic way all the risk factors inherent in its value-creation system. The latter is done through the risk statement, which reports about the status of the inherent risks in a business system.

The risk statement should be oriented on the value-creation system of an enterprise. Its structure will be very similar to the structure of a Tableau de Bord, which should help management to optimize the value-creation processes and to specifically boost the upside to increase the benefits of created intangible assets. The task of the risk statement is to make risk exposure transparent and to initiate risk limiting and risk reducing activities. As part of the enterprise management system, therefore, two measurement tools are required: the Tableau de Bord and the risk statement or risk status report.

But not only managers need information about the risk status of their company. Investors and other stakeholders are increasingly interested in it. A publicly disclosed risk statement would help them and other stakeholders as, for example, banks (especially under the "Basel II" rules[23]), suppliers and employees to better estimate the probability that an enterprise will achieve its planned return on investment and its sales and income targets. Such a risk statement should become therefore a standard statement that companies disclose with their financial statements. Such a risk statement can, for example, look like this:

---

[23] "Basel II" is the name for the new equity rules for banks. They will oblige European banks in the future to define their interest rates for corporate loans according to the individual risk situation of their client.

Strategic and global risks

▶   Demographic changes

▶   Currency and capital market risks

▶   Emerging disruptive technologies[24]

▶   Changes of legal regulations

▶   Strategic information gaps/missing information about major market trends, new competitors, and own competencies

▶   Lacking internal alignment/missing integration power, for which an indication might be, that the company's business units are not aligned with corporate business strategy

Development chain risks

▶   Employee fluctuation/loss of employees with critical knowledge

▶   Reliability of development partners

▶   Technology and engineering risks

▶   Risk of changing markets (during the product development process)

▶   Reliability of marketing partners

▶   Strength of market entry barriers for competitors/speed of competitor reaction to own product announcement

Operational risks (supply chain management)

▶   Supply chain network availability and reliability

▶   Down time/and frequency of disruptions after reconfigurations of the supply chain network (due to demand changes or the introduction of new products)

▶   Reliability of critical supply chain partners

---

[24] "Disruptive technologies" are those new technologies that do not fit into the mainstream business of an enterprise when they emerge. The consequence usually is that a company does not perceive them as important and will often neglect to monitor their further development. This lack of action may threaten the business suddenly in the future. See Clayton M. Christensen (1997) *The Innovator's Dilemma. When New Technologies Cause Great Firms to Fail*, Harvard Business School Press, Boston.

▶ Environmental risks

▶ Purchase price risks/contract risks

Operational risks (customer relations management)

▶ Sales forecast reliability (sales pipeline)

▶ Loss of important customers

▶ Development of customer loyalty in industry

▶ Sales price risks/contract risks

Risks in basis resource

▶ Human resources: retention of the employees with critical skills from a strategic perspective, personnel expense risks (e.g. from employee stock option programs)/contract risks

▶ Alliances: retention of critical alliance partners

▶ IT: system and network crash rate, software bugs, retention of employees with critical system know how

▶ Finance: loss rate in accounts receivables, currency risks, credit risks, interest rate risks, risks in financial investments

Architecture of the new measurement and accounting system

What does the general architecture of an integrated measurement and accounting system for the new economy look like? To answer this question and to develop the blueprint for the architecture, the requirements for such a system should be defined first:

1. Each item (activity, processes, and events), which is of relevance in the assessment of an enterprise's value-creation system, should be captured and quantified along the value-creation chain (such as a change in customer satisfaction or employee loyalty, success or failure in the product development process). The results should be included in selected and/or aggregated form in the Tableau de Bord.

2. The accounting system should recognize expenses for future value-creation potential as investments and should capitalize these investments as soon as the uncertainty of the related benefits is resolved.

3.   The measurement and accounting system should provide drill downs to details and should allow reconstruction of the results reported (audit trail).

To collect and prepare data for the measures of the Tableau de Bord in the most efficient way, the use of a data warehouse[25] is usually recommended. A data warehouse is a good tool to collect data from various sources, eventually restructure and aggregate this data so that it can be presented to support integrated decision-oriented and analytic views. It is, therefore, an important fundament for a measurement system that should support companies to completely capture, quantify, present and analyze information about all relevant value-creation factors of the enterprise. But in order to achieve this target, a data warehouse alone may not be sufficient. To provide accurate, consistent and auditable measures, additional tools and methods are required.

Traditionally, this requirement was the task of the cost and management accounting system. It made sure that data for cost management and for profitability analysis could be collected in a consistent and auditable way. Interestingly, such financial data are still the most used type of business data in data warehouses today – a clear indication of the importance not only of the data itself, but also of the way it is prepared. If companies want to extend their corporate measurement system now to areas not covered so far through general and cost accounting, they have to think about how to provide a similar level of accuracy and reliability for the additional data. Therefore, in addition to a data warehouse system, they will require an extended accounting system able to provide additional views in those areas where similar requirements concerning accuracy and consistency of data exist – as has been the case with cost or profitability data. This could, for example, apply to the area of product innovation, where a company may want to use market and CRM data that provide insight into the development of market opportunities and risk along the development process. Such data should be used for complex value calculations (for example, in a real option valuation) in order to support management decisions. If the company wants to report the results also in its external (supplemental) reports, these results need to be auditable. To do this in an efficient way, the company requires automatic documentation and

---

[25] A data warehouse is a database that is conceived, optimized and structured especially for analysis and reporting. It contains a copy of data from various internal systems, such as transaction systems, as well as from external data sources. A data warehouse serves as the basis for reporting and analytic systems that support those managers and knowledge-workers in analytic tasks and decision processes who require a view on these data across the structure of transactional systems.

account allocation functions, as well as for example valuation and currency translation functions – functions which to date have been usual only in accounting systems.

For sure, such functions can be provided partly as software functions in a data warehouse. This is exactly the concept of so-called analytic software applications that exceed pure reporting functionality by far and enable complex data manipulations. So solutions for financial analytics (e.g. for analytic cost management), for CRM (customer relationship management) analytics, for SCM (supply chain management) analytics, for HR analytics, for PLM (product life cycle management) analytics, etc. are available. The main advantage of this concept is its flexibility. Users are not restricted to the fixed data and analysis structures of transaction systems, but are able to act in a "modelling mode" instead, which can be easily adapted to new analysis requirements. At the same time, the main advantage compared to a pure reporting environment is the availability of ready-to-use more sophisticated functions, such as currency translations, allocations, etc., which can be used in analysis, and planning processes. The main disadvantage of a data warehouse-based analytic system is that data is not auditable (data is copied to a data warehouse and then aggregated or manipulated in other ways, so that its origin can not be determined later). This disadvantage can be reduced, at least partly, when all the raw data is copied to the data warehouse in a so-called operational data store (ODS) and subsequent data manipulations are documented in a log file.

But if different analytic views are to be reconciled with each other and with financial statements, and possible differences are to be explained and documented (for example, via document postings), there is no other solution than to pass this data through the accounting and double entry system and then copy the result to the data warehouse system.

Therefore, between an accounting system and a data warehouse system significant differences exist. These concern the capability of both systems and their basic concepts and functions. This makes sense, because it is not possible to dispose of a high degree of accuracy, continuity, consistency, and comparability of data as in a traditional accounting system and to have, at the same time, a high degree of flexibility and be able to change at any time the structure of the system and to redefine calculation schemes and simulation models.

Therefore, the solution lies in a combination of the two different systems. Data that should be kept consistent across both systems should originate from only one source: from accounting. It will be generated in the accounting system and copied to the data warehouse system, where it will be kept in its original form. This data can then be combined with other data, which originate directly from an operational application (for example, in a report or to calculate another measure), because they are not subject to special requirements concerning their audit ability, consistency, etc. (such as specific market data, customer satisfaction statistics, etc.).

The architecture for the measurement and accounting system should therefore be designed in such a way that the accounting system is able to process all type of data. This to include data from transactions, processes and events that are relevant to assess value creation and performance of the enterprise and its business units and for which consistency, reliability, audit ability and comparability are in focus and which should be able to be reconciled easily with financial statements. The principle of double entry accounting will apply here and additional views will be created through parallel ledgers. It should be possible to copy the results at any point in time to the data warehouse automatically, because for some data, which will not be changed any more through the closing process such as certain cost information, it makes sense to have them available in the data warehouse for analysis before period end closing has been finished.

Data for the measurement system, such as for the Tableau de Bord, originate from the data warehouse, which can process data from the accounting system but also from other sources. The data warehouse and its data form the basis for the analytic applications used for ad hoc analysis in decision support tasks but also for calculating specific measures of the Tableau de Bord or of the risk statement. Conversely, these analytic applications enable detailed analysis of measures of the Tableau de Bord and risk statement (drill down analysis). So the basis architecture of the new measurement and accounting system (see Figure 7.12) consists of three levels: the accounting system (auditable, consistent accounting database, and accounting specific calculations); the data warehouse and analytic applications (analytic world); and the monitoring and reporting level (Tableau de Bord).

The accounting system enables a company to document specific activities, events and transactions in a systematic, consistent way and with a continuity in the methods used, through the creation and posting of accounting documents that allow a detailed audit trail for the values reported in the accounting ledgers. It must provide methods for accounting tasks and processes. For example, it should be possible to reverse easily R&D expenditure postings and to capitalize the same amount as intangible assets (and to post

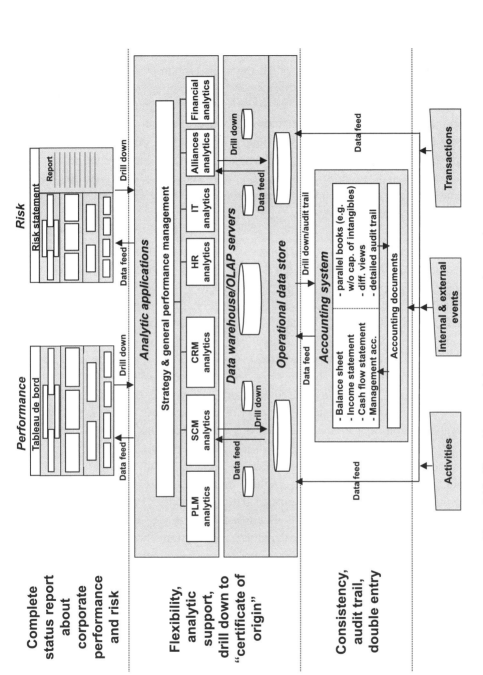

Figure 7.12 The architecture of the measurement and accounting system.

subsequent depreciation automatically) as soon as certain events (such as a successful test of the prototype product) prove that the necessary preconditions are fulfilled. The accounting system should also be able to keep different books in parallel. For example, one in which the capitalization of expenses related to intangibles is executed and another where these expenses are kept as expenses in order to enable companies to report in parallel on both principles. An automatic "Reconciliation Bridge" should explain easily to a user the differences between both ledgers. And, finally, it should be able to process any type of business information for which a company needs accounting logic and a detailed audit trail based on the document principle. So the paradigms of the accounting system therefore are: consistency, double entry principle, and audit trail.

On the level of the analytic applications, that are part of the controlling and measurement system of the enterprise, the system provides for the different value-creation processes of a company calculation methods and algorithms; for example, for the calculation of complex measures, for multidimensional analysis and simulations. In addition, they provide process support for related management processes; for example, the capability to define targets, to identify responsible persons for these targets in the system, to calculate automatically differences between target and actual values, and to store assessments for the actual/target comparisons as well as to enable collaborative communication on these assessments. The technical basis for this is a data warehouse able to capture data from any internal as well as external source that is relevant to monitor a company's value-creation processes. Eventually the large data warehouse is complemented by so called OLAP data marts.[26] The data warehouse is also able to capture data from external sources for the measurement system and may include data from partner transaction systems. Such data, combined with the company's own data, may then serve to form the data basis for an analytic cost management system than spans the entire extended supply chain and enables the company to manage its entire cost stream (collaborative cost management). The data warehouse should also include an operational data store (ODS), where all the incoming data is

---

[26] OLAP = Online Analytical Processing. OLAP-Data Marts represent a data subset of a data warehouse that provide data and functions for multidimensional analysis and simulation for specific views (e.g., an OLAP data mart with CRM data, or one with HR data). Modern data warehouse systems combine both concepts – the one of the large and complete data warehouse and of faster and more flexible OLAP data marts. It is possible in such data warehouse systems, to define several analysis and info cubes (multidimensional data models) independently of each other, but keeping them at the same time consistency of semantics and structures.

stored in its original form – including a "certificate of origin"[27] before aggregation and other data processing takes place. Only in this way can an audit trail for data be effective: this, because it has not been passed through the accounting system and requires a detailed audit trail at any time because of its high importance (for example, due to its use in calculating a measure for the Tableau de Bord). The paradigms for the analytic applications and the data warehouse system are therefore: flexibility in modeling, support for ad hoc analysis and simulation and for a certain level of audit trail through ODS, "certification of origin", and drill down.

At the level of the monitoring and reporting system, the Tableau de Bord and the risk status report form the most important building blocks of the system by providing a comprehensive view on the performance of all relevant value-creation processes of the company, on general or total business performance, on success or failure in executing strategies, and on the actual status of inherent risk in the business system of the company. The paradigms for the Tableau de Bord and the risk status report are: completeness and relevance.

To provide application and problem-oriented performance and risk information that reflects the value-creation system of a company and the necessary analysis tools is the task of the measurement system. The accounting system's task is to provide the necessary services, in the form of valuation, documentation and reconciliation functions. Both systems form the basis for the overall management system of the company. While the measurement system is improving the enterprise's information basis, it does not make sure that the company is really using this information in an effective and intelligent way in order to react to challenges, which single managers may have identified using the measurement system. Therefore, in addition to an appropriate measurement and accounting system, companies have to put methods and processes in place that enable a fast and efficient knowledge exchange between the managers in the enterprise and the extended enterprise around the information provided and the translation of this knowledge, of collaborative data interpretation, and of the resulting insights into coordinated action for the entire organization. This is to ensure that the information is put to its best use, which is enabled by the implementation of suitable management processes. Both management processes and accounting and measurement systems are main elements of the new management system enabling an enterprise to deploy real organizational intelligence.

---

[27] This is a kind of electronic stamp, a log, which can provide later information about when and from which source a data record has been copied to the data warehouse system.

8 New Management Processes and Concepts for the New Management System

That there is a connection between measures and management behaviour is hardly a breakthrough in management science – indeed that is what measures are for. What is new is that if we want managers to be more responsive to market demands and take responsibility for their actions, then budgets are the wrong performance drivers and control systems and must be replaced by steering mechanisms that support a culture of responsibility and enterprise. Such alternative steering mechanisms are not only more relevant to companies today, they release time and energy for more important managerial activities, and they are being practiced successfully by an increasing number of large companies.

Jeremy Hope and Robin Fraser[1]

The management system's task is to institutionalize decisions through management processes on strategy adjustments, but also on adjustments of operational enterprise activities and resource allocation. This should enable the enterprise to continually control and optimize its short- and long-term success in a dynamically changing enterprise environment.

Every enterprise today is challenged by the fast change of market conditions, technologies, or customer behaviour. As Peter Drucker wrote: "One cannot manage change, one can only be ahead of it".[2] Companies and organizations of all kind have to become change leaders if they want to survive in today's market environment. One specific characteristic of a change leader is to perceive change as an opportunity. A change-leader organization is always searching for changes in its environment. It disposes of the necessary "organizational intelligence" that allows it to identify quickly those changes required internally and in the business model/system in order to respond. In addition, change leaders are able to effectively translate required change into action; the objective being to not only maintain actual market position but to extend it by leveraging the changes happening in the markets.

And this is especially true for companies that are based on intangible assets. They are subject to a higher risk exposure, especially to the risk of changing

---

[1] Jeremy Hope and Robin Fraser (September, 2000) "Beyond Budgeting: Managing in the new economy", London: CAM-I/Beyond Budgeting Round Table (BBRT), white paper, p. 12.
[2] Peter F. Drucker (1999) *Management Challenges for the 21st Century*, New York: Harper-Collins, p. 73.

markets. Knowledge-based assets are also often characterized by "spill over effects" where competitors detract from the use of an innovation that its investors have, by copying it. This can be partially restricted by means of patents or protection of proprietary rights, but usually not completely. This is because knowledge-based assets and related products can be copied much more easily than physical assets based value-creation systems, which require considerable capital investments, which not every start-up is able to fund. The problem can often only be solved by use of "time-to-market", where the investors are on the market with the product faster than the competition, and where the investors rapidly increase their own market share. This requires a close link between markets and internal development activities on the one side, and with commercialization activities on the other, with the capability for fast adaptation in the case of changing markets as the key success factor.

But this rule not only applies today to knowledge and R&D intensive companies such as those in the pharmaceutical and high-tech industries. As more and more companies, also in traditional industries, rely on intangible assets, the phenomenon becomes a more common one. Enterprise management systems therefore have to be designed in a way to not only support companies and their managers to monitor and optimize their performance in the area of costs and revenues, but also to enable them to recognize immediately limits to growth in their value-creation system and to eliminate them, as well as to control and manage output – that is, the commercialization process. What is required are management systems which enable dynamic action and reaction and fast, nearly continuous, adaptation of the business system and of business activities to market and technology changes.

The problem with the traditional management process

Traditionally, the cornerstone of the management system of a company is the budget. Budgeting is the central instrument of traditional management systems. All management processes and methods are based on and aligned with it: from strategy planning through resource allocation and cost management to monthly performance measurement and rewards. The budget determines how managers behave and on what activities and objectives they focus. And the main problem today is the inflexibility of the budget-based management system.

These annual budgets, which are absorbing considerable management time and other resources in creating them, are fixed over the following fiscal year as soon as they are released. Through monthly actual/budget comparisons companies check how effective managers are in meeting their budgets. The main target of these managers becomes, therefore, to not exceed their budget, because their bonus is dependent on meeting it.

But a strategic instrument that locks managers into something they thought and found right at the end of the previous fiscal year, cannot be effective in a global knowledge economy with rapidly shifting market conditions and quick and nimble competitors. The monthly actual/budget comparison, which compares financial actuals – actual revenues and expenditures with a budget that is typically already overtaken by reality only after a few weeks of the new fiscal year have passed, locks these managers into the past and in the fictive world of the budget.

Companies are therefore trying to get rid of their inflexible budgets. They are moving instead to continuous rolling forecasting as part of their management processes. These enable fast and coordinated adaptation to anticipated changes in their business environment and help to balance initiated change-management activities with continuity and short-term performance.

The key is an integrated strategy and corporate performance management process, of which the basis is no longer a fixed budget but a dynamic forecasting process (see Figure 8.1).

In contrast to the monthly actual/budget comparison, rolling monthly forecasts of financial performance and for other nonfinancial value drivers related to the different value-creation processes of a company, focus managers on current and future opportunities and risks and not on the past. The forecasting process forces them to look ahead and to achieve market objectives under changing conditions, instead of focusing their attention on how to better meet the budget.

For the company as a whole, an institutionalized rolling forecasting process delivers more realistic estimations, if the organization is able to reach its annual targets. It enables senior management to react in time to negative developments but also to sudden opportunities.

Budgets and forecasts are tools for resource allocation. But resource allocation needs to be consistent with strategy and prevailing business conditions. And that means budgeting and rolling forecasting has to be integrated into the strategy management process. Because a strategy is always, first, a hypothesis of management about how a company can create competitive advantage and value, a strategy has to be adapted continuously as soon as new information

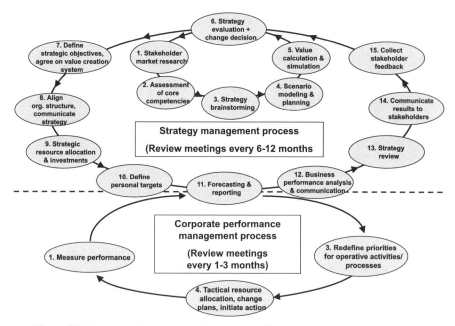

Figure 8.1   Integrated strategy and corporate performance management processes.

about the "reality" is available or as soon as that "reality" changes. For this, a feedback system is required, one that can deliver this information and knowledge on a regular basis. An important element of such a feedback system is the Tableau de Bord, which provides the relevant measures for the forecasting process. The Tableau de Bord can present not only actuals but also forecast information about the possible future development of these important measures. The latter will then trigger strategic and operative adaptation and corresponding coordinated action of the organization. In order to ensure that this happens in an organized way, and continuously, enterprises have to implement in addition to the appropriate measurement and accounting system the necessary management processes.

A model for integrated strategic and operational management processes

In many companies management processes are not very well structured. They are too inflexible in adapting to changes in the environment, and not very much focus is given to market and stakeholder matters. But the capability of a company to execute successfully its stakeholder-oriented strategies and to achieve sustainable business performance in a fast-changing environment, represents a major value driver. This is often the reason that one of two companies with similar "assets" is more successful in generating income and cash flow than the other.

The following paragraphs will therefore describe a model to serve as a blueprint for the integration of strategic, performance, and operational management processes into one enterprise management system. This system should support a company in its efforts to successfully execute its strategies and manage its performance by institutionalizing structured feedbacks and by adaptation of strategy and operational activities and processes.

Strategy and corporate performance management processes

Management processes, through which a company manages its strategies and its total or general performance, are called strategy and corporate performance management processes. The role of strategy is to define how the enterprise wants to create value for its stakeholders and with which assets it wants to do this and how it will combine them to a unique value recipe. The strategy management process should make both this strategy transparent and therefore manageable and should make it a continuous process rather than a one-off and establish a continuous strategic dialogue. Unique competitive positions in the market based on intangible assets can only be retained or even expanded if the enterprise is always one step ahead of external development, which is threatening these positions and has already adapted its own strategy before a change occurs. In addition, a strategy always is first a hypothesis of management. Reality must show, if it can become true or what needs to be changed in order to become successful. The task of strategy management therefore is to establish a strategic feedback loop, which enables an organized adaptation of strategy. The objective of this management process is to make strategies executable within an organization by breaking them down in a structured way to specific detailed targets and responsibilities and by monitoring strategy execution systematically. Variations from targets lead to corrected plans during the strategic planning process, a subprocess of strategy management. Here, methods and techniques such as scenario planning (for identifying and managing long-term strategic risks), real option valuation (for managing larger project and investment risks), and system thinking (for identifying growth restrictions in the system) are used. The strategy management process can also be called the strategic change management process.

In addition, a corporate performance management process that is integrated with the strategy management process is required. This integration is needed to provide more control over the continual conflicts between short-term and long-term performance, which typically increases with the portion of intangible assets in the enterprise. The aim of the corporate performance management process is to optimize the activities and resources of the enterprise with regard to the short-term profit targets (for example, communicated annual turnover and profit targets). The aim of the strategy management process is to create and expand long-term options that will add value. In other words, the task of the performance management process is to optimize the use of existing assets with regards to short-term profit targets, and the task of the strategy management process is to help to manage the creation of such assets (always relative to the market). Although both tasks are normally processed by the same management team but require different methods and a different mental attitude, it would make sense to separate the processes. Holding regular performance review meetings and separate strategy review and planning meetings less often, but also regularly could do this, for example. The reconciliation and integration point between both processes is the monthly rolling forecasting and reporting process based on the Tableau de Bord (see Figure 8.1).

The strategy management process consists of a core process and a subprocess for strategic planning. These provide support for the process step of strategy evaluation and change of the core process. The corporate performance process consists only of one core process. Here, a description of the different process steps is given, as shown in Figure 8.1.

Strategic planning (1–6) as part of strategy management

For enterprises acting in a dynamic business environment it is not enough today to work only once a year on strategy in order to check and to adapt it. Instead, this has to happen more often during the year, meaning management has to do strategic planning and subsequent adaptation of strategy at least twice a year (as in the case of Cisco). Because redefinition of strategy does not mean, necessarily, that people will act upon it nor that it will be executed successfully. Additional and systematic steps have to be taken and processes need to be established in order to make sure that a new or adapted strategy is translated into concrete action and is understood throughout the organization and the broader ecosystem of the company. In consequence, strategy work will become a continuous process, rather than an annual event. It starts with the strategic planning process, as a subprocess for strategy management. The strategic planning process ends with a decision, if the actual strategy is to remain unchanged or if it will be changed and continues with the core strategy management process:

1. The strategic planning process starts with stakeholder-oriented market research. Strategic planning or strategic controlling department staff analyze the expectations of major stakeholders (for example, investors) and actual or developing opportunities in product markets which are related to the company's core competencies.

2. Then the actual status of the company's core competencies is evaluated and analyzed (see Chapter 6).

3. The results of both steps are presented in a strategy-brainstorming meeting of the management team, to which internal and external experts of the areas of discussion may have been invited. The outcome of this meeting will be, say, three to four proposals for new or adapted strategic scenarios.

4. Strategy planning staff will further investigate the selected strategic scenarios and collect additional data and information. Based on these scenarios, different strategy proposals will be modeled reflecting the dynamics and dependencies of the different value drivers and risk factors in each scenario/strategy. This may be done using a systems dynamics model. The different models will be finalized. The management team members add their opinion about these strategies in general and their estimation about the dependencies between the different value drivers and risk factors.

5. Then these models are used to run simulations in order to come to a quantitative valuation of the different strategies and scenarios. This is, again, done together with the management team fine-tuning during the simulation sessions and offering an opinion on the likelihood of certain assumptions (for example, on currency exchange rate changes, on certain price developments, or on the possible speed of reaction of a competitor) in order to end up, finally, with agreed strategies and scenarios. Each strategy, including the actual one, the so-called base case, will be valued, for example using the discounted cash flow model. The outcome will then be compared with stakeholder expectations and with targets defined in Phase 1.

6. Management will then decide in a strategy evaluation meeting whether to leave the existing strategy unchanged, choose a modified version or a

totally new strategy (that is, one of the other proposed strategies). The remaining scenarios and corresponding strategies are kept for future strategic planning meetings, that can directly start to work with them if it turns out that another scenario than the one which has been actually chosen, will come to pass.

The strategy management process (7–15)

As soon as the management team has decided on a new or adapted strategy, it has to make sure that the organization can execute it. Therefore, the strategy has to be broken down into concrete and precise objectives.

7.   First, the related market/product segments will be defined (the "strategy matrix"), in which the company wants to operate. The strategy is then broken down into detailed strategic objectives, related to major stakeholder views, resources, processes and innovation areas. For each of these objectives a responsible person is named. In addition, the management team will decide which major initiatives or projects have to be started in order to support the changes required by the strategic objectives. Also, it has to agree what are the consequences of the new strategy for the configuration of the value-creation system of the company and what are the inherent risks to be included in the risk status report.

8.   Then the organizational structure and management responsibility structure should be adapted, if necessary; for example, to a new market/product segment structure. The newly-defined market/product segment structure, the strategic objectives, as well as a new organizational and management responsibility structure, has now to be communicated to all employees as well as to other major stakeholders.

9.   Financial, human and possible other resources have to be allocated by management to the various management responsibility areas, and to initiatives and projects which are assigned to the defined strategic objectives and agreed priorities. Previous budgets and operative plans need to be changed in order to ensure resource allocation and operative activities are in line with strategy. Every major investment project, such as specific product developments, will be reexamined and it will be decided if the company will continue to invest, or if it will discontinue or even increase, these investments.

10.   After that, strategic objectives are further broken down into personnel targets for all managers and employees playing a role in achieving

these strategic objectives. This will include the definition of incentives, such as bonuses, for personal target achievement, overachievement, and underachievement.

11. Based on regular actuals and forecasts for the measures of the Tableau de Bord, mainly of the Balanced Scorecard view, and of the risk status report, management will be informed about the performance of the organization in implementing the new strategy and about changes of the status of major risk factors in the business system.

12. Continuous communication between managers, employees, and controllers in person, via phone or via the Intranet or email will then take place on the performance and risks reported. For example, managers and employees able to monitor their own performance (related to their personal targets) through a personal scorecard can add comments and ratings to it. Their superiors or colleagues can then react with their comments. The intention of this dialogue across the organization is to come up with opinions about the actual situation and stimulate possible reactions which find a broad support.

13. The management team comes together at this stage. A strategy review meeting takes place, to discuss possible actions and reactions, make related decisions, and to agree on the information policy versus investors and other stakeholders. This can happen for example, in a management cockpit room.

14. Stakeholders are informed about the company's strategic performance through a supplementary report based on a Tableau de Bord scheme, about the actual risks through the risk status report, and about the corresponding actions considered by management. This may happen through flash reports posted on the company website (a web-based stakeholder portal), through email, by fax, printed mailings and so on.

15. Feedback from stakeholders about the company's strategic performance and about the actions considered by management is collected and documented. This forms the basis – besides management and employee opinion – for the evaluation of the actual strategy (phase 6). A new strategic planning cycle is starting.

The corporate performance management process

The task of the corporate performance management process is to control short-term total performance of the enterprise (typically over the actual fiscal year or quarter). Control is achieved by reacting tactically to changes in the business environment within the limits of the defined strategy in order to reach externally communicated annual targets and by adapting activities and resource utilization in the different value-creation processes of the company. This has to happen in a coordinated and in the most effective way. Therefore, a corporate performance management process is needed which helps an organization to manage and coordinate tactical adaptation of plans and resource allocation across different operational processes and functions. That is, a process that will trigger changes in operative management processes and the priorities for them, such as in product development or CRM. The cycle time of the entire process is some one to three months, with the top management team and its staff in charge. The phases of the process can be described as follows:

1. Actual total performance, and performance of operations and of the different operational processes, is measured and presented using the views of the Tableau de Bord (performance of the past reporting period). The top team, but also every responsible operational manager, now analyzes the enterprise performance.

2. In the next steps forecasts are produced for every area. Every manager responsible for one of the underlying value-creation processes is now in charge to deliver an estimation of the performance of his or her responsibility area for the next 12–18 months or for the remaining months of the fiscal year based on the measures of the Tableau de Bord. Then a detailed risk and opportunity analysis follows, by comparing the actual forecast with the last forecast (see Figure 8.2). The results of this analysis are the basis for proposals made by each operational manager for possibly adapting and optimizing measures and activities in their area of responsibility. They run simulations with the help of analytic applications in order to analyze the effects of their proposed changes on the future performance of their own area but also on general/total performance. The result will be reported on the Tableau de Bord showing, for each measure, three values: actual, forecast without adapting activities, and forecast taking into consideration the consequences of proposed adapting activities. If at the end of the actual corporate performance management cycle a new strategy management cycle is starting, the outcome of the risk and opportunity analysis of the forecasting phase will be also used to update the risk measures of the corporate risk status report. This may include also an adjustment of the risk measures, when the forecast analysis reveals that new types of risks and additional

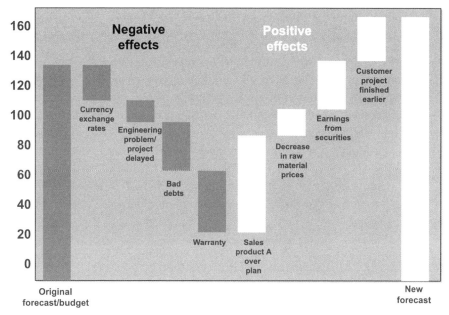

Figure 8.2 Forecast/forecast comparison used to analyze changes of the status of known business risks and opportunities and to identify new risks.

risk measures have to be added. This is, by the way, a good method to keep the risk status report up-to-date and relevant.

3.   Based on these new forecasts (and based on a strategy modification, in case management has just finished the strategy management process) and those of the forecast risk analysis, management redefines priorities for the operative processes and decides on the adaptation measures and activities proposed by operational managers. The objective is to meet the annual/quarterly performance targets communicated to investors and stakeholders under the constraints of the actual strategy. So, for example, management could decide that developers have to support for two months sales in introducing a new product to the customer base (by providing consultancy), instead of continuing with work on the next product version. The reason could be to meet annual sales targets, which may be at risk through competitor action or a late product release, and which may threaten the success of the overall strategy. Here, the management team needs to consider and balance priorities within the operational value-creation system of the company. Does it give priority to sales or to product development in a certain

segment under a specific constellation? To support such a decision, dynamic simulation models ("systems dynamics") might be used again.

4. These changes in the allocation of operative resources may then require changes to operative plans and budgets as well. The revision of operational plans happens in phase 4. To communicate clearly that the related operational budgets are not fixed but might become subject to changes as the year passes by, they may be called "rolling budgets" in contrast to just "budget" – a name that usually implies it is fixed over the fiscal year. But a rolling budget is something different from a rolling forecast. A rolling budget is a regularly adapted (internal) resource utilization plan. A rolling forecast is a regularly adapted forecast from a market perspective.

Management of operational value-creation processes

The operational processes of the business execution system drive total or general enterprise performance. But these operational processes and activities have to be aligned with enterprise strategy and some coordination between them is required. Therefore, a company has not only to properly manage each operational process separately but has to optimize it constantly in order to remain successful. Also it must integrate each operational process with its strategy and corporate performance management process. These two "general management" processes will trigger changes in operative management processes continuously but in a coordinated way in order to optimize the total results and performance of the enterprise (see Figure 8.3). Only in this way can a larger organization achieve positive and sustaining total results.

The operational management processes of an enterprise today typically include a management process that helps to manage and to optimize product and market development and the product portfolio of the company (called product life cycle management). Processes also include supply chain management, customer relationship management, and management of basic resources.

Product life cycle management

Product life cycle management (PLM) is usually related to a specific market/ product segment that has been defined by the strategy management process as a company's core business. It helps to manage the portfolio of existing, new, and future products of such a segment (and of the corresponding development projects) within the constraints defined by management and on the basis of

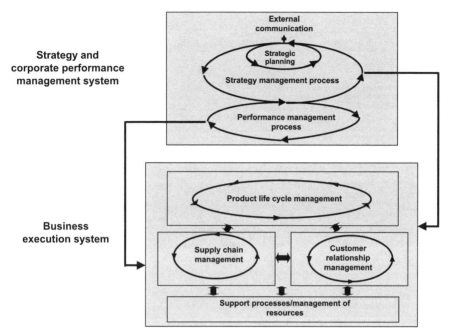

Figure 8.3 The two general management processes of a company trigger change in operational processes in order to optimize total enterprise performance.

the strategic resource allocations made. A product life cycle management process, which also includes business development and market development activities for newly developed products,[3] may consist of the following phases (see Figure 8.4):

1. The product life cycle management process usually starts with product-related market research for the product/market segments under consideration. Statistical information will be collected, such as demand forecasts, forecasts for a company's market share and for those of competitors, forecasts for price developments, etc. Qualitative information about market and technology trends, development of customer behaviour and about so-called lead customers, innovative and leading users of possible new products, and information from user communities will be gathered and analyzed. The result of this first phase will be one or several product idea(s).

---

[3] Market development activities for new products are attributed to the area of PLM, because they typically focus more on the product rather than on a specific customer or specific customer groups which are the target for the CRM process, which may take over at a later stage.

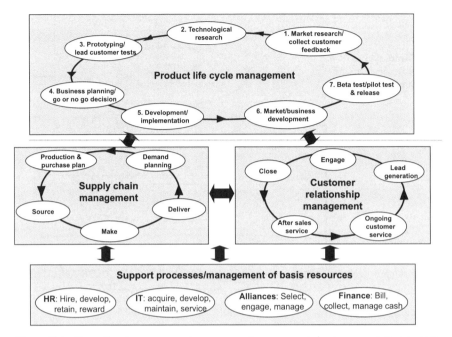

Figure 8.4 Operational management processes of a company's business execution system.

2. Now technological research will start. The objective is to assess and test the technical feasibility of a possible new product. This includes a first rough commercial analysis in order to check if such a product makes any sense at all, taking into account estimated costs and the estimated market potential. On the basis of this information, the responsible managers will then decide if they will continue with prototyping or if they will abandon the new product idea – at least for the moment.

3. In the following phase technical feasibility will be tested. Through the creation of a working prototype, the commercial and market potential will be verified by means of tests with lead customers.

4. If the tests are producing a positive result, a complete business plan will be set up. This will include all necessary expenditures (investments in product and market development for maintenance and continuous improvement of the released product, etc.) and probable revenues and income from the new product over its lifetime. Depending on the outcome of the valuation of this data and its comparison with industry benchmarks and/or economic targets defined by top management, the investment for the development project may be released or the project

will be abandoned. If high development risks are involved, real option valuation techniques might be used here.

5.   If the result of phase 4 is a "go decision", then the new product will be developed and the company will apply for the related patents.

6.   Before the development phase is finished, market and business development activities are begun. For example, the acquisition of marketing and sales alliance partners, the final pricing decision, planning for a possible (re) configuration of the supply chain, planning of marketing campaigns to support the market launch of the new product, and the training of sales people. In this phase, a reconciliation with the operations management processes should be undertaken in order to prepare production and sales for the new product.

7.   The new product will now go into final testing with (pilot) customers in order to make final adjustments and improvements to the product for a successful market introduction. As soon as the product has been released, product-related customer feedback will continuously be collected through customer service and through structured feedback. For example, through user groups or alliance partners in order to continuously improve the product and to collect input for new product ideas, which may lead to a new product development cycle.

When the new product is on the market, the task of market research is to collect market information that allows the company to decide, as soon as new information becomes available, if it should continue to invest in the product. The continuous evaluation of a product's business plan provides a view on the profitability of a product across its entire life cycle, as well as allowing the analysis of the product portfolio of all products. The latter includes existing products and products still under development, the portfolio forming the foundation for product investment decisions and the preconditions necessary for sustaining success in product development. For this, product business plans and data about the entire product portfolio have to be constantly updated and adapted to new market developments. Only in this way can a company systematically release the necessary resources to leverage new market opportunities through new development projects. With such a process in place, a company is able to continuously reduce total risks and increase returns on resources employed in its product innovation chain.

Operations management processes

Management processes related to operations are integrated into the overall management system through integration points linking them with the strategy and corporate performance management processes (see Figure 8.3). And also through integration points which link them with the PLM process (from product development to supply chain management configuration, and from market/business development to customer-related marketing activities). Operations management processes that is, supply chain management and customer relationship management have three tasks:

1.   Coordinate operational tasks and processes.

2.   Optimize operational tasks and processes.

3.   Identify value-creating opportunities and initiate reconfiguration of operational processes accordingly (process innovation).

For these tasks, managers rely mainly on detailed supply chain and customer relationship management information, which is timely and provided through the related cockpits. For the coordination tasks these monitors are used continuously on a tactical level. To optimize processes and identify new value-creating opportunities, managers and their staff should reserve some additional time each month to analyze information about the operational processes in a systematic way from a more strategic perspective (SCM or CRM review meetings). For this, they use analytic tools and software applications, that enable them efficiently and easily to identify opportunities to optimize existing processes or to recognize new value-creating opportunities that can be leveraged by reconfiguring processes (such in SCM) or by initiating certain activities (such as a marketing campaign in CRM).

Support management processes

Management processes that manage activities related to basis resources are integrated into the overall management system by strategy and operational forecasting. That is, by strategic objectives related to these basis resources and by planning and forecasting processes from which the demand and requirements of operational processes for short- and long-term availability and quality of specific resources are a result. The major task of the support management processes, is to manage the efficiency of operational processes and activities, and the effectiveness of the function as a whole.

For managing effectiveness, the responsible manager has to continuously reconcile strategic objectives of the company and operational objectives of other operations with his or her department's own activities. So these managers have to be well-informed, not only about their own function but also about the performance status and forecast of other functions in the enterprise that can lead to increased or decreased resource demands, which will affect workload and activities in their department. So while these functions that manage basis resources are "only" support functions, managers have to be informed about the status of actual total enterprise performance, about the one of each value-creation processes of the company, as well as about all related forecasts. Therefore, these managers have to monitor always the entire Tableau de Bord and they have to continually communicate with their manager colleagues who are responsible for the other processes in the company. The management process for a support function therefore has to include the following two tasks:

1. Monitoring regularly (monthly) the efficiency and effectiveness of the operational processes related to the function; adaptation of these processes if required.

2. Monitoring, at least in the same frequency, the development of the resource demands and requirements of the other functions of the company; reconciling these demands with available and/or planned resource levels and triggering of resource acquisition and development activities. Such resource acquisition and development activities may occur when forecasts will show that available or planned resources will not be able to meet demand in the future.

Innovative management concepts

Some interesting concepts have evolved in the last couple of years in the area of strategy and corporate performance management that enrich these processes and help companies to optimize them. Four of these concepts are:

1. The *Beyond Budgeting* concept, that intends to replace traditional budgeting by a more flexible management system.

2. *Scenario planning*, which intends to enable managers to better manage strategic risks.

3.   The concept of *systems dynamic/systems thinking* that should help managers to understand the dynamics in their business systems and to eliminate limitations for growth.

4.   The concept of the *management cockpit* that should help management teams to work better together and to make better decisions as a team.

The beyond budgeting concept

The Beyond Budgeting Round Table (BBRT)[4] of the Consortium for Advanced Manufacturing International (CAM-I) is an international program funded by more than 50 global companies. The BBRT developed the Beyond Budgeting concept, the objective being to analyze companies that no longer use budgets and to investigate the restriction of budgets in companies that do.

The Beyond Budgeting concept[5] is designed to overcome the barriers of the traditional budget-based enterprise management systems and to create a flexible and adaptive organization that gives local managers the self-confidence and freedom to think differently, to take fast decisions, and to collaborate on innovative projects with colleagues in multifunctional teams both within the company and across its borders (see Figure 8.5).

To support its mission, the BBRT has defined 12 principles that provide a framework for implementing the beyond budgeting model. Principles 1 to 6 are concerned with the performance management *climate*. This involves both the design of the organization and the delegation of power and responsibility to managers. Principles 7 to 12 are concerned with the performance management *processes*. A key element is that goals, measures, and rewards are decoupled – that is, not tied together in a performance contract. (The 12 principles strongly refer to the management system of ABB, as it has been described in Part 2 of this book.)

1.   *Self-governance*. Replacing (bureaucratic) rules and procedures with clear values and boundaries provides front line managers with the freedom they need to make fast, effective decisions.

2.   *Performance responsibility*. Recruiting and developing the right people,

---

[4] For more information see: www.cam-i.org/bb.html and the website of the author at www.juergendaum.com/bb.htm

[5] The following description of the principles of the Beyond Budgeting model and the case studies follows the SAP white paper: "Beyond Budgeting", co-authored by the author, the financial product management staff of mySAP.com and the CAM-I Beyond Budgeting Round Table, SAP AG 2001, pp. 6–9.

Figure 8.5   The Beyond Budgeting model.

those who have the right attitude to serving customers and to taking responsibility for achieving results, is important.

3. *Empowerment.* Authority and responsibility are delegated to front line managers. The defining principle is that decisions should be made as close to the customer as possible.

4. *Structure.* The new organization is based on a network of interdependent units with fast communications up, down, and across the business. The objective is to create as many small entrepreneurial units as possible.

5. *Coordination.* By designing business and management processes that link naturally to deliver customer value, Beyond Budgeting organization's use process and project-based relationships to respond to customer demands in real time. As each unit is responsible for its own results, market-like forces, driven by a network of internal supplier-customer agreements, replace centralized control.

6. *Leadership.* Leaders challenge and stretch managers to make step changes in performance and thus break free from the incremental thinking of the budgeting model. The leadership style changes from command and control to coach and support.

7. *Goal setting.* Only by adopting relative targets that are linked to competitor and market benchmarks will local managers set their sights on
more ambitious goals (they are unable to act totally against a general
market trend, but they are able to do better than the competition).
Moreover, basing targets on a range of key performance indicators
encourages managers to pursue strategic as well as financial goals.

8. *Strategy process.* Managers must be free to think differently, to produce
new ways of delivering customer value and even create new businesses
altogether. New initiatives are derived from strategic goals rather than
from concerns about departmental improvements grounded in the
politics of budgeting.

9. *Anticipatory systems.* Managers need early warning of changes that
impact their business particularly if they spell trouble ahead. Many use
rolling forecasts to keep an eye on the short-term future. An increasingly
important role of anticipatory systems is in managing short-term capacity.
Integrating customer order information with the supply chain means that
capacity need not be fixed far in advance, thus turning fixed costs into
variable ones.

10. *Resource utilization.* Delegating investment and resource decisions to
people close to the action and disconnecting them from the annual
budgeting cycle ensures that such decisions are made only when
needed. Thereby, managers have the freedom to take appropriate
action at the right times. Continuous downward pressure on costs is
maintained by giving high visibility to efficient resource consumption in
the company. Where appropriate, an internal market should be used,
whereby internal supplier-units sell their services to internal customer-
units.

11. *Measurement and control.* Controls need to be multifaceted. They involve
fast actual results, leading indicators, and rolling forecasts – all supported
by fast and open information systems. These measures are disseminated
to all management levels simultaneously with more detail at a local level
and less detail at a higher level.

12. *Motivation and rewards.* Performance evaluation based on relative
measures drives performance improvement. Moreover, the performance
emphasis is on teams or whole companies rather than on individuals. This
approach encourages information and knowledge sharing and ensures
that the whole company pulls in the same direction.

Some companies have already embedded the beyond budgeting principles into their management processes. Most have seen a significant step change in financial performance that has been sustained over many years. Of these first adopters, 14 have so far been the subject of visits and case studies by the BBRT. Here are a few examples.

SKF

SKF is a Swedish company that is the world leader in roller bearings with sales in 2000 of $4.7bn. While TQM had already taken root in the early 1990s, the company launched SKF100 in 1996 – a set of values and targets taking the company up to its centenary in 2007 – based on a multi-level series of balanced scorecards. These provide the broad "stretch" framework within which annual targets are now set for each division and segment. But these targets and measures set the company on a collision course with the traditional budgeting system, which was duly abandoned in late 1995. SKF is now a much more market-focused organization and, after a period of retrenchment, is now growing strongly.

Svenska Handelsbanken

A Swedish universal bank with revenues of around $2bn, 8,500 employees, and 600 profit centres (mostly branches). Svenska Handelsbanken has replaced the fixed annual budget by a system of market driven target setting, continuous forecasting and resource allocation processes for front line profit centres, and market-like relationships between supporting and customer serving units. Since abandoning the budgeting model in the 1970s it has outperformed its Nordic rivals on just about every measure including return-on-equity (ROE), total shareholder return (TSR), earnings-per-share (EPS), cost-to-income ratio, and customer satisfaction. And it has done this consistently, year-in, year-out, for the past 30 years. Svenska Handelsbanken is the most cost efficient bank in Europe and has recently been voted one of Europe's best Internet banks.

Borealis A/S

A Danish company established in 1994 as a joint venture between two Nordic oil companies (Statoil of Norway and Neste of Finland). Borealis is at the leading edge of polymer research and development and is now Europe's largest producer (sales of $2.5bn) and the fourth largest worldwide. The petrochemicals industry is notoriously cyclical with financial success largely dependent on oil prices. The introduction of the Beyond Budgeting model allows the company to react now in a much more flexible way to market changes. Since it abandoned the budgeting model in 1995 Borealis has doubled its shareholder value and reduced costs by 30% over five years.

So, the Beyond Budgeting model requires not only a new approach to budgeting, resource allocation and operational planning, but also a more holistic approach in strategy and corporate performance management: from strategic planning, through target setting, to rolling and event driven forecasting and performance management based on financial and nonfinancial KPIs. To make that happen and to support organizational and management process models according to the Beyond Budgeting principles, organizations are increasingly using advanced information systems like analytical software applications. Essential for the Beyond Budgeting model are continuous management processes which are interlinked by a framework based on a company's individual value-creation system. While the Beyond Budgeting concept is focused more on supporting the corporate performance management process of an organization, the target for the concept of scenario planning is (long term) strategic planning.

Scenario-planning

To act with confidence in major strategic decisions, managers must be willing to look ahead and consider uncertainties. But many people react to uncertainty with denial. They take an unconsciously deterministic view of events. They take it for granted that some things will or will not happen – for example, that oil prices will not collapse or that the Cold War will never end. Not having tried to foresee surprising events, they are at a loss for ways to act when upheaval takes place. Scenarios are used to help managers take a view into the future in a world of great uncertainty. They are a tool to manage strategic risks and opportunities.

Scenario-planning is the process in which managers invent and then consider, in depth, several varied scenarios of equally plausible futures with the objective to bring forward surprises and unexpected leaps of understanding.[6] These scenarios represent a tool for ordering the perceptions of a management team. The point is not to select one preferred future and hope for it to become true. Nor is the point to fund the most probable future and adapt to it. Rather, the point is to make strategic decisions that will be sound for all

---

[6] For more about scenario-planning, see Peter Schwartz (1996) *The Art of the Long View: Planning for the Future in an Uncertain World*, New York: Bantam Doubleday Dell.

plausible futures. No matter what future takes place a company and its management team is much more likely to be ready for it and influential in it, if it has seriously thought about scenarios. Scenario-planning is about making choices *today* with an understanding of how they might turn out.

The concept of scenario-planning first emerged after the Second World War. Used in military planning, it was further developed into a tool for business prognostication. In the early 1970s scenarios reached a new dimension, with the work of Pierre Wack, who was a planner in the London offices of Royal Dutch/Shell. He and his colleagues were looking for events that might affect the price of oil. And they found several significant events that they identified as ''driving forces''. One was that the United States was beginning to exhaust its oil reserves. At the same time American demand for oil was steadily rising and the emerging Organization of Petroleum Exporting Countries (OPEC) was showing signs of flexing its political muscle. Most of the OPEC countries were Islamic, and they bitterly resented Western support of Israel after the 1967 six-day Arab-Israeli war. Looking at this situation, the planning team realized that Arabs could demand much higher prices for their oil and there was every reason that they would. The only uncertainty was when. It seemed likely to happen before 1975 when old oil price agreements were due to be renegotiated. So Pierre Wack and his team wrote up two scenarios. The first story was based on the assumption that the oil price would stay somehow stable – which presented management's opinion at Shell at that time. The second looked at the more plausible future – that OPEC would massively increase oil prices leading to a worldwide oil crisis – and underpinned it by the facts found. This second scenario helped Shell's managers to imagine the decisions they might have to make. And it was just in time. In October 1973, after the Yom Kippur war in the Middle East, there was an oil price shock and of the major oil companies only Shell was prepared for the change. The company's management responded quickly and in the following years, Shell moved from one of the weaker of the seven large oil companies that existed at that time to the second in size and the first in profitability. This was when scenario-planning as a technique for strategic enterprise planning was tested for the first time. It was then further developed by Shell and other companies.

To operate in an uncertain world, managers need to be able to question their assumptions about the way the world works, so that they can see the world more clearly. The purpose of scenario-planning therefore is to help managers to change their view of reality, to match it more closely with reality as it is, and reality as it is going to be. The end result, however, is not an accurate picture of tomorrow, but better decisions about the future.

Peter Schwartz, an expert in scenario-planning, has described the process of scenario-planning. He structured the process into eight phases:[7]

1.   *Uncovering the decision:* In the first phase the company has to identify strategic decisions that might have to be made in the near future. This also includes an identification of the key factors of the business system that influence the success or failure of the decision.

2.   *Information-hunting and information gathering:* This is the research phase. Information about topics and possible future decisions identified in the previous phase is systematically collected.

3.   *Identifying the driving forces of a scenario:* Here, the task is – based on the collected information – to look for driving forces in the macroeconomic environment of the company that influence the key factors of the business system, which in turn will decide about success or failure.

4.   *Uncover the predetermined elements:* According to Peter Schwartz, prede-termined elements are developments and logics that work in scenarios without being dependent on any particular chain of events. That means, a predetermined element is something that seems certain, no matter which scenario come to pass. For example, the most commonly recog-nized predetermined element is demographics, because it is changing so slowly.

5.   *Identify critical uncertainties:* In every plan, critical uncertainties exist that have a significant influence on results. Scenario planning should help organizations to better prepare for uncertainties and to manage them and to react to all possible variants. So critical uncertainties are the variables in scenario-planning and are the basis to create different scenarios in parallel. The task in this phase is to identify these critical uncertainties.

6.   *Composing scenarios:* When all elements necessary for writing scenarios are available, different scenarios are composed that describe – based on assumption of predetermined elements and critical uncertainties – how the driving forces might plausibly behave, and the influence they will have on the key factors of the business system and how this will affect final results.

7.   *Analysis of implications of the decisions according to scenarios:* Once the

[7] Peter Schwartz (1996) *The Art of the Long View: Planning for the Future in an Uncertain World,* New York: Bantam Doubleday Dell.

scenarios have been developed, then it is time to return to the decision identified in the first phase. How does the decision look in each scenario? What vulnerabilities have been revealed? These are typical questions which are discussed now. The task in this phase is to develop possible "reaction strategies" for each scenario related to the decisions identified in the first phase.

8.   *Selection of leading indicators and signposts:* Now, when scenarios and their "reaction strategies" have been developed and thought through, it is important for the management team to know as soon as possible which of several scenarios is closest to the course of history as it actually unfolds. For this, they select indicators that will provide them with early warning information, which scenario will come to pass. These indicators may become part of the risk status report of the company.

The concept of system dynamics or systems thinking

Whereas the objective of scenario planning is to limit the risks of strategic decisions by anticipating possible external developments, the main objective of the concept of system dynamics is to help managers to understand the dynamics in their business systems in order to eliminate limits to growth by recognizing early enough their real limitations. System dynamics, also called systems thinking, is a methodology developed for studying and managing complex feedback systems, such as one finds in business and other social systems. Professor Jay W. Forrester at MIT developed the concept in the early 1960s. At that time, he began applying what he had learned about systems during his work in electrical engineering to everyday kinds of systems.

What makes using system dynamics different from other approaches to studying complex systems is the use of feedback loops. According to the concept of systems dynamics, reality is made up of circles. But people usually see straight lines, which is a major limitation to see and understand the system and make the right decision related to that system. Peter Senge,[8] an expert in systems thinking uses an example from the Cold War to explain that.

---

[8] Peter M. Senge (1990) *The Fifth Discipline: The Art and Practice of the Learning Organization,* New York: Doubleday, p. 70. This book has one of the best descriptions of the systems dynamics concept – or systems thinking as Senge calls it.

The US had a viewpoint to the arms race that essentially resembled the following:

USSR arms ➡ threat to Americans ➡ need to build US arms

At the same time, the Soviet leaders had a view of the arms race somewhat resembling this:

US arms ➡ threat to Soviets ➡ need to build USSR arms

From the American viewpoint, the Soviets were the aggressor, and US expansion of nuclear arms was a defensive response to the threats posed by the Soviets. From the Soviet viewpoint, the United States were the aggressor, and Soviet expansion of nuclear arms was a defensive response to the threat posed by the Americans. But the two straight lines form a circle. The two nations' individual, "linear", or nonsystemic viewpoints interact to create a "system", a set of variables that influence each – with the main reason for this influence being the limited linear view of each party and the fact that neither side had an overview of the total system. Such an overview on the basis of a system dynamics model would uncover the arms race as a perpetual cycle of aggression.

From their individual viewpoints, each side achieves its short-term goal. Both sides respond to a perceived threat. But their actions end up creating the opposite outcome, increased threat, in the long run. The long-term result of each side's efforts to be more secure is heightened insecurity for all, with a combined nuclear stockpile of 10,000 times the total firepower of the Second World War.

The same problem occurs in the business world. Conventional forecasting, planning, and analysis methods are not equipped to deal with dynamic complexity. When the same action has dramatically different effects in the short and the long run, there is dynamic complexity. When an action has one set of consequences locally and a very different set of consequences in another part of the system, then there is dynamic complexity. And the concept of systems dynamic/systems thinking is a way to master this complexity. In order to do that for the object of decision (a business system, strategy, or scenario) first of all its feedbacks are identified. Then further analyzed in order to identify reinforcing feedbacks, balancing feedbacks, and delays – the building blocks of systems dynamics.

Reinforcing feedbacks

These are the engines of growth. Whenever you are in a situation where things are growing, you can be sure that reinforcing feedback is at work. Reinforcing feedback can also generate accelerating decline – a pattern of decline where small drops amplify themselves into larger and larger drops, such as the decline in bank assets when there is a financial panic. In a reinforcing process, a small change builds on itself. Whatever movement occurs is amplified, producing more movement in the same direction.

Balancing feedback

Will operate whenever there is a goal-oriented behaviour. If the goal is to be not moving, then balancing feedback will act the way the brakes in a car do. If the goal is to be moving at 100 kilometers per hour, then balancing feedback will cause you to accelerate to 100 but no faster. In a balancing system, there is a self-correction that attempts to maintain some goal or target. Filling a glass of water is a balancing process with the goal of a full glass. Hiring new employees is a balancing process with the goal of having a target workforce size or rate of growth. Balancing feedback processes underlie all goal-oriented behaviour. What makes balancing processes so difficult in management is that the goals are often implicit, and no one recognizes that the balancing process exists at all. But identifying these balancing processes is crucial for system dynamics modeling.

Delays

Many feedback processes incur interruptions in the flow of influence. This makes the consequences of actions occur gradually. Delays are interruptions between actions and their consequences. Delays can make you badly overshoot your mark, or they can have a positive effect if you recognize them and work with them. Delays exist everywhere in business systems. We invest now to reap a benefit in the distant future; we hire a person today but it may be months before he or she is fully productive. But delays are often unappreciated and can lead to instability or even breakdown, especially when they are long. Adjusting the shower temperature, for instance, is far more difficult when there is a 10-second delay before the water temperature adjusts, than when the delay takes only a second or two. During the 10 seconds after you turn up the heat, the water remains cold. You receive no response to your action; so you perceive that your act has had no effect. You respond by continuing to turn up the heat.

When the hot water finally arrives, it is too hot and you turn away – and after another delay, it's cold again. In general, each cycle of adjustment in a balancing loop with a delay compensates somewhat for the cycle before, so that each adjustment to reach a desired target happens with a delay so that the target will be reached only gradually in steps.

You can model a complete dynamic system by combining these different elements, reinforcing feedbacks, balancing feedbacks, and delays. For example, a model could be built to analyze a business system with limits to growth. A reinforcing process is set in motion to produce a desired result. It creates a spiral of success but also creates inadvertent secondary effects, manifested in the balancing process eventually slowing down the success, if the limiting factor is not recognized and eliminated. Typically, most people react to limits to growth situations by focusing on the reinforcing process and by trying to push harder. But the solution for success lies in the balancing loop – not the reinforcing loop. For example, if a company is successful in selling a new product, sales revenue and profit will grow. It is able to hire more sales personnel and spend more on advertising, driving sales up even more (reinforcing feedback). But growing sales generate higher demands for production. Capacity use in production grows steadily. With growing capacity use failure rate and lead-time in production grows as well, resulting in delivery delays and more frequent customer complaints about product quality. Customer satisfaction deteriorates and the image of the product on the market and of the company will be damaged. The consequence is that customers will buy less and less (balancing feedback). The company cannot solve the problem by investing more in advertising or hiring more sales staff – often the natural reaction – to focus on the reinforcing feedback loop. Instead, it has to invest in more production capacity and has to eliminate the limiting factor of the balancing feedback loop – but this must happen in time (see Figure 8.6).

By using a systems dynamic model, managers can simulate the consequences of certain decisions and actions on specific limiting factors of their business systems over time. The model also checks the consequences the factors have on the output; that is, on the total performance of the system. A systems dynamic-based simulation of scenario or strategy can provide additional insight into the dynamics in the economic/business system. It allows managers to boost the upside – that is the benefits of, for example, an intangible assets-based value-creation process by identifying and eliminating in time the limiting factor for growth. This might be critical to leverage first mover advantages in order to reach market leadership in a new product/market segment and to maintain it.

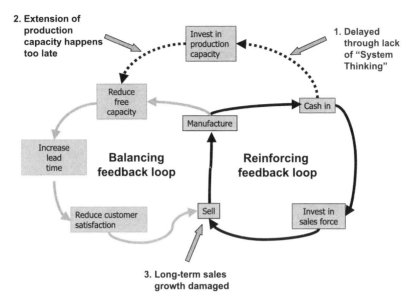

Figure 8.6   Systems dynamics model with limits to growth.

Both concepts, scenario planning and systems dynamics, are very useful tools to support the strategic planning process, in particular if a company has to manage investments in intangible assets. This is especially the case, if both concepts are combined. Scenario planning helps to limit the downside, that is strategic risks of investments in intangible assets; system dynamics helps to boost the upside. Both concepts are the main levers to increase the value of high risk/high opportunity investments.

The Management Cockpit concept

The Management Cockpit[9] is first a concept for the ergonomic design of a management meeting room (see Figure 8.7), but also for the structuring of performance management meetings. It is intended to make management teams more productive by improving communication between team members and by focusing them on strategic issues.

At the heart of the concept is a measurement system of about 100 indicators. These and other critical unstructured business information visuals are depicted

---

[9] The Management Cockpit concept was originally developed in 1989 by Professor Dr. Patrick M. Georges, a neurosurgeon and expert in Human Intelligence Management, based in Brussels. See Patrick M. Georges (2002) *Le Management Cockpit. Pilotez vos affaires avec plus d'efficacité*, Paris: Editions d'Organisation.

Figure 8.7   The Management Cockpit supports efficient management team meetings.

on the four walls of the Management Cockpit room using ergonomically designed graphics. The indicators meet especially the decision support needs of senior executives. During meetings, only those measures and graphs are visible that are relevant to the actual discussion or decision to be made. This display should motivate managers to take action, by presenting them during the meeting with strategic core indicators allowing them to understand relationships between the various underlying business processes and success factors.

The elements of the concept[10] are the four walls with their logical views, the so-called flight deck in one corner of the room powered by a six-screen computer, and training and check lists that should help a management team conduct more efficient team meetings and make faster decisions. The Black Wall depicts the main key performance indicators/measures in six logical views covering all relevant management areas of the company. Each logical view is dedicated to one of the key areas that have to be monitored by the management team. It is oriented on the question and answer principle. Therefore a logical view always represents an answer to a question. For example: Are we in good shape concerning our financial performance? How are we performing on the market compared to the competition? How successful are we in satisfying and retaining customers and acquiring new ones? How efficient are we internally with our business processes? The answer is given through six frames for

---

[10] The intellectual property rights for the concept were acquired in 1998 by SAP AG and the name "Management Cockpit" is now a registered trademark. See also the author's interview with Professor Georges in Chapter 9.

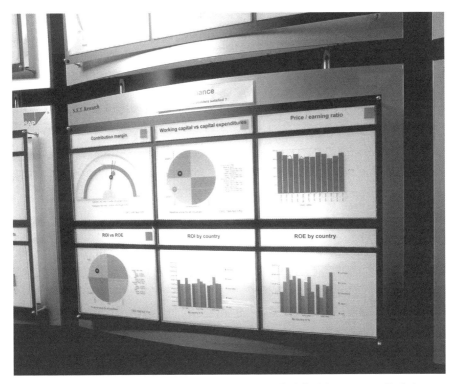

Figure 8.8 A logical view presented on the Red Wall of the Management Cockpit.

each logical view. Each frame presents either a graph or text information (see Figure 8.8).

The other three walls present, each again through six logical views, answers and indicators to more detailed questions. The Red Wall presents information about the market and customers, the Blue Wall about internal processes and resources, and the White Wall about status of important projects and strategic initiatives. So the structure is very much in line with the Balanced Scorecard concept.

Software has been developed, enabling members of the management team to access through their individual web-based portals Management Cockpit data and information. They can use the software to analyze the data and run simulations from their offices or from their homes in order to prepare for the next management meeting.

According to Patrick Georges's concept, the Management Cockpit structure also reflects the structure of the management meetings held in it. The meeting starts with an investigation of the actual status by analyzing and discussing the information from the Black Wall. Moving on to the Blue and Red Wall will then deepen this discussion and analysis. Then the status of the most important projects and initiatives will be analyzed and discussed on the basis of the White Wall. When the meeting is finished, the management team will have made all urgent decisions and will have focused on the really important topics.

So the Management Cockpit is useful to establish a common management information and communication basis in an enterprise through structured communication processes in and around management meetings, such as in the preparation or follow-up phase.

Patrick Georges has supported so far the implementation and operation of a Management Cockpit room in more than 50, mainly European, organizations. One of the first was Iglo-Ola (Unilever Belgium), where Ghislain Malcorps, the former financial controller, promoted the installation of a Management Cockpit room.

Interview with Ghislain Malcorps: experiences in implementing and using the Management Cockpit

Iglo-Ola (Unilever Belgium) is a subsidiary of the Unilever group. Turnover of Iglo-Ola was 6 bn BEF ($169 Mio) at the time of the interview and the company employed 300 people, with some 50% of these in the logistics area. The company operates only in Belgium and Luxembourg and is focused on frozen food and ice cream. It is a purely marketing and sales organization and all products sold are imported from foreign sister companies. The company delivers directly to retailers. The two main functions to be managed therefore are sales marketing and logistics.

I visited Ghislain Malcorps and his company's Management Cockpit room in November 1997. This was a few months after the room went live. He played an important role in introducing this new concept into his organization and in bringing the Management Cockpit to life. He also served as the so called "cockpit officer". The following interview was conducted in spring 2000. In the meantime he has retired.

Jürgen Daum: Ghislain, you had been one of the promoters of this innovative concept of the Management Cockpit in your organization and the responsible person for its implementation. The Management Cockpit Room at Iglo-Ola has now been in use for more than two years and have you gained a lot of experience in this time. Why did you and your management team implement such a corporate "war room"?

Ghislain Malcorps: Well, if we look back to the situation before we used the Management Cockpit, it can be characterized from a manager point of view as a situation where we had an abundance of data but a lack of information and knowledge. There was a lot of data available in the company, but nobody knew exactly at which data he had to look at, what was really important. Often data was not linked to other data, it was difficult to retrieve and to interpret. The available management data did not met the needs of senior and middle management. It was not well prepared for them and not "digestible". It contained many contradictions, many versions, too many figures and there was no visual representation. And very often, there was not enough focus on strategic issues and parameters. The daily experience of the executives and deciders of the company was a lack of knowledge and awareness of the company's strategies and a lack of efficient executive communication about the strategies.

Juergen Daum: I can imagine that this is a typical situation in many business organizations.

Ghislain Malcorps: You are probably right. But I assume that many managers and executives do not know how much better the management system and available management information and knowledge could be – simply because they have no comparison. In our case this came to our consciousness when we found out about the Management Cockpit and learned more about this innovate concept through it's inventor Prof. Georges. The concept of a meeting room and communication tool where the board displays very openly the chosen strategies and which guarantees that everybody is informed, that the strategies and the business fundamentals are clear to and shared by everybody and that short-term decisions are fully compatible with the long-term strategies seemed to us to be the solution for our problem which we just identified to its full extent. Therefore the decision was made by our chairman and the management team to implement at Iglo-Ola such a Management Cockpit room.

Juergen Daum: The adoption of such a different management system in your company – different compared to the management system before, which consisted of the classical financial reports – probably represented a major challenge for everyone in management and in the finance department. How did you proceed in implementing the Management Cockpit room at Iglo-Ola?

Ghislain Malcorps: Yes, it really was a challenge. The Management Cockpit should serve as a unifying and strategy focusing interface between the Chairman and the Board and between the board and the extended board, which includes the managers responsible for the operations. Therefore the first task we had to solve was, to create a common understanding of the company's mission and strategies.

Juergen Daum: Didn't they exist before?

Ghislain Malcorps: Yes, they existed before. But the company's mission and strategies had not been reviewed and re-discussed regularly like it was done with monthly financial reports. The reporting and management system used so far did not stimulate managers to discuss strategies. Therefore every manager and executive had his own understanding of the company's mission and strategies and therefore his own priorities. It was one of the major goals of the Management Cockpit project to create common strategic priorities in the abundance of management information, to make sure that short-term decisions are fully compatible with the long-term strategies. For this, there needed to be first a coherent understanding of the company's mission and then of these strategies within the company.

Juergen Daum: What exactly is the Management Cockpit and what does it look like at Iglo-Ola?

Ghislain Malcorps: The Management Cockpit is a decision centre, where the management team meets on a regular basis to discuss business performance and strategies. It is also a strong communication tool: the board displays very openly the chosen strategies and the cockpit guarantees that everybody is informed. On its four walls, mission, critical success factors and key performance indicators are displayed in graphical form on panels. The Black Wall shows what is important for the company: certainly the trading profit or contribution and all key goals that reflect the strategies and the mission statement, like innovation, growth, etc. The Blue Wall describes the internal environment of the company, like productivity in some sensitive areas (logistics), cost contention, quality of staff, etc. The Red Wall describes the external environment of the company: customer and competitors watch, market shares, macro-economic indicators, evolution of sensitive raw material prices, etc. The White Wall contains the broad action plan of the management team with its strategic thrusts and the three rolling milestones.

Juergen Daum: What are strategic thrusts?

Ghislain Malcorps: The strategic thrusts are the main strategies derived from the company's mission statement. The summary of these main strategies is called "Broad Action Plan". These thrusts are mostly action driven and are represented through one visual with a list of those thrusts at their respective status on the White Wall. The other panels of the White Wall are dedicated to human resources indicators and especially to all the "projects" which are intended to realize the strategies. The follow-up of the various projects was – according to our experiences at Iglo-Ola – a major role of the Cockpit.

Juergen Daum: Can you give us an example of such a project?

Ghislain Malcorps: An example for such a project and for such a visual at the White Wall of the Management Cockpit room is "More Value from SAP" – that is, create more value out of our SAP enterprise resource planning (ERP) implementation. The project is divided into several phases with a deadline for each of them. Among such projects you also find acquisitions, mergers, larger investments, restructurings. On the visual you see one colored bullet that tells you whether the responsible person is on track or not. Each project has of course a responsible person whose variable pay is, generally speaking, linked to the realization in time of his project.

Juergen Daum: Those visuals you mentioned seem to play a key role in the concept of the Management Cockpit. How they are used at Iglo-Ola?

Ghislain Malcorps: Each wall is subdivided into so-called logical views. Each logical view has a title and a question referring to the Broad Action Plan. The question is answered by the six visuals belonging to the logical view, some of them being linked to other visuals in the cockpit. The visual usually represents a single key performance indicator (KPI), like in a scorecard, because the visual should be restricted to one single information: less is more. They are color coded: green, yellow and red make them very easy to read and to digest. There is a natural tendency, mainly in the beginning, to overload the visuals with explicative and quantitative information. In such "patchwork" cases, the visual loses its power and, sometimes, becomes completely ineffective.

Juergen Daum: Are there management responsibilities defined for each KPI/Visual?

Ghislain Malcorps: Each visual and KPI has a sponsor, the director of the concerned department, and a data owner. The controller, who is the head of the management accounting department, me, is responsible for the documentation and the general management of the cockpit. After some experience, the need for a full documentation became very clear. We had to protect our know-how and acquired experience and, at the same time, to offer documentation to every manager who has to understand the visuals. We decided to create a "Visual Guide Book" as soon as the whole cockpit was more or less stable.

Juergen Daum: What did you document?

Ghislain Malcorps: The documentation is composed of a description about the visual owner and data owner, definitions of the visuals with the complete formula, a brief and full description of how to read the visual, how to interpret the data and how often it is updated – the refresh frequency.

Juergen Daum: I can imagine that this type of "management information" is exposed to structural and content changes much more often than traditional management reporting. How often does the content of the Management Cockpit change?

Ghislain Malcorps: Modifications or redefinitions of visuals are generally agreed during board meetings. The frequency of refreshing the visuals is mainly monthly; in some cases, it is every second month such as with the Nielsen indices, or quarterly or even yearly such as with the customer satisfaction survey. One major revamping is organized every year in December, after discussion of the detailed implementation plan for the next year.

Juergen Daum: Let us come back to the implementation phase of the Management Cockpit. You mentioned that the first step consisted in the definition of the mission statement.

Ghislain Malcorps: Yes, the definition of the mission statement was the first step of the process and it was a crucial step because it gave the company an identification, a direction to follow which will be difficult to modify in the future. The questions to answer were "Who are we? What are our values? Our strength but also our weaknesses? What is our role in the company's environment?". But also, "What do we want to be?"

Juergen Daum: How did you come up with a consistent mission statement which was agreed by all the managers? Did you have somebody who facilitated this process?

Ghislain Malcorps: Prof. Georges played the role of the facilitator in the creation of our Management Cockpit at Iglo-Ola. He had many discussions, first with each member of the board, which consisted of six people, thereafter, with the whole board. Group discussions were held at a lower level: the extended board, consisting of 20 people, who helped the board screen and finalize the mission statement; it was also a kind of roll out of the mission statement to the second level of management.

Juergen Daum: What was the next step in the implementation process after you had finished the mission statement?

Ghislain Malcorps: The next step was now to derive the main strategies from the mission statement. This featured the already mentioned "Broad Action Plan", with a list of the 12 main strategic thrusts. Very important was not to define only strategic thrust in general but to define on the time dimension, which strategic thrusts are important very short-term within three months, mid-term within one year and long-term, that is later than one year. For this we defined three visuals on the White Wall of the Management Cockpit with the "rolling milestones", where all the strategic thrusts had been listed with their status. To each strategy or strategic thrust we also assigned then targets like in the area of innovation, where we wanted innovation to represent 20% of our yearly turnover, or in the area of overheads where we wanted to reduce the overheads every year by 0.5% on turnover, during five years.

Juergen Daum: Are these the KPI targets?

Ghislain Malcorps: No. These are the mere targets. To define how targets are measured through KPIs is another step in the implementation process. Very often, this step and the preceding one are combined. To define KPIs and the related targets is also critical and often difficult, leading to long discussions, which you cannot avoid.

Juergen Daum: Can you give us an example? What has to be discussed here?

Ghislain Malcorps: For example, if you want to measure innovation, you have to agree how you are going to measure it. One way could be to count product launches. But then you have to agree if you count them since last year, or since last 12 month, or since the last 24 month. Even if you finish with this, another point has to be discussed explicitly: Do you accept that the past is so dominant in this innovation indicator or should it better include more data of the present or even future outlook? And what about the launches which are not successful, the "flops"? Do we count them as well into the overall number? And do we have to take into account the relative profitability of each innovation or is the turnover a sufficient indication?

Juergen Daum: I see. If you leave the usual common ground of financial figures where everyone can build on his knowledge from business school, you have to define for nonfinancial KPIs much more carefully what you measure and how …

Ghislain Malcorps: … and you have to take into account possible future developments of the underlying business. Or, at least, you have to react to such developments very quickly by adapting the calculation scheme of such indicators to avoid them suddenly becoming irrelevant and useless. Without that reaction managers and executives may not notice it immediately. That means: you need a very experienced active controller.

Juergen Daum: Can you please be more specific on this? Why should an indicator suddenly become useless or irrelevant if it has been selected with such care?

Ghislain Malcorps: I will give you an example. To measure and manage overheads, you have to compare them with another indicator. Absolute overheads do not tell you very much if overheads are too high or not. For example, you can measure overheads as a percentage of turnover. This is in line with common sense. Usually everyone would agree that this is a good comparison, because overheads would increase if operations grow. But the implicit assumption behind this measure is that there is every time a relationship between level of operations and turnover. If you are not aware that this is an assumption and not a natural law, the result could be that management is still using and relying on an indicator, which has become irrelevant if not wrong. What if exploding fish prices due to the shortage of fish catches should boost our frozen fish turnover? If you do not allow for this beforehand, for example by "neutralizing" such effects during the calculation of the indicator, this would account as positive performance for the relevant manager. Another external factor, which has to be taken into account if you want to measure turnover targets, is inflation. You have to agree within the management team, if you don't care or if such effects have to be neutralized. All these questions are important and have to be treated as such, in order to build an efficient tool and to make it credible to the users.

Juergen Daum: Running through all these discussions, indicator per indicator seems to be very important in order that the Management Cockpit is as useful as possible in the future. But do you not risk that people are losing the overview?

Ghislain Malcorps: This is the reason why the next step in the process is the so-called "certification phase". After having had discussions on the performance indicators, we had a certification phase: it consists of a mapping between all the statements of the initial mission statement and the list of indicators. Here we discussed questions like: Does every strategic statement have its performance indicators; how many? Enough? Not too much? Does every indicator fit a strategic statement? If not, should we revise the strategic statement or, on the contrary, drop the indicator? With this "alignment" we make sure, not to lose strategic track by stepping down into operative indicator discussion and, on the other hand, to make sure that every strategic objective is measured in the day to day business.

Juergen Daum: But to define the measures, calculations and possible adjustments is not all. A very important element of the Management Cockpit concept is the visualization of those indicators on the wall panels.

Ghislain Malcorps: Yes, and this is the last step of the process, to choose the most appropriate visual for each indicator. Here too, we had long discussions, because it was the first time that we were confronted with the new displays, the traffic lights etc... These discussions were also part of the learning process. During this step, you have not only to choose the appropriate visual, you also have to define the frequency of updating, the visual owner, etc...

Juergen Daum: What are your conclusions and the summary of your experiences after passing through this process?

Ghislain Malcorps: As you can see, it's not just using some nice visuals to display the status of some accidentally selected KPIs. This is real work and it will take some time. The cockpit room is only the visible part of the iceberg. Do not forget the previous steps, the discussions, the research made on several subjects, the choices that were made and the priorities that were agreed. All that is in fact a first positive result of the cockpit, before even having started the cockpit itself. Even if you should stop the cockpit at that stage, in any case, your management tools would be much better than before. Note that the Cockpit room is the visible part of the iceberg. The conditions of success of the cockpit are in fact included in the implementation steps.

Juergen Daum: How long does it take in total to implement a Management Cockpit?

Ghislain Malcorps: In our case we had to manage some extraordinary hurdles with the result that we needed additional time. For example, the whole board of our company was replaced during the time of implementation – five people had been promoted, one retired. The software we used and struggled with at the beginning caused another problem. At this time, SAP's Strategic Enterprise Management software was not available. Today, it includes standard Management Cockpit software but we had to create our own application using MS Excel.

In more normal circumstances, the duration of the process would have been about nine months in order to create about 100 stable visuals, which is the usual number for a complete cockpit. But as you typically start with the most important ones on the "Black Wall", it is possible to use the cockpit in a prototype version earlier. This is also helpful to gain some experience, which can be incorporated into the final version.

Juergen Daum: How is the Management Cockpit used at Iglo-Ola?

Ghislain Malcorps: The cockpit is used for the board meetings, the extended board meetings and the departmental staff meetings. Each board meeting starts with a two-hour "walk" through the visuals and indicators with a clear focus on the visuals presenting a red or orange traffic light. So the key issues are identified, the "reasons why" are immediately discussed and everybody is immediately informed about problems, the proposed solutions and the actions taken. An important point is that there are no longer discussions about the accuracy of the figures. Because figures are translated into meaningful visuals which compare, for example, actuals with targets and concentrate on the visualization of the variance, the focus is not on the underlying figures but on the situation itself, on the "hot points", where corrective action must be taken in the business itself.

Of course, we have to guarantee a high degree of quality and accuracy of the data behind the visuals, otherwise the cockpit would not be credible. Here is the obvious responsibility of the controller and "cockpit officer". The Management Cockpit has become the only place in the company where all the strategies are written, are visible and where they will be adapted if necessary. Here everybody can also see the rate of success of these strategies. So the Management Cockpit is at the same time the brain of the company with its strategies in it and the muscle of the company where actions are defined, to reach strategic goals or adapt strategies themselves.

Juergen Daum: What happened to the management reporting which was used before? Does it still exist or was it replaced by the Management Cockpit?

Ghislain Malcorps: We thought that the existence of the Cockpit would reduce the amount of paper reporting – that is, our classic monthly financial reports. In fact, the reduction, if any, was very limited, around let's say 2%. The reason is that the cockpit is a strategic tool that replaces nothing; it's additional to the classic reporting that is needed by legal and fiscal authorities, budget controlling and reporting to headquarters. Nevertheless, the cockpit gives strategic weighting to these reports and so helps to structure them or eliminate them, at least partly.

Juergen Daum: What are, according to your experiences, the critical success factors for the implementation and for the use of a Management Cockpit? What would you recommend to other companies that want to implement it?

Ghislain Malcorps: First, you need the full support of the chairman and of the board members and the cockpit has to be perceived as the main management tool, that makes strategies clear to everyone. Also discipline, with respect to updating deadlines, is critical as is patience during the implementation phase. And do not underestimate the amount of necessary resources needed to set up a cockpit and to operate it. Also think about how to buy in other people in the organization in order to tie them into the strategy system of the company.

Juergen Daum: If I asked you for a summary of your experiences with the Management Cockpit, what is your answer?

Ghislain Malcorps: The Management Cockpit is an excellent tool to create strategic focus in a company and enable the management team to much better concentrate on strategic issues in the day-to-day business. It is also an excellent tool to capture and retain management know-how in the organization. The changes in our board during implementation have shown that it makes eventual higher rotations of the board member, which is very usual in a multinational organization, much easier. The reason is that the Management Cockpit captures and stores the experiences and management knowledge of the past and is offering an "intelligent" and efficient documentation for the new incomers.

Juergen Daum: Ghislain, thank you very much for this very interesting interview.

External reporting and communication with stakeholders

Good external relationships, which often represent an important basis for a company to realize the full value of its intangible assets, have become a critical success factor for enterprises today. Therefore, not only management needs better and more comprehensive information than in the past. Also major external stakeholders and the public at large need to be better informed about the status of a company and its strategies. Only in this way can they make appropriate judgments about a company.

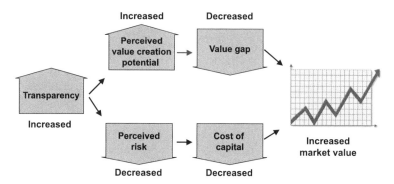

Figure 8.9 Increasing corporate market value by disclosing regularly timely and relevant information to investors.

Research has revealed that companies with an active and professional information policy can expect a "bonus" at capital markets and can achieve higher stock prices. If a company is disclosing regularly and timely relevant business information, investors are better able to estimate its future performance and its potential. Underestimation of a company and of its management is less likely and a so-called "value gap" – that is, a gap between the "real" value of the company and its actual (too low) market value – can be avoided. At the same time, through increased transparency, the risk for investors will also be reduced. This will lead to lower costs of capital, which will in turn lower the threshold for expected shareholder value-added and help a company to achieve a higher market valuation (see Figure 8.9). This is especially the case for enterprises with significant intangible assets, where performance results in value created, which is usually not reported through traditional accounting and financial statements.

According to a study by the German branch of the accountancy group Arthur Andersen, a direct relationship between above-average stock performance and the quality of investor relations does exist.[11] Those companies rated in the top 10 leaders in quality of investor relations were also rated as excellent or very excellent by investors concerning their future shareholder value potential and had experienced in the past an above-average stock price performance. Therefore, the quality of external communication represents for investors a major investment criterion and for management an important value driver.

---

[11] Arthur Andersen (1999) *Stoxx 50 Shareholder Value und Investor Relations in Wettbewerb um institutionelles Kapital*, Eschborn, Germany: Arthur Andersen, p. 30.

Integration of external communication processes and internal management processes

In valuing a company from an investor's viewpoint, the company's potential for the future is the main criterion. Therefore, the availability of reliable information from management about the potential for the future is becoming more important than ever for investors. But management is only able to provide investors with such information if it can rely internally on a management system that can measure and help to forecast business performance and progress in creating potential for the future; that is, of intangible assets – not only for the entire company, but also for products lines and business units. This is important in order to allow management to control and optimize internally what is communicated externally. Only in this way can a company achieve publicly communicated (for example, annual) targets and meet related expectations of financial analysts and investors. So realizing the full value of a company's potential on stakeholder markets does not depend only on the quality of disclosed information, but also on the availability and quality of an appropriate internal management system.

Therefore, both these processes – external communication and internal management – have to be closely interlinked. Without proper external communication, investors are not able to estimate the true value of a company. The company will be undervalued and will become a target for takeovers. And without an appropriate management system, management is not able to measure progress internally and is lacking reliable information "material" to communicate effectively with investors and other stakeholders. But even if both happens, but is executed separately, a company will not be able to achieve its targets. Only if data that is communicated externally is directly taken from data that is used internally, will the company be able to realize the full value of its potential. This is because management needs to know, in order to optimize the total performance of the company, how much each business unit, product line, etc., has contributed to the overall results. This is only possible if it can easily disaggregate total performance (the externally communicated figures) according to internal categories. In addition, strategic objectives of the company must constantly be reconciled with expectations of the major stakeholder groups in the strategy management process. Therefore, for the integration of both processes, a common unified database for performance data and analytic applications is required. It should provide integration through all process steps of external communication/stakeholder relationship management and of strategy and corporate performance management (see Figure 8.10).

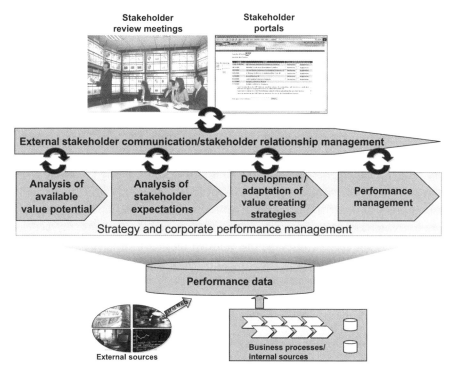

Figure 8.10   Integration of external communication and internal management processes.

The enterprise portal for investors and stakeholders

Communication with a growing number of individual stakeholders on a day-to-day basis – the reality today in many companies – represents a major challenge for most investor relationships and corporate communications departments. Stakeholders will require in the future more interactive communication with companies, for example over their websites or through emails. At the same time the number of information requests handled in the IR or corporate communication department will increase. A common data basis will ensure that data and information for different stakeholder groups are consistent with each other and with internally used management information. In addition, software solutions that support the stakeholder relationship management processes, allowing the automation of not-value-adding tasks in communicating with stakeholders, will not necessarily require human interaction. For example, if individual stakeholders would like to receive certain information to predefined time schedules via email, they can subscribe to such a service through their web-based stakeholder portal on the company's website. The system will automatically send them the required information at the predefined time or in the desired frequency (for example, the next quarterly report directly after release). In the USA, the SEC is planning to oblige the financial community in a similar way. When companies listed on US stock exchanges disclose their reports to the SEC, they will be obliged to publish full details on their website as well, allowing access to all interested companies or individuals.[12]

If companies combine their stakeholder relationship management information systems with web-based enterprise portals for investors and stakeholders, they are able to handle these new obligations in a very efficient way – for example, by updating the related web pages automatically through the system, as soon as the data are released, no matter for which communication channel. In addition, such a system can inform interested stakeholders about the availability of the new report via an automatically generated email, that guides the recipient via a link to the new report on the company's website.

Through such a stakeholder portal a company is able to provide an on-demand, 24-hour, seven-day a week information service providing first-class actual data, for example to investors and financial analysts. In addition, analysts and other stakeholders can run simulations based on the published data and can execute so-called risk stress tests – something for what some experts have asked for after the Enron scandal.[13] Even more complex simulations are possible. For example, investors may want to analyze how net income would look if a company changes its reporting and valuation methods; for example, according to different GAAP rules. Or they may want to review how changes concerning different important external factors such as changing currency rates, raw material prices, interest rates, etc., may affect the future development of the company. Clearly, there is still the restriction for companies listed on a US stock exchange to disclose forward-looking data in order to avoid future claims from investors if they fail to perform according to the published forecasts. But this is currently under discussion and there are proposals to lower the legal barrier in order to enable companies to provide investors with the information they are requiring today: forward-looking data related to major corporate value drivers.

With a stakeholder portal and with a stakeholder relationship management system in place, a company is able to collect regularly structured feedback

---

[12] Securities and Exchange Commission (February 13, 2002) "SEC to propose new corporate disclosure rules". See: www.sec.org

[13] See Baruch Lev's testimony to the US Congress on the Enron case. He asked for companies in the future to be obliged not only to report on their intangibles but also about their risk situation and unexecuted obligations through a risk stress test. See: www.stern.nyu.edu/~blev/

and assessments of the company's performance and strategies from investors and other stakeholders via email and website interaction in a very efficient way. A link in the email will guide the recipients to an electronic questionnaire posted on the company's website, where they can answer questions and make their data entries. As this information is then automatically posted in the central performance database of the company, it may be used directly in the strategy management process of the company. Together with internal forecasts and manager feedback and assessments it can serve as the basis to decide whether the company should continue with its actual strategy, should adapt it, or should opt for a new one.

External reporting based on the Tableau de Bord

Investors and other stakeholders require similar information to that of management in order to get a "true and fair view" of the company. This applies especially if a company is engaged in intangible value creation, where traditional corporate reporting does not provide relevant information. In the USA, a proposal made by the FASB and by many experts in the field of intangibles reporting and disclosure is to disclose nonfinancial information in addition to the GAAP-based financial statement information. This would be in the form of a so-called supplementary report. Only in this way can investors, financial analysts and other interested parties obtain a better understanding about the company's performance and its future perspectives. A task force commissioned by the SEC made the same proposal and stated that such a supplementary report should be based on KPIs oriented on the business model (the value-creation system) of the company.[14] The concept of the Tableau de Bord therefore provides for external reporting on the appropriate framework and structure although it will probably be less comprehensive and more aggregated than one that should support internal management processes. The decision about what should be published or not should be a process step in the strategic management process as I have described it before.

A pioneer in disclosing such KPI-based supplementary reports was the Swedish financial services company Skandia, which started under the direction of its director for intellectual capital management, Leif Edvinsson, to publish supplementary reports in 1997. Figure 8.11 shows an extract from the company's supplementary report for 1998.[15] The concept has become in the meantime

---

[14] See: www.fei.org/finrep/rilesSEC-Taskforce-Final-6-6-2kl.pdf
[15] For more on this Skandia supplementary report of 1998, see:
www.skandia.com/en/includes/documentlinks/annualreport1998/supplements1998.zip

MERICAN SKANDIA

nerican Skandia provides variable annuities and is
e sixth-largest company in the US variable annuity
arket.

	1997	1996	1995	1994
ANCIAL FOCUS				
urn on capital employed (%)[1]	21.9	27.1	28.7	12.2
erating result (MSEK)	1,027	579	355	115
ue added/employee (SEK 000s)	2,616	2,206	1,904	1,666
STOMER FOCUS				
mber of contracts	189,104	133,641	87,836	59,089
ngs/contract (SEK 000s)	499	396	360	333
ender ratio (%)[2]	4.4	4.4	4.1	4.2
ts of sale	45,881	33,287	18,012	11,573
MAN FOCUS				
mber of employees, full-time	599	418	300	220
mber of managers	88	86	81	62
vhom, women	50	27	28	13
ning expense/employee (SEK 000s)	2.7	15.4	2.5	9.8
CESS FOCUS				
mber of contracts/employee	316	320	293	269
. exp./gross premiums written (%)	3.5	2.9	3.3	2.9
xpense/admin. expense (%)	8.1	12.5	13.1	8.8
EWAL & DEVELOPMENT FOCUS				
e of gross premiums written				
om new launches (%)	0.9	23.7	49.2	11.1
ase in net premiums written (%)	31.9	113.7	29.9	17.8
elopment expense/adm. exp. (%)	9.8	9.9	10.1	11.6
e of staff under 40 years (%)	76	78	81	72

anged calculation methods for 1996 and 1997.
renders during the year in relation to the average mathematical
erve, net.

SKANDIA REAL ESTATE

Skandia is one of Sweden's largest property owners,
with about 300 holdings.

	1997	1996	1995	1994
FINANCIAL FOCUS				
Direct yield (%)	5.96	5.93	6.16	6.60
Net operating income (MSEK)	1,130	1,215	1,258	1,399
Market value (MSEK)	19,206	20,092	20,702	21,504
Total yield (%)	7.73	0.62	5.06	4.44
CUSTOMER FOCUS				
Customer satisfaction index				
(max. value = 100)	69	58	56	n.a.
Average lease (years)	n.a.	8.6	8.5	n.a.
Average rent (SEK/m²)	951	960	970	1,041
Telephone accessibility (%)	60	71	60	n.a.
HUMAN FOCUS				
Human capital index				
(max. value = 1,000)	n.a.	615	617	n.a.
Employee turnover (%)	10.0	10.1	7.9	7.7
Average years of service with company	12.0	10.0	10.1	10.2
College graduates/total number of				
office staff (%)	36	32	31	31
PROCESS FOCUS				
Occupancy rate measured by area (%)	93.7	91.8	89.7	89.3
Financial occupancy rate (%)	96.2	94.9	93.0	91.2
Net operating income per m² (SEK)	553	569	590	657
Costs per m², Sweden (SEK)	304	274	276	272
RENEWAL & DEVELOPMENT FOCUS				
Property turnover: purchases (%)	0.2	3.1	3.2	0.8
Property turnover: sales (%)	8.1	1.1	6.1	0.4
Change and development of existing				
holdings (MSEK)	235	311	333	313
Training expense/administrative				
expense (%)	0.8	1.0	1.5	1.0

Figure 8.11 Extract from Skandia's supplementary report for 1997.

part of official disclosure rules for companies in Denmark. Since January 2002
Danish companies that dispose of "significant" intellectual capital are obliged
to publish, in addition to their annual financial reports, an "intellectual capital
statement".[16] The latter guideline is very similar to the concept of supplementary reports as it has been described here.

---

[16] Danish Trade and Industry Ministry (2000) "A Guideline for Intellectual Capital Statements".
See: www.efs.dk/download/pdf/videnUK.pdf

9 Implementing the New Management System – New Roles for Managers

For fifty years, Information Technology has centreed on DATA – their collection, storage, transmission, and presentation. It has focused on the "T" in "IT". The new information revolutions focus on the "I". [...] It is not a revolution in technology, machinery, techniques, software or speed. It is a revolution in CONCEPTS. [...] It is not happening in Information Technology [...] and is not being led by Chief Information Officers (CIOs). It is led by people on whom the Information Industry tends to look down: accountants. [...] And this is leading rapidly to redefining the tasks to be done with the help of information and, with it, to redefining the institutions that do these tasks.

Peter F. Drucker[1]

Most enterprises today are far away from having a management system in place as it has just been described. The reason is not that these companies are not seeing the need to change their management tools, it is simply that the task seems too complex and too difficult. So, many companies are "muddling" through by introducing some singular parts of the new concepts; for example, by extending financial management reports through non-financial indicators in a way that appears to resemble a Balanced Scorecard. But the management processes, the way how managers in the firm communicate with each other, and the overall management culture, often remain unchanged. The result is that the efforts to introduce the new reporting will not pay off and, worse, the company will not make any fundamental progress in moving forward towards having an effective new management system in place in the future. If the new system is not introduced in a systematic way – for example, as was done at Iglo-Ola in Belgium with the introduction of the Management Cockpit by Ghislain Malcorps – its usefulness is at least limited if not damaging. Instead of clarity and strategic focus, confusion might be the result, because the new system is not working yet and the old one has been discarded.

But I am fully convinced that companies today have no choice. If they will not overhaul and extend their management systems in the next couple of years,

---

[1] Peter F. Drucker (1999) *Management Challenges for the 21st Century*, New York: Harper-Collins, p. 97.

the cost of lost opportunity will be tremendous: they will not be able to unleash their full potential under the conditions of the new economy and may lose their competitive edge. The management system of a company will therefore represent an important competitive success factor – a fact that is increasingly recognized by financial analysts and investors. But how should a company start?

If the company does not have an urgent problem with its existing management system, such as that it is not able to publish on a timely basis consolidated financial reports or forecasts, I recommend starting with the definition of the business purpose of the company and of its strategy, as described in Chapter 6. Otherwise, these operational problems should be fixed beforehand, by improving the related processes and by implementing appropriate information systems to support them, because timely and accurate actual and forecast information represents a major building block for a good management system.

Why start with the business purpose and strategy? The answer is: without it the implementation effort is lacking the necessary strategic focus and the company risks the supposed improved management system increasing the chaos by helping to pursue and push forward uncoordinated activities. Unfortunately, in many organizations there exists no strategy and mission statement that is explicitly agreed by all relevant managers. Therefore, strategies often remain too diffuse and abstract because, first, every manager interprets the supposed common strategy in his or her own way, and, second, strategies are not broken down into concrete coordinated action plans and targets. The result is that the company as a whole has no common strategy, because the different departments and units are moving in different directions. Therefore, it is not possible to design a new management system without all managers agreeing on its strategy and mission. Only the strategy and mission determine what is relevant for a company and on what the management system should focus on.

The development and implementation plan

Before a company starts implementing a new management system or improving the existing one, it should set up, first, a long-term project plan. This should provide a common framework for all development and implementation steps and ensure that all activities are coordinated and interlinked and do not work against each other. A development and implementation plan for a new management system could look like this:

1.   The first task is to create a common understanding of corporate strategy

and the company's business purpose in the management team. This requires hard work and takes time. Often hidden conflicts between the perception, thinking and interests of the different members of a management team emerge. Bringing the discussion back to a fact-based level through objective market information that is provided, for example, by an external expert, who at the same time is moderating the most critical sessions, can help to find a solution for these conflicts. This process may take several weeks or even months.

2. During this process the management team also has to come to a consensus of opinion about the company's value-creation system. It has to decide if the internal organization structure still fits with the now agreed strategy. It has to agree how it wants to design its major value-creation processes and how much it wants to collaborate, for example in R&D, with business partners, sharing sometime proprietary knowledge with them.

3. Then a monitoring system has to be set up that integrates strategic and operative views (such as the Tableau de Bord) on the basis of the company's value-creation system. This is an important step because this monitoring system is forming from now on the basis for all business-related communications in the firm and for communication with external stakeholders. It creates a common basis of understanding. And this task cannot be fully delegated to the controlling department. The management team itself has to contribute by making propositions for measures and to discuss their relevance and how data for these measures should be collected. The design of the monitoring system has to be based on original management know-how and selected measures have to be understood and accepted by all managers. In this phase, typically, questions arise as to how the monitoring system should be supported by information systems that help to provide the necessary data timely for all managers, and how the processes for consolidating enterprise data, for setting up rolling forecasts and for reporting should be designed. The implementation of a data warehouse and of appropriate analytic applications for consolidation, planning and forecasting, and for reporting represents therefore an important subproject of this phase.

4. In the next phase, the company has to establish continuous management processes; for example, by institutionalizing regular structured strategy and performance management meetings of the management team. At these meetings, the status of strategic objectives and actual performance

and also important business risks are reviewed, discussed, and necessary decisions taken. This is done on the basis of information provided by the monitoring system in a structured way; for example, according to the Management Cockpit concept. In addition, the company should try to improve support for internal communication processes so as to enable effective communication between management meetings among individual managers and employees involved in these decision processes. This could happen by providing additional web-based software applications for extended strategy and performance management that supports analysis, interactive simulation and communication around strategic and performance management issues.

5.   As soon as the internal basis of the new management system is in place and working, the company should start to improve its external communication processes. In this step, companies start to publish supplementary reports for their investors and stakeholders. Feedback from stakeholders can be collected through the stakeholder portal of the company or by the management team personally in informal meetings with a selected group of stakeholders. These meetings may take place, for example, in the Management Cockpit room of the company, where previously collected feedback from stakeholders is presented in combination with internal company information.

6.   In the follow-up phase, the objective is to move with the management system and management tools to the next level. The company should create an understanding in the management team for the dynamics of its business system by starting with scenario-planning and systems thinking. This step comes last in the process, because it represents probably the most sophisticated area of the new management concept and requires a solid fundament of data, processes and methods, that have to be put in place by the previous steps. With these methods a management team can limit the strategic risks of the enterprise (through scenario-planning) and can boost the upside, the strategic benefits of the business system and can therefore leverage its full growth potential by identifying in time limiting factors through systems thinking and systems dynamic models and simulations. But I would recommend that both concepts start with some very simple exercises in a workshop-type meeting of the management team with an external expert as facilitator. As soon as the management team feels more comfortable in using these methods and as soon as its staff has been trained in scenario planning and systems dynamic

modeling, one can start to integrate these methods into the regular strategic planning and management meetings.

This whole process may take two to three years until the new management system becomes fully productive. So it is very important that some successes become visible in between in order to motivate managers and controllers to continue. Therefore, a company should try to become as quickly as possible productive with a prototype version of the new management system. As soon as the strategy and the value-creation system have been agreed and the first (most important) measures defined, the management team should start with the first performance review meeting on the basis of the prototype, even if not all indicators for all areas have been selected yet. Based on experiences made and based on proposals from participating managers, this prototype will then be improved from meeting to meeting.

In working with the new approach, the management team will come across its limitations and will experience where the monitoring system and strategy have to be adapted or enhanced. So, over time, the management system as well as strategy will be continuously improved and adapted to new realities.

In order to make a start and to collect first experiences that help a management team and the company to move forward, it is not yet necessary to make use of comprehensive IT and software systems. A company is, for example, not able to use effectively sophisticated analytical software to support its management processes until it becomes more sophisticated in its management methods, and before users have made their first experiences with these new concepts. But companies should try to implement from the start a common performance database and an appropriate data warehouse system.

How managers should prepare themselves

To design, to introduce, and to work with a new management system, is not only a challenge for controllers, strategic planners, corporate accountants, and IT experts, but especially for managers. In order to make full use of the new concepts and the new system, managers need to enhance their mental scope.

A main task of management today is to manage value-creation opportunities: that is, those that arise from within the organization, such as through innovations on the basis of existing intangible assets, and those that emerge from the outside of the enterprise, such as through new market opportunities, and opportunities for partnerships and mergers and acquisitions. But opportunity management is something very different from what managers have been used to in the past. Most managers are trained to limit risk and to solve day-to-day problems. Day-to-day problems need to be solved, otherwise a company cannot make progress. But risk should not be avoided at any cost – it should be limited. But more important is to react quickly to new opportunities and to be able to see the broad line of a future development. Therefore, managers have to develop mental agility if they want to be successful under the conditions of the new economy.

Managers should consider putting themselves on a mental learning curve, for example through the following exercises:

▶ Start to monitor the status of intangible assets in your company. By monitoring regularly nonfinancial indicators about the major value-creation processes in the company, you will over time gain understanding about the relationships of these indicators and of the underlying logic that work between your intangibles and between financial results.

▶ Exchange experiences and insights with your peers from other companies. They face similar problems in their existing management systems. Participate in manager working cycles to regularly exchange insights and experiences with managers from other industries. Seeing the problems, challenges and solutions occurred and emerged in other industries helps you to abstract from your mental model which determines your actual view of your own business and management system.

▶ Experiment with new ways of collaboration in the management team. Invite an external expert as facilitator. Try to develop your own style for "Management Cockpit" meetings.

▶ Insist on getting more sophisticated in measurement and to improve it continuously. Engage yourself in understanding and identifying the areas of your company that need management's focus and which performance should be measured regularly and should become part of management reporting. Schedule monthly, or at the beginning even weekly, "research days", where you talk to employees and other managers of your organization about the business processes in which they are involved. Talk also with external people like customers, business partners, industry analysts or even competitors about the company's business and value-creation system.

▶ Start with systems thinking. Subscribe to a systems thinking management introductory training in order to get a first understanding on the basic principles. Start for yourself to design systems dynamics models on paper in order to understand with them smaller business problems better. Then try to model a business process of your company together with your colleagues from the management team using the help of a systems thinking expert.

▶   Start your next strategic planning cycle with scenario-planning. This needs some preparation. Staff members have to do research and to collect data in order to prepare two to three scenarios. Use a scenario-planning expert to guide your staff and to facilitate the meeting.

Interview with Patrick M. Georges: how can executives improve their personal productivity?

Professor Dr. Patrick M. Georges is a senior neurosurgeon based in Brussels and an expert in Human Intelligence Management. Together with neurologists, human intelligence scientists, and computer engineers he designed in 1989 the Management Cockpit. He has installed with his team more than 50 Management Cockpits at companies and non-profit organizations. As a teacher and author in management, he gives seminars for senior managers about techniques for improving their personal intellectual productivity. He is also the Director of the International Institute for Human Intelligence Management at the HEC (Haute Ecole Commercial) School of Management in Paris.

Juergen Daum: Why do you think the idea and the concept of a ''Management Cockpit'' was so well accepted by executives?

Patrick Georges: Because these people were looking desperately for something which really could help them to become more effective in today's ever more demanding business world. Traditional management information systems and other management tools like management reporting had not been really optimized for helping top executives in the tasks they are responsible and paid for: reaching market-related objectives under extreme uncertainty through an often huge and not directly controllable organization.

Juergen Daum: What do top managers need instead?

Patrick Georges: When we started more than 12 years ago to analyze the challenges top managers and especially management teams were facing in their work, we realized that one of the major problems these people and teams were facing is to overcome the information overload they are experiencing everyday. To set focus and to reduce information overload turned out to be the basic necessity for managers to become successful. Scientific studies are demonstrating that the human brain can cope effectively with an information stream, which corresponds to up to 800 characters per minute. According to our studies, managers receive on average 4,000 characters per minute, in the form of phone calls, emails, faxes, meetings and reports. So one element of the solution had to be the intelligent reduction of information overload. The second was to better leverage the common intelligence of a management team through a more systematic approach to how to run the management meetings. The final solution, which came out of this research, was the Management Cockpit. It helps executives and management teams to sort and organize the information overload, respond to the hundreds of questions pertinent in the running of a company, brings added value through collaborative intelligence to the know-how of the single executives and so reduces uncertainty and decision stress.

Juergen Daum: The Management Cockpit, targeted to support management teams, covers only one of the areas of your human intelligence research. Another focus of your work is how executives can increase their personal mental and intellectual productivity. Can you explain that in more detail please?

Patrick Georges: First and foremost it has to be said, that everyone has to live with the intelligence nature has given to him. We can't change this. But we can increase the productivity of human intelligence by means of appropriate work methods and appropriate work environments. And this is exactly where I am focusing in my work.

Juergen Daum: How do you define human intelligence and how can you improve its productivity?

Patrick Georges: For the purpose of practicality I define human intelligence as our ability as human beings to reach our objectives by overcoming obstacles and utilizing our resources. If you want to increase your personal intellectual productivity, you have to investigate what are the weaknesses of human intelligence and what are the "blockers" for its productive use.

Juergen Daum: And what are these weaknesses or productivity blockers?

Patrick Georges: The problem is linked to some specific characteristics of the human brain. Its concentration span is short. Its recognition of form is imperfect and biased. Its short-term memory can only hold very little information at any one time. Its long-term memory stores the information in its own way and often forgets what stock it carries. The brain processes information slowly. It can only do one thing well at a time and is easily overworked.

Juergen Daum: So the human brain seems not to be very efficient. What can we do about it?

Patrick Georges: Unfortunately, there is no wonder weapon available. But if you understand how the brain is working, you can achieve tremendous results. The key to unearth the full potential of a person's intellectual capacities is to provide better support throughout the various stages of the thought process. And this means: you have to increase the power of concentration, focus attention, optimize the perception of forms, better organize the short-term memory, and better organize the knowledge stored in the long-term memory.

Juergen Daum: And how do you make it happen? How can one better support the thought process in the different areas you just mentioned?

Patrick Georges: Take the first topic: concentration. Concentration is what enables us to access the content of our memory. Our level of intelligence depends greatly on this power, for example how long we are able to work productively on a file. But concentration is highly selective and very limited. It is impossible to focus your attention on everything that comes before you. We therefore constantly strive to reduce the cognitive cost of a task by selecting certain sources of information. We filter the information. And ideally, our intelligence should select information on the basis of the task at hand. Unfortunately, that is most often far from being the case. For example, probably triggered by a kind of "safety instinct", the human voice and face immediately capture a large part of our attention if they reach our perceptive areas, even in cases where we receive no useful or desirable information for our work or tasks we are actually executing. We therefore have to assist and protect our concentration in such a way that it selects the right kind of information; information that corresponds to our objectives rather than being based on outdated reflexes or the objectives of others.

Juergen Daum: And how can a person, for example an executive, protect better his or her concentration?

Patrick Georges: Not every person has the same level of natural concentration capability. Selective focusing ability varies from one person to another. It can be measured, for example, by a simple selective listening test. If you have problems in concentrating, you should establish some basic behaviour rules to increase your concentration protection power. One of these rules might be, to never decide to buy in the presence of the seller. The seller, a sales person, captures and focuses the prospects attention by placing his voice and face within the client's field of attention, thus reducing his chances of focusing on the rational elements of the decision-making process. As an intelligent buyer you should always leave the shop for a few minutes before deciding whether to buy or not. Another rule might be, to work free from the sound of voices. The human voice is a priority source of information that the brain cannot help but process. The human voice captures a large percentage of our power of concentration when we are subjected to it, whether consciously or unconsciously. So if you have work to do, for which you need your full concentration, close your office door and unplug your phone. If you are in deep concentration, it will take you up to 20 minutes to regain the same level of concentration you had before an interruption – for example, a phone call. These are only some examples of such rules I teach in my seminars.

Juergen Daum: But to know these rules is one thing. To apply them successfully, another. How can managers make sure they succeed?

Patrick Georges: These things indeed seem to be obvious, but people often have problems to be disciplined enough. My recommendation therefore is: put your three to five main rules on a sheet of paper and check regularly, for example every week, if you are still aware of them.

Juergen Daum: You mentioned that our short-term memory is weak and can only hold very little information at any one time. What can we do about that?

Patrick Georges: Our short-term memory is our working memory. It is the place where it is decided what will be retained for your work at hand and what will be forgotten. It is the poor performance of our working memory, in terms of duration and capacity, that most reduces our intelligence. Our working memory is like a whiteboard on which, during the thought process, information relevant to the situation or to the decision to be made is inscribed. The information comes both from our internal memory, the long-term memory, and from the outside world. But the working memory, probably situated in the frontal lobes, is small and the information inscribed in it is rapidly deleted. The storage capacity of our short-term memory is equal to approximately seven units of information. We can retain seven pieces of information from a few seconds up to 10 minutes, but we have difficulties retaining 10. If information is presented in addition to the initial data that makes us forget the initial data. For a good presentation or for a good management report the conclusion is: you have to give your audience or your readers some time between the presentation of groups of various data so that they can reach a sub-conclusion or group it on the basis of the first packet of information received. This grouping task will empty our working memory and enable the entrance of a new information package without deleting the first. For example, good chess players owe their intelligence to their strong ability to categorize and regroup the positions on the chessboard. This principle is the reason why we conceived the Management Cockpit Walls as divided in so-called "logical views" – each one being easy to distinguish from the other and each consisting of not more than six different single information pieces – the visuals or frames.

Juergen Daum: What would you recommend specifically to managers, who want to start to increase their mental and intellectual productivity?

Patrick Georges: Respect your biorhythm and your intellectual productivity curve over a working day! In the morning, from around 7–11 a.m. you have your most productive time. Reserve this time for your most important project and close your door and do not answer phone calls. Also, never start your day by reading your mail. In the morning your brain is very receptive and "open". You will program it, in reading your mail, with other people's issues and objectives. From 11 a.m. on, you have your "communication peak". Make your important phone calls and have your important meetings. Put the not so important tasks or meetings in the early afternoon, when you have your lowest intellectual performance. Choose your "Business of the Day" every morning, when you wake up. Decide to finish something important before the end of the working day. You will "program" your brain with this objective, so that it will become more likely, that you will achieve it.

Juergen Daum: A manager's task is to make decisions. What is the key to better management decisions?

Patrick Georges: You can increase your decision accuracy as a manager through more hard facts. We are very bad judges of probability. For managers, who have to make every day decisions on the basis of probability estimations of certain favourable or unfavourable business events, this fact can lead to significant damage. If something has a 2% probability of happening in statistical terms, we would intuitively estimate the probability as 10%. If something has a 95% chance of happening, we would estimate it as 80%. Moreover, if a risk is serious, we tend to underestimate it. While when a risk is small, we tend to make it bigger. We are also more sensitive to losses than to gains. We would do much more to avoid a small loss than to make a major gain. Therefore, try to base your decisions on facts. Insist on getting more statistics on company activities. Numerous executives are very surprised when receiving such statistical facts. For example, the fact that certain clients with whom they spend much of their time are not profitable. Or that such and such a sales person systematically sells 80% of the target he sets himself while another always reaches 105% of his objectives. Therefore: take care to acquire more reliable business data.

Juergen Daum: Managers are often constantly under pressure and very stressed persons. How would you conceive an "anti-stress" program for executives?

Patrick Georges: Make sure that every intention is followed by a decision. An intention is a piece of information that creates a desire in us. It is the "I must do this or that", which we get after a meeting. It is the red light in our head, a worry. It cannot be turned off until a decision is made or something is done. You should train yourself to recognize when you have an intention in your head and above all not to let it fall into your subconscious. You should therefore quickly note it down or act upon it directly. The worries, the background stress we have are due to these numerous intentions which we have every day. They clutter our subconscious because they have not been dealt with properly when they were still in our conscience. Executives should therefore always carry a notepad or a Dictaphone where they can collect their intentions, their desires, their worries as and when they arise. They can clean out their memory with it. If you have not got into the good habit of doing that during the day, you should at least push yourself to do it before going to bed. Worries or intentions that are not written down and therefore remain in your memory are a recipe for a bad night.

Juergen Daum: What else would you classify as important to managers concerning their intellectual productivity?

Patrick Georges: Eliminate as many messages as possible which you receive. At least half of the information received by managers today is made up of junk mail, which does not help them to reach their objectives. We have to train our intelligence to mistrust our old reflexes, which tell us that if it is among our mail it is for us, it is for our benefit that we should act on it. And have your regular brief date with yourself every day, your quiet half hour, a brief quiet activity at a regular time. This will recalibrate you, even on busy business days.

Juergen Daum: Patrick, thank you very much for this very interesting interview.

New roles for the CFO and CIO

Beside the business managers, two other corporate functions contribute significantly to the success of companies in the intangibles-based new economy: the chief financial officer (CFO) and the chief information officer (CIO). A company's CFO is the guardian of its financial resources and the economic conscience of the company, responsible for its economic transparency and for "Business Intelligence" – that is, for the design and usefulness of its management system. The CIO is the master of one of the most important basis resources of intangibles-based businesses: the infrastructure for information collection, information storage, and information distribution.

The CFO needs the help of the CIO, who has to provide the new IT and infrastructure for the new management system. The CIO needs the support of the CFO in order to be able to focus resources and expertise of his or her team on those projects that are most relevant to the economic success of the company.

The CFO and CIO therefore share a common bond in providing their companies with the new concepts for information management and for improved business intelligence required for success in the new economy. Both view their mission as that of a partner to business managers and they actively contribute to the business strategy of the company and to its successful execution. Both, too, are experts in their own field and can contribute individually in a significant way to a company's economic success. And when they join forces, the whole is greater than the sum of its parts. The overall benefit for the company will increase exponentially. In order to be able to do that, both have to understand how their role is evolving in the new economy and how they can contribute to the success of their enterprises.

The transformation of the CFO

Traditionally, CFOs are responsible for managing financial processes and the financial resources of a company. Their task is to ensure that the company is not running out of cash to finance the current business, necessary investments and the payment of dividends to shareholders. In addition, they have to make sure that financial transactions such as collection and payments are processed in the most efficient way, and they have to take care in optimizing the company's financing costs and return on financial investments. These tasks are also called financial operations.

The second area for which CFOs are responsible is to account for and document the performance of a company, to prepare financial statements and management reports, to organize and facilitate budgeting, planning and forecasting processes, and to process analysis tasks and support management in major decisions. The role of CFOs today is subject to significant change given the arrival of the intangibles-based new economy.

New collaborative e-business models, as in the example of Cisco described earlier, have a major impact on how companies will organize their financial operations in the future. The e-business models have focused first on improving sales and CRM processes and then on improving supply chain management processes. The focus is now on finance. When customers are able to order online, the also want to pay online or to dispute online an incorrect invoice. And companies are now considering how they can use e-finance models to optimize financial processes in order to cut costs, and reduce financial working capital.

Electronic Bill Presentment and Payment (EBPP) not only reduces costs for invoicing and collection, but can also reduce days-sales-outstanding significantly. So-called payment factories that aggregate payments in a company globally and optimize the routing of these payments through preferred banks across boundaries will not only reduce payment transaction costs but will also reduce the need for cash reserves for payments in operative units. With these new opportunities for optimizing the financial supply chains of companies, active and continuous financial working capital management will move into the focus and will become a proxy for the excellence of a CFO in financial operations.

There will be ample opportunities for e-finance scenarios that offer to outsource operational financial tasks to external service providers and to still keep the integrity of business processes and of the financial picture. The Internet makes it possible, so that it does not matter where accounts receivables are managed – internally or at an external service provider. Business processes at different locations are still interlinked and integrated through the real time flow of information across the e-business network that leverages the Internet.

Those CFOs who take advantage of opportunities to automate such processes using e-business scenarios can cut costs and also release resources to focus on activities that add more value. This can also increase convenience and value for customers in interacting with the company in financial processes. In addition, CFOs who outsource parts or all of these processes to external service providers are able to cut costs for financing, settlement, and payment processes.

Providing business information and decision support

Today, CFOs have to do more than just keep their books in order to provide management and investors with reliable and consistent financial information about the company's performance. Management, investors, and financial analysts need a much broader, keener perspective into both financial and nonfinancial issues, into tangible and intangible assets. It's the task of the CFO to provide these insights across the entire business, across business units, locations and functions – no matter whether this information originates from different sources and if the company has a complicated information system landscape in place. The CFO provides a complete, unified perspective of all financial and business aspects of the enterprise – even of the activities that take place outside the borders of the company, for example in partner companies. This requires an e-business accounting system that can integrate diverse operative systems with the accounting system in real time.

Based on a new accounting system for the 21st century that meets the new accounting requirements,[2] CFOs have to work out, together with their colleagues from the management team, concepts for a new management and performance measurement system that is able to cope with the challenges of the new economy. Their task is not only to support this process, they have to actively manage it and have to make sure that the company is making progress with it. This also requires CFOs to conceive new solutions for an information system infrastructure that meets the requirement of an efficient and effective accounting, measurement and management system for today's enterprises. This has to include a business accounting system that can operate in a heterogeneous system environment, a data warehouse, and analytic software applications to support decision and management processes as well as external communication (see Figure 9.1).[3] In that process, business and cultural considerations have to converge with the technical possibilities that new IT and software solutions provide. Therefore, the CFO has to tightly collaborate with the CIO in this task. They have to put together their expert know-how in economics and business management on the one side and their know-how in IT on the other side in order to make it happen.

The Chief Value Officer (CVO)

As the company positions itself for optimizing value in the knowledge economy, the CFO and the finance function must redefine their roles within the business to determine what kind of organizational structure will best allow finance to fulfil its new tasks. Already, most finance functions have made a significant shift – driven by investment in information systems and shared service centres – toward being less resource-intensive and more efficient

---

[2] See the earlier discussion in Chapter 7.
[3] See SAP AG (2001) *Empowering Finance for E-business – How to Exploit Technology to Optimize Value*, White Paper, p. 15, Walldorf, Germany: SAP AG.

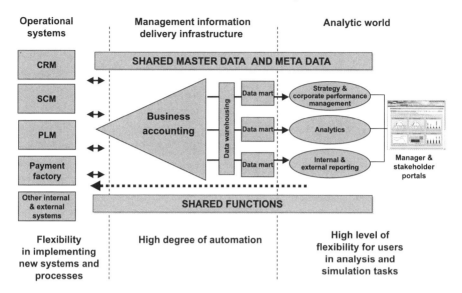

Figure 9.1   The information system infrastructure for the new management and performance measurement system.

teams, particularly in the area of transaction processing, allowing increased emphasis on decision support. In the future, finance will be even leaner. With many front office and analysis tasks being delegated via web-based portals to business managers, back-office tasks being concentrated in shared service centres or outsourced to external service providers, the finance staff will act as management consultants, coordinators, and conceptualists; for example, in maintaining and further developing the concepts for the measurement, management and reporting systems of their company. Standardized, integrated financial processes and systems will be embedded within the business, and they will be available globally to users who can operate them without needing to be aware of where they are located and maintained (see Figure 9.2[4]).

The pressure on the CFO from the management team, to provide better and more reliable business information to meet the requirements of individual managers and to constantly help to adapt the management system to the faster changes in the business environment of the company, will increase even more in the future. So finance departments have to focus on these tasks and try to free up the necessary resources by automating or by out-

---

[4] See SAP AG (2001) *Empowering Finance for E-business – How to Exploit Technology to Optimize Value*, White Paper, p. 11, Walldorf, Germany: SAP AG.

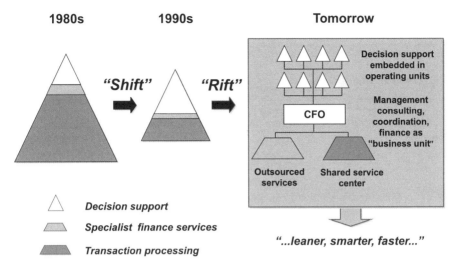

Figure 9.2   Reshaping finance to support the new requirements of the new economy.

sourcing other tasks – such as in financial supply chain management – but also on collecting and consolidating performance data and in preparing rolling forecasts. In the future, CFOs and their staff members have to be able to dedicate much more time to analyzing the company's business processes and its environment, to help managers to understand the economic implications of certain business constellations and situations, and to keep the management systems conceptually up-to-date. So the following scenario may become reality:

▶ Financial supply chain management tasks are completely outsourced to external service providers. The CIO and his or her team are running the accounting system, the data warehouse and the analytic systems, leaving to the CFO and his or her team the task to keep these systems conceptually up-to-date.

▶ Managers as well as external stakeholders will be able to access at any time, via web-based enterprise portals' analytic tools, the performance data of the company and can execute by themselves sophisticated analysis, simulations and what-if scenarios, instead of working through the staff of the finance, controlling, and investor relations department.

▶ The CFO will operate the business intelligence competence centre of the company. Its task is to provide support for managers in understanding new business problems that require in-depth economic knowledge. This will include the collection, editing, and preparation of relevant

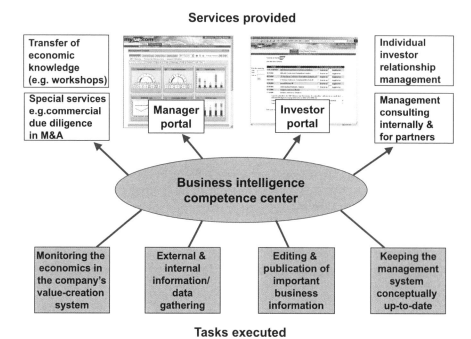

Services provided

Tasks executed

Figure 9.3   To run the Business Intelligence Competence Center of the company will become the main operative role of the new Chief Value Officer.

unstructured internal and external business information that will be supplied to business managers and, for example, investors through the above described web-based self-services. In addition, the centre will provide other services, such as management consulting, training in business issues and economics (for example, in form of online webcasts), M&A services, investor relation services and so on (see Figure 9.3).

So the core competency of a CFO in the future, in order to create maximum value for the company, will be to understand and monitor the economics of the company's value-creation system. Competency has to include the CFO's ability to translate, together with management team colleagues, this understanding into a concept for an appropriate management and reporting system. In addition, the CFO will provide related services to management and investors, rather than merely to manage basic accounting processes and the treasury function of the company. So the traditional role of a CFO will be transformed. The role of a "chief cash manager and chief accountant" will change to that of an agile and active Chief Value Officer (CVO). This means that the CVO will always keeps an eye on the effectiveness of the value-creation system of the company, on the efficiency of its business processes, and on its unrealized value-creation potential and is constantly pressing for its realization. The CFO will be transformed from an administrator of administrative processes to a real business partner, a management colleague directly contributing to the success of the company by ensuring the necessary management transparency.

Challenges for the CIO

The major task of a CIO traditionally was to keep IT operations up and running. Another task was to understand new technologies and convince senior management to invest in them when it becomes crucial for the company.

As a consequence, many CEOs still see their CIOs as "techies" and are skeptical as to whether a CIO belongs in the boardroom. They are especially skeptical about if their IT executives can contribute to the company's business strategy, assuming that IT people are more interested in technology than in business issues. And these concerns are not totally inappropriate. Many IT people have been trained to manage technologies and computers, not the business. But as the e-business network is now becoming the backbone of the business and as companies are moving to online customer and business partner interactions, this culture has to change. And it has changed already in many companies. Most of the CIOs I know are real *information* officers, they develop concepts for *information management* and delegate *technology management* to their chief technology officers.

What are the tasks and what is the profile of a "real" CIO?

First and most importantly, the CIO has to understand the company's business strategy before being able to contribute to it. Because the CIO represents a very critical function in today's companies, I believe that the holder of the position belongs in the boardroom. This, alone, ensures that he or she is always involved in the major strategic decisions that will result in new strategies that the CIO will be expected to support with an appropriate IT infrastructure.

Second, the CIO has to monitor actively, together with the chief technology officer, new evolving technologies. The task is to consider how these new technologies might affect the company's strategy and business and to come up with concepts as to how these new technologies might be used to create competitive advantage.

Third, the CIO has to run operations and the information department as would an entrepreneur. This means he or she has to look always for ways of creating more value for (internal) customers, while at the same time constantly improving efficiency. And indeed, in many companies, IT operations are organized as a shared service centre or profit centre, some are even managed as a separate legal entity or outsourced completely to an external service provider. One way to create value is to guarantee a maximum level of flexibility. Designing and redesigning and changing a company's business system and processes in today's high-risk business environment demands flexibility – and flexibility is a key to success.

Fourth, the CIO must think constantly about ways employees in their day-to-day work, but also business partners and customers in their everyday business, can be helped to become more productive. The major tool that enables companies to convert human capital and individual knowledge into structural capital and organizational capital that can be multiplied is IT.

Today, the CIO can often make a difference, by focusing on the flexibility of IT operations, focusing on improving processes, and on providing the right IT solutions that enable knowledge workers to become more productive. As changes in the business systems of companies are happening faster and faster, and as the major resources for value creation are knowledge capital, intangible assets, and the people who are creating them, productivity improvements are placed top on the agenda of CEOs. If the CIO is able to help the company to develop the productivity of their knowledge workers, business flexibility and continuous business improvement then he or she is making a major contribution to the success and economic performance of the company. Like the CFO, the CIO will become a strategic partner to his or her executive colleagues. The chances of achieving these goals are good, taking into account the latest IT developments.

The flexible, networked and user centric IT infrastructure

Companies that are moving to business network structures and are engaged in knowledge work are more and more dependent on constantly increasing the flexibility of their business and value-creation system and the productivity of their knowledge workers. In this, their IT information infrastructure can be a major obstacle or a major contributor. And this will depend on whether the infrastructure reflects the company's needs, or not. Therefore, an appropriate IT infrastructure for a company today has to be highly *flexible*, has to support the *network* principle, and has to be much more *user centric* than, for example, the traditional mainframe environment. So:

▶   Only a **flexible** IT infrastructure allows quick reconfigurations of business models and business processes that rely on this IT infrastructure.

▶   Only a **networked** IT infrastructure supports the instant and fast interaction between people, no matter if they are located within the four walls of the company or outside. This happens preferably via the Web. An IT infrastructure based on the network principle is also an important precondition for flexibility: it has to allow to plug in fast the IT systems of an acquired company or of a new business partner joining the ecosystem of the company.

▶   Only a **user centric** IT infrastructure can make knowledge workers really productive. To perform their work efficiently, knowledge workers need two things where IT can help: information available at their fingertips at any moment and instant communication and collaboration with other internal or external knowledge workers. But knowledge work is usually not standardized repetitive work – in contrast to many operative tasks of the industrial era enterprise. Therefore, the information provided to knowledge workers has to come not through standardized computer screens, but through user centric, individually configurable web-based portals, oriented on the tasks these people perform and that link them also with the outside world.

A user- and role-based web portal can be seen therefore as the materialization of a user centric IT infrastructure. It provides knowledge workers with a single point of entry to all relevant internal and external information sources and connects them with all required communication and interaction channels.

In addition, an IT platform is required which provides the necessary flexibility in configuring and reconfiguring the existing IT system landscape. It should enable a company to integrate any system into its own information network and any required to be connected with it in the future. So-called exchange-infrastructures, used so far to power electronic marketplaces, can be seen as the materialization of such an open and flexible IT platform that is oriented on the network principle. They allow companies to manage meta and master data of all integrated systems centrally, through so-called meta and master data servers that are a common repository, for example, for customer master data but also for interface characteristics and actual interface configurations of all systems connected to the network. In addition, a message-based information and communication infrastructure, linking all systems and software applications that have to provide specific services for business processes, should automatically trigger the execution of these services on demand via the network by means of an electronic message on the appropriate server where this service is located – wherever that might be. Both, meta and master data servers and the message-based infrastructure, serve as the basis for the integration of various internal and external systems that are used by business and management processes. Their architecture allows a quick and easy reconfiguration of these processes without the necessity to close down and re-build "hard wired" interfaces from system to system every time a process has to be re-configured. Via the message-based network infrastructure each system and software application can be reached via a message and can provide its services directly over the network. Portal and exchange infrastructures represent therefore the main building blocks of the new IT infrastructure.[5]

Another important objective for the CIO is to support the new management system using improved IT. This will help to automate the information flow required to support management processes. The implementation of information and software systems that support these new management processes, and to support managers personally in their tasks, will represent one of the most important projects for CIOs in the future. And, such a project will also provide the CIO with more visibility in front of management colleagues. This includes the deployment of new analytic applications to support strategy and corporate performance management and operative management processes, as well as the implementation of web-based portals for managers, executives and also for investors and other external stakeholders.

IT support for the new management system

On the basis of the new IT infrastructure, which provides and powers open and flexible interfaces, operational systems that support new business processes can be plugged into the e-business accounting system and linked with the data warehouse any time. This provides the information and data basis for the management system, enabling a high degree of configuration flexibility in operations but not restricted by requirements of the accounting and measurement system (as is shown in Figure 9.1).

---

[5] An example is SAP's mySAP Technology: it provides an integrated IT platform that includes a portal as well as an exchange infrastructure and can integrate SAP, third-party, and legacy applications and systems as well as external systems of external service and information providers.

The easy-to-configure business accounting engine will process these incoming data automatically and will translate them into one or several accounting views. Balance sheets, income statements, cash flow statements, and managerial reports based on financial (and even nonfinancial) data processed through the accounting engine will be generated in various versions, each providing a different view. This may, for example, include different views according to different GAAP rules, or one view with capitalization and another without capitalization of investments in intangible assets such as in R&D, where the former might be triggered automatically through the product life cycle management system. The processing of data by the accounting engine will also include the generation of related accounting documents and provides thus the possibility for a detailed audit trail for financial statements and, where required, also for management reports. Through the intelligent and flexible linkage of the accounting system with operational systems, two objectives are achieved at the same time: flexibility for operative systems and process design and more stability for the accounting system that is not disrupted anymore by every change in operative systems. This provides a sustainable high automation level in accounting, which represents an important precondition enabling a virtual or fast close that provides accounting-based information faster and even during the accounting period.

Data from this accounting level are then transferred periodically – or even in real time – together with data and information from other sources to a data warehouse system. This latter provides the necessary management data integrity for views across business functions and across the entire system landscape. In addition, the data structures of the data warehouse system are optimized for multidimensional and time-based analysis via online analytical processing (OLAP). The data warehouse serves therefore as the basis for analytical software applications to support management decisions and management processes as well as controlling tasks and generating the data for the measures of the Tableau de Bord. This includes analytic applications for strategy and corporate performance management, and applications to support operative management processes and analysis tasks (business analytics) as well as reporting. These software tools help to automate support tasks in collecting and preparing timely data to support management processes. This includes, in the area of strategy and corporate performance, functions to automate the financial consolidation and management consolidation process, and budgeting and rolling forecasting. In addition, these systems support KPI-based management reporting and electronic Balanced Scorecards and Tableau de Bords, as well as strategic planning and simulation (for example, based on system dynamics models), external reporting, internal management communication and external communication with stakeholders.[6] Business applications support analytic tasks and management processes in operative areas such as in product life cycle management, customer relationship management, and supply chain management, as well as in managing basis resources such as human resources and finance. Because business analytics applications operate on the same data infrastructure (the data warehouse) as the other reporting, analysis and management tools, it is becoming easy to integrate data for various controlling and reporting tasks (for example, the automatic aggregation of data from operative analytics into the views of the company's Tableau de Bord and again the automatic desegregation for drill down analysis) and to support efficiently cross-functional and cross-business planning and forecasting tasks.[7]

Web-based portals for managers and executives

One important task of the CVO, or of the CFO, is to help to continuously improve the overall productivity of the enterprise. This includes the development of new techniques that will enable a company to manage for value in a systematic way when business conditions are changing. One of the major challenges in initiating a new value-management program is that of training business managers within a given period of time in the new concepts and in using the new measures and tools. In larger organizations this can become a huge task, but even in mid-sized organizations it is not easy. It is often difficult, of course, to get these operational managers to attend an internal training course or seminar and to stay away from their day-to-day business for several days. So the CFO often has no chance of contacting them directly and this often represents a real threat to the success of the program.

One way of overcoming these problems is to use web-based portals instead of courses or seminars. Through a manager portal the CFO can provide so-called management self-services that not only include instant access to the new analytic tools and data, as soon as they are released, but also to information that describes how to use them (e.g. to a recorded training session (webcast)

---

[6] An example of a suite of analytic applications to support strategy and corporate performance management is that provided by SAP's Strategic Enterprise Management (SEM) solution. The author made significant contributions to its conception as the former SAP product manager for SEM.

[7] An example of a suite of analytic applications in the area of business analytics is that provided by SAP's Business Analytics solution. The author was also involved in the conception of this extension to SAP's SEM solution.

about the new Tableau de Bord or to a catalog that provides managers with answers to typical questions). This may include also access to an electronic discussion forum, where managers can discuss with their colleagues from other areas of the company critical issues in the implementation phase, or where they simply can ask questions. Articles related to new performance management concepts, expert presentations and video interviews with external experts might be posted on these web pages. Using such manager and investor portals, the CFO (or now the CVO) is able to create in a very efficient way a virtual community for value and performance management that links different people within the enterprise and within its ecosystem together in a continuous dialog about performance management issues. The community may include managers, controllers and analysts from within the company, but also from partners and may be even investors, financial analysts or representatives from other external stakeholder organizations. The business intelligence competence centre serves as the back-office for this community and provides the necessary services.

The management innovation centre

Leif Edvinsson mentioned in our interview the Skandia Future Center, a "laboratory" for organizational development that is designed to experiment with future organizational concepts, work methods and environments. It is based on the understanding that enterprises need a new approach to organizational and management innovation.

The Skandia Future Center is located in Villa Askudden, near Stockholm, and was built in 1860. Its interior is a clear contrast to the usual high-tech equipped offices of today. The Future Center is a meeting space with a focus on renewal and development, where people from different countries, age groups and professions can meet in a dialogue about enterprising and future organizations. The intention is to generate an atmosphere that stimulates communication and interaction. The Management Cockpit room concept, described earlier, has already demonstrated that ergonomic room concepts are important in helping employees and managers become more productive and to stimulate their creativity. The question therefore is: What is the physical environment that provides the ground for successful innovation work?

But innovation is not restricted to product innovation alone. Today, one of the most important value drivers, beside product innovation, is organizational and management innovation. New business models, new organizational designs and new strategies often have the largest long-term impact on the value-creation potential of companies. In order to innovate successfully and systematically in this area, a company has to provide its management with the right information and has to implement the necessary management processes. While these represent a good foundation, it is not sufficient; companies need to use the right methods and implement the room and environmental concepts. This is what Skandia have done with their Future Center, in order to provide managers with the necessary space and freedom and with a communication environment that enables them to innovate effectively on the strategic level.

For example, about three years ago, a large oil company approached us at SAP asking for someone who could talk about the Management Cockpit concept to their senior executives. I asked for more information about their objectives in order to be able to find the right person. And it turned out that these executives were looking for a concept to establish – what I am calling today a management innovation centre. The concept intended to improve the innovation capabilities of management by helping it to eliminate non-value-adding activities, interactions and information flows.

The oil company wanted to create an environment for its top executives where they no longer sat isolated in their offices at the corporate headquarters, being bombarded with information and reports, and stuck in the day-to-day business. Their main job as top managers was, of course, not day-to-day business but strategy and innovation. It was recognized that for this role to be realized, two things had to happen: an office environment allowing them to be personally and as a team more productive and more creative, and an information and communication infrastructure that allowed them to focus on essentials.

The new corporate centre, as it was visualized by the oil company, should still include personal office spaces, but more open ones, with fewer walls allowing for better communication between people. It should also include coffee corner-type areas, where executives can meet for short chats with managers and with experts working in areas such as strategic planning or from the business intelligence competence centre. The centre should include spaces as in a library, where one could work in silence and in depth on a topic. The whole corporate centre should be wired with the field organization of the company and with its environment through advanced network and video conferencing technology, allowing executives to communicate any time with operative managers, business partners or customers. And, finally, the centre should include Management Cockpit-type meeting rooms, to facilitate management review and strategic planning meetings as well as brainstorming workshops with industry experts, customers, and business partners. What does this story tell us?

Large companies no longer need corporate centres that "administrate" the business. Instead, a management innovation centre should be created, where the top management team can work on new strategies and business models and shape the company's future. In order to stay constantly in touch with reality, appropriate feedback systems, management and communication processes – that is, a management system – has to be set up, that ensures a close link of the top team to the operational business and that can be activated at any time.

For designing, setting it up, and operating such a management innovation centre, the top team needs support not only from ergonomic and human intelligence experts, but also from business intelligence and IT experts. And that is where ultimately the work of the CIO and of the CFO/CVO converges.

Part 4
Epilogue

10 Intangible Assets and the Wealth of Nations

Today's rapid advances in science and technology mean that OECD economies are increasingly based on knowledge. At the same time, countries are increasingly integrated into the world economy, through international flows of goods and services, investment, people and ideas. This has given rise to new forms of competition and co-operation among firms and countries [...]. How well countries respond to these challenges depends on how well business, government and the labor force work together to exploit these key assets.[1]

At the transition from the industrial society to the information and knowledge-based society, not only the corporate growth basis changes from tangible assets to intangible assets but also the economic growth basis of societies and nations. The intellectual capital or knowledge capital embodied in the skills, knowledge, and experiences of its citizens, the organizational procedures, systems and routines of its business enterprises, and its knowledge and innovation infrastructure, constitute the major source of wealth and social welfare of a nation.

This is gaining recognition in governmental and public organizations. An example is the OECD report published in 1996, *Measuring what People Know*. It suggests that learning is a significant source of social and economic development in today's societies and predicts that the public and corporate investments in the development of human capital – here especially education and training – will become a crucial engine for growth, particularly in a world marked by knowledge-intensive activities.

The new wealth of nations

The wealth of a nation, expressed in the growth of its gross domestic product (GDP) – that is, in the total value-added created that can be distributed as

---

[1] Organisation for Economic Co-operation and Development (OECD) (1999) *Technology and Industry Scoreboard 1999: Benchmarking Knowledge-based Economies*, Paris: Directorate Science, Technology & Industry. The passage is taken from the introduction and can also be viewed on the OECD website at: www.oecd.org//dsti/sti/stat-ana/prod/scorebd_summ.htm

income to its citizens – is largely dependent on two factors: on the size of its labor force and on the level of its productivity. The level of productivity is determined in the new economy especially by the quality of the human capital engaged, of the number of brains, and not just hands, of which a nation can dispose of. A nation can influence and improve this quality through education. And it can influence overall productivity through investments in other intangibles – in the information and communication infrastructure, in the science, and in the research and development activities of the country, as the example of the United States demonstrates.

The case of the United States

In a recent study published by The Conference Board, a global, independent research organization, it was revealed that the US economy – despite the actual slowdown – is likely to outpace the rest of the world in the future in terms of productivity, economic growth and income.[2]

The productivity acceleration in the United States that started around 1995 continued unabated into the beginning of the new century. Estimates suggest that US productivity in 2000 rose 3.8% over the previous year. Productivity growth in most other major industrialized nations was relatively sluggish in contrast. For the European Union (EU) as a whole, productivity grew by 1.4% in 2000, and Japan experienced some improvement, at 2.3%. But improved productivity growth in the US is only one part of the story as the country's economy further improved its capability to translate productivity improvements into higher per capita income. The comparison based on actual numbers shows, that the EU's productivity was 82% of US productivity, but its per capita income reached only 69% of the US level. Since the 1970s, the United States has led most other countries in the OECD in translating productivity gains into per capita income. But how is the US economy able to translate productivity in this way?

Translation of productivity into higher per capita income depends on labor participation. That is, on the proportion of the population that is involved in production. And in most countries in Europe the lower translation rate of productivity improvements into per capita income is due to a lower overall participation rate, which means that in Europe the number of people

---

[2] Robert H. McGuck and Bart van Ark (2001) *Performance 2000: Productivity, Employment, and Income in the World's Economies*, New York: The Conference Board. This publication can also be viewed at www.conference-board.org

involved in production of GDP of the total population is much lower than it is in the USA.

There are various reasons why European countries have such lower participation rates. In Norway and the Netherlands it is due to low average working hours. However, in most European countries, unemployment plays a role, but the most important reason is a lower share of the labor force at working age (age 15–64). And this increases the income gap between the EU and the USA by 10 percentage points. Europe clearly has a demographic disadvantage compared with the US. But this is not the only reason for the economic strength of the US economy when compared with other countries. The productivity of the US economy has also been significantly improved in recent years through higher investment in IT.

This dramatic performance is due to success on two fronts:

1. A rapid improvement in productivity, mainly through higher investments in technology-intensive industries – in particular, information and communication technologies.

2. A high level of labor force participation, mainly through more flexible labor markets and the demographic advantage, at least over European countries.

The future wealth of a nation – if we assume that it is dependent on economy wide growth and per capita income – is, among other factors, based on the capability of a nation to continue to achieve productivity improvements through investments in innovation and new technologies and to maintain growth in labor input.

What does this mean for Europe?

The Conference Board states in its study that nations within the EU have to be cautious and not get onto a low-productivity growth track and to concentrate solely on reducing unemployment rates. These nations have to look at productivity as well. Keeping in mind that the rapid acceleration in US productivity growth in the last half of the decade is closely tied to fast technological change and increased investments in new technologies, specifically into information and communication technologies, Europe has to stimulate that type of change too in order to return to higher economic growth rates. Because technological change does not just happen solely through increased investments but is dependent on changes in institutional, regulatory, and legal structures as well, the EU countries have to accelerate the pace of reforming their old structures.

They also have to master the challenge of an aging population which is seriously threatening their capabilities for future economic growth, income and wealth. Keeping in mind that labor force participation rate is an important driver for economic growth and wealth of a nation, Europe has to prepare its population to work more years or to accept immigration – or maybe both.

What about Asia?

The largest Asian economy, Japan, maintained a high level of productivity growth rate throughout the 1990s, despite several recessions, but it did so at the cost of employment growth. Whereas Japan does not stand for Asia in total, it can serve as a kind of "leading example". Countries in Asia also will probably have to face two major challenges in order to become economically more successful and to increase their economic performance:

1.   Improve productivity through investments in new technologies and structures. This requires more flexible product and capital markets that help to reallocate capital to its most productive use. It also requires major investments in education.

2.   Get high rates of its fast-growing population involved in the countries' economic activities. This requires greater flexibility of labor markets.

In the next 20 years, the sheer size of Asia's growing population might catapult it into becoming the most powerful regional economy. If Asian countries are successful in creating the necessary infrastructure (information and communication infrastructure, open markets, democratic political structures), in educating its people, and in reaching and maintaining a high labor force participation rate, this prospect cannot be not avoided.

How should governments react through their economic policies to the new wealth-creating factors?

In addition to labor force participation rate, productivity is a major factor for economic growth and for the future wealth of a nation. And productivity of an economy is driven largely today by the share of its knowledge-based industries versus others, and by the size of its investment in education, in information and telecommunication technologies, and in R&D activities. This list therefore describes the action fields of modern economic policies.

Human capital and its education level

Knowledge is a factor of production and change. Change means that society and business life must always be prepared to adapt to new markets and technological conditions and to develop new organizations in support of development and learning. Knowledge as a new factor of production will help a society or nation as well as its organizations to handle new challenges and ever-changing conditions and to master innovation, which is the success factor in the new economy – not only for companies, but also for nations.

Investment in human capital such as education represents in today's economies one of the first and major drivers for future economic growth and wealth. Without knowing what is already known and without knowing how to work with knowledge and knowledge-creating constellations, people cannot create new knowledge. They will find themselves lagging behind on the continuous innovation and renewal path required in today's global economic competition between nations. Therefore, societies have to invest even more in education in the future.

But economic success will not go simply to those nations investing in education. Because labor markets, especially for highly qualified people, are becoming increasingly open and global – as can be seen in the software industry, for example – countries also have to retain these talents and have to attract in addition others from other countries. The number of available people of working age is a major driver in determining the level of a nation's GDP, the economic growth rate it can achieve, and for the wealth and income of its citizens.

In order to be attractive to talented knowledge workers and to enable them to work with others in productive ways, countries have to offer the right living and working conditions, open labor markets, democratic political structures and, for example, also an appropriate information and communication technology infrastructure.

Information and communication technologies

For nations, as for companies, information and communication technologies are playing the role of enablers for knowledge work. And it is not just PCs per household that is important here. How efficiently these PCs are linked into networks within companies, schools, other public institutions and into the World Wide Web is an important factor. And efficiency is measured today by bandwidth. The more installed bandwidth a country has, the greater its degree of connectivity. The relevant measure is "megabits per capita", how much installed bandwidth it has, divided by the number of its potential users. It tells about the rate of information dissemination within the population and to and from decision makers. Jobs, knowledge, and economic growth will gravitate to those societies that are the most connected, with the most networks and the broadest amount of bandwidth, because these countries will find it easier to amass, deploy and share knowledge in order to design, invent, manufacture, sell, provide services, communicate, educate and entertain.

The ability to create, distribute and exploit knowledge and information seems ever more important and is often regarded as the single most important factor underlying economic growth and improvements in the quality of life. Information and communication technologies are the enablers for it and a pillar of knowledge-based economies. How well and fast countries adopt and master these technologies is thus a key to their future economic performance.

Investment in innovation capabilities

The national R&D effort, a country's science and technology policy, is perceived today by economists as another major driver of economic growth and wealth of nations. And it is not just total R&D expenditure of a society that counts. For example, the number of researchers in its total labor force is an important indicator of a nation's economic growth potential.

Another example is that of the rate of gross domestic expenditures on R&D (GERD) compared with gross domestic product (GDP). In the 1990s, the rate declined in the large economies of the EU (Germany, United Kingdom, France, Italy) in contrast to the United States, which kept its GERD rate not only higher than the average of OECD countries, but also more or less stable over the period. This is seen as another reason for the higher economic growth rate of the US versus the EU.

In most countries the business sector funds and performs an increasing share of R&D, a trend that accelerated in the 1990s. However, today both, government and business enterprises play an important role in science and technology and in creating innovation capabilities. When a government provides support to industrial technology it is more than public funding of R&D. It encompasses financial support through direct grants or through tax relief, a specific public procurement policy, and active science and technology infrastructure and diffusion. Innovation on a national level no longer depends solely on how firms, universities, and research institutes perform independently but, increasingly, on how they cooperate. And even developed countries can differ substantially in their innovation capabilities because of differences in national innovation systems.

Required: a "management system" for nations?

Economic power will not simply flow to those nations who educate their people better, who are the most wired, or who invest most of their GDP in R&D. It will flow to those who, in addition, are the most creative in bringing together business, government, capital, information, consumers and talent in networked coalitions that create value. Some coalitions will be corporate-led to create commercial value; some will be government-led coalitions to create geopolitical value based usually on economic power. And some coalitions will be activist-led to create, or preserve, human values – such as workers rights, human rights or environmental preservation.

So, in today's knowledge and intangible assets-based global economy, nations are increasingly facing similar challenges in the same way as are companies. Nations have to create structural capital that better connects their different institutions, such as business enterprises and universities for value-creating innovation. They have to "manage" basis resources like human capital and related education and development programs. And they have to treat their country as a national brand that allows it to attract the most talented people, the corporations, and those institutional investors interested in their country. And, in order to be able to do that, like companies, they need better information about the real economic value drivers of their economy. Some countries have already started to create the conditions to obtain such information. For example, Denmark is obliging its enterprises from the beginning of 2002 to report on their intangible assets – an important database for the Danish government to monitor and "manage" the development of intangible assets and of intellectual capital in Denmark. An interesting question now might be what kind of "management system" a government needs to better manage its intangibles-based economy and new national value-creation factors and processes. Interested readers may take with them some of the ideas discussed here about the new enterprise management system and may use them as a starting point for their own thoughts about a concept for a new national economic management system.

Bibliography

Aboody, David and Lev, Baruch (2001) R&D productivity in the chemical industry (http://www.stern.nyu.edu/~blev/chemical-industry.doc)

Arthur Andersen (1999) *Stoxx 50 Shareholder Value and Investor Relations in Wettbewerb um institutionelles Kapital*, Eschborn, Germany: Arthur Andersen.

Baghai, Mehrdad; Coley, Stephen and White, David (1999) *The Alchemy of Growth: Practical Insights for Building the Enduring Enterprise*, London: Orion Publishing.

Baum, Geoff (1998) "Cisco's CEO: John Chambers", *Forbes ASAP*, February 23.

Baum, Geoff; Ittner, Chris; Larcker, David; Low, Jonathan, Siesfeld, Tony and Malone, Michael S. (2000) "Introducing the New Value Creation Index", *Forbes ASAP*, April 3.

Branegan, Jay (1997) "Percy Barnevik, Chairman, ABB Asea Brown Boveri; Zurich", *Time Magazine*, March 3.

Bunnell, David and Brate, Adam (2000) *Making the Cisco Connection: The Story behind the Real Internet Superpower*, New York: John Wiley & Sons.

Bürgel, Hans Dietmar (2000) "Flexibilisierungspotenziale in Forschung und Entwicklung", *Frankfurter Allgemeinen Zeitung*, August 14 [in German].

Carlsson, Rolf H. (2001) *Ownership and Value Creation: Strategic Corporate Governance in the New Economy*, New York: John Wiley & Sons.

Christensen, Clayton M. (2000) *The Innovator's Dilemma: When New Technologies Cause Great Firms to Fail*, New York, HarperBusiness.

Collins, Jim (2001) "Good to great", *Why Some Companies Make the Leap . . . and Others Don't*, New York: HarperCollins.

Daley, Zuzanne (2000) "French farmer is sentenced to jail for attack on McDonald's", *The New York Times/International News*, September 14.

Danish Trade and Industry Ministry (2000) A guideline for intellectual capital statements (http://www.efs.dk/download/pdf/videnUK.pdf).

Daum, Juergen H.; Grotheer, Manfred; Heinrich, Claus; Schroeder, Juergen and Stolze, Juergen (1995) "SAP Open Information Warehouse and Self-Controlling: Und was tut noch der Controller", *Controller Magazin*, **6/95** (Gauting, Germany) [in German].

Daum, Juergen H. (1996) "Integration des MIS in Anwendungen für das operative Controlling und die Konzernrechnungslegung", in: Hannig, Uwe (ed.), *Data Warehouse and Management Informations Systeme*, Stuttgart: Schaeffer-Poeschel [in German].

Daum, Juergen H.; Grotheer, Manfred; Funk, Rolf; Hoertig, Juergen and Karl, Stefan (1997) "Anforderungen an ein modernes Konzerncontrolling", *Controller Magazin*, **2/97** (Gauting, Germany) [in German].

Daum, Juergen H. (1998) "Konzernsteuerung mit EC Enterprise Controlling 4.0", *is report*, **04/98** (Munich, Germany) [in German].

Daum, Juergen H. (1999) "Strategic Enterprise Management", *is report*, **02/99** (Munich) [in German].

Daum, Juergen H. (1999) "Strategie-Funktionalitäten", *is report*, **03/99** (Munich) [in German].

Daum, Juergen H. (2000) "SEM-SRM Stakeholder Relationship Management", in: Kueting, Karlheinz and Weber, Claus-Peter (ed.), *Wertorientierte Konzernführung*, Stuttgart: Schaeffer-Poeschel [in German].

Daum, Juergen H. (2000) "Unternehmensmanagement als Prozess verstehen", *is report*, **06/2000** (Munich) [in German].

Daum, Juergen H. (2001) "Leveraging e-business opportunities for finance – how CFOs and IT can join forces to create value", *SAP Insider*, October–December.

Daum, Juergen H. (2002) "Wertreiber Intangible Assets: Brauchen wir ein neues Rechnungswesen und Controlling? – Ein Ansatz für ein verbessertes Management-system", *Controlling*, January (Munich) [in German].

Davis, Stan and Meyer, Christopher (2000) *Future Wealth*, Boston: Harvard Business School Press.

Drucker, Peter F. (1994) "The age of social transformation", *The Atlantic Monthly*, November.

Drucker, Peter F. (1999) *Management Challenges for the 21st Century*, New York: HarperCollins.

Drucker, Peter F. (1999) "The real meaning of the merger boom", *The Conference Board 1999 Annual Essay and Report*, New York: The Conference Board.

Eccles, Robert G.; Herz, Robert H.; Keegan, E. Mary and Phillips, David M. H. (2001) *The Value Reporting Revolution*, New York: John Wiley & Sons.

Edvinsson, Leif and Malone, Michael S. (1997) *Intellectual Capital*, New York: Harper-Collins.

Edvinsson, Leif (2002) *Corporate Longitude: Navigating the Knowledge Economy*, Stockholm: Book House Publishing.

Ernst & Young LLP (1997) *Measures that Matter*, The Ernst & Young Center for Business Innovation.

Friedman, Thomas (2000) *The Lexus and the Olive Tree*, London: HarperCollins.

Garten, Jeffrey E. (2001) *The Mind of the C.E.O.*, New York, Basic Books.

Georges, Patrick M. (2002) *Le Management Cockpit. Pilotez vos affaires avec plus d'efficacité*, Paris: Editions d'Organisation [in French].

Geus, Arie de (1997) *The Living Company*, Boston: Harvard Business School Press.

Ghoshal, Sumantra and Bartlett, Christopher A. (1997) *The Individualized Corporation*, London: William Heinemann Random House.

Guerny, J. de; Guiriec, J. C. and Lavergne, J. (1990) *Principe et mise en place du Tableau de bord de Gestion*, Paris: Masson [in French].

Hagel, John III and Armstrong, Arthur G. (1997) *Netgain: Expanding Markets through Virtual Communities*, Boston: Harvard Business School Press.

Heskett, Ben (2000) Cisco CEO: What, me worry?
(http://news.cnet.com/news/0-1004-200-3989419.html).

Hoch, Detlev J.; Roeding, Cyriac C.; Purkert, Gert and Lindner, Sandro K. (1999) *Secrets of Software Success*, Boston: Harvard Business School Press.

Holson, Laura M. (1998) Whiz kid: young deal maker is the force behind a company's growth (http://www.cisco.com/warp/public/750/acquisition/articles/volpi.html).

Hope, Jeremy and Fraser, Robin (2000) *Beyond Budgeting – Managing in the New Economy*, Beyond Budgeting Round Table White Paper, London: CAM-I.

Hopp, Dietmar (1996) "Globale Strategien der SAP AG", *Strategische Eneuerungen für den globalen Wettbewerb*, Stuttgart: Erich Zahn [in German].

Kagermann, Henning (2000) "Strategische Unternehmensführung bei der SAP AG – Erfahrungen and Lösungen eines Software-Unternehmens", *Wirtschafts Informatik*, April (Wiesbaden, Germany) [in German].

Kaplan, Robert S. and Norton, David P. (1996) "Using the Balanced Scorecard as a Strategic Management System", *Harvard Business Review*, January–February.

Kaplan, Robert S. and Norton, David P. (1996) *The Balanced Scorecard. Translating Strategy into Action*, Boston: Harvard Business School Press.

Kaplan, Robert S. and Norton, David P. (2000) *The Strategy-focused Organization*, Boston: Harvard Business School Press.

Konrad, Rachel (2000) Head-on collision – old and new economies clash in auto industry marketplace (http://news.cnet.com/news/0-1007-201-3412381-0.html).

L.E.K. Consulting LLC (2000) "Making real decisions with real options", *L.E.K.. Newsletter*, "Shareholder Value Added" Series, Vol. XVI.

Leslie, Keith J. and Michaels, Max P. (2000) "The real power of real options", *The McKinsey Quarterly*, Number 3, Strategy (http://www.mckinseyquarterly.com).

Lev, Baruch (2000) New Accounting for the new economy
(http://www.stern.nyu.edu/~blev/NewAccounting.doc).

Lev, Baruch (2000) Knowledge and shareholder value
(http://www.stern.nyu.edu/~blev/knowledge&shareholdervalue.doc).

Lev, Baruch (2000) Communicating knowledge capabilities
(http://www.stern.nyu.edu/~blev/communicating.doc).

Lev, Baruch (2001) *Intangibles: Management, Measurement, and Reporting*, Washington, DC: Brooking Institution Press.

Lev, Baruch and Gu, Feng (2001) Markets in intangibles: Patent licensing
(http://www.stern.nyu.edu/~blev/patent-licensing.doc).

Lev, Baruch and Gu, Feng (2001) Intangible assets: Measurement, drivers, usefulness
(http://www.stern.nyu.edu/~blev/intangible-assets.doc).

Lindahl, Göran (2000) "A new role for global businesses", *Time Magazine Europe*, January 31.

Maister, David H. (1997) *Managing the Professional Service Firm*, New York: Free Press.

McGuck, Robert H. and Ark, Bart van (2001) *Performance 2000: Productivity, Employment, and Income in the World's Economies*, New York: The Conference Board.

Means, Grady and Schneider, David (2000) *Meta-Capitalism: The e-Business Revolution and the Design of 21st-Century Companies and Markets*, New York: John Wiley & Sons.

Muirhead, Sophia A. (1999) *Corporate Contributions: The View from 50 Years*, New York, The Conference Board.

Nakamura, Leonard (1999) "Intangibles: What put the *New* in the New Economy?", *Federal Bank of Philadelphia, Business Review*, July–August.

Nakamura, Leonard (2000) "Economics and the New Economy: The invisible hand meets creative destruction", *Federal Bank of Philadelphia, Business Review*, July.

Nölting, Andreas (2000) "Werttreiber Mensch", *Manager Magazin*, April [in German].

Norris, Grant; Hurley, James R.; Hartley, Kenneth M.; Dunleavy, John R. and Balls, John D. (2000) *E-Business and ERP: Transforming the Enterprise*, New York: John Wiley & Sons.

OECD (Organization for Economic Co-operation and Development) (1999) Technology and Industry Scoreboard 1999: Benchmarking knowledge-based economies (http://www.oecd.org/dsti/sti/stat-ana/prod/scorebd_summ.htm).

Peter, Glen (1999) *Waltzing with the Raptors: A Practical Roadmap to Protecting Your Company's Reputation*, New York: John Wiley & Sons.

Plattner, Hasso; Scheer, August-Wilhelm; Wendt, Siegfried and Morrow, Daniel S. (2000) *Dem Wandel voraus*, Bonn, Galileo-Press.

Porter, Michael E. (1996) "What is strategy", *Harvard Business Review*, November–December.

Rappaport, Alfred (1986) *Creating Shareholder Value*, New York: Free Press (revised edition 1998).

Rappaport, Alfred (1999) "New thinking on how to link executive pay with performance", *Harvard Business Review*, March–April.

Read, Cedric; Ross, Jacky; Dunleavy, Jack; Schulmann, Donniel and Bramante, James (2001) *eCFO: Sustaining Value in the New Corporation*, Chichester, UK: John Wiley & Sons.

Ridderstrale, Jonas and Nordström, Kjell (2000) *Funky Business*, London: Financial Times Prentice Hall.

Rifkin, Glenn (1997) Growth by acquisition – the case of Cisco Systems (http://www.strategy-business.com/thoughleaders/97209/page2.html).

Roach, Stephen (1997) "US: The boom for whom?", Archives of the Global Economics Team of Morgan Stanley (www.msdw.com/GEFdata/digests/19771217-wed.html).

Royal Dutch Shell (2000) Shell Report 2000 – How do we stand? (http://www.shell.com).

Rudis, Esther; Berman, Melissa A. and Mitchell, Chuck (2001) *The CEO Challenge: Top Marketplace and Management Issues*, New York, The Conference Board.

SAP AG (1998) *SAP Strategic Enterprise Management – Enabling Value Based Management*, White Paper, Walldorf, Germany: SAP AG.

SAP AG (1999) *SAP Strategic Enterprise Management – Translating Strategy into Action: The Balanced Scorecard*, White Paper, Walldorf, Germany: SAP AG.

SAP AG (1999) *SAP Strategic Enterprise Management – The Functions – A Closer Look*, White Paper, Walldorf, Germany: SAP AG.

SAP AG (2001) *Empowering Finance for E-Business – How to Exploit Technology to Optimize Value*, White Paper, Walldorf, Germany: SAP AG.

SAP AG (2001) *Beyond Budgeting*, White Paper, Walldorf, Germany: SAP AG.

SAP AG (2001) *mySAP Technology for Open E-Business Integration – Overview*, White Paper, Walldorf, Germany: SAP AG.

Schumpeter, Joseph A. (1949) *Theory of Economic Development*, Boston: Harvard University Press.

Schwartz, Peter (1996) *The Art of the Long View: Planning for the Future in an Uncertain World*, New York: Currency Doubleday.

Schwartz, Peter and Leyden, Peter (1997) ''The Long Boom: A history of the future, 1980–2020'', *Wired Magazine*, July.

Schwartz, Peter; Leyden, Peter and Hyatt, Joel (1999/2000) *The Long Boom: A Vision for the Coming Age of Prosperity*, Cambridge, MA: Perseus Publishing.

SEC Taskforce (2001) Strengthening financial markets: Do investors have the information they need? (www.fei.org/finrep/files/SEC-Taskforce-Final-6-6-2kl.pdf).

Senge, Peter M. (1990) *The Fifth Discipline: The Art and Practice of the Learning Organization*, New York: Currency Doubleday.

Shrimsley, Robert (2000) ''Minister to reassure business over civic duty'', *Financial Times*, May 4.

Skandia Insurance Ltd (1998) *Human Capital in Transformation – Intellectual Capital Prototype Report*, Stockholm: Skandia.

Stewart, Thomas A. (1999) *Intellectual Capital*, New York: Doubleday Dell.

Stewart, Thomas A. (2001) ''Accounting gets radical'', *Fortune Magazine*, April 16.

Strassmann, Paul A. (1996) The value of computers, information and knowledge (www.strassmann.com abgerufen werden kann).

Sveiby, Karl Erik (1997) *The New Organizational Wealth*, San Francisco: Berrett-Koehler.

Thurow, Lester C. (2000) ''If God spoke to John Akers'', *Across the Board*, January.

Vidal, David J. (1999) *Consumer Expectations on the Social Accountability of Business*, New York, The Conference Board.

Index